ABSENT AVIATORS

Donna Bridges

To my grandmother Johanna Bolger (1919–2012), who had a wonderful enthusiasm for life through which she challenged many ideas about gender and became an inspiring role model to us all.

Albert J. Mills

To my granddaughters Harvie Lois and Amber Lulu, may they reach for the stars and know no earthly bounds, and to Maryanne Hardman – financial advisor, friend and female pilot – whose life was cut short when her ultra-light plane crashed in early May, 2014.

Jane Neal-Smith

To my colleagues and friends – Wendy, Chris, Etienne, Chris and Vanessa – a very special thank you.

Absent Aviators

Gender Issues in Aviation

Edited by

DONNA BRIDGES
Charles Sturt University, Australia

JANE NEAL-SMITH
London Metropolitan Business School, UK

and

ALBERT J. MILLS
St Mary's University, Canada

Routledge
Taylor & Francis Group
LONDON AND NEW YORK

First published 2014 by Ashgate Publishing

2 Park Square, Milton Park, Abingdon, Oxfordshire OX14 4RN
52 Vanderbilt Avenue, New York, NY 10017

Routledge is an imprint of the Taylor & Francis Group, an informa business

First issued in paperback 2020

British Library Cataloguing in Publication Data
A catalogue record for this book is available from the British Library

The Library of Congress has cataloged the printed edition as follows:
Absent aviators : gender issues in aviation / [edited] by Donna Bridges, Jane Neal-Smith and Albert Mills. pages cm Includes bibliographical references and index.
ISBN 978-1-4724-3338-1 (hbk)
1. Air pilots--Sex differences. 2. Women air pilots. 3. Airplanes--Piloting--Human factors. 4. Sex role in the work environment. I. Bridges, Donna, editor. II. Neal-Smith, Jane, editor. III. Mills, Albert J., 1945- editor.
HD8039.A4A27 2014
331.4'82913--dc23

2014010730

ISBN 978-1-4724-3338-1 (hbk)
ISBN 978-0-367-67010-8 (pbk)

Contents

List of Figures and Tables

Figures

Tables

About the Editors

Donna Bridges holds a PhD in Sociology from the University of Western Sydney (UWS). Her doctoral thesis, 'The gendered battlefield: Women in the Australian Defence Force', is a qualitative, feminist exploration of gender inequalities in the Australian Defence Force (ADF). She lectures across a range of sociology subjects at Charles Sturt University. She is also co-editor of the qualitative research book *Creative Spaces for Qualitative Researching: Living Research* (with Higgs, J., Titchen, A., Horsfall, D. and Bridges, D. (2011)). Her research interests include qualitative research methodologies; gender, masculinity and feminist theory; culture; peace studies; peacekeeping and women's roles; and military sociology.

Albert J. Mills is Professor of Management and Director of the PhD (Management) Program at Saint Mary's University, Halifax, Nova Scotia, Canada. His 300 publications include numerous books, book chapters and journal articles on gender and commercial aviation. He is Associate Editor of three scholarly journals – *Organization*, *Gender, Work and Organization* and *Qualitative Research in Organizations and Management* – and serves on the editorial boards of several other journals. He is the author of *Sex, Strategy and the Stratosphere: The Gendering of Airline Cultures* and his latest book is *ANTi-History: Theorizing the Past, History, and Historiography in Management and Organizational Studies* (2012).

Jane Neal-Smith has a PhD in Industrial Psychology and Sociology, which explored the working lives of UK commercial women airline pilots. She is currently a senior lecturer at London Metropolitan Business School in the Management, Strategy and Leadership subject group. Her research interests are in aviation psychology and human factors, women in the workplace, gender in employment and organisational behaviour. She is a member of the Royal Aeronautical Society (MRAeS) and the European Association for Aviation Psychology (EAAP).

About the Contributors

Ronald W. Bishop, who is currently undertaking his PhD, is Head of the Aviation programme at Central Queensland University and is Former Operations Superintendent of the Air Force Special Operations and Rescue School with over 5,000 flying hours as an Aircrew member in USAF Special Operations. He began his career in US Air Force rescue and has over 300 saves. He was awarded three presidential presented awards, including the Hoyt and Tunner Award for Aviation Excellence during operations in Afghanistan and Iraq. His research interests are human factors in aviation, mental workload of aircrew, and air quality in aircraft. He is married and has two children. He currently lives in Central Queensland.

Reinhard Braunstingl, who holds a PhD in mechanical engineering, is Associate Professor and leader of the 'Research Platform Flight Simulation' at Graz University of Technology, Austria. He is an experienced commercial pilot and flight instructor, and is Austrian Aerobatics Champion in the Sportsmen category. His research activities focus on human–machine interaction (HMI) design, flight simulation and flight training.

Bridget Cox received her undergraduate degree in Aviation Business with a concentration in Airport Management and a minor in Psychology from Embry-Riddle Aeronautical University. She also went on to pursue her Master's degree in Business Administration from Embry-Riddle Aeronautical University and graduated in the spring of 2011. She began her career in May 2009 as an intern for Business Development at Signature Flight Support and was offered a full-time position as an Operations Analyst in January of 2011. In her current role she is responsible for tracking key metrics for Signature's North American locations, is in charge of the customer loyalty programme and has been involved with the acquisition and transition of new locations into Signature's network.

Klaus Fruehwirth is an aeronautical engineer, flight instructor and commercial pilot with type rating for C525 Series. He is the founder of Brightline Avionics, Austria and is counsellor at Becker Avionics, Germany. He is an expert in the development and usability evaluation of glass cockpits and radio communication systems for aviation.

Group Captain Deanne Gibbon is both an academic and member of the Royal Australian Air Force (RAAF). She has significant experience working in strategic human resource policy development, training management, personnel capability and recruiting. She is completing her final year of a sociology doctorate at the University of New South Wales, where she is examining flying as a field of non-traditional employment for civil and military pilots. She is also currently applying the outcomes of her academic research to an Air Force project designed to significantly increase the number of women in Air Force pilot positions. As the Director of Workplace Diversity, she is implementing a further range of initiatives that are designed to encourage previously untapped demographics towards joining the Air Force. She is particularly passionate about identifying barriers preventing higher numbers of women from joining the ADF and finding creative ways to mitigate those barriers, such that higher numbers of women might enjoy an ADF career.

Erich Grubmueller is an aeronautical engineer at Brightline Avionics, Austria and a PhD student at Graz University of Technology. His research in the field of electronics and computer sciences focuses on embedded systems, airborne devices and human–machine interface. He applies human factors in the specification and development of hardware for airborne devices.

Penny Rafferty Hamilton, who holds a PhD, has academic degrees from Temple University, Philadelphia, Pennsylvania; Columbia College, Columbia, Missouri; and the University of Nebraska, Lincoln, Nebraska. In 2013, she was given Columbia College's Distinguished Alumni Award. In addition to university teaching and business experience, she has written numerous general aviation articles in publications such as *National Association of Flight Instructors: MENTOR* and *Seaplane Magazine*, and in E-zines such as the *State Aviation Journal* and *AV ED Journal*. In 2012, she earned the National Association of State Aviation Officials National Journalism Award. She is the author of two history books, *Granby: Then and Now* and *Around Granby*. She co-holds with her husband, Bill, a World Aviation Speed Record, set on 22 October 1991, awarded by the Federation Aeronautique Internationale and the National Aeronautic Association. In 2011, she was inducted into the Colorado Aviation Hall of Fame. She is an active member of many general aviation organisations. In 2013, she was honoured in the Amelia Earhart International Forest of Friendship in Atchison, Kansas. In 1994, the FAA named a new holding intersection in Colorado at an altitude of 15,500 feet above sea level after her as part of the U.S. aeronautical system. She is the recipient of the FAA Central Region 'Champion of Aviation Education Award'. In 2009, she was named ABC Television-Denver 7 'Everyday Hero' for over 25 years of volunteer community aviation education programmes. She is also the volunteer Director of the Teaching Women to Fly Research Project, which focuses on promoting success for women in general aviation, especially flight training.

Joshua Hirschheimer has been an aviation enthusiast since childhood. He has received two Bachelor's degrees: a Bachelor of Arts in Urban Planning from CUNY Hunter College and a Bachelor of Science in Airport Management and Air

Traffic Control at the Vaughn College of Aeronautics. He continued his education with a Master's degree in Airline Management at Embry-Riddle Aeronautical University, where he served as a research assistant in the areas of labour relations and organisational behaviour. He is a consultant at Sabre Airline Solutions, working with airlines worldwide and specialising in airline network planning and airspace operations. He currently lives in Dallas, Texas.

Giby Abraham Jacob hails from India. He obtained his undergraduate degree in Mechanical Engineering from Mahatma Gandhi University in India. Because of his passion for aviation, he moved to Florida to pursue his Master's degree in Business Administration at Embry Riddle Aeronautical University. He is currently working on his Master's degree with a specialisation in airline and airport operations, and is working as a graduate research assistant.

Ioana Koglbauer, who holds a PhD in psychology, is a pilot, aviation psychologist and human factors expert at Brightline Avionics Austria. Her current research activities focus on gender issues in aviation, human-centred design and evaluation of glass cockpit systems, navigation and collision avoidance devices, and cockpit automation. She has authored scientific papers in the areas of pilot performance and anticipative behaviour, threat and error management training, aviation psychophysiology, simulator and real-flight evaluations.

Alexandra Kristovics received her PhD in psychology. She is currently a lecturer in Organisational Behaviour in the Organisational Studies Programme for the School of Business at the University of Western Sydney (UWS). Prior to her present position, she also taught in the UWS School of Psychology for 10 years. She was also a consultant for an organisational psychology firm and was a practising psychologist. These roles helped her to develop a better understanding of the individual, social and structural factors underpinning both functional and dysfunctional behaviours/attitudes in the workplace.

Siegfried Loesch, who holds a PhD in mechanical engineering, is a hot air balloon pilot and justified expert for aviation technology in Austria. His current research activities include the development of algorithms and software for EFIS and flight simulator applications at Graz University of Technology, Austria. He is also General Manager of LCE Lösch Cellular Engineering Ziviltechniker GmbH, which develops regular cellular metallic materials.

Jean Helms Mills is Professor of Management at the Sobey School of Business, Saint Mary's University, Canada. She is the author of *Making Sense of Organizational Change* (2003) and co-author of *Understanding Organizational Change* (2009). She has presented her work on historiography, critical sense-making, gender, culture and change at numerous conferences and has published in a variety of journals. She is Associate Editor for *Gender, Work and Organization*, serves on the editorial boards of a number of journals and is past divisional Co-Chair of the Critical Management Studies Division of the Academy of Management. She also worked for a major airline for 17 years.

Alexandru Milut is a Revenue Management Analyst with Silver Airways in Ft. Lauderdale, Florida. He is a rated single- and multi-engine Commercial Pilot, as well as a Certificated Flight Instructor. In addition to his practical background in aviation, he earned a Master's in Business Administration and a Bachelor of Science in Aeronautical Science from Embry-Riddle Aeronautical University in Daytona Beach, Florida. During his days as a student, he worked as a graduate research assistant and banner-tow pilot.

Jim Mitchell is Lecturer in Management at the UWS. He gained his PhD in 2000 in industrial sociology and has taught in the management, human resource and aviation programmes. Prior to joining UWS, his work experience included some 30 years in a variety of industries. These include food manufacturing, health insurance and the airline industry in a range of management and administrative roles, mainly human resource management. His main research interests are in gender issues in organisations and aviation in particular from a cross-cultural perspective. He has published in this area in conjunction with international colleagues.

Preven Naidoo began his flying career in the South African Air Force (SAAF) in 1996, where he obtained his wings, and flew the Pilatus Astra and Cessna Caravan. In 2000, he continued his flying career as a commercial pilot, initially for Swazi Express Airways, then South African Express Airways (SAX) and presently with South African Airways (SAA). At SAA he flew the Boeing 747-400, the Airbus A319/320 and currently the Airbus A330/340. He has been with SAA for 10 years and is a Senior First Officer with around 10,000 hours of flight time; presently, he is flight operations CRM training manager and flight instructor on the Airbus A330/A340 fleet. He received a Bachelor of Commerce degree (BCom) in Aviation Management, an Honours degree (BCom Hons) in Business Management, a Master of Philosophy degree (MPhil) in Human Resource Management and a PhD in Organisational Behaviour from the University of Pretoria (South Africa). His research interests are in research methodology, quantitative/mathematical industrial psychology and aviation human factors. He is a research supervisor to MBA students at the University of Pretoria's Gordon Institute of Business Science (GIBS).

Rosemarie Reynolds has obtained her Bachelor's and Master's degrees in management, and her doctorate in industrial psychology. After graduation, she worked as a research psychologist at Naval Air Warfare Systems, Training Division, in Orlando, Florida. She left Naval Air Warfare Systems to join Embry Riddle Aeronautical University. She has been at the Embry Riddle College of Business since 2002, where she teaches classes in organisational behaviour, research methodology and statistics. She has published in a variety of journals, including the *Journal of Aviation/Aerospace Education and Research*, the *Journal of Airport Management* and the *Journal of Air Transportation*.

Air Commodore (Dr) Tracy Smart AM, BMBS, Dip Avmed, MPH, MA, FRACMA, FACAsM, FAsMA, FCDSS, AFACHSM, joined the RAAF as a medical undergraduate in 1985. She has served as a Medical Officer and Senior Medical Officer at bases around Australia, has undertaken overseas postings with the RAF and the USAF, was the first female Chief Instructor and then Commanding Officer of AVMED and was Officer Commanding Health Services Wing. She has had operational experience in Rwanda, Timor Leste, the Middle East and Lebanon, and was awarded a CAF Commendation for her role in a fatal air accident investigation in Malaysia. She attended the Centre for Defence and Strategic Studies as a student in 2008 and was promoted to AIRCDRE and posted into the dual roles of Director General Corporate Health Management and Air Force Health Services within Joint Health Command in February 2009. From 2010 to 2012 inclusive, she performed the role of Director General Garrison Health Operations, in which she managed healthcare at over 70 locations on Defence bases throughout Australia and oversaw a major reform in health service delivery in the ADF. She assumed the role of Strategic Health Coordination in January 2013, with responsibility for policy and research coordination, military medical advice, the Australian Army Malaria Institute and special projects. She has authored 14 published articles and over 70 papers for presentation at scientific meetings, primarily in the areas of aviation medicine, aeromedical evacuation and military medicine. She was made a Member of the Order of Australia in the 2012 Queen's Birthday Honours List.

Emeritus Professor Dr Leopold P. Vermeulen enjoyed tenure in an academic position at the University of Pretoria for 40 years. He was Head of the Academic Department of Human Resource Management from 1986 to 2007 and was involved in various research projects in the military field between 1973 and 1982. From 1982, he shifted his research focus contribution to human resource management, organisational behaviour and aviation psychology. He has authored and co-authored 38 refereed articles, 17 research reports and 12 non-refereed publications. He has delivered and co-delivered 44 conference papers (18 national and 26 international). Twelve PhD and 36 Master's students completed their dissertation successfully under his supervision. Although he retired in 2010, he is still actively involved in research and the supervision of PhD students.

Shannon R. Webb is a PhD candidate in Management (Saint Mary's University) and an LLM candidate (Osgoode Hall). Her educational background includes a BA (Queen's University), an LLB (Western University) and an MIR (Queen's University). She is employed as a labour and employment lawyer. She is also a member of the part-time faculty at Saint Mary's University and has taught with the

Centre for Industrial Relations at Queen's University. She is also a member of the Nova Scotia Labour Relations Board.

Heidi A. Weigand is a PhD candidate in the Management Department, Sobey School of Business, at Saint Mary's University, Canada. She also serves as a management consultant with the Saint Mary's University Business Development Centre. She has been a part-time instructor in both the marketing and management departments at Saint Mary's University as well as the Public Relations department at Mount Saint Vincent University. Her research is in the areas of sport and organisational performance management, goal-setting, employee engagement and motivation, intersectional discrimination studies and human resource social media technology. She is currently investigating the effects of a social media performance model on employee engagement, organisational commitment and psychological capital. She is on the board of directors for the Canadian Centre of Ethics in Public Affairs and serves as part of the research committee. She comes from a private sector background with over 20 years of management experience in the US and Canada with Xerox and IBM.

Acknowledgements

Our very grateful thanks go to the chapter authors for their commitment to this book and to the field of study. We particularly thank them for their patience in seeing the book through to fruition.

We are most indebted to our colleague and fellow author Dr Jim Mitchell from the University of Western Sydney in Australia. Jim envisioned the book and originally it was he who initiated the project to compile it. Through Jim's research and his connections, nationally and internationally, he was able to garner the participation of the diverse and committed group of authors who have contributed to this collection. His dedication to the field of aviation studies and particularly to gender and aviation shaped his vision for the book. We thank Jim for his ambition and for enabling us to play a part in this endeavour.

Many thanks are due also to Guy Loft and his colleagues from Ashgate for their support and guidance in completing this project.

Introduction

Aviation is a worldwide industry that has a significant impact on global and national economies. The industry employs substantial numbers of people and has input into the transportation of people and goods both internationally and domestically. In addition to the visible aspects of aviation such as airports and aircraft, the industry is a major player in areas including manufacturing, supply chains, logistics, hospitality and tourism. The flying component of the aviation industry can be broken down into two domains: civil and military. Military aviation has its own subcategories and these are not addressed here in detail. Civil aviation refers to all other aviation activities. It includes commercial aviation, that is, aircraft operated for profit. These are predominately airlines, but can include operations that do not include fare-paying passengers. General aviation encompasses all other aviation operations (Kumar, DeRemer and Marshall, 2004).

Clearly, airline organisations represent the 'big end' of the aviation industry. With substantial fleets of large and medium-size jets, these organisations dominate the industry in respect of international and domestic traffic. The industry also has smaller airline operations that use smaller jets and propeller-driven aircraft which cater for regional or localised passenger requirements. Competition has increased as both existing and new airlines enter the market as low-cost carriers (LCCs). LCCs are also identified as no-frills, discount or budget carriers or airlines. They generally have lower fares and fewer services, but increase revenue by charging for items provided free on full-cost airlines. This can include passengers paying for food, priority boarding, seat allocation and baggage handling. With electronic facilities, passengers can be required to check in and tag their bags themselves.

Structure of Piloting

Whilst commercial airlines are demonstrably economically and socially important, there are other vitally important components to the overall aviation industry that are sometimes overlooked. These are several subcategories within general aviation, including flying for business, pleasure and sport. Similarly, these can be divided into further subcategories that encompass micro-lights, gyrocopters and gliders (Department of Infrastructure and Transport (DIT), 2008). Each of these categories has significant numbers of aircraft and pilots. There is also a distinction within piloting between those who embrace it as an occupation and those who enjoy it as an activity. People wishing to be employed as a pilot are required to undertake levels of training that means acquiring licences, starting from the basic Private

Pilot's Licence (PPL) and progressing to a Commercial Pilot's Licence (CPL) and then an Airline Transport Pilot's Licence (ATPL). Various endorsements are added as the pilot progresses. This is both a time-consuming and costly exercise for individuals. Many pilots undertake this expense supported by a cadetship or traineeship with an airline or in the military.

Women and Piloting

Piloting is a gendered occupation. Currently women pilots represent less than six per cent of the worldwide pilot population (Mitchell, Kristovics and Bishop, 2010). Despite affirmative action and equal employment opportunity legislation in many countries, piloting remains a domain into which women rarely venture. Traditionally, airline pilots were recruited from the military, where a masculine culture dominates (Cadogan, 1992; Mills, 2006). Aircraft are technologically advanced and represent a high level of capital investment, and it is widely understood that in industries where technology and capital investment are dominant, masculine gender structures are prominent within occupation roles (Walby, 2011). However, rather than a glass ceiling, the aviation domain appears to have glass doors. Many women may look inside and turn away from what they see and hear. Those who do enter can be faced with a strongly masculine, often misogynistic culture (Gardner and Cooper, 1991; Render, 1992). This can manifest itself in jokes and innuendo about women pilots. For example, comments such as 'a woman pilot equals another empty kitchen' (see Mitchell, Vermeulen and Kristovics, Chapter 7 in this volume) and 'if women were meant to fly, the sky would be pink' (Mitchell et al., 2005) have been made in surveys. Even more demeaning is the epithet 'lumpy jumper syndrome' applied to the recruitment of women pilots in a well-recognised airline. Aviation is a dominant masculine occupational culture supported in the context of gendered organisations and continues to keep many jobs segregated on the same gender lines as was common in the early post-Second World War period (Whitelegg, 2007; Williams, Muller and Kilanski, 2012).

Yet, as discussed in the chapters in this book and elsewhere (see also Holden and Griffith, 1991; Lauwick, 1960; Rich, 1993), women have a history as long as men in aviation, including the breaking of numerous aviation records (Lovell, 1989; Mackersey, 1991; Smith, 1988). In the Second World War, women pilots demonstrated their capabilities as pilots in Britain's Air Transport Auxiliary (ATA – see, for example, Smith, 1988) and the US Women's Airforce Service Pilots (WASP – see, for example, Brinley, 1988). Their role was to ferry aircraft to various locations in Britain and the United States. Women pilots flew in treacherous weather conditions and in war zones. Nancy Miller Livingston Stratford flew 50 different types of aircraft for the ATA, including fighters, bombers, transports and other types:

> In the ATA, there were no copilots. Every pilot flew as pilot in command, never knowing what kind of plane they would have next. Because Britain is a small territory, you could fly five different types of aircraft in one day, from light trainers to B-24s, and only log about two or three hours.
>
> There were no radios in the aircraft, and therefore there was supposed to be no instrument flying, although it was impossible to fly in Britain without running into instrument conditions inadvertently. The unpredictable British weather caused a good many precautionary landings, and it could take as many as four or five days to complete an ordinary one-hour delivery flight. (Stratford, 2011, paras 6 and 7)

In Russia, women pilots had their own squadrons, became known as the 'Night Witches', and flew bombing missions against the German military (Bhuvasorakul, 2004; Cadogan, 1992). They routinely exceeded the male regiments in terms of the number of missions and accuracy of their bombing. However, as Krylova points out, many people experienced complex emotional reactions to the success of Soviet women pilots in the Second World War and their service was not automatically commended:

> These women's expectations of their inclusion in history books and fiction were never realised. Women with weapons in their hands, who also excelled at dying and killing, provoked an unexpected popular and intense, disorganised hostility to the female sacrifice. This reaction surfaced in front and home front folk stories and rumours, invaded Soviet literature and survived in memoirs of women fighters. The backlash radically reinterpreted the meanings assigned to female fighting by official culture. In rumours and folk stories, the front women's effort was reduced to prostitution and husband-hunting. Already in Soviet literature by 1943, women fighting at the front and killing the enemy gave way to images of wives and civilian young girls waiting for men to return home. (Krylova, 2004, pp. 649–50)

The women pilots of the three nations made a significant contribution to the war effort, but their actions were not recognised until many years later. At the end of the war, the ATA, WASP organisations and Soviet regiments were disbanded and the women returned to civilian life. Pilot jobs in a rapidly expanding commercial aviation were made available to returning airmen. Women were excluded within the masculine culture of the occupation of pilot (Pugh, 1992). The traditional structures of patriarchy returned women and men to their assigned roles within the sexual division of labour. Women were consigned to their perceived domestic functions related to 'education, care and service' and were denied authority over men. Men retained their 'monopoly of the handling of technical objects and machines' (Bourdieu, 2001, p. 94).

Absent Aviators

The under-representation of women in the occupation of pilot is not simply a concern for gender equality in the workforce and women's rights; low numbers of women pilots directly contribute to the general shortfall of pilots in both military and civil aviation. According to Boeing (2012), 460,000 new commercial airline pilots will be required over the next 20 years in the commercial aviation industry in order to meet increasing numbers of new and replacement aircraft. In the Asia-Pacific region alone, it is estimated that a further 185,600 pilots will be required by 2030, with China requiring 71,300, North East Asia 18,800, South East Asia 51,500, Oceania 12,900 and South West Asia 31,000 (Kelly, 2012). If the commercial aviation industry is to meet the projected level of new pilots, then the recruitment and retention of women into the occupation of pilot will be vital to satisfy demand. Women are needed in both general aviation and the military. Therefore, the aviation industry (both civil and military) needs to make piloting more attractive to women. The industry and military organisations will need to engage with the barriers that deter women from becoming pilots as well as those that cause attrition. The aim of this book is to highlight the many issues surrounding the occupation of pilot and women's place in this male-dominated role; some of the authors explore factors that deter women from flying in general, others shed light on the experience of women within the aviation industry in both contemporary and historical contexts, whilst others explore the debates about gender and work that provide insight into women's roles in aviation. The book also suggests various ways and means to remove barriers to women in the occupation of pilot in order to overcome the potential pilot shortage. In the broader context, this book is about addressing gender issues in masculine occupations.

Overview of Chapters

The chapters that make up this book have been written by a diverse range of authors from several countries. Thus, they present different perspectives on gender and other issues within aviation. The primary focus is on the occupation of the pilot and on matters that impact on the industry as a whole. The book is divided into four parts: Identifying Gender Issues in Piloting; Barriers in Military and Civil Aviation; Technical Issues; and Taking Action.

Part I – Identifying Gender Issues in Piloting

There are four chapters in the first part of the book. We start with a chapter from Heidi Weigand, Shannon R. Webb, Albert J. Mills and Jean Helms Mills from Saint Mary's University in Canada. Chapter 1, 'The Junctures of Intersectionality: Race, Gender, Class and Nationality and the Making of Pan American Airways, 1929–89', addresses a gap in the literature; specifically, it uses intersectionality as a research method to explore the organisational practices of Pan American Airways (Pan Am) in different historical contexts. The authors examine the employment and trading practices of Pan Am in the US and Latin America in a retrospective study that builds on the work of McCall (2005) and Bagilhole (2010). Intersectionality is used here to document change over time and to understand the different lived experiences and social realities of those employed by Pan Am in a specific time period. The authors look at five categories of discrimination – ethnicity, class, race, gender and nationality – and elucidate how institutional and political shifts have impacted upon the experiences and social realities of Pan Am employee and trade partner relationships. They particularly focus upon the issues associated with the building of a white, masculine culture within Pan Am and the impact that this has had on the roles of women and men of ethnicity in the shaping of aviation culture.

The second chapter in this section, 'Difficult, Dangerous, Not a Job for Girls: Factors Impacting Women and Girls' Orientation Towards Pilot Careers' by Deanne Gibbon from the Australian Defence Force, examines why women do and don't pursue flying careers in military and civil aviation. Theory used to explain women's under-representation in fields of non-traditional employment broadly falls into two schools of thought; individual/choice theory versus constraints/barrier theory. This chapter examines women's under-representation in piloting through the lens of the first theory, by identifying why women and girls are reluctant to view aviation as a viable career. The chapter also ascertains a series of factors common to those women who do step outside the stereotype and pursue careers as both military and civil pilots. This chapter draws on data from two distinct sources. The first is a series of focus groups with young women/girls from a range of different contexts to gauge their views of flying as a possible career choice. The second data set is drawn from 75 semi-structured interviews with women pilots, at different careers stages, to ascertain their upbringing, motivation to fly and other key factors that may have influenced their decision to pursue this non-traditional pathway. The chapter concludes that flying remains a heavily gender-stereotyped career in the eyes of most women/girls, with most viewing the job as 'too difficult', 'too dangerous' and gender-inappropriate to even be considered a viable career choice. It also contends that to move past this deeply imbedded stereotype, women must be exposed to a range of factors necessary to incite their passion for this non-traditional employment field.

Chapter 3, 'Fast Women: Or Why Women Who Fly High-Performance Aircraft are Fast But Not Loose', is accompanied by a postscript. This chapter, written by Tracy Smart from the Royal Australian Air Force Institute of Aviation Medicine, examines some of the main issues relating to women pilots, concentrating on the physicality of women and how compatible or not military aircraft is with the female body. This chapter, first written in the late 1990s, looks at objections to women in military pilot roles and in doing so considers four areas of argument: the physiological differences between women and men; the perceived physical weakness of women in comparison to men; health problems specific to women; and squadron cultural issues. The medical and physiological focus of much of the chapter considers women's capacity to fly in the masculine domain of the military in light of scientific evidence. The author also examines cultural barriers that are often found to be contradictory to scientific evidence concerning capacity to fly. The author's postscript, 'Fast Women in the Twenty-First Century', considers innovations in military technology and how these have provided alterations in areas of importance for women, such as cockpit modifications to accommodate a wider range of body sizes and the development of female flying suits that are more suitable for women's bodies than were the designs that were based on the male body but issued to both sexes.

Chapter 4, 'Gender-Based Attitudes Regarding Pilot Behaviour' by Rosemarie Reynolds, Alexandru Milut, Giby Abraham Jacob, Joshua Hirschheimer and Bridget Cox from Embry-Riddle Aeronautical University examines pilot attitudes in the US. The chapter reports on research that was conducted with 113 (89 males and 24 females) Federal Aviation Administration-certificated pilots, all of whom answered an online 34-question Aviation Gender Attitude Questionnaire. The research was designed to understand more about the masculine culture of the aviation industry in the US and specific barriers to women's participation, such as negative attitudes towards women, sexism, harassment and discrimination. The chapter provides a cross-national literature review regarding male pilots' attitudes to women pilots and an examination of literature and research with a focus on pilot behaviours that are based in gender. The authors combine the insights gained from current literature with their own original data to explain gender-based attitudes towards female pilots, The research is based on a series of eight hypotheses that propose that pilot attitudes would vary depending on a number of variables, including: pilots' gender, age, flight experience, opportunity to fly with the opposite gender, level of certification, instructor rating and crew resource management training. The authors found that the general hypothesis that attitudes towards women as pilots would be determined according to gender were correct, with male pilots being more negative towards women pilots than women pilots were themselves.

Part II – Barriers in Military and Civil Aviation

This part presents four chapters that identify and examine the barriers that militate against women pursuing a career in piloting. In Chapter 5, 'Unexpected Turbulence: The Cultural, Gender-Based Challenges Facing Female Pilots in the Australian Defence Force' by Deanne Gibbon from the Australian Defence Force, women's under-representation in flying is examined through the theoretical lens of Kanter's (1977) seminal 'perceptual phenomena' theory. This theory argues that gender-skewed job roles are caused by the efforts of the dominant group to preserve the advantage their group enjoys by making workplaces untenable for female workers. Drawing on data from 46 in-depth, semi-structured interviews with women pilots (past, present and future), this chapter analyses the gender-based barriers and challenges faced by women pilots in both the military and civil aviation contexts.

It is argued that there remain a range of significant barriers and challenges for women that impede their success at all life and career stages, but especially during the training context and at earlier career stages. Motherhood and juggling flying careers with raising young children also presents as a key challenge, especially in the military aviation environment. The chapter concludes that whist civil aviation contexts have become increasingly welcoming and inclusive of women pilots, the military context remains a 'boys' club' where women are viewed as unwelcome intruders into the domain of men. This may explain why women's participation rates in Australian military pilot roles are less than half the participation rate found in civil aviation and why so few women remain in military flying beyond their contracted obligation.

Chapter 6, 'Grounded? Female Pilots, Gender Identity and Integration into the Australian Defence Force' by Donna Bridges from Charles Sturt University, Australia, examines gender issues that arise for women pilots in the Australian Defence Force (ADF) from a military sociology perspective. This chapter provides historical and contemporary contexts associated with women integrating into the military in Australia and analyses the unique difficulties that women in the ADF have encountered when entering into occupations traditionally associated with male gender identity. The author explores the reasons why roles that are defined as masculine do not attract or retain women in anything other than tokenistic numbers. The masculinised cultures of the military and the aviation industry are considered in terms of how they resist women's participation and how they maintain their gendered identity in the face of increasing pressure to integrate women in greater numbers. This chapter seeks to elucidate the barriers and challenges that women pilots face in the ADF. The most complex of these barriers is the masculine culture of the ADF, which constructs military roles as gendered. The chapter places the role of female personnel in the ADF in societal and political contexts, examining how the military constructs the feminine along lines that are discriminatory and illogical, and how the broader belief systems about gender in the ADF thwart progress towards full gender integration.

Chapter 7, 'Another Empty Kitchen: Gender Issues on the Flight Deck' by Jim Mitchell and Alexandra Kristovics from the University of Western Sydney, Australia and Leopold P. Vermeulen, from the University of Pretoria, South Africa, briefly examines historical perspectives relating to women pilots within the context of aviation that have been seen as the bastion of masculinity. Aviation has a long history of heroic deeds performed mainly by men and thus has developed an ethos that recognises 'the right stuff' as an important component of that image. Women pilots are still considered the exception in the industry rather than being accepted as competent contributors. This chapter reports on survey research conducted with pilots across Australia, South Africa and the US. The survey was utilised to ascertain the perceptions of pilots to gender-related issues on the flight deck. While drawing on the results from the quantitative analysis, the main focus is on the results of the qualitative analysis that draws on a grounded theory approach. The analysis identified Flying Proficiency, Safety Orientation, Industry, Gender

Issues, Equity and Survey as themes from the comments. The comments cover a broad spectrum of stereotypical perceptions and prejudices for and against female pilots. The growing numbers of female pilots, albeit still small, is having an impact on the perceptions of pilots and the stereotypical male image of the occupation.

Chapter 8, ‘Flying through Barriers: Identifying Issues for Female Airline Pilots’, by Jane Neal-Smith from the London Metropolitan Business School, explores structural and attitudinal barriers that can affect women but not men on their journey to becoming commercial airline pilots in the UK. The research analysed the experiences of 20 women pilots in the UK, how they became interested in flying, their training experiences and the difficulties they overcame to gain employment within the commercial airline industry. This chapter identifies areas in which women can be discouraged from choosing flying as a career as well as highlighting areas where women pilots can be discriminated against and discouraged from continuing flying as a career. Importantly, the author makes connections between the barriers women face when choosing the role of pilot as a career, retention of women in the industry, and policies that can be put in place which can counteract barriers to employment. The author argues that it is the determination and dedication of the women pilots interviewed for the study that has aided their journey through training to employment as a commercial pilot. However, it is nevertheless important to identify places where other women can be faced with barriers. These barriers are usually the result of gender assumptions about ability and can be visible or invisible.

Part III – Technical Issues

This part consists of three chapters that focus on the changing technologies being introduced throughout aviation. Chapter 9, ‘Automation in Light Aircraft: A Cross-National Analysis’ by Alexandra Kristovics and Jim Mitchell from the University of Western Sydney, Ronald W. Bishop from the Central Queensland University, Australia, and Preven Naidoo and Leopold P. Vermeulen from the University of Pretoria, South Africa, investigates several issues common across two countries. These issues concern the advancement of aviation technology in the form of glass cockpits, an innovation which increases automation. For the past 10 years, glass cockpits have been incorporated into light aircraft at an ever-increasing rate. Research on the impact of the new technology on pilots’ perceptions has been carried out in light of continuing concerns about the efficacy of the technology and pilots’ performance. This chapter seeks to evaluate the Advanced Cockpit Aircraft Survey developed through the National Aeronautics and Space Administration (NASA) (Casner, 2008) and to apply the results in a cross-national comparison of Australian and South African light aircraft pilots. The study also considers gender issues in aviation. Results highlight significant differences between Australian and South African pilots, between women and men pilots regardless of country of origin, and between those who are more or less experienced in glass cockpits. In relation to gender, men generally preferred to use more automated systems than women; however, women tended to be more concerned than men with both the complexity of automated systems and the possibility of misusing them. Both male and female Australian pilots were found to prefer automated systems less than South African pilots, with Australian women pilots tending to prefer them less than Australian men pilots; thus, the authors conclude that culture also plays a role.

Chapter 10, 'Gender Issues in Usability of Glass Cockpit for General Aviation Aircraft' by Ioana Koglbauer, Klaus Fruehwirth and Eric Grubmueller from Brightline Avionics, Austria, and Reinhard Braunstingl and Siegfried Loesch from Graz University of Technology, Austria, considers gender-specific strengths and weaknesses of men and women pilots, such as those that occur in accidents, with the aim of improving cockpit design. Previous accident investigation studies have found significant differences in the incidence of specific flight errors of women and men pilots involved in aircraft crashes. The aim of this study was to optimise the design and functions of an aircraft cockpit using a formative evaluation with male ($n = 10$) and female ($n = 10$) pilots, from Austria, Germany and Switzerland. A new glass cockpit system with manual and automated features was implemented and tested in a flight simulator at Graz University of Technology. Tests involved normal and abnormal aircraft operation scenarios. Pilots' performance, cardiac activity, workload, situation awareness, emotional state, usability and acceptance were evaluated in an experimental design with two matched groups (female and male pilot groups), two operational conditions and two control modes. Gender-specific and overall benefits and limitations in managing automated and manual glass cockpit features are discussed. Conclusions for optimisation of the glass cockpit system to include aspects of gender diversity were drawn out in order to facilitate better and safer flight performance. Results were implemented to optimise the automation functions of an aircraft cockpit developed by Brightline Avionics, which will be installed in general aviation aircraft.

Chapter 11, the final chapter in this part, compares women's and men's perception of glass cockpits in general aviation. 'Glass Cockpits in General Aviation: A Comparison of Male and Female Pilots' perceptions' by Jim Mitchell and Alexandra Kristovics from the University of Western Sydney, Australia and Ronald W. Bishop from Central Queensland University, Australia identifies issues relevant and specific to how each gender perceives glass cockpits. This Australian research builds on similar research carried out in the US. The research used a mixed method approach based on an electronic survey. Quantitative data was drawn from multiple-choice questions and the qualitative data drawn from free comments that participants wrote at the end of the survey. The quantitative and qualitative results are used to complement each other in the analysis. The results indicate, as a community of users, that both men and women pilots generally have positive perceptions of advanced cockpit systems. Results from the quantitative analyses indicate that men preferred to use advanced cockpit systems significantly more than women. Women also tended to be more concerned about not losing their piloting skills and being dependent on these systems more than men. Additional information was also gained through the analyses that suggested that although both men and women pilots were positive and had adopted the new technology, the reasons underlying the use were quite different for men and women.

Part IV – Taking Action

The final part of this book assesses attempts to attract more women to piloting and to advance the occupation so that it becomes less masculine and more open to women pursuing careers in civilian and military environments. 'Leaving Gender "In": The Royal Australian Air Force's Project to Increase the Representation of Female Pilots' by Deanne Gibbon from the Australian Defence Force evaluates a project conducted by the Australian Air Force that aimed to increase the representation of female pilots in all three branches of the ADF. This chapter considers the significant range of gender-based barriers that limit women's progress and alter their propensity to remain in their chosen career (constraints). Only by actively addressing both choice and constraint factors can organisations like the ADF hope to increase their numbers of female pilots in the future. Drawing on theory addressing the issue of increasing women's participation in non-traditional employment roles and data from focus groups/interviews with pilots and non-pilots, this chapter discusses a range of practical strategies and interventions that might be used to encourage higher numbers of women to enter and remain in pilot roles in both military and civil aviation. The Australian Air Force is currently in the process of implementing a range of interventions to diversify its pilot workforce; these are detailed in this chapter as practical examples of initiatives that are already showing some success. This chapter shows that 'bridging the gap' between choice and constraint theory is of paramount importance to removing occupational gender stereotypes and thus ensuring that economies can capitalise on all available human resources in future.

Chapter 13, the final chapter in this book, written by Penny Rafferty Hamilton, a celebrated pilot, businesswoman, author and journalist, and entitled 'The Teaching Women to Fly Research Project', is a practical example of a programme designed to increase the number of women pilots in general aviation. The Project was initiated in the US and was designed to generate positive initiatives and approaches to overcome the impending acute shortage of pilots. The project focused on understanding and learning more about women's motivations to become pilots, their positive and negative flight training experiences and the barriers to their success in becoming and/or remaining pilots. Information was collected using a short open-ended survey consisting of 15 questions for women flight students and pilots, and a 12-question survey for flight instructors. A total of 54 female flight students and women who started flight training but did not certificate, and 157 female pilots volunteered to complete the questionnaire. In addition, 52 female and 33 male flight instructors returned surveys. The study culminated in three outcomes that are useful in understanding barriers to recruitment and retention of women in aviation: the first was to identify and collate the 'Top 10 Barriers That Stop Women From Learning to Fly' and the second was to compile the 'Top Ten

Ways to Increase [women's] Success in General Aviation', while the third was to create the extensive list of '101 Ideas to Increase Women's Success in General Aviation'. All of these outcomes of the research are helpful ways to increase the numbers of women in general aviation.

References

Bagilhole, B., 2010. Applying the lens of intersectionality to UK equal opportunities and diversity policies. *Canadian Journal of Administrative Science*, 27(3), pp. 263–71.

Bhuvasorakul, J.L., 2004. Unit cohesion among the three Soviet Women's Air Regiments during World War II. MA thesis, Florida State University.

Boeing (2012). Pilot and technical outlook. Available at: http://www.boeing.com/commercial/cmo/pilot_technician_outlook.html.

Bourdieu, P., 2001. *Masculine Domination*. Stanford, CA: Stanford University Press.

Brinley, M.B., 1988. *Jackie Cochran. The Story of the Greatest Woman Pilot in Aviation History*. Toronto: Bantam.

Cadogan, M., 1992. *Women with Wings*. London: Macmillan.

Carey, S., Nicas, J. and Pasztor, A., 2012. Airlines face acute shortages of pilots. *Wall Street Journal*, 12 November. Available at: http://online.wsj.com/article/SB10001424052970203937004578079391643223634.html.

Casner, S., 2008. General aviation pilots' attitudes toward advanced cockpit systems. *International Journal of Applied Aviation Studies*, 8(1), pp. 88–113.

Department of Infrastructure and Transport, 2008. The general aviation industry action agenda. Available at: http://www.infrastructure.gov.au/aviation/general.

Gardner, E. and Cooper, A.L., 1991. *Rising Above It. An Autobiography*. New York: Orion.

Holden, H.M. and Griffith, C.L., 1991. *Ladybirds: The Untold Story of Women Pilots in America*. Mt. Freedom, NJ: Black Hawk Publishing Co.

Kanter, R.M., 1977. *Men and Women of the Corporation*. New York: Basic Books.

Kelly, E., 2012. Facing up to the challenge. *Asian Aviation*, 10(10), pp. 20–22.

Krylova, A., 2004. Stalinist identity from the viewpoint of gender: Rearing a generation of professionally violent women-fighters on 1930s Stalinist Russia. *Gender & History*, 16(3), pp. 626–53.

Kumar, B., DeRemer, D. and Marshall, D., 2004. *An Illustrated Dictionary of Aviation*. New York: McGraw-Hill.

Lauwick, H., 1960. *Heroines of the Sky*. London: Frederick Muller.

Lovell, M.S., 1989. *The Sound of Wings: The Biography of Amelia Earhart*. London: Hutchinson.

Mackersey, I., 1991. *Jean Batten: The Garbo of the Skies*. London: Macdonald & Co.

McCall, L., 2005. The complexity of intersectionality. *Signs*, 30(3), pp. 1771–800.

Mills, A.J., 2006. *Sex, Strategy and the Stratosphere: Airlines and the Gendering of Organizational Culture*. Basingstoke: Palgrave Macmillan.

Mitchell, J., Kristovics, A. and Bishop, R. 2010. Glass cockpits in general aviation: A comparison of men and women pilots' perceptions. *International Journal of Applied Aviation Studies*, 10(2), pp. 11–29.

Mitchell, J., Kristovics, A., Vermeulen, L., Wilson, J. and Martinussen, M., 2005. How pink is the sky? A cross-national study of the gendered occupation of pilot. *Employment Relations Record*, 5(2), pp. 43–60.

Pugh, M., 1992. *Women and the Women's Movement in Britain 1914–1959*. London: Macmillan.

Render, S., 1992. *No Place for a Lady: The Story of Canadian Women Pilots 1928–1992*. Winnipeg: Portage & Main Press.

Rich, D.L., 1993. *Queen Bess*. Washington, DC: Smithsonian Institution Press.

Smith, C.B., 1988. *Amy Johnson*, 3rd edn. Bury St Edmunds: Patrick Stephens.

Stratford, N.M.L., 2011. From spitfires to mosquitoes. *Plane & Pilot*. Available at: http://www.planeandpilotmag.com/pilot-talk/more-pilot-talk/guest-speaker-from-spitfires-to-mosquitoes.html.

Walby, S., 2011. Is the knowledge society gendered? *Gender, Work & Organization*, 18(1), pp. 1–29.

Williams, C.L., Muller, C. and Kilanski, K., 2012. Gendered organizations in the new economy. *Gender & Society*, 26(4), pp. 549–73.

Whitelegg, D., 2007. *Working the Skies: The Fast-Paced, Disorienting World of the Flight Attendant*. New York: New York University Press.

PART I
Identifying Gender Issues in Piloting

Chapter 1

The Junctures of Intersectionality: Race, Gender, Class and Nationality and the Making of Pan American Airways, 1929–89

Heidi Weigand, Shannon R. Webb, Albert J. Mills and Jean Helms Mills

Introduction

> Underpinning the arguments here is the acknowledgement that the social differentiations under consideration (gender, race, disability, sexual orientation, religion or belief, and age) do not create homogenous groups … It has now become clear … that there is no longer, if ever, a uniform story of blanket disadvantage for any of these groups. Therefore, *it is timely to acknowledge, confront, and deal with the actual problems of separate and relative deprivation, and sometimes conflicting experiences and interests, both between different categories of disadvantage and even within these categories themselves.* (Bagilhole, 2010, emphasis added)

In 2005 McCall argued that ‘despite the emergence of intersectionality as a major paradigm of research in women’s studies and elsewhere, there has been little discussion of *how* to study intersectionality, that is, of its methodology’ (p. 1771, emphasis in original). McCall then went on to outline three methodological approaches – anticategorial complexity, intrasectionality and intersectionality. Five years later, Bagilhole (2010, p. 270) repeated the point, arguing that despite its theoretical contribution to our understandings of discrimination, ‘there has been little discussion of how it might be operationalized’. To that end, Bagilhole, drawing on McCall’s three methods, ‘set out to consider and analyse its [intersectionality theory] utility as an approach that can further the project of equal opportunities and diversity in the political and policy and policy-making arena’ (2010, p. 270). Building on the work of McCall (2005) and Bagilhole (2010), we attempt to apply the notion of intersectionality retrospectively (Weick, 1995) through a study of one organisation – Pan American Airways (Pan Am) – over time.

We undertake a retrospective study for three reasons: 1) as per Bagilhole (2010), to explore not only the strengths and limitations of the operationalisation of the concept of intersectionality but also the relative viability of McCall’s three methodological approaches; 2) to understand the influence of *categories* of difference on ‘regimes of inequality’ (Acker, 2006), thus revealing the ways in which (single) *categories* of difference serve to compound discrimination; and 3) to examine (and theorise) the role of history and the past (Booth and Rowlinson, 2006) in the development and understanding of categories of difference that, we argue, need to be understood in context.

We undertake our study with a framework that involves three elements: a theoretical categorisation of intersectionality by McCall (2005); a (postpositivist) case study (Mills et al., 2010) of Pan American Airways; and a framing of the past through the heuristic of 'junctures' (Mills, 2010).

Intersectionality and Theoretical Categories

McCall identifies three 'approaches' to the study of intersectionality according to 'their stance towards categories' (2005, p. 1773). The first, *anticategorial complexity* (p. 1773), draws from poststructuralist tradition in an approach that 'deconstructs analytical categories'. This approach argues that 'social life is too irreducibly complex ... to make fixed categories anything but simplifying social fictions that produce inequalities in the process of producing differences' (p. 1773). McCall views this approach as 'the most successful in satisfying the demand for complexity' (p. 1773). However, she goes on to suggest that it falters as a method as it comes up against the issues of categorisation as lived experience and the possibility of identity and voice in a research process that locates subjectivity in multiple identities/voices.

McCall's second – *intracategorical complexity* – approach 'acknowledges the stable and even durable relationships that social categories represent at any given point in time, though it also maintains a critical stance towards categories' (2005, p. 1774). In overly simplified terms, this approach, while questioning the socially constructed character of categories as fixed, draws on broadly established notions of gender, race, class, etc. to 'identify a previously invisible group and reveal the complex nature of its members' daily lived experiences' (Bagilhole, 2010, p. 268). Thus, for this approach, the 'primary subject of analysis [is] typically either a single social group at a neglected point of intersection of multiple master categories or a particular social setting or ideological construction, or both' (McCall, 2005, p. 1780).

McCall's third – *intersectional complexity* – approach (also referred to as the 'categorical approach') differs from the previous (intrasectional) approach in that it uses existing categories strategically. It 'begins with the observation that there are relationships of inequality among already constituted social groups, as imperfect and as ever changing as they are, and takes these relationships as the center of analysis' (McCall, 2005, p. 1785). McCall (2005, p. 1773) sees a tendency for this latter approach to be conflated in the anticategorical approach, while Bagilhole (2010, p. 268), arguing that postmodern theory constitutes 'a retreat from and a failure to engage with political realities', contends 'that the other two approaches to intersectionality offer a useful way back into the political and policy-making arena'. In our case study of Pan Am, we will explore each of McCall's three approaches.

Pan Am: A Postpositive Case Study

McCall's (2005) discussion of appropriate methods to study the complexity of intersectionality suggests – both inadvertently and overtly – the use of case study. In the latter case she mirrors the argument for case study research (Yin, 2009) in the statement that 'intersectionality has introduced new methodological problems [due to] … the complexity that arises when the subject of analysis expand [sic] to include multiple dimensions of social life and categories of analysis' (McCall, 2005, p. 1772). She continues: 'Not surprisingly, researchers favour methodologies that more naturally lend themselves to the study of complexity and reject methodologies that are considered too simplistic or reductionist' (McCall, 2005, p. 1772). Later, in the same regard, she argues that: 'Case studies and qualitative research more generally have always been distinguished by their ability to delve into the complexities of social life – to reveal diversity, variation, and heterogeneity where quantitative researchers see singularity, sameness, and homogeneity' (McCall, 2005, p. 1782). Thus: 'Many feminists who are trained in social science methods and who are interested in intersectionality use the case study method to identity a new or invisible group' (McCall, 2005, p. 1782). In fairness, McCall also counsels that a shift toward studies of complex phenomena of this type 'restricts the scope of knowledge that can be produced on intersectionality' (2005, p. 1772).

With the last caveat in mind, we also embark on a case study to attempt to reveal the complex nature of intersectionality and the attempts to study it. Our approach is 'postpositivist' in that it eschews ontological notions of reality and truth and the adoption of pseudo-natural scientific approaches (Prasad, 2005). In developing an account of intersectionality in a single organisation over time (in our case Pan Am), we recognise the role of the researcher in imposing socially constructed boundaries, frameworks and events on the account that is developed (Mills et al., 2010). Following McCall, we assume 'that different methodologies produce different kinds of knowledge' (2005, p. 1772).

Methods of Study

The study we embarked upon centred on archival research, focused on a large collection of corporate documents (in 1,500 boxes) that constitute the Pan American Airways Collection 341, Series I and II held at the Otto Richter Library of the University of Miami. A team of four researchers visited the Collection on 14 different occasions, ranging from one to two weeks in the period from 2005 to 2010. The research has to date generated two PhD theses, numerous conference papers, journal articles and book chapters, and formed part of a book that focused on the gendering of airline cultures across three airlines. Although some of the research was focused on issues of organisational history, the bulk of the research centred on issues of gender and, to a lesser degree, race and ethnicity. While gender, race, ethnicity and history are all key elements of our discussion of intersectionality, the way in which the materials were originally collected may be a limitation to our findings.

Informed by a feminist poststructuralist approach (Calás and Smircich, 1996), our analysis of the materials for the current intersectionality research project involved the method of critical hermeneutics (Prasad and Mir, 2002) and an historical framing called junctures (see below). Critical hermeneutics involves a process of reading various texts (e.g., minutes, travelogues, company narratives, annual reports, film, diaries, published histories, etc.) to understand the role of: i) the interpretive conditions in which understanding takes place; ii) the researcher in the process of interpretation – his or her situatedness in the process; iii) language and history as conditions and limitations of understanding; iv) the process of textual reading as a form of translation (of researcher to audience); and v) ambiguity as a key outcome of the process to inhibit single readings of a given text or set of texts (Bryman et al., 2011).

Critical hermeneutics thus involved us in reading a series of Pan Am materials to see *what was being said* (the words on or missing from the page), for example, accounts, discussions and absences of different categories of people; *how it was being said* (the use of rhetoric, narrative, emplotment, etc – White, 1985), for example, who and how certain people were being privileged and who and how others were being marginalised; *the historical context in which things were being said* in order to understand both the conditions that allowed certain things to be said and to make sense of how statements were understood at the time, for example, what the conditions were that allowed for use of the term 'Negro' and how the term was understood at a certain point of time; and *the translation of what was being said* (the role of the researcher), for example, understanding and being cautious about the way that the researcher's interpretations construct a sense of what was being said.

The Juncture as a Heuristic for Understanding Intersectionality

Collins (2000, p. 299) argues that: 'Intersectionality refers to particular forms of intersecting oppressions, for example, intersections of race and gender, or of sexuality and nation. Intersectional paradigms remind us that oppression cannot be reduced to one fundamental type, and that oppressions work together in producing injustice'. There is a need for analysis to look at the whole person rather than breaking up a person into component parts. Individuals possess one identity that encompasses multiple and intersecting oppressions, but in order to prevent impotence on inequality, it is important to recognise that different oppressions surface as more important from time to time (Bagilhole, 2006).

We contend that the study of intersectionality needs to be understood as embedded in a changing historical context (or contexts). This is arguable at two levels. First, the concept of intersectionality is itself a concept that needs to be understood in the context of its development. McCall hints broadly at this when she says 'that [i]nterest in intersectionality arose out of a critique of gender-based and race-based research for failing to account for lived experience at neglected points of intersection' (2005, p. 1780). Although an explanation of the development of the idea of intersectionality is beyond the scope of this chapter, we are cautioned to be careful in how we impose our understanding of intersectionality on organisational actors and events in times before the term was invented. People almost certainly felt the pull of varying and conflicting social categories in the past, but how that was understood was different from how we might currently choose to make sense of those experiences. Second, intersectionality is often viewed as a particular way of understanding social location in terms of crisscross systems of oppression. Collins, for example, describes intersectionality as an 'analysis claiming that systems of race, social class, gender, sexuality, ethnicity, nation, and age form mutually constructing features of social organization' (2000, p. 299). We would go further and argue that social location, systems of oppressions and the intersectional features of social organisation can be thought of as outcomes at points in time. To understand those locations, systems and features of oppression, we also need to understand them in context. To understand how they develop, are maintained and change over time, we need to understand how each is/was understood at different points of time. This is for at least two reasons. First, as McCall recognises, the 'artificiality of social categories can be illuminated in history with the method of genealogy, in literature with deconstruction, and in anthropology with the new ethnography' (2005, p. 1778). However, second, what is equally important is the character of artificiality and how its fictitiousness is developed and maintained.

Understanding intersectionality over time involves history per se. Our approach relies on anti-positivist analyses of history where history is viewed as accounts of the past that are invented rather than discovered (White, 1973; Munslow, 2010). To that end, we view the past not as a linear, progressive or evolutionary process, but rather as a series of (dominant) mentalities. To capture that process, we draw on the notion of the juncture (Mills, 2010) as a methodological devise for studying organisational change over time: 'it refers to a concurrence of events in time in which a series of images, impressions, and experiences come together, giving the appearance of a coherent whole that influences how an organization is understood' (Mills, 2010, p. 509). Although not directly related, the approach has something in common with Foucault's (1979) notion of episteme and Febve and Bloch's notion of mentalities (Bloch, 1953).

The concept of juncture is used as a heuristic, the idea of which is that we track a dominant mentality in a particular organisation around the issues of intersectionality. We then follow the mentality over time to assess where and when it appears in corporate imagery, but also where it appears to change. Having identified two differing points of intersectionality, which we label 'junctures', we then work backwards through the documentation to gain a sense of when one ends and the other begins. We then examine events around the apparent change to assess what factors are associated with the change. We then move forward through the material to see if there are signs of different forms of dominant mentalities, identifying new junctures in the process. We hope that the accumulated evidence provides clues to the development, maintenance and changing character of intersectionality over time, as well as its problematisation. The concept was originally developed to make sense of the gendering of airline companies over time (Helms Mills, 2005; Mills, 2006; Dye and Mills, 2012).

Intersectionality, Junctures and Pan American Airways

We follow McCall's (2005) categorical approach of intersectionality using existing categorical distinctions to document inequality across multiple dimensions and document its change over time. Collins (2000) was particularly interested in how intersectionality creates different kinds of lived experiences and social realities. In the case of Pan Am, we will look at five categories of discrimination – ethnicity, class, race, gender and nationality – to explore how the experiences and social realities of Pan Am employees and trade partner relationships are impacted by Pan Am's institutional shifts and political networks during the Great Depression, the Second World War, the immediate post-war era and the era of Women's Liberation.

Relationships are complex and the forces influencing power distribution are constantly shifting due to varying elements such as cultural, economic, political and social events (Acker, 2006). A number of feminist studies emphasise the importance of institutional order and political networks, and how these elements can impact the experiences of identified minority groups through exclusion and subordination (Kanter, 1977; Acker, 1992; Katila and Merilainen, 2002). This chapter uses a case study of Pan American Airways (Pan Am) to analyse the multiple factors influencing the power distribution amongst employees from its early beginnings to its demise at the end of the 1980s. Historically the relationships based on discrimination and domination have been analysed at singular levels of categorisation and impact, creating a broad view that similar groups suffer the same discriminatory injustices. Drawing on the concept of intersectionality (Collins, 2000), this chapter develops what we call a matrix of domination to understand the implications of multiple levels of discriminatory practices and how that influenced people's sense of inclusion, marginality and oppression.

The junctures we identify are: 1) 'A Matrix of Domination' (1927–41). This first juncture examines the period from the airlines' start-up in 1927 through to the imminent threat of war in 1941; 2) 'War time USA: Shifting Boundaries and a Blurring of Roles' (1942–5). This second juncture looks at the impact of warfare on images of men and women in the company; 3) 'The Return of Martin Guerre' (1946–69). This third juncture begins with the impact of the returning (white) service*men* to the airline in the post-war era through to 1969 and the so-called era of modernisation, when increasing numbers of women began to take on more supervisory roles and the impact of the Civil Rights Act was beginning to take effect; and 4) 'The Potential for Change: Social Movements and Legal Advancement' (1970–89). This juncture explores the impact of feminist activism around use of the Civil Rights Act and a series of legal challenges, from the start of the 1970s through to the demise of the airline.

Pan American Airways: An Overview

Our focus on Pan Am is due to its socio-political and economic influence both in the United States and Latin America (Daley, 1980; Bender and Altschul, 1982). In the latter case, Pan Am was for a considerable time close to being *the* airline in and of Latin America (Josephson, 1944; Newton, 1978). With support of the US State Department, the airline operated as the sole US carrier throughout South America until the post-Second World War era. Beginning in 1927, with flights from Miami to Havana, it became the largest international airline in the world, with numerous flights from Florida and Texas into and across Latin America (Trippe, 1930). By 1936, it was a '40,000-mile transportation system in thirty-nine countries and colonies' (Fortune, 1936) that stretched beyond Latin America to China and New Zealand. For most of its existence, the airline was one of the most well-known commercial ventures in the world and its influence extended to the political and cultural realm (Hudson and Pettifer, 1979; Lovegrove, 2000; Pendo, 1985). In 1991, following a series of socio-economic and political problems, the company went bankrupt and never recovered (Gandt, 1995).

In the early years, the company established its mark as a pioneer in mail carrier routes when the manufacturing industry was feeling the impact of the Great Depression (Pan American Airways, 1931a) and expanded its services to include passenger carrier with 9,500 passenger loads in 1927 and growing to 80,536 in 1933 (Pan American Airways, 1934). With the expansion in services and penetration of the Latin American market, Pan Am had established itself as the 'chosen' instrument for the US government (Bender and Altschul, 1982). In the process, it has been argued that Pan Am played a role in 'the idea of Latin America' (Mignolo, 1991), translating images of the Latin America persona for audiences in the United States (Hartt et al., 2010).

Juan Trippe, President and CEO of Pan Am, spoke of the significant role that air power had on the world's economy power distribution and the imminent threat that the European competition presented to the American economy (Trippe, 1938). With the assistance of the US government, Latin American governments and the air carrier industry, Pan Am was able to secure mail carrier routes across Latin American nations, becoming an industry leader and driving foreign trade revenues for the US, which Trippe indicated was the key to future economic sustainability in America: 'they are apt to overlook Pan American's principal value to the United States – its effectiveness in the building up of our foreign trade' (Trippe, 1938).

Pan Am's unprecedented growth and leadership was established in the pre-Second World War years, in great part due the support of the US State Department that worked with Pan Am to ensure its influence throughout the region. An important reason for US government support can be found in growing concerns about the influence of German aviation concerns in South America, concerns that were fuelled by Pan Am's public imaging of the 'German Threat' (Durepos et al., 2008). As we shall discuss, the masculine imagery of the German Threat and of the machismo Latin male played intersectional roles in the company's notion of male and female.

The war years saw a huge growth in the airline's activities as it worked hand in hand with the US military to build airways throughout a number of countries of the world and to provide transportation for a variety of situations, both commercial and military. In the process, the airline's employment of women grew exponentially and began to change the face of gendered relations over the next few decades. The initial post-war era saw the stabilisation of the employment of women. However, those women were viewed as members of the Pan Am 'family' – a powerful metaphor that served to exclude people of colour and to shape images of womanhood in narrow ways (Dye and Mills, 2011 and 2012). Eventually, as the 1970s opened up and companies faced various challenges on the basis of race and gender, Pan Am faced duelling discourses as dominant ideas of the disembodied competitive employee vied with women's liberation. These competing but also overlapping discourses saw changes in the employment and imaging of women/men and white/people of colour against a background of a company that had lost its protected government status and found itself in tightening competition in a period of deregulation. By 1990, it had run out of steam and filed for bankruptcy.

The Junctures

The core of the chapter involves the identification and exploration of four junctures. The first juncture we have called a matrix of domination based on the airline's dominant position in its operations in Latin America and in powerful role as an employer throughout the region and in the southern states of the United States, particularly Florida and Texas. We explore the airline's employment practices in regard to women, people of colour and different groups of Latin Americans based on ethic group and origins throughout this period, which runs from the airline's founding in 1927 until the onset of war in 1941.

The matrix of domination refers to the overall organisation of power in a society. There are two features to any matrix. First, any specific matrix has a particular arrangement of intersecting systems of oppression. Just what and how these systems come together is historically and socially specific. Second, intersecting systems of oppression are specifically organised through four interrelated domains of power: structural, disciplinary, hegemonic and interpersonal (Collins, 2000). Intersectionality motivates us to look at just how our identities are constructed at the expense of others: 'These examples suggest that moral positions as survivors of one expression of systemic violence become eroded in the absence of accepting responsibility of other expressions of systemic violence' (Collins, 2000, p. 247). One final implication of Collins' approach: because groups' histories and inequalities are relational, understanding intersectionality and the matrix of domination means that some coalitions with some social groups are more difficult and less fruitful than others. Groups will more or less align on the issues of 'victimization, access to positions of authority, unearned benefits, and traditions of resistance' (Collins, 2000, p. 248). In our analysis, we looked at 169 articles and documents (represented in two tables) from Pan Am archives to understand the implications of intersectional relationships in Pan Am.

In the second juncture we explore the impact of the Second World War on 'Shifting Boundaries and a Blurring of Roles'. In this period – 1942–5 – Pan Am's female employees went from 390 in 1941 to 1642 in 1942; from routine female-typed jobs to a variety of jobs that include maintenance, operations, traffic, communication and executives (at this period there were as many as 199 women classified as 'executives' – Pan American Airways, 1942c). What isn't clear in these statistics are the other dimensions of a women's characteristic. Race, ethnicity, class, age and nationality are all contributing factors that need to be explored and demonstrate the intricate nature of the intersectionality theory.

The third juncture we call the 'Return of Martin Guerre' (Davis, 1983) because the era deals with the re-entrance of men in the workforce as they return from the armed forces. (It is, of course, a play on words and a reference to the history of a man who returns from the war in medieval France as a much-changed person in terms of his masculinity.) Here we also explore dominant notions of ideal female and male employees (as family members) and the implications for people of colour and non-US employees in various other countries in which Pan Am operated.

The fourth and final juncture focuses on the interface of organisational and legislative changes as companies adjusted to the challenge of the Civil Rights Act and the Women's Liberation Movement and the intersecting debates around class, gender and race.

We conclude with assessments of what history can tell us about intersectionality and how to address it.

Pan Am: A Look at the Early Years through a Lens of a Matrix of Domination (1927–41)

As we enter Pan Am prior to the Second World War, we encounter an airline run and staffed mainly by a group of white male managers and professionals, with a much smaller number of white female administrative and support staff, a group of Latino boys employed as flight attendants on the airline's predominantly South American routes and a growing number of 'foreign nationals' employed as 'locals' in each of the countries where Pan Am operated. There were also less than a handful of black men employed in the US in menial and lowly paid duties.

Three central and interrelated themes – Americanism, European-ethnic associations and masculinity – dominate much of the descriptive and otherwise celebratory material of the era.

Americanism: throughout the era, the company celebrated the many 'firsts' and successes of Pan American Airways, often substituting Pan American (Airways) for Americanism (Hartt et al., 2009). For example, in 1938, John Leslie, an airline director, likened Pan Am flight crews to the 'officers and men of our merchant marine [who a century ago] carried the American flag over new seas and into strange ports … So it is today that American flight crews are undertaking aerial voyages of exploration, carrying the American flag over the seas and into the airports of the world' (Leslie, 1938). A repeated narrative portrayed Pan Am as the quintessential American company, which served not only to privilege US citizens but also to marginalise those of other countries – particularly those in the various countries to the south of the US border.

Whiteness and European heritage: issues of whiteness and, beyond that, maleness, which arguably – outside of census data – have been only broadly thought of as categories and even then more as reactions to and implied contrasts of 'others' with 'white' 'men'. Until recently, whiteness (Jacques, 1997) and maleness (Collinson and Hearn, 1994) have been treated as the norm against which all other people (in various categorisations) have been judged, in practice and in theories of organisation (Hearn and Parkin, 1983; Nkomo, 1992). In Pan Am there was no question that those who ran and organised much of the airline were white – it went without question, but not without some deft identity work. Perhaps the best example of this was Juan Trippe (the Pan Am President for the entire period). Trippe was well aware that his forename was open to confusion. His airline operated from Mexico down through most of Central and South America, where people with so-called Latin names were seen as of a lesser breed than those of those of European (preferably Northern European) heritage. Trippe went to great lengths to make it clear that he did not have an ounce of Latin American blood; sometimes he resorted to calling himself J.T. or J. Terry Trippe, while often he used potted histories and corporate publicity to make it clear that he was an American of 'pure' European heritage (Daley, 1980). The 'whiteness' of the company's small number of senior managers of North European birth was not even called into question. Their whiteness, as we shall see below, was inherent; an essential quality. Yet even here, identity work was also related to deft processes of identity work built into the project of European colonialism that was very much alive and well at this point. Andre Priester, the company's 'Dutch' Chief Engineer, for example, was born in Java and did not move to the Netherlands until he was 17 (Daley, 1980, p. 37).

Masculinity: the notion of masculinity and the role of men at work were largely achieved in the airline as an outcome of a far-reaching gender discourse of the time and the fact that the airline only employed (white) men in all but the lower administrative tasks. To talk of the ideal typical manager, pilot and other employees, as we shall see below, was to talk of men and their characteristics.

The following excerpt from an early edition of *Pan American Airways*, the company's in-house magazine, shows how all the features of Americanism, whiteness and masculinity come together to form a matrix of domination:

> Pan American Airways System has successfully opened the world's longest fastest air mail service, the United States airmail route from the Argentine and Uruguay to Chile and on up the coast to the Canal and so to Miami and the great cities of the United States …
>
> Pan American Airways is not a one man organisation. If the loss of one man could stop the organisation it would have stopped when John Hambleton died. It was a case of John Hambleton and the rest of us. And the rest of us caught his enthusiasm and his loyalty and his courage and Pan American Airways System went right on. And it will go on when all of us now with it are no longer here. And part of the force that carries it along will be the energy and the brains and the loyalty that we give to it and to its destiny.
>
> That's how it is with Lindbergh.[1] It's Lindbergh and the rest of us. And every man counts. You know the mechanic counts who discovers the cracked plug in Lindbergh's engine before the flight. You know the radio-man counts who guards the plane in flight. You know the fellow counts who sweats to get a barrel of gasoline onto a barge so it can be floated seven miles down the coast and hauled ashore to be there when Lindbergh lands for refuelling …
>
> But we all count. It's the team-work, the all-together-now spirit which makes any job with Pan American Airways the best job of its sort in the world … (Pan American Airways, 1930c)

It was against this background (with its related discourses and associated practices) that other employees came to be judged – and judged categorically. To varying degrees, three categories of employee start to emerge in this era – non-US 'local' employees hired to service various aspects of Pan Am's operations south of the border; white (largely US-born) women; and less than a handful of black (US-born) men.

Latin Americans: although a small minority of employees based in the US, there were a number of so-called Latin Americans employed at the airline's various operations, from Mexico down to Argentina. More than most other categorisations

1 Charles Lindbergh, the famed aviator, was a pilot and advisor for Pan Am during this era. His flirtation with Nazi Germany (Wallace, 2003) led to his public absence from the company from the early 1940s to the mid-1940s.

of people, the idea of the Latin American (Mignolo, 1991) loomed large in Pan Am's imagery and discussions of its operations. More often than not, the Latin American image was constructed out of contrasts with Pan Am's ideal typical white manager and professional. In broad-brush terms, the airline tended to paint itself in this era as 'pioneers', evoking the notion of 'discovery' as the primitive is uncovered by the modern, and the uncivilised by the civilised (Durepos et al., 2008). At times this is positively linked with the Conquistadors and their 'discovery' (rather than their conquest and invention) of Latin America (Eakin, 2007; Williamson, 2009). The following is an example:

> Trinidad was discovered by Columbus in 1496. Situated close by the north-east coast of South America, this picturesque island is expected to be one of the most exciting 'discoveries of the countless Americans [who] ... will journey [there] this winter. (Pan American Airways, 1941b)

Within the broad context of the 'idea of Latin America' (Mignolo, 1991), images of the Latin American are located. Analysing the temperament and character of the 'average Latin American', John Leslie opined that he was 'not always well adapted to mechanical work and does not fit easily into a large well-disciplined organization' such as Pan Am (Leslie, 1934). He nonetheless felt that 'great steps had been made in training *such* people' (emphasis added) and that at least one good reason for employing them was because they 'are usually content with their lot, can live healthily and happily, and usually require considerably low wages than America personnel' (Leslie, 1934, p. 70). We note here that, regardless of country of origin in the region, a homogeneous category of Latin American was in play in comments made by Leslie and others. We can also note that, with few exceptions, references to Latin Americans are directed as men rather than women. By way of contrast, Leslie views 'Americans' (i.e., US-born white male citizens) as someone used to a level of social status, 'superior material improvements ... such as modern sanitation, good roads, and speedy communication, radio programs ... the quality of food available and ... the higher degree of sanitation and of healthfulness in the United States' (Leslie, 1934, p. 118).

Blacks/race: the third category of men that Pan Am surfaces in its corporate materials is the black employee. We note that while there is limited evidence that blacks are employed by the airline as early as 1930, there is no discussion or profiling of them throughout the period. We glimpse images of so-called black employees in a picture showing 'Engineering and Operations Personnel of Pan American Airways at Brownsville, Texas, Northern Terminus of the System in the West'. The picture shows 69 male employees (of whom, going strictly on skin tones, seems to include five who appear to be people of colour) and five female employees (Pan American Airways, 1930b). It is not until the post-war years that black employees are even discussed by name. A rare example is a 1946 reference to employee Roy Young, who was employed in 1931 'to tend the grounds' (Pan

American Airways, 1946a). Nowhere in this era are women of colour imaged, let alone discussed.

Race is, however, introduced into corporate discussions by way of a story about applications for employment from two men from the Zulu nation in South Africa (Pan American Airways, 1931c). The Zulu nation is referred to as 'darkest Africa':

> Aviation has gripped the world, it has captured the imagination of men and women in every walk of life, it has spread from the great cosmopolitan cities of the world to darkest Africa, and it is from here that applications for positions with the Pan American Grace Airways were recently received by Mr J.D. MacGregor, Vice-President and general manager of the company. One of the enthusiastic 'Fuzzy Wuzzys' who wrote for a job was so anxious to land it that he explained he would be perfectly willing – in fact, delighted, to subject himself to Mr MacGregor's parental guidance. (Pan American Airways, 1931c)

In both cases the letters are reproduced in full with the apparent aim of exposing them to the amusement of Pan Am's overwhelmingly white employees.[2] The story grounds issues of race in references to Africa and it is not difficult to assume that it serves to invite parallels with US-born people of colour and their supposed heritage.

Women: while (white, seemingly US-born) women are somewhat visible in the corporate materials, they are marginalised against their male counterparts in terms of sheer numbers (fewer female employees), the limited range of positions occupied and the general support (and lower-paid) jobs they occupy. They differ from Latin American men in their ability to access 'Americanism' (i.e., the value of being a US citizen) and great employment in the US operations. They differ from black men in their ability to access 'whiteness', the range of responsible jobs held and their visibility. They differ from other categories of women in the fact that they are the only females who have some visibility. Their supposed feminine characteristics serve to marginalise their importance to the organisation vis-à-vis white men. Images of women initially appear in the same 1930 picture of the Brownsville operations personnel cited above. In October of the same year, a woman's name appears in the published list of 'personnel' that was included in each issue of *Pan American Air Ways*: Helen M. Haynes is listed as joining the maintenance department at Miami.

One of the earliest references to any woman associated with the airline serves to stress essential male and female qualities. A 1931 article on interior decorating, subtitled 'Is Woman's Task She Says', begins: 'Men are all right in the mechanical

2 A similar situation appeared in an earlier edition of *Pan American Air Ways*, with the ridicule of a letter from a 'Chinese resident in San Francisco', a rare mention of anyone who is deemed anything other than white American, Latin American or 'Negro'. See Pan American Airways, 1930a.

side of life, but when it comes to making things comfortable they aren't practical, that's a woman's job, according to Mrs. Guy Murchie who recently departed for Europe to study interior decoration of planes' (Pan American Airways, 1931b, p. 139). Somewhat ironically, an early reference to a female employee appears in 1937 as a story celebrating the first woman to achieve 10 years' employment with the airline. The story begins by noting that 'Pan American's distaff contingent has brought forward its first ten year employee in the charming person of Mrs. Marie Blaske, secretary to Vice-President J.C. Cooper, Jr.' (Pan American Airways, 1937). Having made reference to her feminine charm and informing the reader that her position is clearly women's work ('distaff'), the story linked her obvious, albeit supportive, strengths to the ethos of the company's work ethic: 'Her knowledge of executive office practice, and Pan American Airways methods of doing things enabled her to give Mr. Cooper some very valuable service' (Pan American Airways, 1937). Nonetheless, the author of the story does not seem able to resist the need to end with stress on Blaske's 'role of wife and mother' when she is at home, adding that her 'recreation appears to consist of doing housework', which she is quoted as enjoying (Pan American Airways, 1937). Meanwhile the story underplays the fact that, apart from the airline's President and the Chief Engineer, Marie Blaske was only the airline's third 10-year employee.

The one anomaly in the airline's gendered practices at this time was the 1939 promotion of Ann Archibald, a secretary in the Washington, DC office, to the position of Assistant Vice-President. Her role was that of a political lobbyist for the airline, which may in part explain the need to assign a high-sounding title to her position. Perhaps it is not surprising to find that descriptions of her tended to cross the gender divide. She was seen as 'a smooth-talking, hard headed lady who wore a mink coat' (Daley, 1980, p. 351) and as someone who 'ran the office with the iron whim of a society dowager' (Bender and Altschul, 1982).

At this Juncture

What we would note about this period is the relationship between the organising principles (Acker, 1990) of Pan Am (stress on Americanism and forms of Eurocentric ways of viewing the world) and its formative context (Unger, 1987), i.e., the dominant role of the US, both economically and militarily, in Mexico, Central and South America (Eakin, 2007) and the primary location of Pan Am in Florida. They serve as a kind of vortex in which whiteness, maleness and (US) Americanism serve unquestionably to define desired characteristics of the company employee. In the process, they privilege those who come closest to the intersecting ideals and marginalise those who are the furthest away from the intersection. White women come closest to white men than Latin American men, where the latter's forms of masculinity are seen as not meeting the standards of privileged American masculine forms. In short, there are few spaces for intersectionality *within* the organisation. The process of categorisation is very limited and limiting.

As we shall now see, the relationships between the organisational logic and the formative context in which it operates change dramatically with the advent of the Second World War.

Wartime US: Shifting Boundaries and a Blurring of Roles (1942–5)

> One day last month, Capt. Robert Oliver Daniel Sullivan, bringing the Dixie Clipper in on schedule from Europe, called the radio office at Pan American's LaGuardia Field, NY base, asking for the usual landing instructions: 'North Beach from Dixie Clipper. North Beach from Dixie Clipper. Go ahead'. Came the reply: 'Dixie Clipper from North Beach. Dixie Clipper from North Beach. Go ahead'. Capt. Sullivan turned in his seat, stared at First Officer Calvin Y. Dyer. Without turning off his microphone, the captain broadcast his surprise: 'I'll be darned – it's a woman!' Though he didn't quite believe it at the time, it was a woman – Vera May Dawes Covell, new member of Flight Watch, first woman in Pan American's transatlantic service to occupy such a position. Five minutes later, when Capt. Sullivan reported the Dixie Clipper again, Radiophone Operator Covell snapped out the crisp instructions: 'Dixie Clipper. You are cleared from the New York boundary to LaGuardia tower to cruise ... to LaGuardia – Wind is west northwest IS-Reading: one zero two six point three-repeat – Reading: one zero two six point three. Go ahead'. By this time Capt. Sullivan believed his own ears, repeated the message to operator Covell, ended it with a polite 'Thank you Ma'm'. (Pan American Airways, 1942a)

This example – entitled 'Orders from a Woman' – highlights the shift in women's roles as women took on significant positions in Pan Am's workforce to backfill the men who went overseas during the war, but as the quote demonstrates, the shift was a shock for the entitled white male. Women were popping up in a surprising number of roles. As of 7 December 1941, there were 390 women employed at Pan Am,[3] with the majority based in Miami in maintenance positions. One year later, the Pan Am statistics show 1,642 women employed at Pan Am in a variety of jobs (maintenance, operations, traffic and communication) and 199 as executives (Pan American Airways, 1942c).[4] Among the now numerous images of female

3 It is difficult to assess the overall percentage of women in the company because, with the exception of three employees, the 390 refers only to US-based employees, while the Annual Report for that year lists the total number of employees as in excess of 26,000 across the whole airline – see Pan American Airways, 1941a.

4 It is far from clear what counts as 'executives' as, apart from Ann Archibald (see above), no women are listed as past of the senior management team in Pan Am documents. The annual report for 1942 lists 88,000 employees worldwide, but an internal document refers to a total of 9,441 employees as 'stationed within the Continental United States as of December 31,1942 – Pan American Airways, 1943. This would mean that women constituted around 17 per cent of the airline at this point.

employees, there were some obvious class differences as young women were recruited not only to fill the middle-class hires as secretaries and clerical staff but also to a variety of blue-collar jobs. This, however, seems to be the central core of any changing intersectionality in this period. While much is made of women's 'entry' into a variety of roles, there is no mention of similar increases in people of colour and/or so-called Latin Americans.

In the latter regard, an exception in terms of imagery is the mention of Zoila F. de Carreras, who started as a secretary in the airline's Cubana office in Havana in 1932, but became the Treasurer during the war years (Pan American Airways, 1942b). But the complex dimensions of intersectionality echo loudly in the lack of images portraying the advancement of women of colour and non-American women. In the archival documents there are photos of many white women taking on critical production and engineering roles in the Pan Am workforce, but we find only a single picture of a black woman, Frankie Greenwood, a cleaner polishing an aircraft wing in 1943. Of note as well is that, despite reference to female executives, there was clearly a lack of white women in even middle management, let alone senior management, and executive positions during the war indicated that white women replaced the overseas men in the working ranks, but not in the strategic 'thinking' areas of the organisation.

At this Juncture

At this point of time, for obvious reasons, the company's emphasis on Americanism looms larger than ever and takes on an even more patriotic turn, but the idea of democracy now plays an important role in the story. The latter is still very much linked to the notion of some inherent strength in Americanism and its link to Western thought. Indeed, Pan Am attributes 'their ability to serve the United Nations throughout the world' as due 'in large measure to the fourteen years of pioneering and scientific progress' (Trippe, 1941, p. 3). Nonetheless, it is a concept that blurs the lines of organisational involvement and opens up, however small, spaces for consideration.

Masculinity is explored through a series of stories on men as leaders, warriors and heroes (the assumption remains that such men are white). The links between these characteristics and masculinity are, however, rarely made in an overt way. Masculinity, like whiteness, appears not to need justification and rational (Collinson and Hearn, 1994). The spaces where masculinity per se seems more likely to get defined are through discussions and categorisation of feminine traits.

During this year, the sheer growth in the number of female employees and the range of work they took on became an important story in the airline's discourse, second only to the war itself. Those stories almost invariably addressed the issue of women as occupying 'men's jobs' and the implications for things like skill, professionalism and efficiency – all assumed to be inherently part of men's, but not women's make-up. Lurking behind some of the stories was the concern that the lesser-paid women would end up hanging on to the job that had been temporarily vacated by the men who had gone to war.

The Return of Martin Guerre (1946–69)

The third juncture we call the 'Return of Martin Guerre' (Davis, 1983), as the era deals with the re-entrance of men in the workforce as they returned from the armed forces. Two themes are evident during this time period. First, there is evidence of the continued exclusion of black employees, particularly women, from visible positions within Pan Am. This discrimination was found not only in Pan Am; there was also evidence of discrimination within the very organisations and legal systems that were designed to promote and protect minority groups. The second theme is the return to a portrayal of women in traditional female roles and men in dominant patriarchical positions. We say 'return', but prior to the war, the company had not devoted much time to even discussing female employees. In this case it means a return to the underlying social themes (evident in the pre-war silences) that had been, in part, suspended during the Second World War.

As has been discussed at length elsewhere (Dye and Mills, 2011 and 2012), a major discursive theme during the immediate post-war years was the portrayal, and reinforcement, of men and women in stereotypical gendered roles within the Pan Am 'family'. As men returned to their workplace roles, there was underlying conflict within the organisation as many women had expanded their presence to include valued positions in the paid workforce. Many of these women had entered areas traditionally dominated by male employees. The materials demonstrate a continued under-evaluation of the value that the women played in the organisation and stressed dominant notions of ideal female and male employees. Female employees' role were thus often read from a family rather than a job perspective, with women's jobs portrayed as inherently nurturing roles, associated with motherhood, child care and being supportive to men in positions of authority. Further, women were portrayed in a position of servitude to male employees and customers, a fact demonstrated by photos of women fawning over men. Younger female employees were often sexualised in both text and photos. For example, it was not unusual to reference a women's measurements as key to her identity, and arguably her value to the organisation as an attractive member of the family. For instance:

> Other specifications for this Clipper: Brown hair, five feet five, 34-24-27 fuselage dimensions, from north to south. (Pan American Airways, 1955, p. 2)

This juncture occurred during a time of the unique event of men returning to the workforce. It was a time that has been called a crisis of masculinity as men returned from the armed forces to find that women could and were doing work previously associated with men only, that their military skills (especially those in the lower ranks) did not easily translate into good jobs in civilian life and that they were competing with much younger men as well as women.[5] Unlike previous eras, Pan Am corporate representations of masculinity seem to have needed more definition and justification in this era, and was to be found more in engagement with images of women: the more family-like the woman, the more the dominant form of masculinity was able to emerge. A 1946 story captures some of the ambiguity involved with the title 'Who says women quit? Certainly not this boss':

> Recognition of a boss's bad moods and consideration of a secretary constitute a successful formula for a team working together for more than 13 years. That in substance is the way Frederick L. Culham, head of General Accounting's passenger revenue department, and his pretty secretary, Blanche Jensen Elmore, explain their long, professional relationship.
>
> 'Miss Elmore not only knows her job thoroughly but she knows my bad moods and has sense enough to give me a wide berth when I'm in one', says Culham. He strongly believes that a pleasant personality and good grooming are as important as efficiency in a secretary and in these respects Miss Elmore also fits the bill.
>
> Minimising Culham's claim to being temperamental, Miss Elmore says, 'He is always considerate and that's one of the most important qualities of a boss'. (Pan American Airways, 1946b)

In terms of race, Pan Am had recruited some but very few people of colour and there was little evidence of them in the corporate image in either a public sense or an internal social sense (i.e., in the imagery and discussion of company employees). But race had become an issue for many during the Second World War, including a growing number of men of colour who served in the armed forces, including the air forces (Francis, 1993; Haskins, 1995). In the post-war era, pressure was steadily put on Pan Am from the Urban League and the New York State Commission to employ people of 'colour', but the company continued to resist (Creedy, 1956). Yet, as Pan Am's internal discussions reveal, the company adopted a purposive discrimination towards potential 'Negro' employees. In a confidential memo – 'Buying New Enemies' – John Creedy, Pan Am's Director of Public Relations, links the airline's reluctance to hire more 'Negro flight personnel' to an inability to already hire adequate numbers of white applicants, concerns that 'negro' flight staff would lose the company 'South African and Bermuda business' and that 'integration would make a stewardesses job at Pan American less desirable' (Creedy, 1956). Creedy also opined that there 'would be trouble with Southerners' and that once 'a Negro is hired we will be tagged as a "black" airline' (Creedy, 1956). Weighing up the company's options, Creedy suggests that:

5 This masculine angst is sympathetically captured in the film *The Best Years of Our Lives* – O'Connor, J.E. and Jackson, M.A. (eds), 1980. American History/American Film. New York: Frederick Ungar Publishing Co.

> Pan American already employs, apart from Puerto Ricans, flight service staff who are so dark-skinned as to be indistinguishable from Negroes. We do not appear to have serious scheduling difficulties with them. In addition, it is highly probable that many of our Puerto Rican personnel would qualify as Negroes under Southern rules. Further it is believed that Atlantic Division has already unwittingly hired a Negro stewardess. We are quite willing to restrict the scheduling of Nisei crews. It may be, therefore, that we have already faced and solved the problems of colored flight service staff.
>
> As to the pilot problem, we have spent more than 25 years of work proving that dark-skinned Brazilians, Venezuelans, Colombians, Cubans and Mexicans are 'second to none' as pilots, to say nothing of our current projects with dark-skinned Turks, Pakistanis and Thailanders. Are we being consistent? (Creedy, 1956)

Creedy ends by suggesting 'why not take the position that we never had a qualified Negro applicant, but that if we did we would hire her. Then, when one comes along, hire her. This position has the additional virtue of being the only legal one to take in New York State' (Creedy, 1956).

It is not clear who was the recipient of this memo, but around this time the *New York Amsterdam News* (10 March 1956) announced: 'Pan American World Airways announced this week that it does not intend to hire Negro stewardesses because "we don't want to subject them the sort of treatment they would get in foreign countries". John Creedy is cited as stating: "No Negro girls qualified" for a flight crew position' (Creedy, 1956).

The refusal to hire qualified black personnel appeared to be industry-wide, as was referenced by Everett Goulard in a note to Pan Am Vice-Presidents Cledhill and Leslie. The letter discussed the issue of race discrimination as referenced in a panel. Goulard, Pan Am Vice-President, noted:

> It is apparent that the Federal, State and private organizations concerned with fair employment practices are campaigning against all air lines for the sole purpose of forcing us to integrate Negroes into the flight crews. The pressure is being kept on us and the organizations involved have no intention of allowing us to adopt a 'gradual' approach. Mr. O'Brien has learned from the staff of the President's Committee that Secretary of Labor Mitchell, who had virtually assured the air lines last November that the President's Committee would not press the flight crew matter if the air lines continued to make satisfactory progress in regards to ground crews, is wavering under the pressure of the Urban League and State Commission. (Goulard, 1956b)

As evidenced by the reference to Secretary of Labour Mitchell's allowance of discriminatory treatment, arguably the most troubling event during this time period, a theme that is also carried into the next juncture, was the failure of organisations designed to advance the rights of disadvantaged members of society to assist in this endeavour. For instance, an employee who pursued a discrimination claim was advised to accept another, less visible, position by the New York Commission on Discrimination. Further, labour unions suppressed potential black employees' opportunities with Pan Am by threatening workplace upheaval (Goulard, 1956a).

Women who were members of visible minorities were subject to multiple elements of intersectionality, namely on the basis of ethnicity, race and gender. Women who were members of ethnic-minority groups were subject to further exclusion and marginalisation in the Pan Am family. The *Pan Am Clipper*, an internal newsletter, provides evidence of this disparate treatment. An interesting element was the exclusion of women of ethnic and racial minorities from the cartoons. This has interesting points of intersectionality for the few women of colour in the organisation at the time. On the one hand, many cartoons would show images of white men and women interacting over issues that would poke fun at the company, the customers and/or their managers. Here those considered racial or ethnic minorities would be left out of the joke and thus not included in important aspects of the airline. On the other hand, there were numerous examples of what would later come to be classified as blatant sexism and/or sexual harassment where white women are shown being lusted after or physically grabbed by white men to make a graphic joke about the sexual purpose of women. In this case sexuality is seen as something that white women have and others do not, but on the downside, white women are the ones being sexually constructed and the subject of objectification. This further exemplifies the social and political stratification felt by individuals with multiple dimensions of intersectionality (Hancock, 2007).

At this Juncture

During this period of time, there seems to have been two central foci – one internal, as man and women attempt to adjust to changing post-war conditions and the implications for masculinity, and the other external, as anti-discriminatory organisations form part of a changed and changing environment that no longer unquestioningly accepts discriminatory practices. Unlike previous eras, masculinity and whiteness are far less stable and cannot simply be 'handled' through references to Americanism. In the changing social discourse, Americanism was coming to be understood as something far more inclusive than Pan Am had earlier expressed. In the first case, a form of stabilisation was achieved through a discourse of family (Dye and Mills, 2012), but it was a discourse that embraced whiteness and exasperated the growing external pressures. Nonetheless, we can detect in this period the opening up of intersectional spaces, both in terms of the instability of notions of gender and race and the changing practices that saw women as a stable or 'normal' part of Pan Am employment and the beginning of greater numbers of so-called racial and ethnic hires.

The Potential for Change: Social Movements and Legal Advancement (1970–89)

During this time period, US society began to undergo a reformation with respect to recognising issues related to human rights. The late 1960s, 1970s and 1980s was a time of widespread social reform that saw the advent of the Second Wave feminist movement alongside numerous organisations advocating change. The era saw a number of challenges and changes to the law that impacted a number of organisations, including airlines. Pan Am flight attendants made some of the earliest challenges to women's rights at work and the era saw the development of such organisations as Stewardesses for Women's Rights (Barry, 2007; Sanderson et al., 2010). The era also saw speed-up and increasing competition throughout the industry as a result of deregulation and a period of oil crisis (Whitelegg, 2007). One of the outcomes was a willingness of airlines such as Pan Am to focus on the disembodied employee – preferring to hire the cheapest, more skilled, more efficient and also the more socially acceptable in terms of legal requirements – as a more ideal candidate for employment. As we argue below, this did not end discriminatory practices, but it does seem to have provided a set of external pressures, which combined economic necessity with legal requirements. It was left to employee groups to battle over the details. Somewhat ironically, opportunities were being opened up by established and growing pressure groups that were more often than not organised along categorised lines, e.g., women's groups, groups for racial equality and so on. Thus, in many cases an increasing number of intersectional spaces opened up in Pan Am as activism, and legal challenges and legal concerns forced changes in practices as well as in a growing discourse of competition, often relied on categories of employee or categorised employees to vie for space in the company.

Some of the legal protections advanced at this time included forms of protection for women on the basis of sex (for rights related to maternity leave) (Pan American Airways, 1985), changes to the Civil Rights Act and protecting individuals from sexual harassment. However, these advances appear largely illusionary, as Pan Am continued to disparately pay female employees (Hanlon, 1985) and objectify female employees, evidenced by an advertisement in *Playboy* magazine using an employee as the model (Pan American Airways, 1971a). Men were also now using the law to redress discrimination, on the basis of gender, for steward positions, and in a notable case against Pan Am were successful in challenging the discriminatory practice on the right to be employed as stewards (*Wall Street Journal Reporter*, 1971).

Publicly, Pan Am made efforts to adopt employment equity practices where 100 black stewardesses were to be hired in 1971 (Pan American Airways, 1971b). However, this veiled the organisational practices, which continued to undermine the possibility of allowing black employees to advance into visible positions in the organisation (Price, 1973). Price, Corporate Director of Personal for Urban Affairs and Equal Opportunity, wrote a memorandum in preparation for the Annual Meeting regarding Pan Am's involvement with minority assistance programmes to the Vice-President, Miller. The memo detailed, in addition to other things, 'what we said we would do vs. what we did' (Price, 1973, p. 2):

> To what extent is the company involved in the affairs of the community in which it is located?
>
> The company is not involved *per se*. Pan Am has become involved primarily through the work of Pan Am employees, not because of but in spite of the company. We have no minority assistance programs, no participation in urban renewal programs, and no financial (or very little) involvement in community programs.

The memorandum provides evidence of internal recognition of poor treatment of Pan Am employees, and potential employees, on the basis of race and ethnicity. In the same time period, class actions were filed on the basis of sex or race, including a claim advanced by three black female employees who were subject to multiple grounds of intersectionality (Pan American Airways, 1974). The legal claim initially advanced discrimination on the basis of race. However, on an application to the courts, the magistrate denied their requested amendment to pursue a claim both on the basis of race and sex. However, the claims are noteworthy in that they demonstrate (not necessarily surprisingly, as noted in the last juncture) that the instruments developed to protect those being oppressed by injustices, including at the hands of the employers, were failing to protect these individuals. Specifically, the courts failed to acknowledge that the individuals might be subject to multiple dimensions which might lead to further marginalisation of these individuals.

At this Juncture

In this fourth broad juncture, changes to the organisation were largely the result of external pressures linked to various legal challenges and social movement activism from within but also outside of the organisation. An increasing number of intersectional spaces were identified and created alongside organisations and laws designed to gain greater opportunities for categories of employees. In a sense, these very challenges to narrowly defined categories of people served to strengthen those categories as people took up the specific challenges category by category, but it was also the era which, by its close, had led to the identification of the growing importance of intersectionality research.

Conclusion

This chapter has addressed a gap in the literature; specifically, it has focused on intersectionality and organisational practices *over time*. In particular, we studied 'organizations in historically specific contexts', examining Pan Am over different historical contexts over time, taking up issues of 'intersectionality and globalization', examining the employment and trading practices of Pan Am in the US and Latin America, and examining 'embodied intersectionality' following the segmentation of forms of intersectionality in Pan Am over time.

Through the use of junctures, we set out to 'reassemble' a particular organisation to explore intersectionality over the course of its existence. The junctures provide insight into the examination of the impact of events on employment practices and how the practices related to race, ethnicity and gender change over time in response to external events, such as war, post-war adjustment and widespread social conflict. These changes in the workforce shift the power relations within subsets of the working population and amplify the overt and covert discriminatory employment practices adopted by Pan Am in the early junctures by the continuation of the hegemonic American white male. In the first juncture, intersectionality reached a high peak with the voices of multiple dimensions silenced through non-existent hiring practices. Persons of race and ethnicity are virtually non-existent in the workforce, with the exception of the so-called Latin American man who is employed largely in the company's Latin American branches. White women's role in the workplace is predominately supportive and secretarial in nature until the war years. In the second juncture, we see a dramatic shift in the role of white women replacing men in the workforce, which sets the tone of change into the evolving workplace as women's knowledge and expectations for employment begin to change. What is of concern is again the silenced voices of race and ethnicity (e.g., black men and women, Latino and Asian women and Asian men) who are not represented in the workforce. In the third juncture, we see the impact of the return of the traditional employee, the American white male, to the workforce following a period of absence during a time of conflict. Pan Am displayed two predominant themes during this time: the continued exclusion of black individuals, particularly women, from the workforce; and the organisation's tendency to frame male and female employees in traditional gendered roles. The fourth juncture, turned attention to social movements and the legal framework that protects workers. Throughout the junctures, we used Pan Am's globalisation to illustrate how intersectionality influences the construction of normative, (de)valued, sexual and able bodies in organisations. While there is some privileging of groups over others, such as the hegemonic American white male, the experience and social construction of individuals or groups of individuals is complex due to the matrix of domination in intersectionality theory.

In terms of McCall's (2005) notions of intersectionality, we have tried to note how categorisations are the outcome of discursive processes, which develop out of a matrix of domination. In other words, we need to take an anticategorical stance to categories as systems of oppression. As people are categorised through sets of relationships, they come to stand in more or less privileged/more or less marginalised positions vis-à-vis the categorising group. This much was clear from our first juncture. However, it is not enough, as McCall (2005) suggests, to simply reject categories; they need to be understood in context. We need to examine not simply the categories per se and how they are problematic for those involved. Such an intersectional approach is inadequate for dealing with categorisation itself and its changing character. Nor is a strategic exploration of categories-in-use – an intrasectional analysis of the relationships between categorisations – enough. What is needed, we contend, is an historical approach to anticategorisation that seeks to understand how the categorisation of people is performed over time. In that way we can gain a sense of how categorisation can both be used as a resource to develop intersectional strategies while ultimately undermining the underlying divisive character of discriminatory categories (Calás and Smircich, 1992).

References

Acker, J., 1990. Hierarchies, jobs, bodies: A theory of gendered organizations. *Gender & Society,* 4(2), pp. 139–58.

——. 1992. Gendering organizational theory. In: A.J. Mills and P. Tancred (eds), *Gendering Organizational Analysis.* Newbury Park, CA: Sage, pp. 248–60.

——. 2006. Inequality regimes: Gender, class and race in organizations. *Gender & Society*, 20(4), pp. 441–64.

Bagilhole, B. 2006. Exploration of UK equal opportunities and diversity legislation and implementation agencies through the lens of intersectionality. *European Conference on Equal Opportunities.* University of Antwerp.

——. 2010. Applying the lens of intersectionality to uk equal opportunities and diversity policies. *Canadian Journal of Administrative Science*, 27(3), pp. 263–71.

Barry, K.M., 2007. *Femininity in Flight: A History of Flight Attendants*. Durham, NC: Duke University Press.

Bender, M. and Altschul, S., 1982. *The Chosen Instrument. Juan Trippe. Pan Am. The Rise and Fall of an American Entrepreneur.* New York: Simon & Schuster.

Bloch, M., 1953. *The Historian's Craft*. Toronto: Random House.

Booth, C. and Rowlinson, M., 2006. Management and organizational history: Prospects. *Management & Organizational History*, 1(1), pp. 5–30.

Bryman, A., Bell, E., Mills, A.J. and Yue, A.R., 2011. *Business Research Methods. First Canadian Edition.* Toronto: Oxford University Press.

Calás, M. and Smircich, L., 1992. Using the 'F' word: Feminist theories and the social consequences of organizational research. In A. Mills and P. Tancred (eds), *Gendering Organizational Analysis.* Newbury Park, CA: Sage, pp. 222–34.

——. 1996. From 'the woman's' point of view: Feminist approaches to organization studies. In S. Clegg, C. Hardy and W. Nord (eds), *Handbook of Organization Studies.* London: Sage, pp. 218–58.

Collins, P.H., 2000. *Black Feminist Thought: Knowledge, Consciousness, and the Politics of Empowerment*, 2nd edn. New York: Routledge.

Collinson, D.L. and Hearn, J., 1994. Naming men as men: Implications for work, organization and management. *Gender, Work and Organization*, 1(1), pp. 2–22.

Creedy, J., 1956. Confidential memo: Buying new enemies. Draft by Cready to SP. Pan American Airways.

Daley, R., 1980. *An American Saga. Juan Trippe and His Pan Am Empire*. New York: Random House.

Davis, N.Z., 1983. *The Return of Martin Guerre*. Cambridge, MA: Harvard University Press.

Durepos, G., Helms Mills, J. and Mills, A.J., 2008. The Pan American dream and the myth of the pioneer. In M. Kostera (ed.), *Organizational Epics and Sagas: Tales of Organizations*. London: Routledge, pp. 131–43.

Dye, K.E. and Mills, A.J., 2011. Dueling discourses at work: Upsetting the gender order. *Canadian Journal of Administrative Science*, 28(4), pp. 427–39.

——. 2012. Pleading the Fifth: Refocussing Acker's gendered substructure through the lens of organizational logic. *Equality, Diversity and Inclusion: An International Journal*, 31(3), pp. 278–97.

Eakin, M.C., 2007. *The History of Latin America: Collision of Cultures*. Basingstoke: Palgrave Macmillan.

Fortune, 1936. Pan American Airways. *Fortune*, April, pp. 79, 159– 60.

Foucault, M., 1979. *Discipline and Punish: The Birth of the Prison*. New York: Vintage Books.

Francis, C.E., 1993. *The Tuskagee Airmen*. New York: Branden Publishing Co.

Gandt, R., 1995. *Skygods. The Fall of Pan Am*. New York: William Morrow and Comany, Inc.

Goulard, E., 1956a. Meeting on fair employment practices.

Goulard, E. 1956b. Note to Vice-Presidents Gledhill and Leslie.

Hancock, A., 2007. When multiplication doesn't equal quick addition: Examining intersectionality as a research paradigm. *Perspectives on Politics*, 5(1), pp. 63–79.

Hanlon, P., 1985. Note to corporate communications staff (letter) (personal communication).

Hartt, C.M., Mills, A.J., Helms Mills, J. and Durepos, G., 2009. Guiding the space age from the ground up: Pan Am, Cold War and guided missiles. *Management & Organizational History*, 4(3), pp. 1–17.

——. 2010. Markets, organizations, institutions and national identity: Pan American Airways, postcoloniality and Latin America. Paper presented at the Latin American and European Meeting on Organizational Studies, Buenos Aires.

Haskins, J., 1995. *Black Eagles: African Americans in Aviation*. New York: Scholastic Inc.

Hearn, J. and Parkin, P.W., 1983. Gender and organizations: A selective review and a critique of a neglected area. *Organization Studies*, 4(3), pp. 219–42.

Helms Mills, J., 2005. Representations of diversity and organizational change in a North American utility company. *Gender, Work & Organization*, 12(3), pp. 242–69.
Hudson, K. and Pettifer, J., 1979. *Diamonds in the Sky: A Social History of Air Travel.* London: Bodley Head/BBC Publications.
Jacques, R., 1997. The unbearable whiteness of being: reflections of a pale, stale male. In P. Prasad, A.J. Mills, M. Elmes and A. Prasad (eds), *Managing the Organizational Melting Pot: Dilemmas of Workplace Diversity.* Thousand Oaks, CA: Sage, pp. 80–106.
Josephson, M., 1944. *Empire of the Air*. New York: Harcourt, Brace and Company.
Kanter, R.M., 1977. *Men and Women of the Corporation*. New York: Basic Books.
Katila, S. and Merilainen, S., 2002. Metamorphosis: From 'nice girls' to 'nice bitches': Resisting patriarchal articulations of professional identity. *Gender, Work & Organization*, 9(3), pp. 336–54.
Leslie, J., 1934. The building of the Pan American Airways maintenance organization. MA thesis, Massachussets Institute of Technology.
——. 1938. Remarks on the officers of the Samoan Clipper, funeral services, 24 January, Pan American Airways Collection 361, Box 29/11. Miami, FL: Otto Richter Library, University of Miami.
Lovegrove, K., 2000. *Airline. Identity, Design and Culture*. New York: teNeues Publishing Co.
McCall, L., 2005. The complexity of intersectionality. *Signs*, 30, pp. 1771–800.
Mignolo, W. D., 1991. *The Idea of Latin America*. Oxford: Blackwell.
Mills, A.J., 2006. *Sex, Strategy and the Stratosphere: Airlines and the Gendering of Organizational Culture*. Basingstoke: Palgrave Macmillan.
——. 2010. Juncture. In: A.J. Mills, G. Durepos and E. Weibe (eds), *Sage Encylopedia of Case Study Research.* Thousands Oaks, CA: Sage, pp. 509–11.
Mills, A.J., Durepos, G. and Wiebe, E., 2010. *Sage Encyclopedia of Case Study Research* (two volumes). Thousand Oaks, CA: Sage.
Munslow, A., 2010. *The Future of History*. Basingstoke: Palgrave Macmillan.
Newton, W., 1978. *The Perilous Sky: U.S. Aviation Diplomacy and Latin America, 1919–1931*. Coral Gables, FL: Florida University of Miami Press.
Nkomo, S., 1992. The emperor has no clothes: Rewriting 'race in organizations'. *Academy of Management Review*, 17(3), pp. 487–513.
O'Connor, J.E. and Jackson, M.A. (eds), 1980. *American History/American Film*. New York: Frederick Ungar Publishing Co.
Pan American Airways, 1930a. All he wants is a job. *Pan American Air Ways*, 3(9) (15 August).
——. 1930b. Engineering and operations personnel of Pan American Airways at Brownsville, Texas, Northern Terminus of the system in the West. *Pan American Air Ways*, 1(8) (3 July).
——. 1930c. The rest of us. *Pan American Air Ways*, 1(6), (19 May), p. 34.
——. 1931a. Grumblling ballyhoo. *Pan American Air Ways*, 2(2), p. 90.

——. 1931b. Interior decorating job on S-40 being done by Mrs. Guy Murchie. *Pan American Air Ways*, 2(6), p. 139 (August).

——. 1931c. Zulus apply for airway jobs. *Pan American Air Ways*, 2(3), (April), p. 100.

——. 1934. Total passengers carried each year (letter, personal communication, 30 September).

——. 1937. Mrs. Marie Blaske is first secretary to serve 10 years. *Pan American Air Ways*, 8(7), (August), p. 7.

——. 1941a. *Annual Report*. Miami, FL: Pan American Airways.

——. 1941b. Trinidad. *New Horizons*, XI(4).

——. 1942a. Feminine touch. *New Horizons*, January, p. 15.

——. 1942b. First eleven. *New Horizons*, June, pp. 9–10.

——. 1942c. Women of the year. *New Horizons*, December, p. 10.

——. 1943. Internal document: Pan American Airways system employees stationed within Continental United States as of December 31, 1942.

——. 1946a. Pins. *Clipper Latin American Division*, 3(8) (May).

——. 1946b. Who says women quit? Certainly not this boss. *Pan American Clipper*, 3(4), p. 4.

——. 1971a. Untitled. *Clipper*.

——. 1971b. Why the big emphasis now? More black stewardesses. *Pan American Clipper*.

——. 1974. *Annual Report*. Pan American Airways.

——. 1985. National Airlines Inc., maternity leave claims. Notice of federal court ruling against National regarding maternity benefits. Women. *Pan American Clipper* (May).

Pendo, S., 1985. *Aviation in the Cinema*. Metuchen, NJ: Scarecrow Press, Inc.

Prasad, A. and Mir, R., 2002. Digging deep for meaning: A critical hermeneutic analysis of CEO letters to shareholders in the oil industry. *Journal of Business Communication*, 39(1), pp. 92–116.

Prasad, P., 2005. Crafting qualitative research. working in the postpositivist traditions. Armonk, NY: M.E. Sharpe.

Price, W., 1973. The annual meeting (letter) (personal communication).

Sanderson, K., Parsons, D.B., Helms Mills, J. and Mills, A.J., 2010. Riding the second wave: Organizing feminism and organizational discourse – Stewardesses for Women's Rights. *Management & Organizational History*, 5(3–4), pp. 360–77.

Trippe, J.T., 1930. Memorandum to Department Heads and Division Officials – December 29. Box 17, Folder 31.

——. 1938. America's place in world air commerce, National Aeronautic Meeting Pan American Archive. Miami, FL: Otto Richter Library, University of Miami.

——. 1941. *The Wings of Democracy*. Pan American Airways Annual Report, Pan American Airways, p. 3.

Unger, R.M., 1987. *Social Theory: Its Situation and its Task*. Cambridge: Cambridge University Press.

Wall Street Journal Reporter. 1971. Court lets stand order that airlines end anti-male bias in hiring cabin attendants. *Wall Street Journal*, 10 November, p. 2.

Wallace, M., 2003. *The American Axis. Henry Ford, Charles Lindbergh, and the Rise of the Third Reich*. New York: St. Martin's Griffin.

Weick, K.E., 1995. *Sensemaking in Organizations*. London: Sage.

White, H., 1973. *Metahistory: The Historical Imagination in Nineteenth-Century Europe*. Balitimore, MD: Johns Hopkins University Press.

——. 1985. *Tropics of Discourse. Essays in Cultural Criticism*. Baltimore, MD: Johns Hopkins University Press.

Whitelegg, D., 2007. *Working the Skies. The Fast-Paced, Disorienting World of the Flight Attendant*. New York: New York University Press.

Williamson, E., 2009. *The Penguin History of Latin America*. London: Penguin.

Yin, R.K., 2009. *Case Study Research. Design and Methods*, 4th edn. Thousand Oaks, CA: Sage.

Chapter 2

Difficult, Dangerous, Not a Job for Girls: Factors Impacting Women and Girls' Orientation Towards Pilot Careers

Deanne Gibbon

> … when I think of women on planes, I don't think of women as pilots. I think of them more as the tray carriers and stuff. (High school focus group participant)

Introduction

Around ANZAC Day in 2011, I was invited to speak about my Air Force career at my daughter's co-ed primary school. Sadly, my own career as an Education Officer hasn't exactly consisted of the stuff primary school students would find thrilling, unless they have a particular bent for strategic policy development. To cleverly deflect attention away from my office-bound military existence, I invited an Air Force colleague 'Jessica'[1] to share some of her adventures as an operational Hercules and C17 pilot.

Jess was fantastic. Wearing her flying suit and a hot pink cap, she regaled her wide-eyed audience with tales of flying home victims of the horrific 2002 Bali bombings and of hair-raising dirt-strip landings in Afghanistan and Iraq. The children enjoyed every minute, their eyes shining with awe throughout her presentation. Once she had finished speaking, I asked how many children in the audience were interested in becoming pilots in either Defence or commercial aviation. About 15 or so children, around a third of the audience, put up their hands … all boys. Not one girl raised her hand.

'Come on', I cajoled, 'surely there is one girl in this class who wants to be a pilot when they grow up?' Eventually, one small, orthodontically challenged girl raised her hand: 'I don't want to be a pilot Dee, but I would like to become an air hostess'. This provoked a chorus of 'me too' and nods from some of the other girls.

Jess and I looked at each other, slightly exasperated. 'Why do you want to be an air hostess and not the pilot?' Jess pondered, genuinely intrigued. 'Well I just think it would be too hard and also too dangerous … you know, in case you crash', the girl replied. Jess explored this further. 'But you'd still be in the crash if you were

1 Not her real name.

cabin crew at the back of the aircraft … wouldn't you rather be flying the plane so that you could control what's happening?' 'No', the girl replied quite firmly, 'I think that would be more of a man's job'. Jess sighed and conceded defeat.

This little girl unwittingly summarised the findings of this research project: that girls view piloting as 'difficult, dangerous and not a job for girls'. These perceptions may contribute to the persistently low numbers of women in piloting roles worldwide. In Australia, women comprise only five per cent of the piloting workforce,[2] which approximates estimated percentages in other countries (Neal-Smith and Cockburn, 2009; Turney et al., 2002). At just 3.2 per cent,[3] the ratios of women in Australian Defence Force (ADF) piloting roles are even lower. Women pilot ratios compare unfavourably with other fields that are also considered 'non-traditional' for women, such as policing (18 per cent), bus/tram driving (12 per cent) and mining engineering (seven per cent) (Marchbank, 2008).

While women's under-representation in non-traditional occupations can be examined from a range of perspectives, this chapter focuses on qualitative research that has explored flying as a career choice for women and girls. The first perspective examines findings that relate to factors that are important to women pursuing flying. Germain et al. (2012) note the importance of research focusing on women's motivation for entering male-dominated industries. The second perspective examines findings that pertain to non-pilot women/girls' attitudes towards flying as a possible career choice, another primary consideration for researchers examining occupational gender segregation (Miller and Budd, 1999).

Beyond contributing to academic debates about non-traditional employment, this research is also practical and timely. The world is facing impending pilot shortages (Carey et al., 2012; O'Connor, 2012) borne from post-global financial crisis economic recovery. Ongoing globalisation, significant growth in Asia's aviation industries and an aging commercial pilot population is further exacerbating pilot population shortfalls (Craver, 2007; Blakely, 2008). Women are already viewed as a currently untapped source of future pilots (Turney, 2004; Bennett, 2006; Brown, 2008), but there is little research available to support their recruitment to this non-traditional career. Understanding female pilots' career motivations and women and girls' perceptions of piloting is critical to informing the pilot recruitment strategies of the future.

Theoretical Perspectives

Despite years of government and industry initiatives to reduce occupational segregation, women still tend to be clustered into stereotypical 'female'

2 Approximated by combining CASA licensing data with other estimations (Marchbank, 2008; Mitchell et al., 2005).

3 Based on data extracted from Defence's Personnel Management Database, as at April 2013.

occupations, while men dominate in traditionally 'male' occupations (Anker, 1998). Occupational segregation by gender is found in all countries, 'in every region, at all economic development levels, under all political systems, and in diverse religious, social and cultural environments' (Anker, 1997, p. 315).

Researchers generally differentiate between 'labour supply and labour demand factors when explaining occupational segregation by sex' (Anker, 1997, p. 316). Supply theories argue that women *prefer* to work in certain types of occupations, while demand focuses on *why employers/industries stream* women and men into different employment roles. Irrespective of their different theoretical positioning, occupational-segregation experts seem united in believing that no one theory offers a complete, inarguable explanation of the ongoing phenomena of gendered occupations (Bagilhole, 2002; Padavic and Reskin, 2002). Accordingly, both supply and demand considerations are important when analysing women's low representation in non-traditional roles. While supply factors are the focus of discussion here, demand considerations are considered as part of the wider study from which this data is drawn.

At a micro-theoretical level, there is little available research addressing factors that are important to women and girls choosing, or not choosing, flying careers. Studies of girls' career preferences offer some indicators: pilot was listed as one of girls' 'least preferred' careers in one study of children's occupational preferences (Stockard and McGee, 1990). While little girls may find flying undesirable, boys' childhood flying dreams are often cited as an influence determining male pilots' decisions to fly (Frederick-Recascino and Hall, 2003).

There is some evidence that girls who become pilots also have childhood aspirations, with Mills observing that for commercial pilots, 'in nearly every case the female pilot had an early association with flying' (1998, p. 176). McGlohn et al. (1997) reported similar findings when focusing on military pilots in the US. While childhood influences may be an important factor influencing female pilots' career selections, other considerations and influences have not been well-documented.

The dearth of literature addressing flying as a career choice for women mandates examining literature addressing women's perceptions of other non-traditional fields. Unfortunately, many of the hypotheses offered to explain women's low numbers in other occupations do not seem applicable to piloting. The work is not remote (Office for Women and Minerals Council of Australia, 2007), requiring significant physical strength (Jurik, 1985) or saddled with an unfortunate image problem (Gale, 1994; Fielden et al., 2000).

Although possibly less prestigious than in years past, flying is still perceived to be an exciting and relatively well-paid career (Hansen and Oster, 1997). It certainly doesn't seem to suffer from the 'geeky', 'isolated' image apparently preventing women from pursuing other technologically orientated fields (Outlay et al., 2012; Spertus, 1991). Lepore (2011) speculates that women's low representation in piloting may be attributed to flying being incompatible with raising a family whilst being away for long periods of time. This argument is seemingly countered by women's disproportionately high representation as cabin crew (currently estimated at around 72 per cent),[4] who work the same shifts and fly the same routes as pilots.

A lack of science, technological and mathematical exposure purportedly prevents higher numbers of women from pursuing careers in other technical fields (Kongar et al., 2009; Oakes, 1990). It could therefore be hypothesised that the technological and mathematical aspects of flying may serve as a deterrent to women. Court and Moralee (1995) cite a lack of visibility as a factor explaining women's low representation in construction, but pilots are an integral and highly visible aspect of life in the vast land of Australia. While visibility of pilots generally may not be a factor, the visibility of *female* pilots must be considered, noting their extremely low representation in all aviation contexts.

From a career image perspective, past research into gender and aviation offers some clues. Hansen and Oster note that 'aviation suffers from image problems that may hamper its attempt to diversify its workforce' (1995, p. 8). The most notable of these image problems relates to the highly masculine image of aviation, as emphasised by Ashcraft (2005); Davey and Davidson (2000); Kristovics et al. (2006), Mills (1998) and Mitchell et al. (2005). This highly masculine image may render flying an unattractive option for women and girls.

Blog commentators and journalists have speculated as to why women are reluctant to become pilots (Collins, 2012; Goyer, 2010; Pawlowski, 2011), but these forums are based purely on personal opinion. This research seeks to create a more rounded, researched view of why women do and do not pursue flying careers.

Method

Qualitative Interviews

Women's perceptions of flying careers were explored from two quite different perspectives. The first was based on qualitative data drawn from 75 semi-structured interviews with female pilots, past, present and future, from a wide range of Australian aviation contexts, including university aviation programmes. Further detail regarding the construct and methodology of these interviews is outlined in the Chapter 12 of this book.

Data used to inform this discussion was primarily drawn from the first part of each interview. Questions addressed early life, motivation to fly, hobbies and interests, alternative career choices and a range of other biographical and vocational considerations. Pilots were also asked why they selected their particular career pathway, which provided a wealth of data pertaining to women's preferences for civil or military flying. Quotes from pilots are described by aviation context; Air

4 Based on Open University Webpage data. Available at: http://www.open.edu.au/careers/transport/flight-attendants.

Force pilots are differentiated from their Navy and Army colleagues. Navy and Army pilots are described collectively as Australian Defence Force pilots, as their low numbers would make them too easy to identify if their service was specified.

Focus Groups

The second perspective examines women and girls' perceptions of flying as a potential career choice. Data for this aspect of discussion was drawn from a series of 12 focus groups, or 'group interviews' (Barbour, 2007), held at various locations around Australia. Although focus group findings are not reliable when creating generalisable data (Barbour, 2007), the method was useful to gaining a preliminary insight into women and girls' perceptions of piloting. Other researchers may choose to test or build on the preliminary 'hypotheses generating' findings detailed here.

Each focus group had between four and 10 women and girl participants, aged between 14 and 21. Participants were selected to encompass perspectives from three different groups. The first group comprised girls from public high schools with no institutionalised association or known exposure to aviation or the military. The second group of participants who had joined Defence through the Air Force's gap year programme, but were yet to make an occupational selection. The other group were students from Brisbane's Aviation High School, a school dedicated to preparing young people for a range of future aviation careers.

The focus groups were highly interactive discussions that ran for approximately 40–60 minutes. Discussion was framed around very open questions, which were designed to be free of any preconceptions or existing hypotheses. Some standard questions were 'What come into your mind when you hear the word "pilot"?', 'What do you think would be the best/worst thing about being a pilot?' and 'Is flying a career you might consider?'

After each series of focus groups or interviews, the data was transcribed, coded and analysed to identify the themes that are discussed in this chapter. Coding and analysis followed a grounded theory approach, where patterned responses and meanings were determined 'from the bottom up' through systematic discourse analysis (Charmaz, 2006). The quotes used in this chapter were selected to encapsulate representative perspectives of the topic under discussion. All participants have been de-identified.

Context

Military flying contexts have been described in the Chapter 12 of this book. There are two primary ways by which pilots can become qualified in civil aviation. The first of these entails undertaking a cumulative series of flying lessons and examinations at private flying school. The flying school pathway generally takes around 12–36 months to gain a commercial licence and is likely to cost in the range of $60,000 to $120,000 (Civil Aviation Safety Authority, 2013).

The alternative to the flying-school model for flying training is a university-based 'Bachelor of Aviation' course, which has theoretical and practical flying components. A recent initiative has been the government's introduction of 'fee-help', which enables students to defer paying the cost of flying until their income reaches a certain threshold. This relatively recent initiative has made flying more accessible to students without independent financial means.

Pilots intending to pursue a career in aviation must attain sufficient flying hours, experience and the appropriate licences and ratings to progress their career. Most early-career pilots are poorly paid, with many working a series of different jobs in order to fund additional flying hours, lessons, ratings and licences. There are very few genuine fully funded flying cadetships or scholarships offered in Australia, which makes the early years of piloting quite financially (and sometimes emotionally) taxing for many civilian pilots.

Factors Important to Selecting a Flying Career

> Choose a job you love, and you will never have to work a day in your life. (Confucius)

Past studies of women in traditional employment have determined three primary influences on women's career choices. These include family and parental characteristics, childhood socialisation and external support towards career choices (Fitzpatrick and Silverman, 1989). Studies have also determined that key influences on women's non-traditional career choices include parental attitudes and encouragement, support, school subject choices, teacher and guidance-counsellor support, media portrayals and everyday exposure to occupations (Andrew, 2009; Gadassi and Gati, 2009; Gottfredson, 1981; Lent et al., 2008; Tang et al., 2008). The impact of these factors on female pilots' career selection is addressed through this section.

Motivation to Fly

Michie and Nelson observe that 'work interests and self-efficacy expectations begin to develop in early childhood and are influenced, often inadvertently ... through the process of socialisation' (2006, p. 13). The assertions made by Mills (1998) and McGlohn et al. (1997) about most female pilots having childhood dreams of flying were certainly confirmed through this study. While some pilots discovered a love for flying through adult flying experiences such as university gliding clubs, the majority articulated a clear childhood *epiphany moment* when they first decided to be pilots. Epiphany moments were triggered by direct exposure to flying – visits to the flight deck during a flight to see Grandma, watching aircraft take off from the local airfield or on a joy-flight while on vacation:

> I guess, it was just always there, the fact that when you're a kid you could always go and visit the flight deck. That was one of the things that was really influential to me just going up there and meeting pilots. (Nada, commercial pilot)

> So I grew up on the Darling Downs. When I was small we had a glider actually land on our farm. So I think that just sort of sowed a seed. I was really small at the time. (Delia, general aviation pilot)

> I grew up on a cane farm in North Queensland and we've got an air strip up there … we had movies made, like war movies, so there'd be lots of planes in that. And then my Dad's just really obsessed! (Callie, Bachelor of Aviation student)

The age at which these epiphany moments occurred may be theoretically relevant. Most interviewees cited between five and 10 as the age at which they first decided to become a pilot. Vocational choice theorists contend that 6–8 are critical ages in terms of career decision making, as this is the period when children 'orientate themselves to sex roles' and decide what is 'appropriate for one's sex' (Gottfredson, 2002, p. 96). Clearly the women in this study did not rule flying out as being 'gender inappropriate' as children, thus enabling them to orientate themselves towards a non-traditional career as teenagers.

This early orientation towards flying also confirms that flying is not a career choice made after attending a career fare, flipping through a vocation guide or hearing from a guest presenter at school. *None* of the pilots in this study made their career decision based purely on high school career guidance. This finding suggests the need for more creative and imaginative approaches when inciting girls' interest in aviation.

Childhood dreams of flight were almost always solidified through a tangible 'hands-on' flying experience during teenage years. Parents often helped to facilitate and fund these practical flying experiences. Exposure was attained through flying lessons, scenic joy-flights and/or gliding club participation through Air Force cadets or university flying programmes. Some interviewees suspected their parents facilitated exposure to flying as a means of deterring them, which clearly backfired!

> So Mum and Dad weren't that keen but I think once they saw how fixed I was in my mind that that's what I was going to do they would then became very supportive and they gave me my first $1,000 towards flying lessons. (Margaret, commercial pilot, former Air Force pilot)

> I'd already obviously been talking about flying and so Dad said to my uncle, 'Do you think we could get her a lesson and see?' So they organised someone to take

> me up, I was about 15. I think Dad thought I'd probably hate it, but I loved it. (Vera, commercial pilot)

Practical exposure has been identified as a factor positively impacting women's entry into other non-traditional fields (Bourne and Özbilgin, 2008; Whittock, 2002). This premise guides the development of experiential school camps (Doerschuk et al., 2007; Gilbride et al., 2007; Yilmaz, 2010) and targeted schemes designed to provide hands-on exposure to other non-traditional roles (e.g. Queensland's 'Women in Hard Hats' programme). Aviation organisations seeking to increase female pilot participation should actively consider sponsoring programmes to generate exposure for teenage girls, for example, through an experiential 'school camp' concept. Air Force is certainly investigating this option through its 'jet camp' programme, which is described in Chapter 12 of this book.

The gender stereotyping of girls into traditional occupational roles is frequently offered as an explanation for women's disinclination towards non-traditional roles (Bourne and Özbilgin, 2008). The degree to which parents supported their daughters' access to flying may indicate interviewees' non-gendered upbringing. Interviewees spoke of feeling that there were no limits as far as their professional choices were concerned. Women in this study spoke of growing up feeling empowered, being told they 'could do anything' and of being actively encouraged to pursue non-traditional careers:

> [My parents] were both very conscious to make sure that there was never anything that we felt like we couldn't do. 'Like you can't do that 'cause you're a girl', or, 'Well I want to be a plumber', 'well why don't you think about hair dressing?' I never felt like I couldn't do anything. (Prinny, commercial pilot)

Fathers were cited as key influencers in many interview reflections. Pilots spoke of having 'aviation-obsessed' fathers, who actively or inadvertently triggered their daughters' childhood orientation towards flying. The significance of fatherly encouragement is noted in several studies of women's participation in non-traditional employment (Fitzpatrick and Silverman, 1989; Lemkau, 1979; O'Donnell and Anderson, 1978):

> I've just always loved planes like Dad sort of has a thing for planes. When I was really young, maybe five or something and dad would actually bring me to Archerfield … and you can see through the fence and see all the planes taking off and we just used to come here and chill … (Narine, Bachelor of Aviation student)

> And then dad took me to War Birds over Wanaka, which is a big air show in New Zealand … so massive air show, and I watched it and I'm like, 'That is so cool'. And I was probably eight or nine, and I'm like, 'That's what I want to do' … When I was little, yeah, I was really little. (Erica, Air Force pilot)

A significant point of difference between this and other studies of pilot motivation is that the 'aviation-obsessed' fathers were rarely pilots themselves. Only seven of the 75 women interviewed had pilots in their immediate or extended family; just three of these pilots flew professionally. This presents a point of departure from other studies citing pilot-family members as invoking women's initial interest in flying (Davey and Davidson, 2000; Mills, 1998). Most interviewees only made personal connections with other pilots once they began flying themselves.

In terms of family background, interviewees' parents hailed from a wide variety of professional backgrounds, ranging from truck driver to surgeon. The majority of pilots came from modest backgrounds that might be described as working or lower-middle class. This finding debunks the myth that flying is the preserve of the wealthy. The only noticeable correlation between parent's careers/ backgrounds and women becoming pilots was that military pilots tended to have a family association with military service, although not necessarily to military *pilots*.

Another unexpected finding was the over-representation of pilots from rural backgrounds. Around half of all interviewees grew up either on farms or within rural communities. One explanation for this may be that children engaged in 'androgynous or masculine play' are more likely to proceed into non-traditional fields (Standley and Soule, 1974). Farming children tend to grow up engaging in non-gender stereotyped activities and generally lead more adventurous lives than their city-bound peers.

Farming parents' role modelling may also be a factor. As one interviewee astutely observed, 'on farms, there is no women's work or men's work, there is only farm work'. Renata noticed the influence of her mother as a strong, 'emancipated' role model:

> I think on a farm I think my mother, for her generation, was quite an emancipated woman and I think also the role of the man and woman on a farm … I mean, the woman has got to do the jobs that men do. (Renata, commercial pilot)

Rural children's attraction to flying may be borne out of sheer exposure. In Australia, aviation forms an integral aspect of rural life. Farm children are likely to have greater everyday access to flying than their city-bound peers and thus more opportunity to create those all-important 'epiphany moments':

> I don't know; I just was one of those … I think I saw a plane, 'cause I was from a farm in Perth in the country, and I used to always saw – like, we had lots of planes flying over and stuff and I guess being a farm girl and stuff I'm into … (Roxy, general aviation pilot)

> Not really, like we always had the day off school 'cause I was from the farm, so we always had a day off school when the ag [agriculture] pilot came and like

> fertilised, and we'd jump in with him and go for a burn and think it was pretty cool. (Tori, regional commercial pilot)

Elements of all explanations may hold some truth. Irrespective of which hypothesis is correct, women and girls from rural areas clearly present a demographic worth targeting when seeking to recruit female pilots.

Beyond parents, teachers and school guidance counsellors are also reported to 'influence gender stereotyping of roles and choices through their interactions with students' (Adya and Kaiser, 2005). Encouragement for girls to step outside gender stereotypes was also found in many school environments. Many younger interviewees attended school with highly supportive teachers and a strong empowerment focus. Maths and science teachers were especially influential to many interviewees.

> he was my maths teacher, so that was my favourite subject and stuff so he was really supportive. I've never met someone so supportive, so that was like, that's sort of the only person like outside of my family that was really fully into the whole idea of it. Where everyone else was supportive but he was like encouraging me more. (Tamson, Australian Defence Force Academy cadet)

While many senior pilots experienced adversity from both schools and parents, younger women spoke of being encouraged towards non-traditional careers. This generational shift suggests a welcome cultural change regarding women's encouragement into non-traditional roles. Senior pilots spoke of being persuaded into nursing, teaching, flight attending and other occupations deemed 'gender-appropriate'. The lack of encouragement resulted in some pilots commencing alternative career/study pathways, before reorientating themselves towards their original dream:

> Yeah, my career teacher at school absolutely tried to talk me out of it … he thought that it wouldn't be a very stable job and that it wasn't something you know that was a normal thing for women … Mum and Dad weren't very keen on the idea at all as well then either. (Margaret, commercial pilot, former Air Force)

> I had a lot of trouble even just financing my flying. My dad was always supportive but my mother was completely flabbergasted at the choice of career and couldn't even really discuss it with me. So there wasn't a lot of help there … I had a lot of obstacles. (Vera, commercial pilot)

> I can't say my parents were fully supportive. Dad didn't really think that I could do it … he just laughed and said: 'Don't be so stupid'. (Barb, commercial pilot)

Vera directly attributed a lack of parental encouragement and financial support as a key limitation to women's flying careers, observing that parents may be more prepared to fund aviation training for sons. Mitchell et al. (2005) support Vera's view, noting parents' reluctance to fund women's careers in male domains. Women without parental support, both emotional and financial, had to fund their own flying. Before fee-help, only the most dedicated and motivated pilots could achieve their career aspirations:

> Fee-help is such a good thing and I think that will probably boost female interest because that takes out … that expensive aspect and makes it more achievable. (Bella, Bachelor of Aviation student)

> [Without fee help] I probably would have done some other degree first so that I could, I could get a job and earn the money and then do the flying after that but it would have been a much, much longer process and who knows where I would have gone? I might have just not worried about it. (Faith, Bachelor of Aviation student)

Fee-help has certainly opened the piloting door to many more women. The convener of Griffith University's Bachelor of Aviation course directly attributes fee-help with Griffith's inordinately high ratios (30 per cent) of female pilots.[5]

Pilot Personality and Recreational Preferences

Personality traits play a significant role in determining both men and women's vocational choices (Chusmir, 1983; Holland, 1966). Novello and Youssel's study of pilot personality determined that irrespective of gender, pilots are 'courageous and adventuresome' and 'orientated toward demonstrating competency, skill and achievement' (1974, p. 633). Focus and drive are also cited by Mitchell et al. (2005) as characteristics necessary for women to succeed in aviation.

Our study determined some personality commonalities across the pilot population of interviewees. Interviewees demonstrated a high degree of 'self-efficacy', or the innate belief or expectation that they could succeed in their chosen profession. Self efficacy is known to be a common personality trait in selecting non-traditional fields, especially those entailing mathematical aspects (Betz and Hackett, 1983).

Farmer et al. (1995) note the strong correlation between women who view themselves as 'self-reliant' and choosing careers in science and technology fields. Accordingly, a high degree of independence and self-reliance might also be expected from women pursuing flying careers, as was confirmed through this study. Pilots also commonly described themselves as *adventurous*, *highly competitive*, *motivated*, *resilient*, *determined*, *driven* and in some cases *rebellious*.

5 Participation data provided by Griffith University Bachelor of Aviation course convener in March 2010.

Women in other non-traditional fields share similar qualities to the pilots in this study (Chusmir, 1983; Lemkau, 1979):

> We all go through that in teenage years, so I was the typical, naughty, rebellious teenager [laughs]. (Sheila, general aviation pilot)

> Yeah, I'd definitely say we're competitive people and you have to be I think driven, motivated and ambitious to work hard … (Tania, Air Force pilot)

> I'm pretty competitive. (Aviation high school student)

> Yeah, I'd definitely say we're competitive people and you have to be I think driven, motivated and ambitious to work hard and to put up with some of the crap and to get there I think. (Roberta, Air Force pilot)

Research into cultural and structural barriers impacting female pilots suggests that qualities such as resilience and determination may indeed be necessary to 'surviving and thriving' in the highly masculine world of aviation (Ashcraft, 2005; Davey and Davidson, 2000).

Being competitive also manifests in pilots' recreational preferences, with most interviewees playing competitive sports to high levels during their high school years. Coates and Overman (1992) noted parallels between competitive sports and women succeeding in non-traditional employment. Interviewees certainly spoke of participation in competitive activities as being helpful to managing the rigours of a flying career.

> I think that that discipline from martial arts and the ability to focus when there's so much going on around you and the shit's hit the fan the ability to sort of go whoa, hang on a sec, what am I actually doing, that came from martial arts, definitely. (Mindy, Australian Defence Force pilot)

As both children and adults, most female pilots also engaged in a range of adventurous recreational pursuits. Motorbike riding, drag-cart racing, mountaineering, hiking, water-skiing and wake-boarding, sailing, hang-gliding and sky-diving were all listed as pursuits enjoyed by pilots in this study. Adventure and sporting clubs might be another rich source of future female pilots.

In terms of masculine/feminine identity and orientation, pilots happily described themselves as either 'tomboys' or 'girly-girls'; there was equal representation of both extremes in this study across all aviation contexts:

> I'm definitely a girl. I like to do my girlie things. I love doing all my girlie stuff. I like to go get my hair done. But it doesn't mean I don't love flying, and I like the adrenalin rush. (Aviation high school student)

> No, I was a bit of a tomboy, yeah, I was one of those, you know, and I suppose that's probably something I guess you've probably seen a lot of in this industry [laughs]. (Mindy, Australian Defence Force pilot)

Many pilots spoke of preferring the company of boys and engaging in 'boyish pursuits' in their teenage years. This is not unusual for women who seek non-traditional careers, with Coates and Overman finding that 'girls who had played more with boys were likely to choose non-traditional professions as adult women' (1992, p. 269).

Women who described themselves as lifelong 'tomboys' seemed, at least to me, overtly quite feminine. Although interviewees referred to other 'butch' pilots (their words, not mine), I did not meet any overtly 'butch' pilots in this study. This leads me to suspect the prevalence of another myth: that of the *butch* woman pilot. Sonya agrees this is an inaccurate stereotype:

> a lot of people stereotype that a typical female pilot is a bit of a 'you know' butch type. Yeah we're not. We're not, we're just normal girls who seem to like planes, you know, it's as simple as that. (Sonya, commercial cadet pilot)

Subject Selections and Alternative Careers

Anker (2001) contends that decisions made in early life can be very limiting to women's access to non-traditional roles, especially high school subject selections (Melkas and Anker, 1997). Bagilhole (2002) also contends that girls' propensity towards humanities and arts subjects limits their future access to scientific and technical careers. The link between school subject selections and piloting was also analysed in this study.

Most of the *military* pilots interviewed in this study situated their academic preferences to achieve their preferred career, undertaking maths, physics, technology and science at high school. Unlike their military peers, interviewees in civil aviation hailed from a wide range of academic backgrounds, including maths/science, as well as dance, music, humanities, art, human movement and sports science. The lack of a maths/science high school background did not seem to impede success in civil aviation, although women without high school maths and physics found aspects of ground school more challenging. Civil pilots' success, without strict maths/science backgrounds, suggests that Defence's stringent educational requirements may be limiting the pool of potential female pilots.

When discussing alternative careers, pilots in this study had a strong orientation towards careers that were not deskbound and 'boring'. This was a key attribute of flying and numerous other non-traditional jobs cited as viable alternatives by female pilots:

> That's mainly why I always wanted to be something different. I didn't want to just be … another accountant or another something. (Roxy, general aviation pilot)

> So I thought, you know, I'll be a fire-fighter or a policeman or something like that … something practical that I just always wanted to be doing things. (Gina, Bachelor of Aviation student)

Several civilian pilots initially pursued careers as professional dancers, which I found quite surprising. Bella, a former dancer, drew a connection between performing arts and flying, noting extreme discipline and tenacity required to succeed in both fields:

> [Ballet dancing] is just such an unrealistic career and it means that you have to really want it … the discipline required is ridiculous and your social life is just gone … in aviation it's similar. (Bella, Bachelor of Aviation student)

Other pilots felt that dancing had a natural connection to flying, as both require an understanding of physics, spatial awareness and a degree of physicality. As unlikely as it may seem, dance studios might be another source of future pilots!

Choosing a Flying Pathway

While a small number of civilian pilots expressed ethical and/or moral issues pertaining to military flying careers ('I just, I have a problem with your job being to kill people'), the vast majority actively investigated a military pathway to flying. The lengthy contractual obligation (currently 12 years), or 'return of service obligation' (ROSO), was cited by almost all interviewees and some focus group participants as the major deterrent to military flying:

> When I started to learn to fly, I rang them [Defence recruiting] up and they said it was an eight to 10 year return to service and when I was 18 that just seemed like forever. Because you know, I'd be like 28 by the time I got out. [Q. Do you think you might have joined if the commitment was shorter?] Yes, definitely, because that was the reason why I didn't do it. (Tiff, commercial pilot)

The single most effective measure Defence could take to attract higher numbers of female pilots would be to remove, reduce or mitigate the negative perception of the lengthy contractual obligation. Interviewees did not even attempt applying for the Australian Defence Force after realising the length of the contractual commitment. It is difficult to ascertain whether this obligation is similarly demotivating for young men, but it seems likely, noting 'Generation Y's' apparent adversity towards long-term employment commitments (McKrindle Research, 2006).

In terms of military pilot motivation, most Defence pilots joined the military to fly – it was pilot first, military second. The military was viewed as a means of accessing affordable, high-quality flying training and an exciting aviation career. Army pilots were the notable exception, as for many interviewees, becoming a pilot was secondary to becoming an Army officer. Many Army pilots only considered an aviation career after discovering they had an aptitude after undertaking voluntary pilot aptitude testing whilst undergoing Army training.

The aptitude-testing pathway may explain the Army's increased female pilot ratios as compared to the two other services. This present possibilities for organisations seeking to attract female pilots; epiphany moments *can* be created in later life, especially if women have an 'I can do this' experience.

Pilots from all three Defence arms felt a strong orientation towards their preferred service and expressed clear preferences for flying either rotary or fixed-wing aircraft. Civil pilots also expressed a clear orientation towards their preferred career pathway, targeting either commercial or non-commercial aviation. A large of number of interviewees at all career stages expressed an interest in Angel Flight or Royal Flying Doctor Service (RFDS). This may support the finding by Francis (2002) that girls and women tend to have more of an orientation towards humanitarian/carer roles than boys.

Somewhat ironically, the RFDS pilots interviewed in this study were intent on pursuing commercial aviation careers, citing low pay, inhospitable shifts and general employment conditions as primary factors for leaving their current context:

> My dream was to be an RFDS pilot … but very soon in GA, you realise GA's just … you've got to get out of it. The only career you can really have in aviation seriously is to be an airline pilot. There's just not the money in it. (Nada, commercial pilot)

Pilots seeking commercial aviation careers with larger airlines stated an affinity towards their preferred airline:

> Qantas is definitely the one for me I think … I sort of always grew up wanting to fly for Qantas. (Callie, Bachelor of Aviation student)

> Because I am now facing an issue where I'm trying to get into Virgin, because at the end of the day it's the best of the three. (Ellen, RFDS pilot)

Virgin Australia is viewed by some pilots as the 'more progressive', 'female-friendly' and 'family friendly' airline. Qantas is considered more prestigious, but somewhat staid and conservative. Qantas has a reputation amongst non-Qantas female pilots as not being very family-friendly, which seems more of a misconception than actuality, based on data from other aspects of this research. Qantas should address these inaccurate perceptions, noting its goal to increase female pilot representation (Brown, 2008).

Women and Girls' Perceptions of Flying as a Possible Career

While pilot backgrounds, motivations and personality characteristics provide an insight into factors that are important to women pursing flying careers, that is only part of the story. Another important factor to understanding women's entry into flying is to ascertain how non-pilot women and girls view flying as a possible career choice. Researchers contend that gendered career perceptions warrant 'research attention if the negative consequences of gendered perceptions are to be tackled' (Bourne and Özbilgin, 2008, p. 321). This section examines women and girls' perceptions of flying as a possible career choice.

Positive Attributes Associated with Flying

Participants cited numerous positive attributes associated with flying careers. Flying is seen as very prestigious and elite, with numerous girls and women describing how proud they would feel to tell people they were pilots. Other perceived positives were the amount of travel, opportunities to explore the world and, in a military context, being able to serve your country in a meaningful way. Being a 'different' career was also very attractive to participants:

> I think just 'cause it's different. Like it's just not a typical, I don't know, it's just not an everyday job. You know, it's just different, I think that would be pretty good. (High school student)

> I think like 'cause it's not something everyone does, like just to be able to do something that – like doing something different that nobody can do it's, like, oh I can fly a plane. (Gap-year cadet)

While participants readily spoke of the positive attributes of being a pilot, very few actually thought they might like to pursue this career for a range of reasons.

Not a Job for Girls

Occupational stereotyping entails 'holding images of occupations … including the personalities of people in those occupations, the work they do, the lives they lead … and the appropriateness of that work for different types of people' (Gottfredson, 2002, p. 85). Archer and Lloyd (2002) suggest that stereotypes, which are often formed as children, can directly discourage women from entering certain professions.

Numerous studies have demonstrated children's ability to classify occupations as either 'masculine' or 'feminine' from early childhood, with results generally mirroring similar gender classifications afforded by adults (Hartung et al., 2005; Morgan et al., 2001). Focus group data suggests that flying remains a deeply gender-stereotyped occupation, with participants from all contexts expressing a view that flying is masculine, requiring 'male qualities':

> Just, whenever I think about pilots, I always think about men, mainly, pilots. (High school student)

> I guess I've always thought of it as a guy's kind of thing … but like I always just thought it was a guy like, 'cause like in the movies and then like, just everything, it's always just males. (High school student)

> … it's like, well, why would you – like, that's a man's job. You've got to leave a man to do a man's job. (High school student)

Where piloting was seen as a masculine profession, flight attending was stereotyped as being a gender-appropriate role for women. Numerous high school participants referenced cabin crew as being their initial reaction when considering flying, with a number of girls actively citing flight attendant as one of their vocational considerations:

> Yeah, like, well, females wouldn't really choose, like, a pilot, they seem to choose say, an air hostess or something, like, who's not actually flying the plane. (High school student)

> I wouldn't want to be a pilot but being an air hostess would be really awesome … for the travel and stuff. (High school student)

The lack of exposure to female pilots and role models was a major factor influencing girls' views. Participants referenced movies like *Top Gun* and other Hollywood blockbusters as confirming their views of flying as being a masculine career. Vermeulen and Mitchell (2007) and other researchers have also noted that the image of aviation generated by films such as *The Right Stuff* and *Top Gun* may be detrimental to the recruitment of female pilots. Beyond media portrayals, few women or girls had ever seen a female pilot in *real life*, which certainly contributes to the perceptions of flying being gender-inappropriate for women:

> But I actually don't think I've ever met a female pilot in the Air Force. It just feels really unachievable. (Gap-year cadet)

> I don't know, it just seems like more of a guy job. I've never really seen a girl flying a plane and stuff. (High school student)

> When you've got all of this media and film, newspaper articles, ra, ra, it's all about boys, boy pilots, boys this, boys that. It's difficult to inject yourself into that world … (Gap-year cadet)

Barry also noted the lack of exposure as being problematic to women's recruitment into aviation, stating that 'women don't often get exposure to flying and don't get to meet many pilots … when they do, those pilots tend to be male … a little arrogant, macho and with strong views, which further enhances the perception' (cited in Bennett, 2006, p. 52).

Barry's (cited in Bennett, 2006) view about pilot personas being off-putting to girls and women was absolutely reinforced through the focus groups with Air Force's gap-year students. This group expressed strong views about flying as a career choice on the basis of their less-than-positive interactions with some Air Force pilots. While there were exceptions, gap-year women described pilots, especially fighter pilots, as being 'sleazy', 'self-absorbed', 'arrogant' and generally quite unreceptive to the prospect of female pilots:

> Like we felt like pieces of meat because all the pilots just stared at us … (Gap-year cadet)
>
> Yeah, it was like, they, the pilots found it easier to talk to the boys that were interested rather than the girls. Like if a girls like, 'Hey, I'm interested in pilot', they're like, 'Yeah, righto' … You have to go like, 'No, I'm serious'. (Gap-year cadet)
>
> If you've a female they'll pay a lot of attention to you. In a very sleazy way.
>
> [Q. And what about if you're trying to talk to them about their jobs?] They're really into it. They are always into it; they'll happily talk about themselves for hours. (Gap-year cadet)
>
> Well, they [fighter pilots] like to get drunk and destroy things … at Williamtown whilst we were there. And they destroyed the pool table and all that sort of stuff. And they were breaking glasses, and then they blamed gap year, because we were there. They blamed it all on us. (Gap-year cadet)

It is perhaps easy to see why gap-year students may have felt disinclined towards choosing flying careers in the Air Force. Beyond negative perceptions garnered through interacting with individual pilots, flying was clearly viewed as a 'boys club' by gap-year students, which was a major disincentive for many students. Even women who joined the gap year programme to pursue flying careers changed their views through the year-long programme:

> But the hard thing is, is that even if you've only got one or two girls in I … they're going to be thought as the crap, even if there is 80 per cent guys that are worse than them … all the extra pressure, and the boys club as well. (Gap-year cadet)

> Every single boy would be finding an excuse to try … to show you up … make a mistake, or show you up, or to prove that you're – it's still a boy's job. 'Cause I think that's the impression at the moment … it's a boys' job. It's only allowed to be a boy's job sadly. (Gap-year cadet)

> But I think the stigma with flying is totally different because I think everyone's really supportive of women in the Air Force, but not necessarily flying. (Gap-year cadet)

Girls at the Aviation High School, who also had some exposure to pilots, shared similar concerns:

> Well, the worst thing would probably be, most are male pilots. So the intimidation of them thinking they're better than you. (Aviation High School student)

> They [the boys] try and bring you down because, I mean, we take all the hard classes … we're smart but I feel like I have to work harder to get the same job that another guy in my class that wants to get as well. (Aviation High School student)

Another major contributor to women and girls feeling that flying was gender-inappropriate was the strong view of what constitutes a 'typical pilot'. Aviation High School and gap-year students, some of whom actually selected that pathway due to their interest in flying, questioned their 'legitimacy' as potential pilots because they weren't as 'obsessed' as their male peers. Girls spoke of their peers as 'living, sleeping and breathing' aviation, and were concerned they lacked similar dedication:

> I think to have a job like that you've got to have the passion for it, it's got to be your calling … the people that are pilots they've dreamt of being pilots since they were a little kid and I wouldn't want to be in a class with them. (Gap-year cadet)

This might be a perception worthy of addressing, possibly through exposure to female pilots who do not 'live, sleep and breathe' aviation, but still absolutely love flying. There are many professional female pilots who fit this criterion.

A number of participants also raised concerns about flying being 'family friendly' for women, confirming Lepore's (2011) hypothesis that this is a factor impacting girls' views of this career pathway:

> I reckon that's just like [name removed] said, you have to think about a family if that's what you want. And I think that for a very big percentage of women, that's what would stop them. (Gap-year cadet)

Aviation organisations have introduced so many flexible employment options for female pilots that really make this career achievable for women with families. Defence is currently introducing similar measures. Aviation organisations could market these flexible work practices to reposition flying as a family-friendly career.

In terms of mitigating negative perceptions, Aviation High School staff has worked very hard to counter girls' views of aviation as being a gender-inappropriate job for them, which has definitely had a positive impact on some of the students at that school. The School has introduced an all-girls aviation awareness programme called 'Aviation Angels', which actively encourages girls towards piloting. The programme facilitates flying exposure, access to female pilot role models and industry awareness. This programme is fairly new, but seems to be very popular with the students who participated in the focus groups. Groups like Aviation Angels might be similarly beneficial in other contexts in order to counter the perception that flying is simply not a career for women.

Difficult

Researchers have determined that male-stereotyped occupations may be perceived by women as being 'more difficult' than female-stereotyped roles (Eccles, 1986; Michie and Nelson, 2006). Michie and Nelson (2006) also contend that women had a reduced belief in their own ability to perform job duties in male-dominated technologically based occupations, even when they were academically competent in aligned subject areas. Apparently, gender rather than ability is still a major factor impacting women's occupational choices (Francis, 2002).

The perception of flying as being 'too difficult' was absolutely affirmed through the focus groups. Even academically superior participants pursuing hard sciences and maths worried that they wouldn't be 'smart enough' to become pilots:

> Yeah, my family kept trying to tell me, like, 'If you get an opportunity go for pilot, go for pilot', but I'm not, well I'd, I'm not smart enough [laugh]. Not that I'm not smart. (Gap-year cadet)

> You have to be really smart and confident to be a pilot. (High school student)

> Like, you're going on a plane, something goes wrong, you just have to depend on yourself to save a whole plane of people. And, maybe, I'm not that brainy enough to do that. (Aviation High School student)

The perception of difficulty was also a deterrent to Aviation High School students when considering Air Force flying careers:

> [Q. So have you thought about Air Force?] You need to be really smart to be that … it's just the pressure that they put – like, you have to have an OP1, and be good at physics and all the sciences, maths, and all that stuff. And I think that,

> personally, it would be a bit – pressure. It would be too much pressure for me. So, I guess, boys can take that a bit more … But girls would just freak out, I guess. (Aviation High School student interested in a civil flying career)

This lack of self-efficacy was worrying in contexts like Aviation High School, especially when this school was selected primarily due to their interest in aviation. Many students on the Air Force's highly competitive gap year programme were exceptionally bright and orientated towards careers in other scientific, technical or mathematical disciplines. They too deemed piloting as unattainable due to perceived difficulty and were not even prepared to attempt pilot aptitude testing to establish whether they had a flying aptitude. The belief that becoming a pilot is 'too difficult' in the Air Force was exacerbated by exposure to Air Force personnel, both pilot and non-pilot, who reiterated this perception:

> And so, whereas the rest of us are just like, 'Oh', like that's so far out of reach, and because of the massive failure rates and all the massive hype about it, we all kind of go, 'Oh, that's unobtainable'. (Gap-year cadet)

> Such a high fail rate … I've heard lots of stories where you stuff up one day, you're gone the next. I don't know, there's like no second chances. (Gap-year cadet)

> And it's just like, 'Oh yeah, the girls don't ever get this far and then they don't get much further' and things like that. So I just, it was like, I couldn't really be bothered. [Q. So where did you get that impression from?] Yeah, everyone says that. I know there was one bit that they said the girls usually don't get past … this one last test that the girls never get past. [Q. Who told you that?] Our Flight Lieutenant. (Gap-year cadet)

Becoming a military pilot is definitely difficult, so the perceptions are not totally unfounded. However, where young men might be confident enough to 'give it a go' irrespective of the perceived difficulty, women are seemingly reluctant to proceed down a pathway with very low prospects of success. Women's underestimation of their own capabilities is thought to be a major factor limiting women's progression into non-traditional careers (Fassinger, 2002). This certainly seems to be the case with women and flying.

Again, ensuring higher numbers of women and girls have positive exposure and develop a sense of 'I can do this' might help to reframe piloting as a realistic possibility. Presenting 'risk-free' opportunities to at least undertake pilot aptitude testing could be very helpful in this regard. Access to flying in simulators, 'hands-on' experiential flying exposure and positive experiences with aptitude testing might also reposition flying as more attainable.

Given that girls also 'avoid jobs which involve "masculine" scientific and technical aspects' (Francis, 2002, p. 86), promoting flying as a 'doing' active career, rather than as a technical career, may also improve girls' willingness to consider this career option.

Dangerous

Barucky and Stone's focus group study of minority group's perceptions of flying determined that 'the youth's strongest perception of a flying career was that it is a dangerous and therefore undesirable activity' (1999, pp. 20–26). The view that flying is dangerous was certainly reiterated through this study, but only in groups without any direct exposure to aviation:

> It's like, it'd be a good job, but there's heaps of disadvantages that you have with it. Like it's really dangerous. (High school student)

> Crashing. Yes, crashing would be the main negative about being a pilot. (High school student)

Students with exposure to aviation were seemingly more educated about the risks of a flying career because *danger* was not cited as a concern in most focus groups with Aviation High School or gap-year students. This finding suggests that exposure might mitigate the 'danger' perception of flying.

High school participants initially commented that flying would be 'dangerous' because of the risk of crashing. However, when challenged further regarding their perceptions, the danger factor was actually less important than the degree of responsibility held by pilots. In response to being asked if they thought being an aircraft passenger was also 'dangerous', participants revealed that their fears were more about being responsible for a large number of other people's lives.

It is difficult to ascertain whether boys and men also view this degree of responsibility as a deterrent. Their much higher numbers in flying suggest they may be more willing to proceed down a flying pathway, irrespective of any concerns they might have regarding risk and responsibility. The degree of responsibility held by pilots, and assuming accountability for passenger safety were huge disincentives by girls and women from many focus groups:

> If something goes wrong, they'll usually blame you, even though, it might not even, actually, be your fault. (High school student)

> Because if you think about all of these lives that you're carrying every time that you fly a plane … you're responsible … if your plane crashed, you'd be like … blamed. (High school student)

> Not your – you would have the crashes, like what if your plane crashes and you're gone, or if like passengers die, you'd kind of feel responsible. (High school student)

It is difficult to ascertain where this antipathy towards holding responsibility and being 'blamed' stems from. Recent televisions shows such as *Air Crash Investigation* were mentioned by a number of participants, suggesting these programmes may negatively influence young women's perceptions regarding flying careers. The threat of terrorism was also raised in a number of high school focus groups – perhaps growing up in a post-9/11 world has impacted young women's views of flying?:

> I don't know 'cause I've been watching a lot of those air crash investigation thingy, yeah, on Foxtel. And you just think back to 9/11, even though it was in America, but like there's been a lot of terrorist stuff in the news lately. (High school student)

> Terrorist stuff would be probably like another thing that would scare me. Like you don't know who's getting on your plane. (High school student)

Mitigating these fears and perceptions through targeted marketing may be important to increasing women and girls' tendencies towards flying. Flying is statistically far less risky than driving (Podmore, 2011), a point that should be reiterated to high school students. Girls may need to be reassured regarding the high calibre of pilot training in Australia, which mitigates the degree of risk for all pilots. Providing assurances that pilots are supported by other crew members, including co-pilots, might also help ease girls' concerns.

Conclusion

In an amusing satirical article, pilot and journalist Garth Wallace notes that flying clubs of the past were 'nothing but smelly airplanes, filthy washrooms and dirty old men' (2004, p. 10). While the washrooms these days may be more sanitary, their patrons are still 'mostly men, some old, some dirty, some not' (Wallace, 2004, p. 10). Wallace asks 'where are the women?' (2004, p. 10) and this is an excellent question. It seems there are still innumerable barriers to women's entry into aviation careers, many of which were ascertained through this study.

As the mother of city-dwelling daughters, I do find it worrying that girls seem so fearful of responsibility, viewing handling emergencies as a masculine role. Does a farming childhood provide girls with opportunities to develop feelings of competence and responsibility through activities such as riding horses, driving tractors and other active pursuits? This may be a theme warranting further investigation, especially the link between rural upbringing and entry into non-traditional employment into other non-traditional roles.

The 'not a job for girls' sentiment was quite startling coming from maths and science-inclined girls already within an aviation or Defence context. The perception of flying as a masculine career has been shaped by exposure to 'typical' pilot identities and stereotypes, which may seem unwelcoming to young women. Views about what constitutes a 'typical pilot' were extremely strong – a number of participants expressed a belief that they wouldn't suit flying because they lacked the *typical* pilot traits of arrogance, overt confidence and a lifelong obsession with aviation. Exposure to male pilots reinforced this view, especially in the military context. Providing access to relatable female pilots would be extremely helpful to changing these negative perceptions; this should be focused in aviation-inclined contexts such as Aviation High School, aviation work experience programmes and through the Defence recruiting process.

Perception of role and perception of potential have clearly been shown to be important in career choices. In the Australian Defence Materiel Organisation recently, a discussion around recruiting more women into engineering and military technical roles became quite light-hearted. One suggestion was to sponsor a television soap opera, in which the main female characters were shown, every third scene, welding a submarine. The Hollywood effect of showing certain career choices as 'exciting' and gender-appropriate seemingly has a wonderful effect on career choice and recruitment. Women's representation on US Forensic Science courses currently sits at 78 per cent (the highest of any scientific field), which Houcka (2009) attributes, in part, to popular television programmes showcasing women in this field. The positive image of male pilots created by *Top Gun* saw an increase in recruitment to US Navy pilots for many years; it remains a benchmark image of masculine fighter pilots. The aviation industry could benefit from a television series showcasing female pilots.

Ascertaining female pilots' backgrounds, career and subject orientations and motivation to fly revealed some unexpected insights that may be helpful to organisations seeking to increase their representation of female pilots. Positioning recruiting campaigns to target likely groups of potential pilots may be quite fruitful to prospective employers, especially Defence. It seems that future pilots might be found in rural communities, through university flying clubs, Air Force cadet programmes and in sporting/adventurous activity clubs. Influencer support is necessary for women's progress into aviation, so parents, teachers (especially maths/science teachers) and guidance counsellors should also be a focus of campaigns designed to increase women's interest in flying.

Focus group findings determined that while girls felt that piloting was an exciting and prestigious career, there are some clear negative perceptions preventing them from considering an aviation career. Organisations may need to reposition flying as a career that is accessible, achievable and suitable for women if they seek to radically increase the numbers of girls and women pursuing flying careers. Reinforcing the high level of training, the crew support and comparative safety of flying (as compared to other modes of transport) may also help to mitigate girls' fears about holding too much responsibility in the event of an aircraft emergency.

The perceived level of difficulty was a factor impacting girls' view of both military and civil aviation careers, with numerous focus groups respondents stating they 'wouldn't be smart enough' to become a pilot. This is especially true of Air

Force aviation, which was viewed as simply unattainable by all focus groups. It seems the carefully garnered 'elite' image of Air Force pilots may prove counter-intuitive when it comes to recruiting future pilots of both sexes. This perception might be mitigated by encouraging potential applicants to 'just give pilot testing a go' (without risk) or providing access to online practice tests to remove the fear of the unknown. Marketing along the lines of 'anyone can fly' (whether true or not!) might bring higher numbers of potential candidates to recruiting for assessment.

In terms of making the findings from this study practical, the Air Force has actively applied research findings to developing a range of innovative activities designed to attract female pilots. Removing the lengthy contractual obligation, encouraging women already proceeding down a flying pathway to consider Defence and extending aptitude testing to more broadly are key initiatives underway in the Air Force. Exposure and practical access is also being facilitated through the 'Jet Camp' concept, which is modelled on the success of other school camp programmes targeting non-traditional fields like engineering and information technology. These programmes may show some success, but based on the findings of this study, the Air Force will need to work inordinately hard and creatively if it is to change young women's negative perceptions of military flying and flying generally. This will take resources, effort and time.

This study reveals that without dedicated, targeted efforts to change women and girls' perceptions of flying as a tangible career choice, there is unlikely to be an influx of women into piloting in the near future. Unfortunately, *Top Gun*'s Maverick seems unlikely to have a female 'wing-man' at any stage soon. Perhaps what the aviation industry and Defence Aviation needs is a thrilling movie about women fighter pilots … or maybe a reality television series. Watch this space!

References

Adya, M. and Kaiser, K.M., 2005. Early determinants of women in the IT workforce: A model of girls' career choices. *Information Technology & People*, 18(3), pp. 230–59.

Andrew, A., 2009. Challenging boundaries to 'employability': Women apprentices in a non-traditional occupation. *Social Policy and Society*, 8(3), pp. 347–59.

Anker, R., 1997. Theories of occupational segregation by sex: An overview. *International Labour Review*, 136(3), pp. 315–40.

——. *Gender and Jobs: Sex Segregation of Occupations in the World.* Geneva: International Labour Office.

——. Theories of occupational segregation by sex: An overview. In: M. Fetherolf Loufti (ed.), *Women, Gender and Work: What is Equality and How Do We Get There?* Geneva: International Labour Office, pp. 129–56.

Archer, J. and Lloyd, B., 2002. *Sex and Gender.* Cambridge: Cambridge University Press.

Ashcraft, K.L., 2005. Resistance through consent? Occupational identity, organizational form, and the maintenance of masculinity among commercial airline pilots. *Management Communication Quarterly*, 19(1), pp. 67–90.

Bagilhole, B.M., 2002. *Women in Non-traditional Occupations: Challenging Men.* New York: Palgrave Macmillan.

Barbour, R.S., 2007. *Doing Focus Groups.* London: Sage.

Barucky, J.M. and Stone, B.M., 1999. Difficulties in accessing a representative pilot force: The demographic challenge and views of minority pilot focus groups. *RTO HFM Workshop on Officer Selection,* RTO MP-55, pp. 9–11.

Bennett, S., 2006. *A Sociology of Commercial Flight Crew.* Aldershot: Ashgate.

Betz, N.E. and Hackett, G., 1983. The relationship of mathematics self-efficacy expectations to the selection of science-based college majors. *Journal of Vocational Behaviour*, 23(3), pp. 329–45.

Blakely, R., 2008. Safety fears as staff shortage hits aviation. *The Times*, 10 May. Available at: http://business.timesonline.co.uk/tol/business/industry_sectors/transport/article3904546.ece.

Bourne, D. and Özbilgin, M.F., 2008. Strategies for combating gendered perceptions of careers. *Career Development International*, 13(4), pp. 320–32.

Brown, K., 2008. *Qantas Group Annual Report for the Equal Opportunity for Women Agency*. Sydney: Qantas Airways Ltd.

Carey, S., Nicas, J. and Pasztor, A., 2012. Airlines face acute shortage of pilots. *Wall Street Journal*, 12 November, p. A1.

Charmaz, K., 2006. *Constructing Grounded Theory: A Practical Guide through Qualitative Analysis.* London: Sage.

Chusmir, L.H., 1983. Characteristics and predictive dimensions of women who make non-traditional vocational choices. *Personnel and Guidance Journal*, 62(1), pp. 43–7.

Civil Aviation Safety Authority, 2013. Learning to fly. Available at: http://casa.gov.au/scripts/nc.dll?WCMS:STANDARD::pc=PC_90018#howlong.

Coates, P.B. and Overman, S.J., 1992. Childhood play experiences of women in traditional and nontraditional professions. *Sex Roles*, 26(7–8), pp. 261–71.

Collins, R., 2012. The great debate: Boy vs girl pilots. Available at: http://airfactsjournal.com/2012/01/the-great-debate-boy-v-girl-pilots.

Court, G. and Moralee, J., 1995. *Balancing the Building Team: Gender Issues in the Building Professions*. Lobdon: Institute for Employment Studies.

Craver, M.L., 2007. The Kiplinger Letter: Deepening pilot shortage to raise fares. Available at: http://www.ardis-creative.com/clients/rjdirect/media/documents/Kiplinger97.pdf.

Davey, C.L. and Davidson, M.J., 2000. The right of passage? The experiences of female pilots in commercial aviation. *Feminism & Psychology*, 10(2), pp. 195–225.

Doerschuk, P., Jiangjiang L. and Mann, J., 2007. Pilot summer camps in computing for middle school girls: From organization through assessment. In: *ITiCSE*

'07 Proceedings of the 12th Annual SIGCSE Conference on Innovation and Technology in Computer Science Education. Dundee, 23–27 June, 2007, p. 4.

Eccles, J., 1986. Gender roles and women's achievement. *Educational Research*, 15(6), pp. 15–19.

Farmer, H.S., Wardrop, J.L., Anderson, M.Z. and Risinger, R., 1995. Women's career choices: Focus on science, math, and technology careers. *Journal of Counselling Psychology*, 42(2), pp. 155–70.

Fassinger, R.E., 2002. Hitting the ceiling: Gendered barriers to occupational entry, advancement, and achievement. In: L. Diamant and J.A. Lee (eds), *The Psychology of Sex, Gender, and Jobs: Issues and Solutions*, 2nd edn. New York: Praeger, pp. 21–45.

Fielden, S.L., Davidson, M.J., Gale, A.W. and Davey, C.L., 2000. Women in construction: The untapped resource. *Construction Management and Economics*, 18, pp. 113–21.

Fitzpatrick, J.L. and Silverman, T., 1989. Women's selection of careers in engineering: Do traditional-nontraditional differences still exist? *Journal of Vocational Behavior*, 34(3), pp. 266–78.

Francis, B., 2002. Is the future really female? The impact and implications of gender for 14–16 year olds' career choices. *Journal of Education & Work*, 15(1), pp. 75–88.

Frederick-Recascino, C.M. and Hall, S., 2003. Pilot motivation and performance: Theoretical and empirical relationships. *International Journal of Aviation Psychology*, 13(4), pp. 401–14.

Gadassi, R. and Gati, I., 2009. The effect of gender stereotypes on explicit and implicit career preferences. *Counselling Psychologist*, 37(6), pp. 902–23.

Gale, A.W., 1994. Women in non-traditional occupations: The construction industry. *Women in Management Review*, 9(2), pp. 3–14.

Germain, M.L., Herzog, M.J.R. and Hamilton, P.R., 2012. Women employed in male-dominated industries: Lessons learned from female aircraft pilots, pilots-in-training and mixed-gender flight instructors. *Human Resource Development International*, 15(4), pp. 435–53.

Gilbride, K., Kennedy, D., Waalen, J. and Zywno, M., 2007. A proactive strategy for attracting women into engineering. *Canadian Journal of Counselling and Psychotherapy*, 39(3), pp. 4–8.

Gottfredson, L.S., 1981. Circumscription and compromise: A developmental theory of occupational aspirations. *Journal of Counselling Psychology*, 28(6), pp. 545–79.

——. 2002. Gottfredson's theory of circumscription, compromise and self-creation. In: D. Brown (ed.), *Career Choice and Development*, 4th edn. San Francisco, CA: Jossey-Bass, pp. 85–148.

Goyer, M., 2010. Why so few women pilots? Webinsider; Aviation's Most Informative Blog, 27 September. Available at: http://www.avweb.com/blogs/insider/WhySoFewWomenPilots_203344-1.html.

Hansen, J.S. and Oster, C.V. (Committee on Education and Training for Civilian Aviation Careers) (eds.) 1997. *Taking Flight: Education and Training for Aviation Careers*. Washington, DC: National Academy Press.

Hartung, P.J., Porfeli, E.J. and Vondracek, F.W., 2005. Child vocational development: A review and reconsideration. *Journal of Vocational Behavior*, 66(3), pp. 385–419.

Holland, J.L., 1966. *The Psychology of Vocational Choice: A Theory of Personality Types and Model Environments.* Waltham, MA: Blaisdell Publication Company.

Houcka, M.M., 2009. Is forensic science a gateway for women in science? *Forensic Science Policy & Management: An International Journal*, 1(1), pp. 65–9.

Jurik, N.C., 1985. An officer and a lady: Organizational barriers to women working as correctional officers in men's prisons. *Social Problems*, 32(4), pp. 375–88.

Kongar, E., Kontagiorgis, P., Russo, N.L. and Sobh, T.M., 2009. Women in science, engineering and technology: Changing roles and perceptions within the technical services industries. *Journal of Engineering and Applied Sciences*, 4(1), pp. 46–50.

Kristovics, A., Mitchell, J., Vermeulen, L., Wilson, J. and Martinussen, M., 2006. Gender issues on the flight deck: An exploratory analysis. *International Journal of Applied Aviation Studies*, 6(1), pp. 99–119.

Lemkau, J.P., 1979. Personality and background characteristics of women in male-dominated occupations: A review. *Psychology of Women Quarterly*, 4(2), pp. 221–40.

Lent, R.W., Lopez Jr., A.M., Lopez, F.G. and Sheu, H., 2008. Social cognitive career theory and the prediction of interests and choice goals in the computing disciplines. *Journal of Vocational Behavior*, 73(1), pp. 52–62.

Lepore, M., 2011, Female pilots are few and far between: Here are some reasons why. Grindstone Blog and Discussion Forum, 7 July. Available at: http://www.thegrindstone.com/2011/07/07/mentors/female-pilots-are-few-and-far-between-here-are-some-reasons-why.

Marchbank, M., 2008. A career with altitude. *Flight Safety Australia*, July–August, pp. 9–14.

McGlohn, S.E., King, R.E., Butler, J.W. and Retzlaff, P.D., 1997. Female United States Air Force (USAF) pilots: Themes, challenges, and possible solutions. *Aviation Space Environmental Medicine*, 68, pp. 132–6.

McKrindle Research, 2006. *New Generations at Work: Attracting, Recruiting, Retraining and Retaining Generation Y*. Baulkham Hills: McKrindle Research.

Melkas, H. and Anker, R., 1997. Occupational segregation by sex in Nordic countries: An empirical investigation. *International Labour Review*, 136(3), pp. 341–63.

Michie, S. and Nelson, D.L., 2006. Barriers women face in information technology careers: Self-efficacy, passion and gender biases. *Women in Management Review*, 21(1), pp. 10–27.

Miller, L. and Budd, J., 1999. The development of occupational sex-role stereotypes, occupational preferences and academic preferences in children at ages 8, 12 and 16. *Educational Psychology*, 19(1), pp. 17–35.

Mills, A.J., 1998. Cockpits, hangars, boys and galleys: Corporate masculinities and the development of British Airways. *Gender, Work and Organization*, 5(3), pp. 172–88.

Mitchell, J., Kristovics, A., Vermeulen, L., Wilson, J. and Martinussen, M., 2005. How pink is the sky? A cross-national study of the gendered occupation of pilot. *Employment Relations Record*, 5(2), pp. 43–7.

Morgan, C., Isacc, J.D. and Sansone, C., 2001. The role of interest in understanding the career choices of female and male college students. *Sex Roles: A Journal of Research*, 4(5–6), pp. 295–320.

Neal-Smith, S. and Cockburn, T., 2009. Cultural sexism in the UK airline industry. *Gender in Management*, 24(1), pp. 32–45.

Novello, J.R. and Youssef, Z.I., 1974. Psycho-social studies in general aviation: II. Personality profile of female pilots. *Aviation, Space, and Environmental Medicine*, 45, pp. 630–3.

O'Connor, E., 2012. Airlines face the worst pilot shortages in decades. *Time Magazine* newsfeed, 3 March. Available at: http://newsfeed.time.com/2012/11/14/airlines-face-worst-pilot-shortage-since-the-1960s.

O'Donnell, J.A. and Anderson, D.G., 1978. Factors influencing choice of major and career of capable women. *Vocational Guidance Quarterly*, 26, pp. 214–21.

Oakes, J., 1990. *Lost Talent: The Under-participation of Women, Minorities, and Disabled Persons in Science.* Santa Monica, CA: RAND Corporation.

Office for Women and Minerals Council of Australia, 2007. *Unearthing New Resources: Attracting and Retaining Women in the Australian Minerals Industry*. Canberra: Office for Women and Minerals Council of Australia.

Outlay, C., Ambrose, P. and Chenowith, J., 2012. Overcoming gender stereotype entry barriers to computing degree programs: The cybergirlz program experience. *Journal of Computing Sciences in Colleges*, 28(1), pp. 33–8.

Padavic, I. and Reskin, B., 2002. *Women and Men at Work*, 2nd edn. Thousand Oaks, CA: Sage.

Pawlowski, A., 2011. Why aren't more women airline pilots? CNN. Available at: http://edition.cnn.com/2011/TRAVEL/03/18/female.airline.pilots/index.html.

Podmore, S., 2011, Flight fear? Air travel is less dangerous than car and road travel, statistics show. *News.com*. Available at: http://www.news.com.au/travel/travel-advisor/overcome-your-fear-of-flying/story-fn6yjmoc-1226042220391.

Spertus, E., 1991. *Why are There So Few Female Computer Scientists?* Cambridge, MA: Massachusetts Institute of Technology.

Standley, R. and Soule, B., 1974. Women in male-dominated professions: Contrasts in their personal and vocational histories. *Journal of Vocational Behavior*, 4, pp. 245–58.

Stockard, J. and McGee, J., 1990. Children's occupational preferences: The influence of sex and perceptions of occupational characteristics. *Journal of Vocational Behavior*, 36(3), pp. 287–303.

Tang, M., Pan, W. and Newmeyer, M.D., 2008. Factors influencing high school students' career aspirations. *Professional School Counselling*, 11(5), pp. 285–95.

Turney, M.A., 2004. Tapping diverse talent in aviation: A must of the new century. In: M.A. Turney (ed.), *Tapping Diverse Talent in Aviation*. Aldershot: Ashgate, pp. 3–10.

Turney, M.A., Bishop., J.C., Karp, M.R., Niemczyk, M.S., Sitler, R.L. and Green, M.F., 2002. National survey results: Retention of women in collegiate aviation. *Journal of Air Transportation*, 7(1), pp. 69–92.

Vermeulen, L.P. and Mitchell, J.I., 2007. Development and validation of a measure to assess perceptions regarding gender-related pilot behaviour. *International Journal of Aviation Psychology*, 17(2), pp. 197–218.

Wallace, G., 2004. Where are the women? *COPA Flight*, June.

Whittock, M., 2002. Women's experiences of non-traditional employment: Is gender equality in this area a possibility? *Construction Management and Economics*, 20(5), pp. 449–56.

Yilmaz, M., 2010. Hands-on summer camp to attract K-12 students to engineering fields. *IEEE Transactions on Education*, 53(1), pp. 144–51.

Chapter 3

Fast Women: Or Why Women Who Fly High-Performance Aircraft are Fast But Not Loose[1]

Tracy Smart

Introduction

Women entering a male-dominated sphere for the first time will always encounter difficulties. Some of these problems relate to the physical or physiological attributes of the women themselves. Others relate to the attitudes of the men whose world they wish to enter. The Royal Australian Air Force currently has its first woman attempting to break into one of the last bastions of male domination left in today's military – the fast jet world.

The concept of flying women is not new. A brief look back at the history books tells us that women played a large role in the early history of aviation. Early pioneers included the Wright brothers' sister Katharine, Harriet Quimby in her purple satin flying suit, who was the first woman to fly the channel, and household names such as Amelia Earhart and Amy Johnson. Australia even had its own pioneer aviatrix, Nancy Bird, who learned to fly in 1933 at the age of 17 and flew one of this country's earliest airborne ambulance services.

Women have also played a major part in the military in general; however, the role of female aviators in Western militaries has been an area of controversy, particularly when enough men were available to do the job. Despite this, thousands of female pilots were called upon in the Second World War to fill vacant cockpits and free men up for fighting duties.

In the US, the Women Airforce Service Pilots (WASPs) based at Avenger Field, Sweetwater, Texas, kept the home planes flying from 1943. Eventually over 2,000 women flew over 70 types of aircraft in non-combat roles, mostly performing ferrying, training and transport duties. Seventy of these women were killed or injured whilst flying, but it was not until 1977 that the WASPs were granted

1 Originally published as: Smart, T.L., 1998. Fast women: Or why women who fly high performance aircraft are fast but not loose. *Institute of Aviation Medicine*, 7(1), pp. 8–16. Reprinted here with permission thanks to the Australian Military Medicine Association.

Veterans status by Congress (International Women's Air and Space Museum, 1997).

The British kept female aviators out of uniform, but had them fulfilling similar functions to the WASPs as part of the civilian Air Transport Auxiliary. It wasn't until 1953 that the first RAF pilot, Jean Bird, a reservist, was given her first set of wings. By this time she had been flying for 20 years, had over 300 hours on 90 aircraft types and had a Senior Commercial Pilot's licence. In fact, she had more experience than most of the instructors who trained her for her wings. Unfortunately, the Royal Air Force Volunteer Reserve, the only arm of the military in which these women could serve, was disbanded in 1957 due to an early Defence reform plan (Eliot, 1990). The Russians were far more progressive in the Second World War, allowing women to fly in a combat role and creating and entire female bomber and fighter regiments.

After the war, the surplus of fully qualified male pilots meant that women, who were still unable to take on a combat role, were relegated back to their 'proper' positions as wives and mothers. The one exception to this was in the USSR, which continued to allow women to fly and in 1962 put the first woman in space: Valentina Tereshkova.

The role of females in society gradually changed over the following years and in the 1970s female aviators once again began training in Western Defence forces. In the late 1970s and early 1980s, the Canadians conducted the 'Servicewomen in Non-traditional Roles' (SWINTER) study, culminating in the first female CF-18 pilots undergoing training in 1987. The US soon followed and now most Western militaries allow women to fly all aircraft types.

Australia lagged a little behind in this area. Some women apparently managed to slip the shackles and fly in the UK during the war with the Air Transport Auxiliary (ATA), but our first female military pilots did not graduate until 1988. Fast jets were opened to women in 1995; however, the first candidate unfortunately failed the Introductory Fighter Course (IFC). In 1997 a former transport pilot passed the IFC and began F-111 conversion. As of August 1997, the Royal Australian Air Force (RAAF) had eight female pilots flying most aircraft types, including two Qualified Flying Instructors and a test pilot. Five pilots were completing training at No. 2 Flying Training School. The RAAF also had three female navigators and several non-commissioned aircrew, including three air-borne electronics analysts, a load master and a flight engineer. As a result of these small numbers, the concept of female aircrew is still a relatively novel one within the Australian military environment.

This chapter examines some of the main issues relating to these fast women, concentrating on those areas where we as military health professionals may be called upon to provide support. The particular areas of concern are the four traditional arguments as to why women shouldn't be flying: their physiological differences, their perceived physical weakness, specific women's health problems and squadron cultural issues.

Physiological Issues

> Women can't fly fast jets – their tits will sag and their wombs will fall out. (Crusty Old Jet Jockey, RAAF Pearce, 1991)

Hypoxia

As in many areas of female physiology, studies into differences in response to hypoxia between the sexes have been conflicting, but have overall shown little significant difference. Some differences do exist in terms of physiology. Women have smaller values across a wide range of lung parameters and generally have smaller lung capacities than men. Women also have several haematological differences, including reduced haemoglobin, and therefore oxygen-carrying capacity compared with their male counterparts. However, women exist at sea level under normal circumstances with these differences and presumably have similar coping mechanisms to men when exposed to hypoxia.

Most studies in this area have been performed in mountaineers and therefore focused on chronic hypoxia. These studies have demonstrated no real differences between the sexes in terms of overall acclimatisation, although some minor differences in response have been reported (Drinkwater et al., 1982). In fact, women appear to tolerate chronic hypoxia better and have also been shown to be less susceptible than men to the symptoms of Acute Mountain Sickness (Harris, Shields and Hannon, 1966). The limited studies comparing the response of men and women to acute hypoxia have shown little difference in performance between the sexes at altitude relative to their differences at sea level (Wagner et al., 1979).

Decompression Illness

Various studies have shown that women are susceptible to Decompression Illness (DCI) compared with men, with reported increased incidences of between three and four times in both altitude-induced and diving DCI (Bangasser, 1987; Bassett, 1980). Dixon et al. conducted separate studies on men and women, which involved exposure to a chamber altitude of 16,500 ft for six hours, breathing a mixture of 50 per cent N_2 and 50 per cent O_2 (Dixon, Adams and Harvey, 1986; Dixon, Krutz and Fischer, 1988). These studies revealed that although more bubbles were detected in men compared with women (73 per cent versus 43 per cent of subjects), women experienced more symptoms (17 per cent versus 3 per cent). A relationship between DCI and the stage of the menstrual cycle has also been reported, with an apparent increased incidence early in the cycle (Rudge, 1990). Yet another study suggested that women were more likely to present with complicated DCI (Davis et al., 1997).

Several reasons for this difference between the sexes have been postulated. The most popular theory is that, as women on average have increased body fat compared to men, they therefore have an increased nitrogen load. In addition, hormonal changes occurring as a result of the normal menstrual cycle or due to the oral contraceptive pill may result in reduced venous tone and this may exacerbate the effects of nitrogen bubbles.

Despite the differences, DCI is still a relatively rare event in aviation, and therefore even with this increased risk, the overall risk of female aircrew developing DCI when flying is still acceptably low. However, the risks associated with chamber training are of some concern.

Effects of G

Centrifuge studies by Gillingham et al. exposed subjects to rapid onset runs to +7 G_z and gradual onset runs up to +8 G_z (Gillingham et al., 1986). No significant differences in relaxed or straining G tolerances were noted between the sexes in this series; however, there was some evidence that there was a significant difference between the sexes when matched for height. In addition, a later study examining retrospective data did report a significant difference at higher levels of G (Fischer, Wiegman and Bauer, 1992). Two reasons were postulated for this difference. The first is that women have reduced body strength compared to men and therefore have difficulties in sustaining an anti-G straining manoeuvre, particularly at high G. Another possible explanation is inadequate G suit fit, particularly as these garments are designed for men.

In a recent study utilising custom fit G-suits, eight women were tested and their results were compared with data on ten male subjects (Heaps, Fischer and Hill, 1997). No significant differences were demonstrated *in time to fatigue* between the sexes. This study also examined performance across the menstrual cycle in women on the contraceptive pill. It had been postulated that the theoretically increased vasodilatation seen as a result of an oestradiol surge during the mid-follicular phase may have resulted in a slightly reduced tolerance; however, no significant difference was noted.

Specific female health issues in relation to high G have not been studied, despite the uninformed claims of some. Many studies have shown the potentially damaging effects of oscillatory motion on breast tissue; however, breast discomfort has not been reported in centrifuge studies and there is no evidence that unidirectional motion is likely to cause long-term damage. The Gillingham study deliberately screened out women with pre-existing gynaecological conditions, but two of the 24 women in the study reported urinary incontinence while undertaking an anti-G manoeuvre (Gillingham et al., 1986). This symptom has not been reported in men. The effect of G on the uterus in older women and on *in situ* intrauterine devices has also not been adequately studied to date, nor have effects on menstruation.

Tolerance to Thermal Extremes

Men and women tend to respond differently to hot environments. Some studies have demonstrated that men have a greater work capacity in heat; however, women sweat less than men and therefore conserve their water stores more effectively. A negative side-effect of this latter difference is that women have been shown to react more severely on exposure to hot environments; however, there seems to be little difference between the sexes once acclimatisation has occurred (Avellini, Kamon and Krajweski, 1980; Wyndham, Morrison and Williams, 1965). It has also been suggested that many of the reported differences may not be significant if subjects are controlled for physical fitness (Avellini et al., 1980).

Cold environments are also encountered in aviation, especially in the survival situation. Women tend to tolerate cold better that men, possibly due to their greater average fat stores. On average women contain 25 per cent fat, while men only contain 15 per cent, and these differences remain even with training (Sperryn, 1983); thus, women have greater buoyancy, insulation and energy stores compared with men and are therefore better prepared physiologically in a survival situation, particularly at sea. This theory was supported by Mannino and Kaufman, who reported a significant decrease in core temperature drop in men compared to women when exposed to a reduction in torso temperature. However, if controlled for percentage fat (and especially fat distribution), there is probably little difference between the sexes (Mannino and Kaufman, 1986).

Motion Sickness and Disorientation

Studies utilising questionnaires have reported that women are significantly more susceptible than men to the symptoms of motion sickness (Lentz and Collins, 1977). A male to female ratio of 3.5 has been calculated (Lawther and Griffin, 1988) and this gender difference appears to be further exacerbated during menstruation (Benson, 1988). Differences have also been reported in rates of simulator sickness (Kennedy et al., 1995).

The reason for this difference is not entirely clear, although hormonal factors have been proposed (Mannino and and Kaufman, 1986). Other factors may also be of significance, including field dependence – that is, when in an unstable environment (for example, when stationary in a moving environment), women are more likely to experience conflicting perceptual cues than men (Heaps, Fischer and Hill, 1997), field dependency correlates with both nausea and disorientation. This area clearly requires more study, but is supported by the fact that men are more stable than women on tests for ataxia such as the Sharpened Romberg Test (Wyndham et al., 1965). Another possible explanation is that women are more likely than men to report symptoms of motion sickness, as has been reported to be the case with other medical conditions (Fischer, Wiegman and Bauer, 1992).

This difference in susceptibility to motion sickness may be of significance in selecting potential aircrew; however, apart from questioning for a history of significant motion sickness, screening for sensitivity is not routinely performed on aircrew applicants. If students do fail to adapt to the motion environment, they are able to undergo motion sickness desensitisation, usually with good effect. Each individual is managed on a case-by-case basis and therefore a demonstrated increased incidence in women as a group is not viewed as a reason to bar all potential female aviators.

Physical Issues

> Men do not *believe* us capable. (Amelia Earhart, 1930s)

Physical Strength

Women are, in terms of physical strength, the weaker sex. In fact, depending on the muscle group, they have only between 35 and 85 per cent of the strength of men (Baisden, Pokorski and Meyer, 1995). This can be improved somewhat by weight training; however, the effects of weight training in female student pilots has not always produced benefits. When women first began flying training in the US Navy, they were scheduled extra physical training sessions as part of their curriculum. This was in fact found to be detrimental to their training as it distracted them from their studies and actually produced no real benefits in terms of strength (Hutton, 1990).

Both manoeuvring an aircraft and performing an anti-G straining manoeuvre in a high-G environment require a high degree of muscle strength and endurance. Therefore, it would appear that a greater percentage of women compared to men will experience difficulties in this area. However, it is also true that a percentage of men will also have difficulties, particularly when flying at the aircraft limits. Therefore, in this area, as in many others, fitness to fly high-performance aircraft should be judged on a case-by-case basis, with the acceptance that not all people are capable of flying all types of aircraft and all types of missions.

As well as assessing the ability to fly the aircraft, several occupational health and safety considerations may be of concern due to these strength differences. These include the potential for neck injuries under high-G loads and the ability to initiate the ejection sequence in an emergency.

Women have decreased neck strength compared to men (60 per cent), but have a 12 per cent greater range of movement and 11 per cent faster neck muscle reaction time (Whitley et al., 1995). As all three probably play a role in determining resistance to injury under G, the overall risk is believed to be similar for both sexes.

Ejection initiation requires a reasonable degree of physical strength; however, the general consensus of opinion is that most people will have the strength to initiate the ejection sequence in an emergency. Specific studies examining these issues do not appear to have been undertaken.

Anthropometry

As well as being physically weaker, women are also smaller on average than men across all parameters considered important in the cockpit. These include sitting height, buttocks-heel, buttocks-knee and functional reach. There is also an interaction between size and strength, as problems of reduced strength will be compounded when maximum force is required at maximum reach. In fact, it is estimated that as many of 50 per cent of women may be excluded from flying current US military aircraft on the basis of anthropometry alone (Lyons, 1992).

Women are not only smaller than men, but also have different dimensions in different places. For example, women have greater hip breadth by 5 cm on average, whilst men are wider across the shoulders by at least 2.5 cm (Robinette, 1995). These size differences are not only important when considering fit in the cockpit and ability to control the aircraft, but also the fit of safety equipment. This includes aircrew helmets, oxygen masks, flying suits and Nuclear, Biological, Chemical defence (NBC) ensembles, and necessitates either changes or modifications to this equipment to accommodate these size differences.

Ejection

Concerns have been raised regarding safety in ejection. Women have a smaller cross-sectional area of vertebrae compared to men. In addition, seat charges are designed for the male weight range and therefore women's vertebrae are exposed to greater force per unit area than those of men. This suggests an increased risk of spinal column injury in women. Evidence to support these theories is, however, somewhat contradictory. One study using mannequins demonstrated that the risk of vertebrae fractures was significantly greater with smaller mass dummies (Chiou and Kellogg, 1993); however, a statistical analysis of real-life ejection data revealed that the risks were increased in taller and heavier ejectees (Edwards, 1996).

With modern ejection seats being designed to reduce the overall force and particularly the onset of the force to which the aviator is exposed, the overall risk for women is probably not unacceptable. Despite this, several nations do not train women on an ejection set rig during initial aviation medicine training, although the RAAF has continued to do so.

Other differences in shape between women and men may result in increased risk of other injuries, such as fracture of the femur; however, this has not been thoroughly investigated at this stage.

Also to be examined further are the implications for the older woman, particularly the post-menopausal effects on bones and the possibility of osteoporosis. Early indications are that hormone replacement therapy will be mandatory for post-menopausal women.

Solutions

Many of these physical problems can be overcome. Future aircraft are being designed to accommodate a larger percentage of the female population. An example of this is the design of the new Joint Primary Aircraft Training System (JPATS) aircraft and the F22 fighter for the US military. By order of the US Congress, the JPATS was to accommodate 95 per cent of female pilots; however, the reality will see perhaps only 80 per cent compatibility (Slabodkin, 1996). In addition, the fact that most modern aircraft these days utilise fly by wire control inputs means that the physical demands required to control aircraft are much reduced and are therefore within the capabilities of a larger proportion of the population. However, this may be countered by the fact that the new generation fighter aircraft will be capable of sustaining much higher levels of G and thus will place greater demands on the aircrew in terms of sustaining an anti-G straining manoeuvre.

Safety equipment can also be modified, and in some cases in the past this has been attempted illegally. Legal modifications in the RAAF include applying darts in the waist, thighs and calves of G-suits, and the removal of links from oxygen mask suspension chains, thereby tightening the fit of the mask. Illegal modifications include the use of seat padding in the ejection seat and cutting holes in helmet liners to accommodate hairbuns.

As mentioned above, ejection seats have already been designed to reduce the maximum force and rate of onset of force to which the aircrew are exposed. Some seats have also been designed to tailor the force to the individual by dialling in the recipient's weight prior to take-off.

In summary, most of the problems resulting from the physical differences between men and women can be solved, but generally at a considerable cost. Much effort and expense is being applied throughout the world at the present time in order to accommodate women in all types of aircraft. As far as the RAAF is concerned, the extent to which these modifications will be adopted will probably depend on both the need to adhere to the principles of equality and the overall cost of the measures involved.

Medical Issues

> Women are temperamentally unfit to fly and prone to panic in any calamity.
> (Claude Graham-White, 1911)

General Health

Some medical conditions are more common in women. These conditions include migraine, varicose veins and urinary tract infections. There is also evidence to suggest that women report more symptoms and attend medical facilities more frequently than men (Rice et al., 1992). However, women have a lower incidence of serious and potentially permanently incapacitating disorders, such as ischaemic heart disease.

Women's Health

Specific gynaecological problems may also compromise fitness to fly. These include menstrual abnormalities, where the risk of sudden incapacitation may be of concern. Studies of female pilots before and after flight have demonstrated that flight has some influence upon the secretion of female hormones (Dongyun and Yumin, 1990); however, the significance of this is unknown. It has also been reported that menstrual cycles in female flight attendants may become disrupted during transmeridian flight and that a significant percentage of these individuals suffer from heavier menstrual loss whilst flying, although most report normalisation of their cycles with time (Cameron, 1969). Effects on pilots of high-performance aircraft have not been examined.

Pre-menstrual syndrome is another problem specific to women that may produce a variety of effects, some of which may be of significance in the aviation environment. Symptoms include pain and discomfort, oedema, abdominal bloating, nasal and sinus congestion, increased incidence of migraines and psychological effects such as general irritability. The latter may not necessarily be a disadvantage, as few pilots would want to go into combat against an ace fighter pilot with PMT! However, there is some evidence that increased rates of accident-proneness occur during this stage of the menstrual cycle.

The most important aspect when considering these specific women's health problems is that they should be managed in a similar way to any other medical problems which may impact upon flying safety and operational effectiveness. The conditions should be screened for at recruiting, and trained aircrew suffering from severe symptoms or incapacitating conditions should be grounded, investigated and treated.

The Oral Contraceptive Pill

It is of course possible to successfully treat many of these menstrual disorders by use of the oral contraceptive pill. The pill is cleared for flight despite its potential side-effects, such as hypertension and deep vein thrombosis. In the ADF and many other air forces, these risks are considered acceptable; however, a ground trial of one month is required to eliminate the possibility of other systemic effects.

Pregnancy

Pregnancy is of course not an illness but a natural phenomenon. However, it does represent a change to the body's physiology and, as far as female aircrew are concerned, it should be considered as a medical condition with respect to fitness to fly. Areas of concern include flying safety (risks of sudden incapacitation, safety equipment and ergonomic issues), risks to operational effectiveness (psychological and physical distraction) and occupational health and safety issues (stresses on the foetus). The risks associated with these various considerations vary depending on the stage of the pregnancy and particularly trimester by trimester.

First trimester The risks of sudden incapacitation are especially high during the first trimester due to complications such as spontaneous abortion, ectopic pregnancy and morning sickness. Also of concern are the potential effects on the embryo in its most delicate stage of development. Some of these aviation stressors are discussed below:

- *Hypoxia*: Severe hypoxia in certain periods of development has been shown to produce foetal malformations in animals (Ingalls, 1973). Most aircrew will only be exposed to mild hypoxia under normal flying circumstances and there appears to be no evidence to suggest concern at these levels of hypoxia (Cameron, 1973).
- *Vibration*: Once again, animal studies have demonstrated the sensitivity of the embryo to this type of stress, with an increase mortality rate in chick embryos and intrauterine growth retardation in mouse embryos (Bantle, 1971; Shannon, Moran and Mason, 1994).

These effects are more evident at certain frequencies.

- *Decompression illness*: Bubbles formed in decompression illness have the potential to cause more effects in the foetus because of a patent foramen ovale. In addition, there is a hypothetical increased risk in mothers due to increased fat stores and blood flow. Animal studies have also demonstrated that untreated DCI in the mother is likely to produce teratogenic effects in the foetus, but that the incidence of these problems is reduced with hyperbaric treatment (Gilman et al., 1983; Jennings, 1992). Studies in female divers have reported low birth-weight babies and an increased incidence of birth defects (Bolton, 1992; Magaletta, 1986). The significance of this for aviators is unknown; however, due to this theoretical increased risk, pregnant women are not permitted to undertake hypobaric chamber training.
- *'G' effects*: The effects of accelerative forces on the foetus have not been established despite theoretical concerns expressed of a bungy-jumping foetus! Physiologically one would predict effects on placental blood flow and placental integrity may be of concern here.
- *Other aviation toxins*: The aviation environment contains many potential toxins, some of which have the potential to cause effects on the foetus. The effects of exposure to cosmic radiation have been examined at some length

> in the literature. Concerns include the risk of foetal malformations and the possible increased risk of neoplasms in childhood (Lyons, 1992).

Most studies looking at overall risks to the foetus in this trimester have been carried out on female flight attendants. There does not appear to be a significant risk to pregnancies in this group of individuals when all factors are controlled for (Daniell, Vaughan and Millies, 1990); however, this type of flying environment is vastly different from that of high-performance aircraft.

Of greatest concern for medical practitioners are the medico-legal aspects if complications occur during or after a flight. For all of these reasons, most military forces ground pregnant aviators during their first trimester.

Second trimester Maternal complications likely to cause incapacitation are less common in this trimester. However, other effects of the pregnancy may become significant, including anaemia and fatigue. Ergonomic issues begin to become an issue during this period, including the fit of the G-suit and other safety equipment. Nevertheless, it is a relatively safe time for the foetus. Overall the risks are minimal and as such flying, at least in a multi-crew role, could be permitted on a case-by-case basis. Flying in high-performance aircraft would still be of some concern.

Third trimester Risks to both mother and foetus increase again in this trimester. Specific risks include pre-eclampsia, premature labour and abruptio placentae, and ergonomic problems are exacerbated. In addition, psychological distraction is known to be a problem as the pregnancy progresses. It is therefore common practice to ground aircrew from the start of their third trimester until after the birth.

In summary, ADF policy is that all female aircrew, including those flying fast jets, will be grounded as soon as the pregnancy is diagnosed until after the birth of the child. This in itself may be a problem for the military as considerable time and money has been invested to train such aircrew, only to have them become unfit to fly for a prolonged period. However, all aircrew are required to perform ground jobs at some stage of their career and therefore female aircrew should be able to manage their family along with career demands.

Cultural Issues

> You would not want to fly a combat mission with a woman. (Ex-USAF Chief of Staff, 1992)

Squadron Bonding

The issue of squadron bonding appears to be the major concern touted by the leaders of the RAAF fast jet squadrons of today. Squadron morale, and therefore theoretically its fighting ability, is dependent upon the extremely strong bonding that occurs between squadron members. This is also the case for ground troops. Many men consider that the presence of women within this environment will upset this delicate balance by introducing the issue of sex, and that the essential bonding fabric will be rent asunder. However, evidence from overseas does not appear to support this idea. A survey conducted amongst USAF pilots revealed that 97 per cent of men and 98 per cent of women felt comfortable flying in combat with both genders. In addition, 77 per cent of men and 74 per cent of women believed that squadron mission effectiveness had not been changed by mixed-gender flights (McGlohn et al., 1997).

Protective Instincts

Another concern raised by male fast jet aircrew is that of the protective instincts of men in both combat and prisoner-of-war situations. This appears to be a problem even if women elect to take the risk to place themselves in such dangerous situations. In the study mentioned above, 73 per cent of men reported that they would be more protective of one gender in combat (compared with 6 per cent of women) (McGlohn et al., 1997).

Public Perceptions

One of the major concerns expressed by governments when deliberating on the women in combat issue was fear of the public's reaction to women returning home from war in body bags. It would appear from recent experience such as during the Gulf War that this is no longer an issue.

Trailblazers

At present, only small numbers of female aircrew are being trained by the RAAF. This means that many of these women are still 'blazing the trail' for other women and this in turn often attracts media attention. This not only has the potential to cause jealousy amongst colleagues, but also the belief that a double standard or quota may apply to these women. Many male instructors also believe that there is increased pressure to pass these women and that the women have to be treated differently from their male counterparts.

Solutions

There are no easy solutions to many of these issues, especially as most relate to the perceptions of male aircrew. However, many of these problems seem to have been resolved in overseas militaries by such elements as good leadership, time and the emergence of increasing numbers of female aircrew. This has also become evident in RAAF experience as some flying instructors have noticed that concerns currently evident during introductory fighter training have ceased to be issues during initial flying training.

Perhaps these aspects are best summarised in a quote by Major Deanna Brasseur, one of the first female F-18 pilots in the Canadian Forces. Major Brasseur reports experiencing more difficulties as one of her country's first female air weapons controllers than as a pioneer 'fast woman':

> As the first woman on my crew I experienced the stares, the snide comments, the questioning of my abilities and purpose for wanting to be a member of such a previously male environment ... Once I had established my credibility ... and demonstrated that their crude language and bad jokes did not bother me, I was accepted. (Brasseur, 1990, p. 491)

Current Issues in the RAAF

Much research is ongoing in the area of female aircrew in general and in particular those flying high-performance aircraft. The RAAF Institute of Aviation Medicine has so far been consulted on the following subjects.

F111 Relief Bags or 'Piddle Packs'

In the F111, sorties lasting several hours are possible and a male relief bag with a condom-like attachment is in common use. Unfortunately, this system is not suitable for female use and therefore a variety of other options have been suggested. These range from a simple nappy-like pad to a small collecting device that somehow must be manoeuvred into position in the close and less than private confines of the F111 cockpit.

Saline Breast Implants

A recent enquiry from an ADF Recruiting Centre requested information as to a young woman's fitness to train as aircrew after having undergone a single saline breast implant. This condition is not covered in the ADFP 701 (Recruiting Standards) and little information is available on this subject in the aviation environment. The USAF does have a policy on this condition for currently serving aircrew, allowing them to return to flying nine months after surgery. This particular potential applicant elected not to apply.

Long Hair

This issue has become a case of Equal Employment Opportunity (EEO) meets flying safety. The problems of long hair are those of adequate helmet fit, risk of entanglement in the ejection seat and fire risk. A draft Defence Instruction on aircrew dress and grooming implied that all aircrew should have short hair to prevent these problems. This caused some concern amongst our female aircrew and prompted one enterprising female pilot to develop an alternative, a hair bag. This consists of a Nomex cover that can be tucked down into the back of the flying suit, thus solving the risks of fire and entanglement. It does not necessarily solve the fitment problems as long hair worn in any style at the back of the head may interfere with nape strap grip. It also poses other problems, particularly the concern that neck movements may be restricted during manoeuvering under high G. A project to assess the virtue of such a bag has been put on hold at present as a further draft instruction avoids comment on hair length, preferring to emphasise the necessity of an adequate fit.

Conclusions

There is no doubt that women are different in many ways from men. Many of the physiological differences probably require more research to determine their significance, particularly the problems facing older women. The problems relating to physical differences between the sexes can be solved by re-engineering both aircraft and safety equipment to accommodate a larger percentage of the population. Most of the specific women's health issues really should be considered on a case-by-case basis and treated like any other fitness to fly issue.

This was confirmed by the findings of the United States Commission on the Assignment of Women in the Armed Forces (1992), which stated that there were no physical or physiological reasons why women could not fly combat aircraft (Draude, 1995). It has also been proved by the experience of many other nations.

The main reason why the issues surrounding female fast jet aircrew are still of concern in Australia is the novelty aspect – we are dealing with small numbers and the very male fast jet world doesn't know quite what to do with these strange creatures. It is interesting to note that the first two women streamed to fast jets were heading for F111s and not FA-18s. Entry of women into the fighter world will be the final stumbling block, but provided she is good enough and strong enough, our first female FA-18 pilot is probably not far away.

A final quote from an article entitled 'Females, Girls, and Fighting Marines' from the US *Marine Corps Gazette* summarises the major problems confronting our prospective female fighter pilots: 'It is not the psychological fortitude of women marines that concerns me but the men they might be serving with' (Freeman, 1991, pp. 66–7).

References

Avellini, B.A., Kamon, E. and Krajewski, J.T., 1980. Physiologic responses of physically fit men and women to humid heat. *Journal of Applied Physiology*, 49, pp. 254–61.

Avellini, B.A., Shapiro, K.B., Pandolf, K.B., Pimental, N.A. and Goldman, R.F., 1980. Physiologic responses of physically fit men and women to dry heat exposure. *Aviation Space Environmental Medicine*, 51, pp. 1081–5.

Baisden, A.G., Pokorski, T.L and Meyer, S.G., 1995. Development of gender-neutral occupational standards II. Job demands and physiological issues. *SAFE Journal*, 25, pp. 22–7.

Bangasser, S.A., 1987. Decompression sickness in women. In: W. Fife (ed), *Women in Diving: Proceedings of the 35th Undersea and Hyperbaric Medical Society Workshop*, 21–22 May. Kensington, MD: The Undersea and Hyperbaric Medical Society.

Bantle, J.A., 1971. Effects of mechanical vibrations on the growth and development of mouse embryos. *Aerospace Medicine*, 42, pp. 1087–91.

Bassett, B.E., 1980. Twelve-year survey of the susceptibility of women to altitude decompression sickness: Preprints of the Aerospace Medical Association Annual Scientific Meeting, Alexandria, VA. *Aerospace Medical Association*, pp. 12–13.

Benson, A.J., 1988. Motion sickness. In: J. Ernsting and P.F. King, *Aviation Medicine*. London: Butterworths.

Brasseur, D.M., 1990. A Canadian female CF-18 pilot's experience. *AGARD Conference Proceedings No. 491 1990. Recruiting, Selection, Training and Military Operations of Female Aircrew*. 2-1–2-5.

Cameron, R.G., 1969. Effect of flying on the menstrual function of air hostesses. *Aerospace Medicine*, 40, pp. 1020–23.

——. 1973. Should air hostesses continue flight duty during the first trimester of pregnancy? *Aerospace Medicine*, 44(5), pp. 552–6.

Chiou, W.Y., Ho, B.L. and Kellogg, D.L., 1993. Hazard potential of ejection with canopy fragmentation. *Aviation Space Environmental Medicine*, 64, pp. 9–13.

Daniell, W.E., Vaughan, T.L. and Millies, B.A. 1990. Pregnancy outcomes among female flight attendants. *Aviation Space Environmental Medicine*, 61(9), pp. 840–4.

Davis, J.C., Sheffield, P.J., Schuknecht, L., Heimbach, R.D., Dunn, J.M., Douglas, G. and Anderson, G.K., 1977. Altitude decompression sickness: Hyperbaric therapy results in 145 cases. *Aviation Space Environmental Medicine*, 48, pp. 722–30.

Dixon, G.A., Adams, J.D. and Harvey, W.T. 1986. Decompression sickness and intravenous bubble formation using a 7.8 psia simulated pressure suit environment. *Aviation Space Environmental Medicine*, 57, pp. 223–7.

Dixon, G.A., Krutz, R.W. and Fischer, J.R., 1988. Decompression sickness and bubble formation in females exposed to a simulated 7.8 psia suit environment. *Aviation Space Environmental Medicine*, 59, pp. 1146–9.

Dongyun, S. and Yumin, W., 1990. Flight influence on the plasma level of sex hormones of women pilots. *Military Medicine*, 155, pp. 262–4.

Draude, T.V., 1995. Women in combat. *Aviation Space Environmental Medicine*, 66, pp. 1207–11.

Drinkwater, B.L., Kramar, P.O., Bedi, J.F. and Folinsbee, L.J., 1982. Women at altitude: Cardiovascular responses to hypoxia. *Aviation Space Environmental Medicine*, 53, pp. 472–7.

Edwards, M., 1996. Anthropometric measurements and ejection injuries. *Aviation Space Environmental Medicine*, 67, pp. 1144–47.

Eliot, P., 1990. The RAF's first women pilots. *Air Clues*, pp. 170–4.

Fischer, M.D., Wiegman, J.F. and Bauer, D.H., 1992. Female tolerance to sustained acceleration: A retrospective study. *SAFE Journal*, 22(2), pp. 31–5.

Freeman, A.Z., 1991. Females, girls and fighting marines. *Marine Corps Gazette*, October, pp. 66–7.

Gillingham, K.K., Schade, C.M., Jackson, W.G. and Gilstrap, L.C., 1986. Women's G-tolerance. *Aviation Space Environmental Medicine*, 57, pp. 745–53.

Gilman, S.C., Bradley, M.E., Greene, K.M. and Fischer, G.J., 1983. Fetal development: Effects of decompression sickness and treatment. *Aviation Space Environmental Medicine*, 54, pp. 1040–42.

Harris, C.W., Shields, J.L. and Hannon, J.P., 1966. Acute altitude sickness in females. *Aerospace Medicine*, 37(11), pp. 1163–7.

Heaps, C.L., Fischer, M.D. and Hill, R.C., 1997. Female acceleration tolerance: Effects of menstrual state and physical condition. *Aviation Space Environmental Medicine*, 68(6), pp. 525–30.

Hutton, L.V., 1990. The integration of women into US Navy aircrew training and squadron assignments. *AGARD Conference Proceedings No. 491: Recruiting, Selection, Training and Military Operations of Female Aircrew*, 1(1), pp. 1–5.

International Women's Air and Space Museum, 1997. Women Airforce Service Pilots. Available at: http://wingsacrossamerica.us/wasp.

Jennings, R.T., 1992. Women and the hazardous environment: When the pregnant patient requires hyperbaric oxygen therapy. *Aviation Space Environmental Medicine*, 58, pp. 370–4.

Kennedy, R.S., 1995. Motion sickness questionnaire and field independence scores as predictors of success in naval aviation training. *Aviation Space Environmental Medicine*, 46, pp. 1349–52.

Kennedy, R.S., Lanham, D.S., Massey, C.J., Drexler, J.M. and Lilienthal, M.G., 1995. Gender differences in simulator sickness incidence: Implications for military virtual reality systems. *SAFE Journal*, 25, pp. 69–76.

Lawther, A. and Griffin, M.J., 1988. A survey of the occurrence of motion sickness amongst passengers at sea. *Aviation Space Environmental Medicine*, 59, pp. 399–406.

Lentz, J.M. and Collins, W.E., 1977. Motion sickness susceptibility and related behavioural characteristics in men and women. *Aviation Space Environmental Medicine*, 48, pp. 316–22.

Lyons, T.J., 1992. Women in the cockpit: Aeromedical considerations. *Aviation Space Environmental Medicine*, 63, pp. 809–18.

Magaletta, G.E., 1986. Diving and sports medicine for women. In: W. Fife (ed.), *Women in Diving. Proceedings of the 35th Undersea and Hyperbaric Medical Society Workshop*. Bethesda, MD: UHMS Publications, No. 71, p. 68.

Mannino, J.A. and Kaufman, M.S., 1986. Comparative cold responses of men and women to external and internal cold stimuli. *Aviation Space Environmental Medicine*, 57, pp. 27–30.

McGlohn, S.E., King, R.E., Butler, J.W. and Retzlaff, P.D., 1997. Female United States Air Force (USAF) pilots: Themes, challenges, and possible solutions. *Aviation Space Environmental Medicine*, 68, pp. 132–6.

Robinette, K.M., 1995. Female anthropometry and the implications for protective equipment. *SAFE Journal*, 25, pp. 35–45.

Rudge, F.W., 1990. Relationship of menstrual history to altitude chamber decompression sickness. *Aviation Space Environmental Medicine*, 61, pp. 657–9.

Shannon, S.G., Moran, A.W. and Mason, K.T., 1994. Effect of vibration frequency and amplitude on developing chicken embryos. *UAAARL*, Report No. 95.

Slabodkin, G., 1996 Summary of Cessna's JPATS protest. *Inside the Air Force*, 12 January 1996, pp. 13–14.

Sperryn, P.N., 1983. *Sport and Medicine*. London: Butterworths.

Wagner, J.A., Miles, D.S., Horvath, S.M. and Reyburn, J.A., 1979. Maximal work capacity of women during acute hypoxia. *Journal of Applied Physiology*, 47, pp. 1223–7.

Wyndham, C.H., Morrison, J.F. and Williams, C.G., 1965. Heat reactions of male and female caucasians. *Journal of Applied Physiology*, 20, pp. 357–64.

Postscript to Chapter 3
Fast Women in the Twenty-First Century[1]

Tracy Smart

Introduction

Although basic physiology hasn't changed since I first explored this area in 1998, many other aspects have. At that time, there were only small numbers of female aircrew and none flying fast jets, although it looked probable that our first fast jet pilot was not too far away.

Fifteen years later, the numbers of female aircrew have increased and we have had our first female fast jet aircrew, with F-111 Navigators (now Air Combat Officers – ACO) Flying Officer Brooke Chivers and Pilot Officer Aroha Fifield graduating in 2000 (Department of Defence, 2000). As of April 2013, there are 142 qualified female aircrew (37 pilots) and a further 24 under training (12 pilots) across the three services (see Table 3b.1). Female RAAF pilots now fly the C-17 Globemaster, B737-AEW&C Wedgetail, C130J Hercules, AP-3C Orion, KA350 King Air, KC-30A MRTT, CT-4 and PC-9 aircraft (Royal Australian Air Force, 2013) and four serving female ACOs are qualified on fast jets, two of them on the F/A18F Super Hornet. The Air Force has also had its first female Commanding Officer of a flying squadron – WGCDR Linda Corbould of 36 Squadron. However, 17 years after these roles were first made available to women, and despite an aggressive recruiting campaign, the RAAF has yet to see its first fast jet pilot (Dodd, 2009).

While the basics haven't changed, some things have. This postscript provides an update on some of these emerging issues and the potential solutions that will break down the remaining barriers to women serving in all aircrew roles in the ADF.

Women on Operations

In my previous chapter (Chapter 3), I mentioned that one of the barriers to frontline female pilots was the public perception about women in war. Although the 2012

1 A version of this chapter was originally published as: Smart, T.L., 2003. Women as aviators: A favourable view. *Touchdown*, 2 August, pp. 14–17. The modified version of this chapter is reprinted here with permission thanks to *Touchdown: The Fleet Arm Safety and Information Magazine*.

Table 3.1 Qualified ADF female aircrew (as at April 2013)

	RAN	Army	RAAF	TOTAL
Pilot	3 (+2)	13 (+3)	21 (+7)	37 (+12)
Aviation Warfare Officer/Instructor	3 (+2)			3 (+2)
Air Combat Officer			37 (+3)	37 (+3)
Aircrewman	2	2	-	4
Loadmaster			4	4
Airborne Electronics Analyst			6 (+1)	6 (+1)
Crew Attendant			51 (+6)	51 (+6)
TOTAL	8 (+4)	15 (+3)	119 (+17)	142 (+24)

Note: Numbers in brackets are those under training.

announcement that all ADF jobs are now open to the women produced major media coverage (Department of Defence, 2012), even the Returned and Services League (RSL) support women on the front line, and certainly female aircrew on operational roles are no longer a novelty. The wars in the Middle East saw many female aviation firsts, including the first female B-2 pilot to fly a combat mission, a fully female team who conducted a KC-135 Stratotanker air refuelling mission and the first female RAF Tornado pilot to fly in operations against the Taliban (*Daily Mail*, 2010). In 2008, Merlin helicopter pilot Flight Lieutenant Michelle Goodman became the first female Royal Air Force (RAF) pilot to win a Distinguished Flying Cross (RAF Museum, n.d.). ADF women are no exception, with women from all three Services serving on operations in recent years.

Anthropometric Differences

As discussed previously, women are smaller than men on average across all parameters considered important in cockpit and flying clothing design. Women were not flying in military aircraft when most of the aircraft in the ADF inventory in 1998 were designed. In addition, the last anthropometric survey of aircrew conducted in the ADF was in the RAAF in 1977, well before women were allowed to operate military aircraft. The result is that both aircraft and aircrew flying clothing were designed purely with men in mind.

In the past 15 years, the ADF has substantially renewed its fleet of aircraft, with plans to replace many others with newer airframes designed since female military aviators have become a reality (Brown, 2012). As a consequence, these aircraft have being designed to accommodate a larger percentage of the female population. An example of this is the design of the new Joint Strike Fighter (JSF), which will have a fully adjustable seat and adjustable cockpit and rudder controls, and will accommodate the median 95 per cent of all eligible US military pilot candidates (Next Air Combat Capability Project, 2003).

Flying clothing and equipment has traditionally also been designed just for men. A 2001 survey of Canadian female aircrew indicated that a large percentage 'made do' with ill-fitting helmets, hearing protection, masks, flight suits and other protective suits (e.g. G suits), gloves and boots; however, very few complained about these issues, which were a possible flight safety risk (Breek, 2001). The ADF has undertaken a major anthropometric survey of aircraft workstations and of current and potential aircrew. This study, and others undertaken since that time, has ensured that appropriate sizes of flying clothing are available to all. A specially designed female flight suit has been in use in Western militaries for some time and modern G suits such as the Combined Advanced Technology Enhanced Design G Ensemble (CombAT EDGE) and Advanced Technology Anti-G Suits (ATAGS) have also been designed to accommodate women.

Pregnancy

The policy on pregnancy and flying as aircrew has not significantly changed since 1998. Health Directive 235 identifies that female aircrew are to be grounded (A3 – unfit to fly as aircrew) as soon as they are diagnosed as pregnant (Department of Defence Health Directive, 2013). The rationale is as follows:

> Stresses of flight (noise, vibration, thermal stress, hypoxia, g-loading), ionising/non-ionising radiation exposure, workload issues, accidental injury, problems with fitting protective equipment.

Pregnant women are also regarded as unfit to fly high-performance or rotary wing aircraft as a passenger; however, they can fly in pressurised fixed-wing transport aircraft up to 32 weeks, and possibly up to 36 weeks with medical officer clearance. This somewhat conservative stance has been questioned by some based on concerns about discrimination and the effects that time off flying will have on the individual's career. Others have urged us not to risk the health of their unborn child by exposure to the aviation environment. Of greatest concern for medical practitioners are the medico-legal aspects due to the unknown risks to the foetus. It is my experience that any complications that occur with the pregnancy or in the child's development will be blamed by the mother on her flying while pregnant. For all of these reasons, there has been no real impetus to change the approach of the ADF, which is not dissimilar to that of other militaries.

Female Bladder Relief

Even in fast jets, sorties lasting several hours are possible, especially with air-to-air refuelling; however, onboard toilet facilities are non-existent. Even aircraft with more spacious toilet facilities, such as the C-130, present difficulties to female aircrew wearing traditional flight suits, who may need to disrobe almost entirely to use the facilities.

As discussed in Chapter 3, 'piddle packs' of various types have been in use by male aircrew for some time, and condom catheters have been used by aircrew flying high-performance aircraft for more 'hands-free' operation. Obviously, this system is not suitable for women and therefore a variety of other options have been suggested. NASA developed the Disposable Absorption Containment Trunk (DACT), effectively a glorified nappy. Female U2 aircrew use a specially designed absorptive pad with tubing connected to their pressure suits. For other female aircrew, the only options in the past were to dehydrate themselves (Voge, n.d.), pass a catheter or just hold on.

In 2001 the USAF undertook a market survey to find a solution to this problem. The result was the choice of the Travel John as the device of choice for female aircrew to relieve themselves in flight (Smart and Elliott, 2001). This simple and cheap device consists of a plastic bag with a harder plastic lip designed to fit the female anatomy. Inside the bag is an inner bag containing absorbent polymer powder which instantly gels and deodorises liquids within seconds. The bag can then be rolled up, put in a re-sealable bag and stored for the duration of the flight.

However, finding the right device was only part of the solution. It was also evident that the flight suit itself required alteration in order to use such a device without disrobing. The simple solution was to design a flight suit with a longer zipper and this change was incorporated in the new female flight suit then under development. In the meantime, flight suits can be modified by adding another zipper under the current midline zipper.

This device and the associated modification met with great success with USAF aircrew in all aircraft types; however, it was not the final solution. The USAF created an Operational Requirements Document for a female bladder relief capability in the hope of producing a hands-free, constant-wear device that is compatible with NBC and other flying clothing ensembles. Such a device has been developed in the US and has now been certified for all US military aircraft (Reid, 2006). An option for male aircrew has also been developed.

Cultural Barriers

From the developments that have occurred over the past 15 years, it is somewhat surprising that there are not more female aircrew and that the RAAF still doesn't have its first fast jet pilot. While at the time I stated that I thought many cultural issues could be overcome by good leadership, time and increasing numbers of female aircrew, it would appear that some barriers remain.

Some of these barriers may have a particularly dark side. In Chapter 3 I quoted Major (retired) Dee Brasseur, the first female F-18 pilot in the Canadian military, who reported receiving a lot of hostility in her early flying days, but ignored the jibes and was eventually accepted by her peers. In more recent years, Major Brasseur has admitted that she was subject to unwanted sexual advances, including by an instructor, and actual sexual assault (O'Hara, 1998). Elizabeth Broderick heard similar tales from women serving in non-traditional roles in the ADF (Broderick, 2012).

The Broderick Review also documented a number of barriers that female aircrew still face, such as the inability of command to handle pregnancy, the difficulties in operating as one of few women in the 'boys' club' environment of flying training, the feeling of continuously being in the spotlight and the need to over-achieve to succeed (Broderick, 2012, p. 219). Some women even reported being told in recruiting that they couldn't be fast jet pilots due to the effects of G forces on the female body (p. 171)! Broderick also cited statistics that, particularly in the RAAF, rates of completion of the initial term of service in aviation were far lower for women (76.2 per cent) than for men (100 per cent) (p. 416).

The ADF response to this review, *Pathway to Change: Evolving Defence Culture*, details many strategies to overcome these problems, such as trying to increase numbers of women overall, but with particular attention to non-traditional roles, changes to policy to better cater to the needs of women, the development of mentoring and support networks, and a zero-tolerance policy to sexual harassment and abuse of any kind (Defence Committee, Department of Defence, 2012). What sort of effect this may have on the numbers and types of female aircrew in the ADF in the coming years remains to be seen.

Summary and Conclusions

Women and men will continue to be different, and these differences will continue to result in female-specific issues being raised in the aviation world. This is not a reason to restrict aircrew opportunities, but to rethink our current ways of doing business, and in some cases the result may be improvements for both genders. Although significant cultural barriers remain, there is no reason why appropriately qualified women cannot achieve as much or more than their male counterparts in both peacetime and on operations, and this has now been proved by experience. Women are now an integral part of our military flying force and are here to stay.

References

Breek, K., 2001. Unpublished survey data regarding Canadian female aircrew reporting on ill fitting flight gear (personal communication).

Broderick, E., 2012. *Review into the Treatment of Women in the Australian Defence Force*. Available at: http://humanrights.gov.au/defencereview/ADF_report/index.html.

Brown, G., 2012. ASPI 'Dinner with the Chiefs' – Chief of Air Force: Air Marshal Geoff Brown, speech, 5 June. Available at: http://www.aspi.org.au/

admin/eventFiles/CAF%20address%20-%20ASPI%20Dinner%20-%205%20 Jun%2012.pdf.

Daily Mail, 2010. Meet Juliette, the RAF bombshell who terrified the Taliban in her fighter jet, 27 January. Available at: http://www.dailymail.co.uk/news/article-1246237/Shock-awe-Female-RAF-Top-Gun-pilot-tells-beat-Taliban-deafening-noise-instead-bombs.html.

Defence Committee, Department of Defence. (2012). Pathway to change – evolving defence culture. Available at: http://www.defence.gov.au/pathwaytochange/docs/120410%20Pathway%20to%20Change%20-%20Evolving%20Defence %20Culture%20-%20web%20version.pdf.

Department of Defence Health Directive 2013. 235: Management of pregnant members of the Australian Defence Force. Canberra, ADF.

Department of Defence, Defence Jobs Website, 2012. Removal of gender restrictions. Women in the Australian Defence Force. Available at: http://www.defencejobs.gov.au/women/RemovalofGenderRestrictions/15.

Department of Defence Press Release. 2000. RAAF women graduate to fast jets. Press release, 18 February 2000.

Dodd, M., 2009. Women: RAAF wants you for its top guns. *The Australian*, 11 September. Available at: http://www.theaustralian.com.au/national-affairs /defence/women-raaf-wants-you-for-its-top-guns/story-e6frg8yo-122577 1738475.

Next Air Combat Capability Project. 2003. Discussion regarding the new Joint Strike Fighter which will adjustable seat, cockpit and rudder controls (personal communication).

O'Hara, J., 1998. More rape in the military. *Canadian Encyclopedia Website*, 1 June Available at: http://www.thecanadianencyclopedia.com/articles/macleans /more-rape-in-the-military.

RAF Museum, (n.d.). Michelle Goodman's biography. Available at: http://www.rafmuseum.org.uk/research/online-exhibitions/women-of-the-air-force/women-in-the-raf-today/michelle-goodmans-biography.aspx.

Reid, J., 2006. AMXD: A new extended-wear bladder relief system developed for the U.S. Air Force. *SAFE Europe Symposium.* Warsaw, Poland, 2006. Available at: http://www.safeeurope. co.uk/media /3592/jerry_reid.pdf.

Royal Australian Air Force, 2013. Becoming a pilot. Available at: http://www.airforce.gov.au/Our_People/Careers/Becoming_a_Pilot/?RAAFAn2hMAOE EYLxlX7puIXHAd6J4qTRM7DQ.

Smart, T.L. and Elliott, J., 2001. Operational requirements for female urine relief devices in tactical aircraft. *Aerospace Medical Association 72nd Annual Scientific meeting*. Reno, Nevada, USA, 6–10 May.

Voge, VM., Self-reported waste collection problems of US Air Force and US Army rated men and women. *Safe J*, 25(3), pp. 213–20.

Chapter 4
Gender-Based Attitudes Regarding Pilot Behaviour

Rosemarie Reynolds, Alexandru Milut, Giby Abraham Jacob, Joshua Hirschheimer and Bridget Cox

Introduction

Women have flown aircraft since the eighteenth century, when Jeanne Labrosse first soloed in a balloon. Five years after the Wright brothers' first flight at Kill Devil Hills, North Carolina, Therese Peltier soloed an aircraft in the Military Square in Turin, Italy. Two years later, Baroness Raymonde de Laroche became the first licensed female pilot. In 1929, 20 women flew in the first women's National Air Derby from Santa Monica, California, to Cleveland, Ohio, and Elizabeth MacGill became the first woman in the world to qualify as an aeronautical engineer (Wilson, 2004; Women in Aviation International, 2012).

But these female aviation pioneers have been the exception, rather than the rule. When Raymonde de Laroche earned her pilot's licence in 1910, three per cent of all pilots were women. A hundred years later, women represent less than five per cent of the worldwide pilot population and six per cent of the pilots in the US (Mitchell, Kristovics and Bishop, 2010; Wilson, 2011). The aviation industry is still dominated by masculine values and practices, negative attitudes towards women in aviation, and isolation, sexism and harassment for female pilots (Davey and Davidson, 2000; Mitchell, Kristovics and Bishop, 2010; Vermeulen, 2009; Wilson, 2004). In fact, a recent case study by Hynes and Puckett concluded that: 'The results of this study indicate that female pilots and captains in the aviation industry faced real gender-related roadblocks to their career paths, as had their predecessors over the past forty years' (2011, p. 5).

For a significant amount of time, women were discouraged (and at times barred) from becoming pilots and pursuing aviation as a career option. Changes in societal attitudes regarding women as a whole, combined with the passing of anti-discrimination and equal opportunity legislation, have removed many of the legal barriers that women faced in pursuing flying, whether for recreation or as a career. However, it is one thing for women to be legally allowed to pursue careers as aviators and something else entirely for them to do so in the face of hostility and suspicion from their male peers.

Previous studies have attempted to gauge the attitudes towards female pilots in South Africa, Australia, Norway, South America and the US. Despite a wealth of information gathered in English-speaking aviation communities around the world, US pilots' attitudes regarding gender-related behaviour are still not very well understood.

Such research on gender attitudes is required for a number of reasons, with safety of flight being the most important one; if the crew members of an aircraft distrust their teammates' abilities and judgment, they will not be able to function adequately as a team. In addition, at a time when declining standards in professionalism and the quality of the pilot pool are at the forefront of the debate on pilot certification and hiring standards, the aviation community cannot afford to shun future members due to preconceptions and prejudices. Finally, an accurate understanding of these attitudes would be useful in developing training materials, particularly with regard to crew resource management (CRM).

Thus, in this study, our purpose was to examine gender-based attitudes in a sample of US pilots. We proposed that pilot attitudes would vary as a function of a number of variables, including pilots' gender, age, flight experience, opportunity to fly with the opposite gender, level of certification, instructor rating and CRM training. We chose these biographical variables because they have been used in previous studies on gender-based attitudes in aviation.

Literature Review

Previous studies on gender in aviation have focused on two major themes: attitudes in relation to gender and actual differences in pilot behaviour based on gender. In the following sections we will review some of the findings from both sets of studies.

Attitudes

In 2002, Vermeulen and Wilson began to develop the Aviation Gender Attitude Questionnaire (AGAQ), which was designed to gauge attitudes, stereotypes and prejudices regarding female aviators. The AGAQ has since gone through several revisions, as well as validation across different cultures. The original questionnaire contained 72 questions with two dimensions. The questionnaire was subsequently refined by Vermeulen and Mitchell (2007) in order to reduce the number of questions and was expanded to four dimensions: flying proficiency, safety orientation, flight confidence and flight standards. Vermeulen et al. (2009) collected data from South African and Australian pilots in order to establish the intercultural equivalence of the AGAQ, and found no item bias for the AGAQ across the two cultures.

Wilson (2004) used the AGAQ to compare the means of South African and US respondents, as well as factors such as gender, level of education, pilot certification, age, total flying time, position of the pilot and opportunity to fly with the opposite gender. Pilot gender was the only variable that had a significant impact on gender-related attitudes.

Mitchell, Kristovics, and Vermeulen (2006) used the AGAQ to survey 1,114 pilots in Australia. They found more negative attitudes towards female than male pilots, although opportunity to fly with the opposite gender improved male attitudes regarding female pilots' safety orientation. Kristovics et al. (2006) used the AGAQ to compare responses from samples in the US, South Africa, Australia and Norway. Female pilots were scored more negatively than males on all factors, although the opportunity to fly with the opposite gender and completing CRM training led to more positive attitudes towards female pilots.

Vermeulen (2009) examined how flight instructors and commercial pilots in South Africa differed in their attitudes regarding female pilots, and found that flight instructors and commercial pilots differed significantly in their assessment of female pilots' flying proficiency, but not in their safety orientation. Finally, Mitchell et al. (2005) analysed attitudes regarding female pilots in four different countries – South Africa, Australia, Norway and the US – using both the AGAQ and qualitative analysis of the comments from the surveys. They found that there was bias and prejudice towards female pilots, but that the growing number of female pilots was having an impact on the attitudes of pilots and the masculine stereotype of a pilot.

Behaviour

Although there has not been a great deal of research on differences in pilot behaviour based on gender, there has been enough research to indicate that there are, in fact, some differences. With regards to flight performance, McFadden (1996) found female commercial pilots had significantly higher accident rates than male pilots. However, when McFadden adjusted for experience and age, the accident rates of men and women were not significantly different. In general aviation (GA) accidents, Vail and Ekman (1986) found that male pilots had higher accident rates than female pilots and were more likely to have accidents that resulted in fatalities. Twenty-five years later, Baker et al. (2001) also examined GA accidents and found that male pilots were more likely to crash due to inattention or flawed decision making, while female pilots were more likely to crash because they mishandled the aircraft. More recently, Bazargan and Guzhva (2011) looked at over 40,000 GA incident reports in the US from 1983 to 2002 and found no relationship between gender and pilot errors, although they did find, as did Vail and Ekman (1986), that men had accidents that were more likely to result in fatalities.

Sitler (2004) examined gender differences in how pilots learn to fly and found that female pilots were slower learners in a number of areas (gaining confidence, understanding aerodynamics and solo flight) and were more fearful of stalls and spins. However, once women learned a procedure, they tended to be more consistent and had fewer fatal aircraft accidents.

Fischer and Orasanu (1999) found gender differences in the way that female and male pilots communicated with their aircrews – findings supported by Turney and Bishop (2004). In the Fischer and Orasanu study, female pilots stated the problem before issuing a command or suggestion to their co-pilot, a technique that can help develop shared understanding, but may be inefficient in high-risk situations. Turney and Bishop (2004) found that male pilots were more confident and task-oriented, while female pilots were seen as better communicators and negotiators. In addition, male pilots viewed themselves as better leaders, had difficulty seeing female pilots as professionals, and considered situational awareness and the ability to listen and evaluate critical, while women considered shared decision making, conflict resolution and patience important in decision making.

King, McGlohn, and Retzlaff (1997) examined gender differences in personality as a major variable, using the Big Five dimensions of neuroticism, extraversion, openness to new experiences, agreeableness and conscientiousness to compare male US Air Force (USAF) pilots, female USAF pilots and a female non-pilot comparison group. Female pilots scored higher on the extraversion, agreeableness and conscientiousness scales than both male pilots and the female comparison group.

The Present Study

We selected the variables examined based on a number of previous studies utilising the AGAQ. In the following sections we will discuss the hypotheses, method, sample and instrument.

Hypotheses

We proposed a number of hypotheses based on biographical variables. Specifically, we hypothesised that:

- H_1 attitudes regarding female pilots will vary depending on gender (same sex vs. opposite sex);
- H_2 male pilots' attitudes regarding female pilots will vary with the male pilots' age;
- H_3 male pilots' attitudes regarding female pilots will vary with the male pilots' experience as measured by total flight hours;
- H_4 male pilots' attitudes regarding female pilots will vary with the male pilots' experience as measured by years of flying;
- H_5 male pilots' attitudes regarding female pilots will vary depending on the amount of opportunities male pilots have had to fly with female pilots;
- H_6 male pilots' attitudes regarding female pilots will vary with the male pilots' level of certification;
- H_7 male pilots holding flight instructor ratings will have more favourable views of female pilots than male pilots without instructor ratings;
- H_8 male pilots' attitudes regarding female pilots will vary depending on whether the male pilot had received CRM training.

Method

Our method was a survey, hosted online using the Survey Monkey software and its web hosting option. The Survey Monkey software automatically collected and catalogued the data, which was then interpreted using Statistical Package for the Social Sciences (SPSS) statistical analysis software. Traffic to the website was generated by contacting various pilot and aviation organisations via email and telephone calls, through a viral campaign on the Facebook social networking site, and through notices on various online pilot- and aviation-related forums.

Sample

We used the AGAQ to sample the pilot population of the US. For the purposes of this study, we defined the pilot population as 'anyone who holds a valid Federal Aviation Administration (FAA) pilot certificate'. This definition includes student pilots, who are, within certain limitations, allowed to act as pilot-in-command of aircraft.

We obtained a total of 113 complete responses to our survey. The descriptive statistics for the entire sample are set out in Table 4.1.

Table 4.1 Sample characteristics

Variable	Groups	Number of respondents	Percentage of respondents
Sample size	Men	89	78.8%
	Women	24	21.2%
Instructor rating	Yes	38	33.6%
	No	75	66.4%
Flight hours	350 or less	75	66.4%
	351 or more	38	33.6%
CRM training	No	41	36.3%
	Yes	72	63.7%
Age group	18–30	91	80.5%
	31–64	22	19.5%
Experience	6 years or less	77	68.1%
	7 years or more	36	31.9%
Opportunities to fly with opposite gender	Few	82	72.56%
	More	31	27.43%

Note: $n = 113$

Table 4.2 shows the descriptive statistics for the male portion of the sample.

Table 4.2 Characteristics of male sample

Variable	Groups	Number of respondents	Percentage of respondents
Instructor rating	No	55	61.8%
	Yes	34	28.2%
Flight hours	350 or less	55	61.8%
	351 or more	34	38.2%
CRM training	No	30	33.7%
	Yes	59	66.3%
Age group	18–30	68	76.4%
	31–64	21	23.6%
Experience	6 years or less	55	61.8%
	7 years or more	34	38.2%
Opportunities to fly with opposite gender	Few	74	83.15%
	More	15	16.85%

Note: $n = 89$

Of our respondents, 89 were men (79 per cent) and 24 (21 per cent) were women. The age of our sample ranged from 18 to 64, with an average age of 27. Of the pilots surveyed, 81 per cent (n = 91) were 18–30 years old. The majority of our sample (61 per cent) had a commercial pilot or higher rating, with an average flight experience of eight years. The average number of flight hours was 2,723.85; however, the modal number of flight hours was less than 350. Sixty per cent of the sample had a bachelor's degree and 64 per cent had CRM training.

The biggest difference between the pilot population in the US and our sample was the average age and the high percentage of women. In addition, the sample had significantly more pilots with commercial pilot or higher ratings (61.4 per cent) than the certificate-level distribution among the US pilot population, indicating that our sample consists, to a large extent, of individuals who are either currently working as professional pilots or intend to do so, thus increasing the applicability of our findings with respect to the commercial aviation industry. At the same time, it is important to remember that most of our sample consisted of pilots with low flight time (less than 350 hours total time) and less than eight years of flying experience.

Instrument

We used the 34-question version of the AGAQ, which has been shown to have acceptable factorial validity, unidimensionality and appears to be a valid and culturally unbiased tool across different Western, English-speaking cultures (Vermeulen and Mitchell, 2007; Vermeulen et al., 2009). The AGAQ asks pilots to evaluate different statements regarding pilot behaviour, in a training environment as well as regular operations, and to agree or disagree with them using a five-point Likert scale, with lower scores indicating more positive attitudes.

The AGAQ covers four dimensions: (1) flying proficiency; (2) safety orientation; (3) flight confidence; and (4) flight standards. Flying proficiency consists of items related to general piloting skills, decision making in flying and the pilot's comfort level with controls. Safety orientation concerns the level of safety awareness among pilots and a pilot's attention to detail. Flight confidence includes pilot confidence, assertiveness, emotional stability and coping with flight demands. Flight standards referred to the perception that female pilots are given some latitude when they are tested for their licences and when they are given access to flying positions.

We altered the biographical data section (Section I of the AGAQ) to apply to US pilots. A number of subject matter experts and pilots were asked to review and provide feedback as to whether the altered content was appropriate.

Analysis

Where appropriate, the answers to the AGAQ were reverse-coded and the individual question scores were then aggregated according to the four factors. Reliability analysis was carried out by calculating Cronbach's alpha (α = .94). Most of the biographical variables that offered more than two answer choices were consolidated prior to statistical analysis. Based on their age, respondents were divided into 18–30 year olds (which comprised the majority of our sample) and 30 year olds and above. Education level was divided between 'no college degree' (to include associate and technical degrees) and 'college degree or higher'. Certification levels were consolidated into 'private pilot and below' and 'commercial level and above'. Flying experience in years was divided into 'six years and below' and 'seven years and above'. Flight time was analysed by comparing pilots with fewer than 350 hours (the majority of the pilots that responded to our questionnaire and, coincidentally, a number of hours that is characteristic of young commercial pilots or flight instructors at the beginning of their career) to those with more than 350 hours. Pilots were also divided according to their opportunities to fly with the opposite gender. In order to explore this possibility, participants' responses to questions about their gender and their opportunities to fly with the opposite gender were combined to create a variable that divided our sample into four: (1) male pilots with relatively few opportunities to fly with female pilots; (2) male pilots with more opportunities to fly with the opposite gender; (3) female pilots with relatively few opportunities to fly with male pilots; and (4) female pilots with more opportunities to fly with male pilots. There were only three female pilots who had relatively few opportunities to fly with male pilots. This group was ignored due to the small sample size.

Results

Independent sample t-tests were used to compare means for the various groups. The t-tests revealed only four statistically significant differences. One set of differences was based on pilot gender as the independent variable; for all pilot biographical subgroups, significant differences were found with respect to male and female attitudes regarding female flying proficiency, flight confidence and erosion of standards. There were no significant findings with respect to safety orientation. In addition, male pilots with more flying experience in terms of years had significantly more positive attitudes with regards to female flying proficiency.

Hypothesis 1

Our first hypothesis stated that attitudes regarding female pilots would vary by gender. T-tests were performed to test the hypothesis. The mean scores and results of the t-tests are shown in Table 4.3. There was no difference in attitudes for of safety orientation; however, for the remaining three dimensions, there were significant differences based on gender.

Table 4.3 Attitudes regarding female pilots by gender

	Mean		***t***	***p***
	Men[1]	**Women**[2]		
Flying proficiency	43.37	26.96	.5	<.01
Safety orientation	19.97	18.46	.14	ns
Flight confidence	22.63	16.75	.52	<.01
Erosion of standards	11.63	8.21	.58	<.01

Note: [1] $n = 89$ [2] $n = 24$

Hypothesis 2

Our second hypothesis stated that male pilots' attitudes towards female pilots would vary with the male pilots' age. We divided our sample of male pilots into two groups: those between 18 and 30, and those between 31 and 64. T-tests were performed to test the hypothesis that mean scores would vary by group. The scores and results of the t-tests are shown in Table 4.4. There were no significant differences based on age.

Table 4.4 Male pilot attitudes regarding female pilots by age

	Mean		*t*	*p*
	18–30[1]	31–64[2]		
Flying proficiency	44.56	39.52	.74	ns
Safety orientation	19.85	20.33	34	ns
Flight confidence	23.07	21.19	.32	ns
Erosion of standards	11.68	11.48	23	ns

Note: [1] $n = 68$ [2] $n = 21$

Hypothesis 3

Our third hypothesis focused on the effects of experience, as measured by fight hours, on male pilots' attitudes regarding female pilots. We divided our sample of male pilots into two groups: those with 350 hours or less, and those with 351 hours and more. T-tests were performed to test the hypothesis that mean scores would vary by group. The scores and results of the t-tests are shown in Table 4.5. There were no significant differences based on experience.

Table 4.5 Male pilot attitudes regarding female pilots by number of flight hours

	Mean		*t*	*p*
	350 hours or less[1]	351 hours or more[2]		
Flying proficiency	43.85	42.59	.49	ns
Safety orientation	19.36	20.94	1.3	ns
Flight confidence	23.25	21.62	1.3	ns
Erosion of standards	11.58	11.71	.16	ns

Note: [1] $n = 55$ [2] $n = 34$

Hypothesis 4

Our fourth hypothesis focused on the effects of experience, as measured by years of flying, on male pilots' attitudes towards female pilots. Respondents were grouped into those with six years and below, and seven years and above. T-tests were performed to test the hypothesis. The mean scores and results of the t-tests are shown in Table 4.6.

Table 4.6 Male pilot attitudes regarding female pilots by years of flying

	Mean		*t*	*p*
	6 years or less[1]	7 years or more[2]		
Flying proficiency	45.80	39.44	2.56	<0.05
Safety orientation	19.92	20.03	0.08	ns
Flight confidence	23.41	21.35	1.6	ns
Erosion of standards	11.92	11.15	1.0	ns

Note: [1] $n = 55$ [2] $n = 34$

There were no significant differences for three of the dimensions. For flying proficiency, there was a significant difference, with male pilots with more experience having more positive attitudes.

Hypothesis 5

Our fifth hypothesis stated that attitudes regarding female pilots would vary depending on the number of opportunities male pilots had to fly with the opposite gender. Male pilots were grouped into those who had fewer (or no) opportunities to fly with the opposite gender (50 per cent of the time and below) and those who had more opportunities to fly the opposite gender (50 per cent and above). T-tests were performed to test the hypothesis. The mean scores and results of the t-tests are shown in Table 4.7. There were no significant differences in attitudes based on the opportunities male pilots had to fly with the opposite gender. Although not statistically significant, opportunities to fly with the opposite gender actually resulted in less favourable attitudes regarding female pilots.

Table 4.7 Male pilot attitudes regarding female pilots by opportunities to fly with the opposite gender

	Mean		*t*	*p*
	Few opportunities[1]	More opportunities[2]		
Flying proficiency	42.80	46.20	1.03	ns
Safety orientation	19.86	20.47	.38	ns
Flight confidence	22.53	23.13	.37	ns
Erosion of standards	11.46	12.47	1.03	ns

Note: [1] $n = 74$ [2] $n = 15$

Hypothesis 6

Our sixth hypothesis stated that attitudes regarding female pilots would vary with male pilots' level of certification. Certification levels were consolidated into private pilot and below, and commercial level and above. T-tests were performed to test the hypothesis. The mean scores and results of the t-tests are shown in Table 4.8. There were no significant differences based on level of certification.

Table 4.8 Male pilot attitudes regarding female pilots by level of certification

	Mean		*t*	*p*
	Private pilot and below[1]	**Commercial level and above[2]**		
Flying proficiency	43.27	43.57	0.11	ns
Safety orientation	20.085	19.73	0.28	ns
Flight confidence	22.41	23.07	-0.5	ns
Erosion of standards	11.71	11.47	0.31	ns

Note: [1] $n = 59$ [2] $n = 30$

Hypothesis 7

Our seventh hypothesis stated that pilots holding flight instructor ratings would have more favourable views of female pilots than those who did not. T-tests were performed to test the hypothesis. The mean scores and results of the t-tests are shown in Table 4.9. There were no significant differences based on flight instructor ratings.

Table 4.9 Male pilot attitudes regarding female pilots by flight instructor rating

	Mean		*t*	*p*
	Pilots without instructor rating[1]	**Pilots with instructor rating[2]**		
Flying proficiency	43.02	43.94	0.72	ns
Safety orientation	19.47	20.76	0.29	ns
Flight confidence	22.73	22.47	0.84	ns
Erosion of standards	11.65	11.59	0.93	ns

Note: [1] $n = 55$ [2] $n = 34$

Hypothesis 8

Our eighth hypothesis stated that attitudes towards female pilots would vary by CRM training. T-tests were performed to test the hypothesis. The mean scores and results of the t-tests are shown in Table 4.10. There were no significant differences based on CRM training.

Table 4.10 Male pilot attitudes regarding female pilots as a function of CRM training

	Mean		*t*	*p*
	No CRM training[1]	**CRM training**[2]		
Flying proficiency	42.33	43.89	.59	ns
Safety orientation	19.17	20.37	.97	ns
Flight confidence	22.47	22.71	.19	ns
Erosion of standards	10.70	12.10	.83	ns

Note: [1] $n = 30$ [2] $n = 59$

Discussion

The main limitation of our study is the small and somewhat skewed nature of our sample. Many of our respondents were people with similar flying backgrounds. Because of this, there are doubts as to how accurate a representation our sample is of the actual pilot population of the US.

The fact that the survey was posted online was not judged to be a significant impediment, as Internet access is generally taken for granted in the aviation community in the US, as shown by the fact that one of the two official FAA sources of weather and flight information is a web-based flight planning tool, and that in recent years the FAA has made the Airman Certificate and/or Rating Application (ACRA) available online and has encouraged its use.

The fact that attitudes regarding female pilots differed by gender and that male pilots viewed female pilots' flying proficiency, flight confidence and the standards that they were held to in a more negative light than female pilots is indicative of a certain level of distrust from male pilots regarding female pilots. For all pilot biographical subgroups, significant differences were found with respect to flying proficiency, flight confidence and erosion of standards. The fact that such a division exists and, more importantly, exists to such an extent seems to indicate that even after more than 100 years of female participation in aviation, female pilots are still not perceived in the same way as male pilots. The only other statistically significant difference was in male pilots' attitudes towards female pilots by years of flying, where pilots with seven or more years of experience flying had more positive perceptions of female flying proficiency.

Our findings corroborate those found in previous research, indicating that there are indeed differences in attitudes regarding female pilots based on gender (Kristovics et al., 2006; Vermeulen, 2009; Wilson, 2004). Although these findings are somewhat disheartening, they do point out areas in which further work needs to be done.

Future research should focus integrating the results of this study with those of previous studies using the AGAQ in order to obtain a more complete view of pilot attitudes regarding female pilots. Only when a complete and accurate picture of how various subsets of the pilot population view gender-related pilot behaviour is obtained can the roots of such attitudes be identified and addressed.

Knowledge of gender-based attitudes can help airlines develop better recruitment strategies and emphasises the need to recruit and retain experienced female pilots to serve as role models/mentors for inexperienced female airline pilots. Understanding attitudes regarding female pilots will allow for the development of more accurate training materials that include such topics as communication differences, gender sensitivity, diversity training, gender-based stereotyping, sexism and occupational gender segregation. This is also applicable to CRM training, and particularly applicable to instructors, who play a formative role in the development of students' perceptions and behaviour (McFadden, 1996; Vermeulen, 2009; Vermeulen and Mitchell, 2007; Vermeulen et al., 2009; Wilson, 2004).

In conclusion, the AGAQ's reliability has been confirmed once again and our findings corroborate those of previous research, which found that there are differences in attitudes regarding female pilots based on gender. In addition, despite the limitations of our sample, we were able to obtain information on pilot attitudes from a section of the US pilot population that had been largely absent from previous studies, namely young male pilots.

References

Baker, S.P., Lamb, M.W., Grabowski, J.G., Reebok, G. and Li, G., 2001. Characteristics of general aviation crashes involving mature male and female pilots. *Aviation, Space & Environmental Medicine*, 72(5), pp. 447–52.

Bazargan, M. and Guzhva, V.S., 2011. Impact of gender, age and experience of pilots on general aviation accidents. *Accident Analysis and Prevention*, 43, pp. 962–70.

Davey, C.L. and Davidson, M.J., 2000. The right of passage? The experiences of female pilots in commercial aviation. *Feminism and Psychology*, 10(2), pp. 195–225.

Fischer, U. and Orasanu, J., 1999. Cultural diversity and crew communication. In: 50th Astronautical Congress. Amsterdam, 4–8 October 1999.

Hynes, G. and Puckett, M., 2011. Feminine leadership in commercial aviation: Success stories of women pilots and captains. *Journal of Aviation Management and Education*, 1, pp. 1–6.

King, R.E., McGlohn, S.E. and Retzlaff, P.D., 1997. Female United States Air Force pilot personality: The new right stuff. *Military Medicine*, 162, pp. 695–7.

Kristovics, A., Mitchell, J., Vermeulen, L.P., Wilson, J. and Martinussen, M., 2006. Gender issues on the flight-deck: An exploratory analysis. *International Journal of Applied Aviation Studies*, 6(1), pp. 99–119.

McFadden, K.L., 1996. Comparing pilot-error accident rates of male and female airline pilots. *Omega: International Journal of Management Science*, 24, pp. 443–50.

Mitchell, J., Kristovics, A. and Bishop, R., 2010. Glass cockpits in general aviation: A comparison of men and women pilots' perceptions. *International Journal of Applied Aviation Studies*, 10(2), pp. 11–29.

Mitchell, J., Kristovics, A. and Vermeulen, L., 2006. Gender issues in aviation: Pilot perceptions and employment relations. *International Journal of Employment Studies*, 14(1), pp. 35–59.

Mitchell, J., Kristovics, A., Vermeulen, L., Wilson, J. and Martinussen, M., 2005. How pink is the sky? A cross-national study of the gendered occupation of pilot. *Employment Relations Record*, 5(2), pp. 43–60.

Sitler, R., 2004. Gender differences in learning to fly. In: M.A. Turney (ed.), *Culture, Gender and Diversity*. Aldershot: Ashgate, pp. 77–88.

Turney, M.A. and Bishop, J.C., 2004. Women's learning and leadership styles: Implications for air crews. In: M.A. Turney (ed.), *Culture, Gender and Diversity*. Aldershot: Ashgate, pp. 61–75.

Vail, G.J. and Ekman, L.G., 1986. Pilot-error accidents: Male vs. female. *Applied Ergonomics*, 17(4), pp. 297–303.

Vermeulen, L., 2009. Flight instructors' perceptions of pilot behaviour related to gender. *SA Journal of Industrial Psychology*, 35(1), pp. 819–27.

Vermeulen, L. and Mitchell, J., 2007. Development and validation of a measure to assess perceptions regarding gender-related pilot behavior. *International Journal of Aviation Psychology*, 17(2), pp. 197–218.

Vermeulen, L. and Wilson, J. (2002). The measurement of perceptions with regard to gender-based issues in aviation. Unpublished research report. Pretoria, South Africa: University of Pretoria.

Vermeulen, L., Schaap, P., Mitchell, J. and Kristovics, A., 2009. Exploring the equivalence of the Aviation Gender Attitude Questionnaire (AGAQ) for South African and Australian pilots: A cross-cultural comparison. *International Journal of Aviation Psychology*, 19(4), pp. 367–90.

Wilson, I., 2011. Local pilot works to introduce women to aviation. *McClatchy – Tribune Business News*, 15 February. Available at: http://search.proquest.com.ezproxy.libproxy.db.erau.edu/docview/851576588?accountid=27203.

Wilson, J., 2004. Gender-based issues in aviation, attitudes towards female pilots: A cross-cultural analysis. PhD thesis, University of Pretoria.

Women in Aviation International, 2012. WAI announces Pioneer Hall of Fame inductees for 2012. Available at: http://www.wai.org/news/press/12_wai_02.html.

PART II
Barriers in Military and Civil Aviation

Chapter 5

Unexpected Turbulence: The Cultural, Gender-Based Challenges Facing Female Pilots in the Australian Defence Force

Deanne Gibbon

> Gender integration amounted to a double assault on their manhood: first you had women thinking they should join in this manly sport of war, now they wanted to fly your goddam air-plane too! (Gandt, 1997, p. 35)

Introduction

Research into the barriers and challenges facing women working in fields of non-traditional employment has proven that women face stressors, both structural and cultural, beyond those found in more gender-balanced workplaces (Andrew, 2009; Gale, 1994; Greed, 1991; Whittock, 2000). Cultural barriers are those created through organisational 'symbols and meanings, which are negotiated and shared' (Whittock, 2002, p. 114). In male-dominated organisations, workplace cultures are often 'hierarchical, patriarchal, sex-segregated, sexist, misogynistic, resistant to change and as encompassing gendered power structures' (Whittock, 2002, p. 115).

This chapter explores the gendered culture of Australian military aviation through the lived experiences of women pilots, who find themselves very much *visitors* to the dominant masculine culture. Through sharing their stories, this chapter contributes women military pilots as a *case* in the rich and growing literature addressing the gender-based cultural challenges faced by women operating as a small minority of a gender-skewed workforce. This chapter focuses only on cultural barriers; structural barriers are addressed elsewhere in this book.

As a case in the study of women in non-traditional employment, military pilots offer some valuable insights that are not limited to military or flying contexts. Women pilots must negotiate their femininity through intertwined layers of hegemonic masculinity, which is an idealised form of masculinity that subordinates, or makes inferior, images of femininity or other masculinities (Connell, 2005). The Australian military institution creates an overarching masculinised context in which women pilots must function. Militaries, by their very nature, are *highly gendered* in accordance with Acker's theoretical framework, where 'advantage and disadvantage, exploitation and control, action and emotion, meaning and identity are patterned through and in terms of a distinction between male and female, masculine and feminine' (1990, p. 146).

The aviation context presents yet another layer of masculinity that must be negotiated by female pilots. While hegemonic masculinity abounds in commercial aviation (Mills, 1998), within the military aviation context it has been described as 'extreme' (Barrett, 1996). This masculinity perhaps stems from the *Top Gun* image of military pilots, who reek 'self-confidence, privilege and the conviction that they are the best' (Kellner, 1995, p. 77). Militaries are patriarchal bureaucracies dominated by men, and aviation contexts show masculinity at its most extreme. These findings raise questions as to how female pilots negotiate their femininity in such an intensely masculine world.

The voices of military women pilots have, until now, been neglected in discussions about the gendered nature of flying and women in other fields of non-traditional employment. The perceptions that male pilots have of their female colleagues have been thoroughly documented in a number of academic studies (e.g. Ashcraft, 2005; Davey and Davidson, 2000; Kristovics et al., 2006; Mitchell et al., 2005) and in popular discourse (PPRuNe Forums, 2010, 2012). However, women's voices rarely feature in the subsequent reporting.

The few past sociological studies exploring female pilots' lived experiences have focused on commercial and civilian training contexts, (Davey, 2004; Davey and Davidson, 2000; Neal-Smith and Cockburn, 2009, Sitler, 2004; Turney et al., 2002; Turney, 2004). The experiences of *military* female pilots rarely feature in sociological research. When researchers have actively sought Australian Defence Force (ADF) pilot participation, their access has been denied (Kristovics et al., 2006). The military seemingly distrusts outsider research.

Past internal research on military pilots and gender has predominantly focused on detecting any gender differences in flying skills, physiology, aptitude and personality traits (King et al., 1997; McGlohn et al., 1996; Smart, 1998). Non-academic literature paints a glowingly positive picture of women's participation in military flying (Debenham and Stafford, 2001; Grant, 2002; Williams, 2003). These depictions sit in stark contrast to the far less rosy stories shared through female pilots' biographies (Cummings, 1999; Flinn, 1997; Spears, 1998). The disparity between different accounts makes it difficult to gain an accurate understanding of women's experiences in military aviation.

This chapter discusses research that has captured the lived experiences of female military pilots in the Australian Navy, Army and Air Force, and contributes their voices to the growing dialogue on gender in military aviation and other non-traditional employment fields. As an actively serving officer in the Australian Air Force, my insider status has afforded me access to participants that has been denied to researchers in the past. My researcher positioning as a feminist sociologist enables the experiences of Australian military female pilots to be shared, in their own voices, for the first time. This chapter and the empirical data used throughout sit within the context of a much broader research project addressing women's under-representation in military aviation from a range of perspectives.

Theoretical Perspective

The broader research project sits firmly within a feminist epistemology. While there are divergent views regarding what constitutes modern feminism (or feminisms), there are common threads that unify feminists as both theorists and activists. One of the major premises of all forms of feminism is that 'traditional accounts of socio-political life are prejudicial to women' (Gatens, 1991, p. 1), which is supported by an underlying belief that gender is socially constructed rather than biologically pre-determined (Sprague, 2005). Feminist research is usually conducted for women rather than about women (Hesse-Biber and Yaiser, 2004) and has an overarching commitment to take action to remedy women's disadvantages (Morawski, 1997).

Discussion of cultural barriers is framed around Kanter's seminal 1977 'perceptual phenomena' theory, which remains an authoritative theory for studies of organisational dynamics in workplaces with minority groups of workers. Kanter's theory discusses the dynamics of groups with different numerical constructs. Female pilots fall into a 'skewed group', where they comprise less than 15 per cent of the workforce. A skewed group is comprised of 'dominants' and 'tokens'. With Australian Defence Force (ADF) female pilot ratios at less than three per cent, they are clearly tokens according to this theoretical position, with such low representation rendering them 'virtually alone' (Kanter, 1977, p. 968).

Kanter's theory describes the interaction dynamics of skewed groups, describing three 'perceptual phenomena' – visibility, boundary heightening and assimilation – as expected responses by dominant groups to the tokens in their midst. Kanter notes that these perceptions 'determine the interaction dynamics … and create the pressures dominants impose on tokens'. This study ascertains the degree to which this 1977 theory is pertinent to female pilots in the ADF.

Theoretical perspectives on women in non-traditional employment have illuminated this analysis, providing a helpful point of comparison across other highly masculine fields, including Andrew (2009), Bagilhole (2002, 2006), Bennett et al. (1999), Bennett (2006), Gale (1994), Powell et al. (2006), Whittock (2000, 2002) and Williams (1989). Past studies of the barriers and challenges facing female pilots in other contexts have enabled an assessment of whether barriers identified here are unique to Australian military aviation or are prevalent in other aviation contexts. Neal-Smith and Cockburn's examination of cultural sexism in the UK airline industry (2004) and Davey's study about human factors on civilian flight training *ab initio* (2004) show significant similarities with the findings from this project. Mitchell et al.'s cross-national study (2005) provides insights into Australian male pilot's perceptions of their female colleagues that certainly resonate with findings from this study.

Method

Feminist principles were adhered to at all stages of this research. Semi-structured interviews were selected to empower respondents to construct data about their lives through creating the personal, empathic connections that are a defining feature of feminist research (Reinharz, 1992). Women's voices, captured through the interview process, have driven the research; their concerns, thoughts and feelings were of paramount importance at all stages. The data reflects only women's perspectives; as noted previously, male pilots' perspectives have been thoroughly documented in other sociological studies.

The findings reflected in this chapter were extracted from a larger study of female pilots across all aviation contexts. Forty-six Australian military pilots, past, present and future (i.e. students undertaking pilot training), contributed their stories to this study, through 40–90-minute interviews held between 2009 and 2011. Pilots were recruited to this study via informal emails and snowball recruiting, where interviewees invited other women in their piloting to participate. Initial emails were sent from my university address and did not identify me as a military officer in order to avoid anyone feeling obliged to participate. I did mention my military status prior to each interview, as required by ethical governance.

To equalise the status between interviewer and interviewee (a hallmark of feminist research), interviews were, where possible, conducted away from the workplace, sometimes over a shared meal or drinks in a restaurant or bar. Interviews were very relaxed and informal in order to create the intimacy and rapport so necessary to encouraging open, free-flowing conversation. Interviews followed a loose, semi-structured format, detailing early life and family construct, upbringing, schooling, alternative career preferences, motivation to fly and other aspects of participants' personal and professional lives.

Data used in this chapter was garnered through open questions about working and training experiences, such as: 'Can you tell me about your experiences as a pilot?' Some women needed little encouragement to speak openly about their lives and experiences, while others required promoting through open questions. Questions were carefully constructed so as not to meet any predefined outcomes. For example, questions like 'what barriers did you face in your training?' were strictly avoided, as the question presumes the existence of barriers. Hypothesis-free questions were important to ensuring that all responses were freely given in accordance with the principles of grounded theory research (Charmaz, 2006).

Interviews were digitally recorded, listened to once, transcribed, de-identified, analysed and coded using a grounded approach (Strauss and Corbin, 1997), where themes and sub-themes were identified and grouped. Themes around cultural barriers and challenges provide the basis for the discussion in this chapter. Data and themes were shared with a number of pilots/former pilots as a means of creating ownership of the data collected (Reinharz, 1992), as well as ensuring that the findings resonated with women who actually 'living the experiences' under discussion. The synergies between research outcomes and Kanter's theoretical framework were only identified after the coding was complete and I began referencing my findings against other studies of women in non-traditional fields.

Brief pilot descriptions have been attached to the quotes used in this chapter. Where interviewees did not succeed in military flying training or voluntarily sought an alternative career, they are referenced as 'former trainee'. Where pilots have left the ADF, they are described as 'former Air Force (AF) or ADF pilots'. AF is specified in the quotes, but Navy and Army pilots are generically referenced as 'ADF' to avoid compromising women's identities, as they are so few in number. All names have been changed. 'Junior' denotes less than six years of post-training flying experience.

Context

To situate readers, this section provides a brief overview of the Australian military aviation context. ADF pilot selection is highly competitive. Candidates must meet high standards in mental acuity, hand-eye coordination and academic ability in order to be selected. Trainees are usually under 23 years of age, with minimal life experience beyond the military. The initial phase of flying training is at Tamworth (Basic Flight Training School (BFTS)) and pilots may commence their training with former coursemates from one of the military colleges or be placed on a course with peers who are unknown to them.

Most courses will have few women trainees, if any at all. All key leadership and instructional roles are currently undertaken by men, with the exception of the BFTS psychologist. The course is deliberately insular; trainees eat, study, socialise and live together for the duration of their course. Flying training is extremely expensive and in such a small Defence Force, with minimal room for aircraft wastage, highly skilled pilots are a critical capability requirement. As such, only the most skilled trainees, capable of learning at an accelerated pace, can progress. Fifty per cent course failure rates are common; students unable to cope with the training's intensity and performance pressured are quickly 'scrubbed' from training.

Army pilots graduate from 1FTS to rotary conversion. For Navy and Air Force pilots, the next stage of training takes place in Western Australia and focuses on flying jets (2 Flight Training School, or 2FTS). Navy graduates proceed to rotary wing conversion. Air Force graduates of 2FTS are ranked in order of skill; the highest ranked pilots may have an option of fast jet conversion, while others are posted to a range of different flying squadrons to continue their training. Current platforms encompass large, medium and small transport/cargo, maritime patrol, refuelling/multi-role tankers and airborne early warning and combat.

Barriers and Challenges

The one key factor unifying all pilots and trainees interviewed in this study is their absolute love of and passion for flying. For most, becoming a pilot fulfilled their long-held childhood dream and they have worked for most of their teenage and adult lives to achieve that dream. Flying seems more of an *obsession* than a *profession* to pilots and, as such, this is not an easy career aspiration to dismiss, irrespective of the challenges that might emerge along the way. Pilots absolutely love flying and will stop at nothing to remain airborne in a career they have worked incredibly hard to achieve:

> I love my job at the moment … being a pilot in the Air Force is the best job in the world. (Erica, AF pilot)

It is this enduring passion for flying that enables female pilots to succeed in their chosen profession, despite encountering significant gender-based challenges along the way. The majority of pilots interviewed in this study cited at least a few gender-based challenges, although a small number of pilots did not observe any barriers at all. The pilots unable to cite any gender-based challenges attributed their success to being 'lucky', and luck does seem to play a critical role in women's success, especially in the flying training context. Being placed on a course with mature and welcoming peers, or with close friends from previous training contexts (such as the Australian Defence Force Academy or Royal Military College), makes an enormous difference to women's acceptance by the dominant group.

Beyond luck, women best able to 'perform masculinity', either naturally or as a deliberate integration strategy, are likely to experience fewer barriers than those who can't or won't. Women's overall acceptance into aviation contexts is perhaps slowed by their enduringly low numbers and the very poor retention of female pilots; as such, few female pilots means that each new recruit remains a 'pioneer' in most military aviation contexts. Loneliness was a recurring theme through many interviews, as female pilots in Defence have very few female role models and peers.

Until this study, female pilots' gender-based barriers were largely unknown outside those personally facing them. Women who fight for acceptance and work to become fully fledged members of the team are highly unlikely to ever share their struggles with other military personnel and especially not their superiors. A number of women spoke of finding our interview 'cathartic' and 'a bit like therapy'. For many women, this was the first time they could speak of their lives without judgement or possible consequences with an empathetic military listener.

This invoked some unexpected reactions, including women choosing to speak about traumatic past experiences, sometimes for the first time.

Visibility

> I wish we had as many women as men … because then each one wouldn't be unique, a cause celebre. (Senior pilot, quoted in Gandt, 1997, p. 35)

Visibility is an issue for women who work in non-traditional roles, with Whittock (2000), Bagilhole (2002) and Zimmer (1988) all noting the consequences of being a highly visible woman in workplaces dominated by men. 'Capturing a larger awareness share' (Whittock, 2000, p. 177) was an issue for military pilots throughout all career stages, but most predominantly during training and in early career postings. Pilots spoke of being the subject of intense scrutiny, but not in a positive way. As Kelly, a more senior ADF pilot succinctly phrased it: 'You're not a highlight, but you're highlighted, do you know what I mean?'

Where visibility may be an annoyance or mild frustration in some work contexts, for pilots, it may have tangible consequences on achieving their flying dream. There is an adage in military training that if you can't be one of the 'high flyers', you need to be the 'grey-man', a gendered term which means 'fly below the radar' and try to pass training without drawing attention to yourself. For female pilots, it is impossible to be 'grey' from the outset; they are such a small minority, their female voices are obvious on the radio and their mistakes are the source of ongoing discussion:

> Pretty much every girl that I know tries to be the grey man and it's impossible. So you have saddled yourself with failure straight away. (Grace, junior ADF pilot)

> I mean all your mistakes on the radio and stuff was always very obvious, there was no hiding. (Lisa, former AF pilot)

> As a girl I felt you were talked about more, your mistakes were noticed more. If a guy made a mistake it would be forgotten the next day, but mine would be brought up 10 years later, you know and I've forgotten about it. (Margaret, former AF pilot)

Such intense scrutiny can be very damaging to self-confidence, adding additional pressure to an already intense course. Kerryn, a young woman who was unsuccessful through military flying training, attributed this intense scrutiny to her losing confidence, ultimately resulting in failing the pilot's course. Although she has forged a successful piloting career outside Defence, she still struggles with the confidence issues she attributes to her military flying training experiences.

Gossip and Rumours

Their rareness, coupled with the incestuous nature of military flying, means female pilots' social lives, relationships and piloting skills are an ongoing source of fascination. Nearly all pilots and trainees are the subject of much (usually inaccurate) gossip pertaining to their flying abilities, sexual escapades, romantic relationships and daily activities. This degree of intense scrutiny was dismissed by some as an expected consequence of being a woman pilot, whilst others found the gossip to be yet another stressor in an already stressful occupation:

> Your personal and professional life is so intertwined it's not funny ... unfortunate. You can't just fly. You can't just get on with the job and do what you need to do. (Andrea, junior ADF pilot)

> But anyway, so I actually found it quite difficult on course because a lot of the guys were talking behind my back ... [Q: About you?] Yeah, being one of the only females, in a sexual connotation ... that put a great deal of strain on ... (Bianca, AF pilot)

> Rumours for every girl, and I knew that ... When I realised there were rumours about me it was almost ... but why, I haven't done anything? ... There's nothing that you can do as a person to prevent it. (Grace, ADF pilot)

Beyond the standard negative connotations brought about by rumours and gossip, in Defence it may result in a formal investigation and possibly disciplinary action. Margie spoke of the indignity of being formally investigated on the basis of untrue rumours about her being promiscuous whilst on a deployment overseas – gossip that was utterly unfounded, as proven through the investigation. Margie certainly was not alone in enduring an investigation or being punished on the basis of untrue rumours. Andrea notes that men are not afforded the same treatment.

> ... if you're single and you sleep with someone, oh my God! I have been dragged in going you shouldn't be sleeping with him. The guy doesn't get treated like that. Not a hope in hell. (Andrea, ADF student pilot)

Pilots' social lives and informal interactions are the source of valuable information-sharing and team bonding. During flying training, some women found they were unable to have drinks and socialise with male instructors without incurring gossip and accusations of 'sleeping your way through the course'. Missing these social interactions can be detrimental to their training experience, as women are unable to benefit from the much-needed 'bar side advice' afforded to their male peers. This also impacts the male instructors, who are also justifiably wary of incurring gossip. This wariness from both women and instructors can impact female pilots' training experience:

> I came here initially, was, you know, with instructors talking to me, they had 10 minutes and then they had to go. It was like, I was walking sexual harassment claim, like it looked like that, every now and then I felt that people were just 'no, I can't be seen with a girl for too long'. (Peta, AF student pilot)

> One of the big things I found … is the friendship male students develop with male instructors. They bond and build these great relationships that us girls can just never have. It's a real disadvantage. If you're too friendly or if others see you get on with instructors, there will be rumours. (Carmel, former ADF trainee)

Performance Pressures

Beyond gossip, another common consequence of heightened visibility is the performance pressure placed on token women (Bagilhole, 2002; Hogue and Yoder, 2006; Rabe-Hemp, 2008). In an already intense learning context, additional performance pressures are yet another impediment to women succeeding:

> I find being the girly thing, it just destroys my confidence to the point you don't perform. It was, and I don't know how you find, to get through that, I don't know how. (Leslie, junior ADF pilot)

> You've got to be better. Even if you only have one screw-up, you're stuffed … you have to fly harder, fly better, not allowed to screw-up. (Andrea, ADF student pilot)

A number of pilots spoke of 'scraping through' 2FTS towards the lower end of the graduation order, with their confidence being dashed in the process. Some women took many years to rebuild the confidence lost through their flying training and early career. Does this pressure stem solely from being a woman or, rather, an inability to 'perform masculinity'? Interviewees reported that many men, somehow deemed 'less masculine' or 'different' by the dominant group, are often subject to similar pressures. One interviewee was grateful to have an effeminate man on her pilot's course, as he attracted the bullying and harassment that would normally be levelled at her (he ultimately failed the course). Harriet described similar treatment being levelled at a colleague:

> There's a guy at work at the moment … he's not deemed as suitable by those people who deem people as suitable … So they just don't get him so therefore, they don't want him … his confidence has just eroded … you know, a few little egotistical blokes felt challenged by him and how much he did know and had to take him apart. (Harriet, junior AF pilot)

How many highly competent and capable pilots, both men and women, have been 'taken apart' and had their flying dreams dashed due to their inability to 'perform masculinity' in the way expected by their flying peers?

One of the Boys?

In highly masculinised environments, women are 'forced to make severely constrained choices between accommodation and resistance', which requires 'taking on, to the extent possible, the attributes of their male colleagues' (Britton, 2000, p. 427). Numerous studies describe the efforts women make to *limit visibility* by blending into masculinised cultures (Chusmir, 1983; Gale, 1994; Robinson and McIlwee, 1991). Reimer (1979) and Yount (1991) found that 'tomboys' were the most likely to gain acceptance in the highly masculinised workplaces studied through their research.

The same is also true of military aviation; pilots who were most accepted by their colleagues were those women best able to 'perform masculinity'. For some women, being 'one of the boys' is their natural, preferred state; they proudly describe themselves as 'tomboys', prefer the company of men to women and enjoy operating in male domains:

> I have an older brother, and sort of grew up around a lot of boys … I wouldn't necessarily call myself a tomboy, but I'm very comfortable with guys and interacting with them. (Irene, junior AF pilot)

> Yeah. I was one of the boys … I didn't have a bad relationship with any of the guys. And I ended up being, one of the guys at my pilots' course, his best man at his wedding. (Renee, ADF pilot)

> Well, I think I probably managed a bit easier because I wasn't a girly-girl from my childhood doing all my soccer and running and stuff. I think that I just kind of fit in with the boys, as one of the boys, I guess. (Anne, junior ADF pilot)

Others had to work harder at performing masculinity, making a conscious decision to adapt to the masculine context, but not necessarily enjoying taking on what was for them an unnatural persona. Women employed a wide range of strategies to fit in, but did not always relish being in 'disguise':

> I changed my gestures. When you sit, when you talk, the way you gesticulate, the way you slide your shoulders, the way you go drinking, the way you slap somebody's back … I behaved as if I was a boy. I drank with the boys, I out-drank them, I played sport with them, team sports, touch footy and as much as I hated it … I did it. (Grace, junior ADF pilot)

The inability to adopt of masculine façade was cited by Cindy as a key reason why women might struggle during flying training:

> … they don't have the knowhow, they haven't learnt to put on that façade … being one of the boys, fitting in with the boys, all of that sort of stuff … I think

> that is one thing that makes pilot's course more – more challenging for the girls 'cause they're also trying to learn what personality they need to make it. (Cindy, ADF pilot)

The degree to which women adapt to their masculine context may seem extreme, but assimilation was cited by numerous pilots as absolutely essential to succeeding in aviation, especially during training:

> If you can't assimilate, then you stand out like dog's balls. And that's not what you want. You want to assimilate with those boys so that you're part of the group because … if you can't assimilate, you don't get help and you're not going to pass. (Cindy, ADF pilot)

> It's very much a man's world. It's almost like you pretend to be man, so like you have to be one of the boys. If you're not one of the boys, you don't make it. (Lilly, junior ADF pilot)

Some interviewees didn't assimilate and still managed to pass their flying training, but for others, failure to assimilate had dream-ending consequences. Carmel directly attributed her gender-based inability to assimilate as a primary factor impacting her inability to succeed in training. Perhaps the experiences of Carmel and numerous other women who were unsuccessful at flying training might explain women's comparatively lower success rates at both BFTS and 2FTS:

> The guys who weren't welcoming, I had to live with and see around, it was a constant discomfort … I feel like I'm living in a foster home and my adopted parents don't want me. I just don't belong. And the feeling is unrelenting, you get no break. It is where you work, where you live, where you eat … it just feels like a constant fight, and you just get sick of having to fight all the time when men around you are having a ball. (Carmel, former ADF trainee)

Acker notes the struggles faced by women when attempting to adapt to the dominant culture: 'women's bodies cannot be adapted to hegemonic masculinity; to function at the top of male hierarchies requires that women render irrelevant everything that makes them women' (1990, p. 153). True to Acker's theory, women who did manage to 'perform masculinity', assimilate and succeed by altering their natural state and pretending to be 'one of the boys' found the experience absolutely exhausting. Interviewees spoke of feeling emotionally drained, confused about their identity and 'lost' at different time during their career. Many also spoke regretfully of repressing their femininity and actively mourned their lost years of womanhood:

> I think what – the negative of that is how unbalancing it is to being a whole person. So how do you balance that? I don't know. (Pauline, junior AF pilot)

> I became extremely masculine trying to fit in … and I found in the end I was actually quite empty. I didn't know what that emptiness was and it was because I wasn't balancing it with my femininity. (Bianca, AF pilot)

> … you miss out on becoming a girl, if that makes sense. Like, you … all the things that you would normally learn and talk about with other girls as you're growing up … just as you're, sort of, growing up and developing as a young woman. I, kind of, missed all that because I was hanging out with guys. (Jen, junior AF pilot)

Being deprived of women's company during their formative adult years further impacted some pilots' emotional development; one pilot described this as 'being stunted' in her journey to womanhood. This overt suppression of femininity created something of a backlash in some women as they gained confidence and started to feel more secure in themselves. A number of women spoke of their strong need to express overt femininity and of becoming 'girlier' to counter the masculinity so prevalent in their early years of flying:

> I used to be [one of the boys] but I think as time went on, I just rebelled against it more and more because I was so sick of it, yep. I have definitely gotten girlier and girlier. (Margie, junior ADF pilot)

As well as feeling more comfortable with overt displays of femininity, as women grew in experience, confidence and credibility, they also felt less compelled to assimilate; their need to be 'one of the boys' lessened once they felt more comfortable saying 'no' to the dominant majority:

> I think now that I'm older, that's not so much of an issue, 'cause it's not the same anymore. I go home on Friday night, I don't need to be one of the boys … I think you reach a point when you're like, 'I don't need to be one of the boys anymore'. And for me now I don't. (Erica, AF pilot)

> … they'd say, 'Come on let's go, let's go', and I'd say, 'no, this is – this is going to be a boys' night I'm not coming'. And I just started detaching myself from trying to be one of the boys, which was the way I thought I had to be … and it just made life so much easier. (Isobelle, ADF pilot)

Extension of Consequences

A number of women confirmed another consequence of visibility, the 'extension of consequences', where tokens are expected to carry 'the burden of representing their category' (Kanter, 1977, p. 973). Interviewees believed their failures would be attributable to all other female pilots and vice versa, creating even more performance pressure in already pressurised contexts. Women felt compelled to prove themselves, not only for their own reputation, but also for the reputation of female pilots generally. For this reason, less competent pilots were very much resented for 'giving all of us a bad name'. This extension of consequences could also work in female pilots' favour, as interviewees who followed well-respected female pilots into squadrons noted far fewer issues with being accepted and having to prove their competence.

Unwelcome

Performance pressures are exacerbated by an unwelcoming culture. Female pilots have proven themselves in a range of aviation contexts, excelling in both military and civilian flying endeavours (Gilmartin, 1992; Grant, 2002; Haynsworth and Toomey, 1998; Pateman, 1997), yet some men remain overtly sceptical regarding women's flying abilities. Generalisations about women's flying ability or expressing a belief that women do not belong in military aviation are exceptionally jarring when coming from men in positions of power as flying instructors or senior staff:

> … there were a few older instructors … one particular one; I think he is still there and every girl who has flown with him has had problems and he has said that girls are not meant to fly. (Grace, junior ADF pilot)

> 'I don't want her down here at the squadron taking a place of someone that can actually do the job'. He goes, 'I don't want to fly with her', and all this sort of shit. And he stood up in front of the CO [Commanding Officer] and said that at morning brief in front of 100 people. (Tara, AF pilot)

Davey and Davidson's study of commercial aviation also detected an overt negativity towards female pilots, with men pilots 'openly admitted hating female pilots' and being 'consistently difficult with female pilots' (2000, p. 214). While it is difficult to determine the impact of male pilots' negative views on women's ability to succeed in aviation, when critics hold instructing, testing or leadership positions, fair and impartial treatment seems most unlikely.

Downplaying Competence

Tokens can be subjected to another form of visibility pressure – avoiding 'making the dominants look bad' (Kanter, 1977, p. 974). Female pilots suffer the paradox of having to be 'that bit quicker, that bit harder, that bit faster' (Mindy, junior ADF pilot) to be deemed competent, whilst possibly suffering the negative consequences of outshining dominants. Nowhere is this more acutely felt than during military pilot training, where men's masculinity and pride can be diminished by high-flying women:

> Yeah, but most of the young guys on course were okay. But they hate … a girl doing better than them. (Lisa, former AF pilot)

In his study of hegemonic masculinity in the US Navy, Barrett ponders the following question: 'if gruelling tests separate the men from the boys, what does it mean if women can pass them?' (1996, p. 133). It seems that high-performing female pilots must be put in their place. Numerous pilots highlighted the threat attached to doing well:

> I think a lot of the reason why the alpha male, the guys like that, do that [sexually harass women] … it's 'cause they're so threatened by the fact that they've got a girl there that can actually do the same as they can. (Ellie, ADF pilot)

To avoid outshining dominants and fearing retaliation (Kanter, 1977), some women actively and deliberately downplayed their flying success:

> A lot of the guys would come back and brag, so as a girl if you come back and say, 'Honestly, I stuffed this up or I stuffed that up', none of the guys would say that. (Bianca, AF pilot)

Where men would brag about an 'awesome flight' (even if it wasn't!), female pilots remained quiet about their successes and kept tendencies towards overt confidence in check. Pauline even spoke of counselling another pilot to downplay her confidence to minimise a backlash from men who might feel threatened.

Unfortunately, in a context where overt confidence and machismo are rewarded in men, downplaying ability can result in women being viewed as less than adequate by their superiors and peers. This situation is not unique to pilots, with Kimmel observing a similar lose-lose dilemma in military cadets (2000, p. 504). Interviewees spoke of being told to 'grow some balls' and 'be more aggressive' in response to their perceived under confidence. One wonders if Australia's inability to produce a single woman fast-jet pilot might be partially attributed to their inability or unwillingness to demonstrate overt confidence, a key selection criterion for fighter pilots.

Sexual Harassment

A number of high-performing, self-assured and outwardly confident pilots found themselves diminished through insidious means, including harassment, bullying and in extreme cases assault. Research offers some explanations for this behaviour, noting the link between men's masculinity, paid work and the significant threat to their masculinity when outperformed by women (Cockburn, 1985). Sexual harassment enables men to 'reassert dominance and control over women colleagues who would otherwise be their equals' (Bagilhole, 2002, p. 126), cutting 'emergent and potentially powerful women down to size by sexual means' (Cockburn, 1991, p. 141). Burton notes that 'the fact that the presence of women constitutes a threat to "manhood" is a frequent theme in the literature on the military' (Burton, 1996, p. ES-10). There are also 'psychological rewards' associated with harassing women en masse as a form of 'fraternity and solidarity' bonding, especially in male-dominated contexts (Chamberlain et al., 2008).

Further supporting this literature, a number of pilots shared heartbreaking stories of harassment and assault in various aviation contexts. Incidents were particularly prevalent during flying training. The women who seemed to suffer the most abject forms of physical and psychological abuse were the most competent pilots, with perpetrators tending to be 'alpha males' who were struggling themselves. Sexual abuse was used as a means of diminishing powerful women to protect men's fragile masculinity.

Margaret was subject to repeated episodes of abuse through her career, resulting in her leaving the Air Force as soon as her contracted period was up, despite being widely viewed as a high flyer destined for senior leadership roles. She bears the emotional scars of her time in the Air Force and became very emotional during our interview when recounting some events of her past. Andrea, Margaret and numerous other pilots noted the link between harassment and struggling men:

> I found I got the hardest time from the guys who were struggling because they just needed to take it out on somebody. Whereas the guys who were doing well just didn't have an issue with me … (Margaret, former AF pilot)

> You really have to have a degree in psychology to understand how the alpha male ego actually works to be able to try and pat the ego and make sure you don't get in the firing range of it because, quite frankly, once you're in their line of sight, you're screwed. You're really screwed. (Andrea, ADF student pilot)

Harassment in the training context can escalate towards graduation. One interviewee was sexually assaulted on the night before her final check ride; this timing seems telling. Kerry, another successful pilot who left Defence at her earliest opportunity, described being 'close to breaking point' after experiencing severe stalking by another course member during her training. The impact of this on her performance and emotional resilience was profound; she failed her first flight during a week when the harassment escalated in frequency and severity. Through this adversity, some women do manage to pass their training, but can suffer significant emotional scarring from their past treatment.

Bullying

Bullying was far more prevalent than sexual harassment and tended to be more extreme during training and in those squadrons where the culture was hostile and unwelcoming towards women generally, not just female pilots:

> It was good flying but a horrible place to be as a girl, it was just terrible ... they [the men] were very, they were just horrible, absolutely horrible … you would go in there [the women's toilet] to cry. And [another female pilot] would be crying and I would be crying and [other female aircrew] would be crying and the other girls in there would be crying … (Leanne, AF pilot)

> ... he was just really threatened by me … one of his little followers would sit on the other side [of the desk] and throw darts at the board in between us. It would feel like he was throwing them at me. He had like this axe handle thing in the little office and they would walk in the office and pretend to hit me over the head with it. (Tania, junior AF pilot)

> Oh yeah, the guys hated me. They were trying to get me off-course … they just didn't want me there … he used to tell me stories about how all the chick pilots he ever flew with were shit, except for one. [Q. So how did you react to that?] I just tried to ignore it. It was shit. [Crying] It gets me upset all the time. (Margie, junior ADF pilot)

This small selection of stories, extracted from a larger cache, do not portray a welcoming and inclusive workplace. It is difficult to fathom how anyone succeeds in the face of such treatment. I found it extremely confronting witnessing the extent to which these incredibly strong women had been traumatised by their military experiences. Many interviewees who had experienced bullying and harassment stated they were biding their time until the end of their contractual obligation and intended to leave Defence at their earliest opportunity. This may explain female pilots' poor retention statistics, especially in the Air Force.

Non-reporting of Abuse

I questioned interviewees about why they chose not to report cases of bullying, sexual abuse and harassment when there are extensive procedures and protocols in place for dealing with such occurrences. Tania, like many of her peers, didn't report extreme harassment because she didn't want the perpetrator punished by being removed from the course:

> I didn't really let on a lot to the hierarchy, because I didn't want to be the reason that someone was scrubbed off the course. I didn't want that to happen … it's emotionally hard to talk about it now … because you try block it out a bit. I feel really sorry for that person that I was. (Tania, junior AF pilot)

Tania's desire to protect her peer from being 'scrubbed' may be difficult for non-military outsiders to understand. The *team* ethos in Defence is incredibly strong and many women in this study did not report because they want to *protect* team members, while also believing they will be held responsible if team members are punished. Interviewees had very little trust in 'the system' and felt that reporting would result in negative consequences for their own careers. There may be some truth in this, as interviewees who *did* report harassment ultimately regretted doing so due to recriminations from peers and supervisors.

Other reasons cited for non-reporting include women's strong desire for acceptance, not wanting to draw any further attention (gossip and rumours) to themselves, feeling uncomfortable reporting to an all-male command chain and believing that nobody would believe their story, especially if there was no tangible 'evidence' of an incident occurring. Women in many contexts are reluctant to report harassment (Austin, 2000; Fitzgerald et al., 1995) for similar reasons cited by women in this study.

There is hope for a brighter future. Criminal behaviours in the ADF are being actively addressed through several recent review recommendations, including the Review into the Treatment of Women in the ADF Phase 2 Report (Australian Human Rights Commission, 2012). In June 2013, the ADF will introduce a support service for victims of abuse that guarantees their anonymity until they feel ready to place a formal report. The service will also provide large-scale education reforms designed to improve ADF culture in terms of appropriate behaviours, directly targeting sexual misconduct, bullying and systemic abuse. These measures, if effective, will positively impact the culture in military aviation and the ADF more broadly.

Perceptions of Favouritism

Another masculinity-preservation technique employed by male pilots is to actively diminish the achievements of women. Many interviewees spoke of accusations of special treatment, being called 'a quota' and having any achievements (like graduating from the pilot's course or gaining captaincy) attributed to gender-based favouritism rather than their flying skill. There are even colloquial terms for this; 'tit-assist', 'playing the chick card' and 'lumpy jumper syndrome' were expressions referenced throughout this study.

> Even my first posting to a flying squadron, like I did fairly well early out and I got my aircraft Captaincy very early … it definitely started then … 'Oh you've got to have a set of boobs around here to get anywhere'. (Mia, junior ADF pilot)

> I don't think our gender helped us to succeed, but when we succeeded, that was something for the blokes to say to us, oh, you know, they call it the 'tit assist' or something. Yeah, and that was, that was prevalent. (Mia, junior ADF pilot)

Female pilots tried very hard to avoid, where possible, any action that might be perceived as preferential treatment, knowing that it would invoke resentment from their male colleagues and diminish their success. Sometimes, however, they were powerless to prevent perceptions of favouritism occurring, especially when it stemmed from their Commanding Officers or higher-ranking personnel. Pilots spoke of being selected for media opportunities, being chosen to fly high-profile officers and of generally being 'paraded around like a prize'.

Perceptions of favouritism or special treatment always invoke highly unpleasant reactions from male peers, who perhaps don't realise just how much women actively avoid being on the receiving end. Many women interviewed refuse to undertake any media activities for this reason, which certainly doesn't help with promoting piloting careers for women in Defence. The perception that female pilots have it easier than their male colleagues, even if they do attain an occasional gender-based privilege, seems difficult to fathom in the context of the research detailed in this chapter.

Barrier Heightening/Polarisation/Exaggeration of Differences

> Their space had been violated. A woman. She was the intruder, the outsider, the unwanted. (Gandt, 1997, p. 37)

Following on from visibility, Kanter's second perceptual phenomenon is polarisation or the exaggeration of differences between the token and the dominant group (1977). The aim of polarisation is to render the token isolated, whilst reinforcing the commonality between dominants. Exclusion from social gatherings, male-only sporting events, sexual innuendo, salty language and practical jokes at the token's expense (e.g. stealing women's underwear and removing toilet seats such that women cannot sit down) were common forms of polarisation found in this study.

Socialising

A number of women attempted to assimilate by ensuring they were included in any social/bonding activities, to varying degrees of success. Context makes a huge difference to women's acceptance, as does women's willingness to 'be one of the boys', which, as discussed earlier, is perceived as necessary to succeeding as a military pilot. Interviewees spoke of watching porn, attending strip clubs, playing football and engaging in other 'barrier heightening' activities orchestrated by dominants:

> So even on the weekends you live with the guys and they were gross. They were standard guys, who are watching porn when you wake up in the morning, but whatever. Like if you want to play in their domain then you have to accept that. (Ellie, ADF pilot)

Despite their best efforts to fit in and socialise with *the boys*, there were times when some women were made to feel very unwelcome, kept away from social occasions or quarantined (Kanter, 1977, p. 978). The need for all-male bonding sessions might be valid, noting that women's networks are designed to enable women to feel comfortable without the presence of men. Men may also have a need for 'all-male' bonding; however, in situations where female pilots have no social alternative, such as on deployments or trips away, their exclusion from team-activities seems pointed:

> They would just make me feel excluded. If there was something going on, on a Friday and one of my [male pilot] friends would invite me along to it they, obviously, in front of me say: 'Why'd you invite her? We don't want to see you there'. (Tania, junior AF pilot)

> Say they all decided to go out on the piss one night and don't invite you, you probably weren't going to go anyway, but if they just specifically don't invite you, you're going to feel unwelcome. You feel unwelcome, you're not going to be able to perform as well. (Mindy, junior ADF pilot)

> You get ostracised, socially, the crew would land and you would like either check into the base or at the hotel accommodation and you'd all meet up an hour later for dinner, well I would never be included in the plans ... so I'd sort of find myself going 'Oh'. And then you know, I'd go out and grab a bite to eat and they would be there. And so I'd sort of join them and I had people say women don't fly in the Air Force and they certainly don't fly in this place … and we'll do our best to get you out. (Harriet, junior AF pilot)

Margie described an incident of the most extreme isolation; as the only woman undertaking a highly sought-after conversion course, she noticed that nobody would speak to her. She eventually discovered through a so-called *friend* (who swore her to secrecy) that the entire course was holding a contest to see who could last the longest without speaking to her, led by the alpha male of the group who had played a pivotal role in her ongoing bullying and harassment. The entire group's behaviour towards one of their highly competent peers demonstrates a level of immaturity that seems unfathomable in professional pilots. Abject, intense loneliness was a prevalent theme throughout many women's descriptions of life as a military pilot.

Friendships with Men

This loneliness is exacerbated by an inability to foster friendships with men, as was the case with a small number of interviewees. Carmel spoke of the intense loneliness she experienced while on her flying course; sexual insinuations about her platonic friendship and the teasing of her male friend compromised their entire friendship. Like Margie's supposed *friend*, some men also face pressure to side with the dominants against the token or risk their own place in the male pack:

> And even then, in private, the other guys will be, 'Oh yeah, we're really sorry about that, or whatever', but they will never stand up to the other blokes. (Ellie, ADF pilot)

Many interviewees did form close, platonic and enduring friendships with men, with some female pilots even being 'best men' at the weddings of their friends. The women best able to form these friendships were those adept at 'performing masculinity' and thus able to integrate with the broader group of men. In the intense pack-mentality training context, beyond women's own agency and ability to integrate, acceptance by the alpha 'pack leader' makes an enormous difference to women's success.

Loyalty Tests

Loyalty tests are another form of barrier heightening, designed to force tokens to pledge allegiance to the dominant group by 'siding against' other tokens. Sometimes 'the price of being "one of the boys" is a willingness to turn occasionally "against the girls"' (Kanter, 1977, p. 979). The 'women-against-women' dynamic is not unusual in male-dominated workplaces (Bagilhole, 2002) as there are significant 'psychological pressures on tokens to side with the majority' (Kanter, 1977, p. 980). Female pilots on the 'inner' were sometimes expected to side with dominants to ensure their own acceptance:

> When I rocked up at [removed] squadron, I was told by the senior co-pilot there 'If you're friends with her you won't be friends with us … and it will affect your friendship with everyone else here at the squadron' … I remember just looking at this guy thinking: 'You are the biggest idiots I've ever met. I cannot believe you're sitting there threatening me not to be friends with someone'. (Tara, AF pilot)

While Tara held firm against this collusion, some pilots did express contempt towards their flying female colleagues, denigrating their character, flying skills, morals and personalities. Younger pilots, still fighting for acceptance and working through complex negotiations of femininity, seemed more inclined to speak negatively about their aviatrix peers. More mature, experienced pilots seemed more willing to actively champion female pilots, highlight their positive traits and stand up for others and also themselves when publicly denigrated. They also became more willing to call out poor behaviour:

> But I think we established early on where the line was … when I first started, I usually would always back down because I figured that I didn't have the experience. I hadn't been in for that long, and all that sort of stuff. So it wasn't my place to do that. But as soon as I got to a point where I felt comfortable and

> was that, I could just go: 'Right, no, that's it. You're out. This is how it's going to be'. (Ellie, ADF pilot)

A number of interviewees spoke of wanting to share their lessons learned with younger female pilots in order to help them to avoid some of the mistakes they had made in their own early flying years. Throughout this research, I detected a tangible and growing sense of 'sisterhood' across the female pilots' network, primarily driven by more experienced pilots actively seeking to make aviation culture more inclusive for women.

Self-degradation

Tokens can also side with dominant groups by making derogatory, humorous remarks about their own ability and the ability of other tokens (Kanter, 1977). There was little direct evidence of this perceptual phenomena through the empirical data; however, sometime after our interview, a senior pilot emailed a photo of an embroidered flying suit patch that had been created by a group of female pilots to wear on their flying suits or sport bags.

The patch said 'No Longer the Cockpit, Welcome to the Box Office' and the emblem was of two movie tickets saying 'Admit One'. I found this difficult to process from a feminist perspective. Were pilots actively reclaiming the term 'box-office' ('box' being a slang term for female genitalia, and the source of many 'cockpit' jokes aimed at female pilots) in the same way that feminists have reclaimed the word 'slut' through organisations such as Slutwalk? Was this women banding together, showing overt unity through standard military banter? Or, more insidiously, was this a crude, sexually charged ('admit one') means of siding with dominants through self-degrading humour? The patch polarised female pilots; it was enthusiastically embraced by some as a show of humorous unity and 'giving as good as we get', but rejected by others who found it demeaning and inappropriate.

Role Entrapment or 'Gender-Appropriate' Social Roles

Kanter's last perceptual phenomenon is *assimilation*, which 'involves the stereotypes or familiar generalisations about a person's social type' (1977, p. 971). One form of assimilation is 'status levelling', where women are assumed to belong to more gender-appropriate roles, for example, doctors being mistaken for nurses. While commercial pilots interviewed for the wider study were often assumed to be cabin crew, this rarely happened to military pilots. This could be because the military flying suit pilot brevet is so distinguishable or, perhaps more realistically, because their extreme visibility means they are very widely known across the ADF and thus unlikely to mistaken for a non-pilot.

Far more common was another form of assimilation called 'role entrapment', where women are categorised into gender-appropriate 'female caricature roles' and are treated accordingly (Kanter, 1977). There was ample evidence of three of Kanter's four roles in this study: mother, seductress and iron maiden. There was no data suggesting the 'pet' role is prevalent in military aviation; however, an unexpected fifth role, which I have termed 'mob wife', was overwhelmingly prevalent in the data. This new role may be worthy of further investigation by researchers addressing other fields of non-traditional employment.

Mothers/Sisters

Some pilots who were viewed as sexually unavailable (perhaps because they were married or engaged) or were slightly older than their colleagues found themselves cast in the role of 'mother' or 'older sister'. Mothers/sisters were required to provide emotional support, advice and reassurance to their male colleagues at all levels of the organisation:

> I found the biggest thing is that the guys … the guys would use you for all sorts of advice. I feel like a Dear Ellie column … [laughs]. (Ellie, ADF pilot)

Adopting this role is not problematic in and of itself; however, similar to Davey's study, where 'despite being isolated and unsupported themselves, women are expected to meet the emotional needs of their male colleagues' (2004, p. 644), interviewees found the emotional support so willingly extended to male colleagues was rarely reciprocated:

> And they'll accept that you want to listen to them because you're a girl, but they won't accept the fact that you need to speak to them, to unload stuff that they're not even going to listen about. (Cindy, ADF pilot)

> I had been there emotionally for a bunch of them for stuff that happened. They came and sat in my room and had a teary, and the ones that I thought I had a good friendship with, turned out to be useless in providing support when I needed it … (Pauline, junior Air Force pilot)

The lack of reciprocation invoked anger in some interviewees. Younger pilots valued their confidante advice-giving as a means of gaining acceptance and forging a bond with their colleagues. As women became more experienced and self-confident, they grew increasingly tired of not receiving emotional support themselves. When they reached this point, their enthusiasm for providing womanly counsel and playing 'agony aunt' waned considerably. Female pilots want to be seen as legitimate equals, seeking acceptance and respect on the basis of their flying skill and contribution to airpower, not as emotional care-givers.

Seductress

Perhaps the most common gender stereotype detected in the data was Kanter's 'seductress' or 'sexual object'. Women inadvertently stereotyped into this role can be rewarded for their *femaleness*, but if their attentions are cast too widely, may become Freudian whores to the more motherly Madonnas (Kanter, 1977). As stated previously, if perceived as 'sexually available', female pilots become a source of rumours regarding their sexual exploits, whether true or otherwise. Pilots spoke of denying themselves possible relationships in order to protect their reputations, but to little effect; they were gossiped about anyway:

> I think I was a lot more careful than I would have liked to have been in my life. I would have liked to have had more fun if you understand what I'm saying [laughs]. But I was – I worked really hard to not get a bad reputation because I know some of the girls have had bad reputations and so I kept myself clean and just didn't want anyone to have anything to talk about me. (Margaret, former AF pilot)

Margaret's statement 'I kept myself clean' infers that to have sex is to be dirty, a perception perhaps reinforced through a culture constantly denigrating any woman who may be sexually active. Kanter's theory notes that for attractive women stereotyped as seductresses, 'men may adopt the role of protector', which serves to 'put up further barriers to a solitary women's full acceptance' (1977, p. 983). Pilots certainly spoke of being 'owned' by the group of dominants, who decided 'their woman' was in need of protection from other men:

> Yeah and so the other guys wouldn't have let me talk to anybody else out in public anyway because they would look after me … (Nelly, junior ADF pilot)

> Yeah, I was definitely included [in social activities], but it was definitely known that I was sort of owned, you know what I mean. (Bianca, AF pilot)

> So no one messed with me. I'd be out, and if anyone came up to me, they would deal with it … I would then be looked after by everybody on my crew and no one went near me. (Tara, former AF pilot)

Some women felt quite proud of their protected status, viewing this as the ultimate sign of acceptance. Nevertheless, being in need of protection does not suggest *equal* status within the group. *Protecting* may indeed be a *gentlemanly*, brotherly gesture, showing inclusion towards their female peers, but in the context of other empirical data and Kanter's assertions, this could also be another means of diminishing tokens. Playing protector allows men to assert their manly strength and masculine dominance by 'looking after' the weak, fragile woman.

Iron Maidens

Women inducted into this caricature role were certainly not in need of or desirous of men's protection and would likely never be offered it; men would not dare even try! 'Iron maidens' (Kanter, 1977, p. 983) are afforded the most professional respect in the military aviation context, as they demonstrate the tough, emotionless, cool persona that is so highly valued. This differs somewhat from Davey's study of the commercial aviation training context, where the more feminine pilots were viewed more positively than women who did not conform to female stereotypes (2004). In military aviation, strong, forthright women who patently refuse to adopt more feminine stereotypes are rewarded with respect and sometimes awe by both men and female pilots alike:

> … the guys already have a view of her [another female pilot], you know, they respect her. It's very different. They respect her because she, you know, she comes across as cold and blunt and she will tell them, you know, in no two ways … so therefore they don't mess with her, they don't stuff around with her. (Mindy, junior ADF pilot)

Interviewees respectfully described 'iron maidens' as 'not taking any shit from the boys' while also being 'one of the boys'. It seems that women in this category are those quite proficient at 'performing masculinity' (Cross and Bagilhole, 2002) and, like the women in Kanter's original study, were stereotyped as perhaps being tougher and more militant than they actually were (1977). Some of the women in this category, perhaps due to minimising their sexual availability and adopting masculine traits, were also branded 'lesbians' or 'butch':

> So I always was in control of myself … so yes, some of the boys would go hey … even at some stage there was this perception that I might be a dyke. (Grace, junior ADF pilot)

> They thought I was gay to start off with because I cut my hair short [both laugh]. (Andrea, ADF student pilot)

Interviewees seemed largely ambivalent regarding false rumours about their sexuality and accepted this as a consequence of maintaining their sexless persona. They did, however, express enormous pressure to maintain their 'hard arse' image, lest they lose the respect of other pilots. Tears and/or other emotional (womanly) reactions were absolutely unacceptable; pilots described techniques they and other women used to hide any 'weaknesses' from their colleagues. The women's bathrooms in some flying squadrons hold many secrets.

Mob Wife

While women readily spoke of being tough, feeling sexualised and providing emotional support to men, there was no evidence of Kanter's fourth role: the 'pet', mascot or 'cute amusing little thing' (Kanter, 1977, p. 983). A fifth category did emerge clearly, though – the role of being 'married to the mob' or, in shortened form, 'mob wife'. A woman could only be inducted into this privileged role by marrying a male pilot.

Mob wives were afforded respectful treatment and equal-peer status, irrespective of how they had been perceived or treated prior to their marriage. Anne, a junior ADF pilot, experienced virtually no gender-based issues throughout her career, which she attributed to being 'Married and into boy stuff [laughs]'. Marrying a pilot was cited as a turning point for many interviewees; this role seemingly enabled them to escape the shackles of any gender roles that had plagued them previously:

> Oh, I don't care anymore. Like I don't [laugh] ... it was more difficult ... now that I'm married it's easier. (Anne, AF pilot)

> Because I said, 'How did you deal with this [gossip and rumours]?' … and she [another female pilot] goes, 'Oh, it all got better once me and [a male pilot] got together, and then it was all fine'. (Margie, junior ADF pilot)

> I was married by then as well. And I think it does sort of help once you're married, especially if you marry a pilot … (Gen, former AF pilot)

This data might suggest that marriage itself is the panacea, as it removes any 'seductress' role issues pertaining to sexual availability, thus allowing 'safe' relationships to occur between men and women. However, women married to non-pilots did not experience the same level of acceptance. Unrelated focus groups held with AF women in other non-traditional employment roles also demonstrated this finding; fire-fighters, technicians and police women married to men from the same profession experienced far greater acceptance than unmarried women or those who were married 'outside the mob'.

I initially hypothesised that perhaps marriage was the ultimate form of acceptance by a dominant group member, thus formally confirming a woman's status as 'insider'. However, when discussing this finding outside the parameters of this research project, some male pilot friends speculated that the finding was probably more attributable to female pilots being afforded a status held by all pilots' wives. Squadron code mandates that pilots look after each other's partners and families, due to the nature of operational flying and military service. While I remain unsure as to which explanation is correct, the 'mob wife' finding warrants further exploration in other non-traditional occupations outside the close-knit military context. Do women firefighters married to other firefighters also experience enhanced levels of acceptance?

Issues with Gender-Appropriate Roles

Most interviewees accepted the gender-appropriate roles they were stereotyped into, or had stereotyped themselves into, as an expected part of working in a non-traditional role. As Kanter observes, 'it is often easier to accept stereotyped roles than to fight them' (1977, p. 984). Unfortunately, conforming to gender-appropriate stereotypes, however benign or inoffensive, means that women can never be accepted just as pilots and equals. If women are typecast into caricatured roles, they remain 'othered' and will never be valued as legitimate and equal peers, judged in the context of their competence as pilots and military officers. A frustrated Andrea expressed this so very succinctly:

> ... you're either a bitch or a slut. Choose one. Unfortunate. You can't just fly. You can't just get on with the job and do what you need to do. (Andrea, ADF student pilot)

Implications and Conclusion

Kanter's theoretical framework has once again been tested through this research and, somewhat disappointingly, appears as salient in military aviation today as it was to corporations of the 1970s. The extremely low numbers of female pilots in the ADF means that woman are still very much 'tokens' and 'pioneers' in most military aviation contexts. An unwelcoming, unchanged military culture means that many women today experience exactly the same barriers, challenges and workplace behaviours experienced by the pioneering aviatrixes of the last century.

There is no doubt the barriers faced by many female pilots impacts their ability to fly, with a number of unsuccessful former trainees implicating gender barriers such as heightened visibility, intense loneliness, harassment and bullying, and extreme performance pressures as key contributors to their demise:

> You're so emotionally battered, lacking in confidence and feeling isolated, how can you possibly overcome that and perform well? (Carmel, former trainee).

> [Q. Do you think it (bullying) impacts on your ability to fly the aircraft?] Of course, it definitely did, because I was just like, well, they think I'm shit. I must be shit. And right at that point, I did fail a flight just because I just couldn't handle it. (Liz, junior ADF pilot)

Only a few women succeed in military aviation; they have exceptional skills which they adapt and use to survive, though not all do so without paying a personal price.

While it could be argued that this is part of a necessary weeding-out process to ensure high-calibre pilots for the ADF, female pilots face so many more challenges than those experienced by their male counterparts.

Young women with minimal life experience outside Defence must negotiate their femininity in an intense, hyper-masculine context, with minimal acknowledgement that many of the difficulties they face are attributable to their gender. Until very recently, female pilots have not had role models, models, mentors or even peers to help guide them through the complex negotiations of femininity that are so prevalent in the earlier years of ADF flying. They have been virtually alone through their struggles in the ADF, like their peers in other non-traditional fields, both within Defence and beyond. While women have not been readied for the environment that awaits them, more significantly, Defence culture has not been readied for their arrival.

Until only recently, Defence has upheld a staunch philosophical belief of 'equality as sameness', which means that women entering non-traditional occupations 'must be treated the same as men' (Bagilhole, 2002, p. 134). In a military context, this 'equality as sameness' is intensified in war-fighting roles such as pilot. Women seeking warrior status are required to *perform masculinity* in order to integrate into the dominant culture, where women employed in supporting roles in health, logistics and administration simply do not experience this same pressure.

The 'equality as sameness' has cultural implications across the entire Defence force, preventing much-needed cultural reform and any targeted measures designed to enhance women's entry and retention in non-traditional roles. Neal-Smith suggests that rather than 'promoting pseudo gender neutrality by ignoring gender differences and focusing on an organisational identity', 'gender awareness is highlighted and diversity promoted' (2009, p. 43) when seeking to promote greater gender equality.

Previous reports into Defence culture have offered similar suggestions, most notably Clare Burton's seminal report urging Defence to stop viewing 'equal treatment' as being equitable (1996), because women do have differing needs to their male counterparts. She also implored Defence to introduce a range of measures to create a more inclusive culture for women and built equity through the 'reasonable accommodation to a person's wishes and needs' (1996, p. 171). While Burton's excellent report has had minimal enduring impact, there has recently been a renewed interest in gender equity, prompted by several reviews into ADF culture, including the Australian Human Rights Commission's two reviews into women's treatment in the ADF (AHRC, 2011 and 2012).

In 1996, Burton wrote that 'ADF policy on employment equity needs to achieve a fine balance between recognising the special needs of the gender pioneers it introduces into its work force' and issues pertaining to remediating these needs within the ADF's framework of organisational rules and regulations (1986, p. 61). It has taken 17 years, but I do believe that the ADF is finally heeding this advice through implementing a range of *carefully managed and communicated* cultural reform and targeted gender equity programs across Defence. While there is still some resistance to any form of 'different treatment', there is a growing acceptance that the current 'sameness as equity' programmes have been disadvantageous to women's integration.

This research has made 'women's invisible experiences visible' (Gray, 2007, p. 225), a key goal of feminist research. Findings from this study have been used to inform cultural change programmes and human resource interventions that will fundamentally change the Air Force, and the other Services, for the better. The ADF's senior leadership is absolutely committed to removing or mitigating many of the barriers and challenges ascertained through this and other recent research (Australian Human Rights Commission, 2012). In the Air Force, a large-scale cultural reform programme, '*New Horizon*', was introduced in 2012 to build a more inclusive, welcoming culture across the organisation. The other two services have similar cultural reform programmes in place.

As the Service with the most pilots, the Air Force is also directly tackling many of the issues detailed in this chapter. In 2012 and on an ongoing basis, it has/is implementing targeted measures to attract, retain and progress higher numbers of female pilots, as well as women in other non-traditional employment roles, such as non-pilot aircrew, technical trades, engineering and fire-fighting. It is building schemes that create a greater understanding of women's gender-based barriers in training and work contexts, and is actively applying initiatives designed to support women in non-traditional roles. There has already been a positive impact from these measures. More senior female pilots, perhaps inspired by this research and other role models, seem far more willing to actively champion these programmes when once they would have resisted any gender-exclusive activities for the many reasons discussed in this chapter.

Senior interviewees spoke of the desire to share their experiences with younger women coming through and to provide them with the support and guidance that they themselves had no access to as younger pilots. The Air Force has actively embraced this feedback by developing mentoring, role modelling and support structures that will enable more senior women from all non-traditional roles to share their wisdom with the more junior women who most need it. These networking and mentoring schemes are detailed more fully in Chapter 12 of this book.

The visibility of female pilots' experiences has created an impetus for much-needed change that will profoundly alter many aspects of Air Force and Defence culture. I am enormously hopeful that the negative accounts detailed in this chapter are the legacy of a past Defence force, not a reflection of a Defence force being built for the future. This research has deeply impacted me as a woman, a military officer and an academic. I remain personally and professionally committed to ensuring that Defence women entering all non-traditional occupations will encounter cultures that are radically different from the one made visible through this research.

References

Acker, J., 1990. Hierarchies, jobs, bodies: A theory of gendered organizations. *Gender and Society,* 4(2), pp. 139–58.

Andrew, A., 2009. Challenging boundaries to 'employability': Women apprentices in a non-traditional occupation. *Social Policy and Society*, 8(3), pp. 347–59.

Ashcraft, K.L., 2005. Resistance through consent? Occupational identity, organizational form, and the maintenance of masculinity among commercial airline pilots. *Management Communication Quarterly*, 19(1), pp. 67–90.

Austin, W., 2000. Getting round, over, under and through the barriers to women's integration in front line operational activities: The Australian Police Service. In: K.L. Spurling and E. Greenhalgh (eds.), *Women in Uniform: Perceptions and Pathways*. Canberra: School of History, University College, UNSW, pp. 127–40.

Australian Human Rights Commission, 2012. *Review into the Treatment of Women in the Australian Defence Force, Phase 2 Report*. Sydney: Australian Human Rights Commission.

Bagilhole, B.M, 2002. *Women in Non-traditional Occupations: Challenging Men.* New York: Palgrave Macmillan.

——. 2006. Not a glass ceiling more a lead roof: Experiences of pioneer women priests in the Church of England. *Equal Opportunities International*, 25(2), pp. 109–25.

Barrett, F.J., 1996. The organizational construction of hegemonic masculinity: The case of the US Navy. *Gender Work and Organization*, 3(3), pp. 129–41.

Bennett, A., 2006. Doing a man-sized job: A study of women in non-traditional trades, *The Australian TAFE Teacher*, 40(2), pp. 12–13.

Bennett, J.F., Davidson, M.J. and Gale, A.W., 1999. Women in construction: A comparative investigation into the expectations and experiences of female and male construction undergraduates and employees. *Women in Management Review*, 14(7), pp. 273–92.

Britton, D., 2000. The epistemology of the gendered organization. *Gender and Society*, 14(3), pp. 418–34.

Burton, C., 1996. *Women in the Australian Defence Force: Two Studies*. Canberra: Director Publishing and Visual Communications, Defence Centre.

Chamberlain, L.J., Crowley, M., Tope, D. and Hodson, R., 2008. Sexual harassment in organizational context. *Work and Occupations*, 35(3), pp. 262–95.

Charmaz, K., 2006. *Constructing Grounded Theory: A Practical Guide through Qualitative Analysis.* London: Sage.

Chusmir, L.H., 1983. Characteristics and predictive dimensions of women who make non-traditional vocational choices. *Personnel and Guidance Journal*, 62(1), pp. 43–7.

Cockburn, C., 1985. *Machinery of Dominance: Women, Men, and Technical Know-how.* London: Pluto Press.

——. 1991. *In the Way of Momen: Men's Resistance to Sex Equality in Organizations.* Basingstoke: Macmillan.

Connell, R.W., 2005. *Masculinities*, 2nd edn. Berkeley, CA: University of California Press.

Cross, S. and Bagilhole, B.M., 2002. Girls' jobs for the boys? Men, masculinity and non-traditional occupations. *Gender, Work & Organization*, 9(2), pp. 204–26.

Cummings, M., 1999. *Hornet's Nest: The Experiences of One of the U.S. Navy's First Female Fighter Pilots.* San Jose: Writer's Showcase.

Davey, C.L., 2004. The impact of human factors on *ab initio* pilot training. *Gender Work and Organization*, 11(6), pp. 627–47.

Davey, C.L. and Davidson, M.J., 2000. The right of passage? The experiences of female pilots in commercial aviation. *Feminism & Psychology*, 10(2), pp. 195–225.

Debenham, I. and Stafford, S. (eds.) 2001. *Women with Wings: Portraits of Australian Women Pilots*. Sydney: Powerhouse Publishing, New South Books.

Fitzgerald, L.F., Swan, S. and Fischer, K., 1995. Why didn't she just report him? The psychological and legal implications of women's responses to sexual harassment. *Journal of Social Issues*, 51(1), pp. 117–38.

Flinn, K., 1997. *Proud to Be.* New York: Random House.

Gale, A.W., 1994. Women in non-traditional occupations: The construction industry. *Women in Management Review*, 9(2), pp. 3–14.

Gandt, R.L., 1997. *Bogeys and Bandits: The Making of a Fighter Pilot.* New York: Viking.

Gatens, M., 1991. *Feminism and Philosophy: Perspectives on Difference and Equality.* Indianapolis: Indiana University Press.

Gilmartin, P., 1992. Women's performance in desert storm helps lifts barriers in military civilian market. *Aviation Week & Space Technology*, 136(2), pp. 62–4.

Grant, R., 2002. The quiet pioneers. *Air Force Magazine,* 85(12), pp. 34.

Gray, P.S., 2007. *The Research Imagination: An Introduction to Qualitative and Quantitative Methods.* Cambridge: Cambridge University Press.

Greed, C., 1991. *Surveying Sisters: Women in a Traditional Male Profession,* London: Routledge.

Haynsworth, L. and Toomey, D., 1998. *Amelia Earhart's Daughters.* New York: Morrow and Company.

Hesse-Biber, S.N. and Yaiser, M.L., 2004. *Feminist Perspectives on Social Research.* New York: Oxford University Press.

Hogue, M.B. and Yoder, J.D., 2006. Tokenism theory: What happens when few women work with many men. In: M.F.Karsten (ed.), *Gender, Race and Ethnicity in the Workplace*. Westwood, CT: Greenwood Publishing Group, pp. 199–216.

Kanter, R.M., 1977. Some effects of proportions on group life: Skewed sex ratios and responses to token women. *American Journal of Sociology*, 83, pp. 965–90.

Kellner, D., 1995. *Media Culture: Cultural Studies, Identity and Politics between the Modern and Postmodern.* London: Routledge.
Kimmel, M., 2000. Saving the males: The sociological implications of the Virginia military institute and the citadel, *Gender and Society*, 14(4), pp. 495–516.
King, R.E., Callister, J.D., Retzlaff, P.D. and McGlohn, S.E., 1997. *Pilot Personality: Gender and Career Level Differences.* Brooks, TX: United States Air Force Armstrong Laboratory, Brooks Air Force Base.
Kristovics, A., Mitchell, J., Vermeulen, L., Wilson, J. and Martinussen, M., 2006. Gender issues on the flight deck: An exploratory analysis. *International Journal of Applied Aviation Studies*, 6(1), pp. 99–119.
McGlohn, S.E., King, R.E., Retzlaff, P.D., Flynn, C.F. and Butler, J.W., 1996. *Psychological Characteristics of United States Air Force Pilots*. Brooks, TX: Air Force Materiel Command, Brooks Air Force Base.
Mills, A.J., 1998. Cockpits, Hangars, boys and galleys: Corporate masculinities and the development of British Airways. *Gender, Work and Organization*, 5(3), pp. 172–88.
Mitchell, J., Kristovics, A., Vermeulen, L., Wilson, J. and Martinussen, M., 2005. How pink is the sky? A cross-national study of the gendered occupation of pilot. *Employment Relations Record*, 5(2), pp. 43–7.
Morawski, J.G., 1997. The science behind feminist research methods. *Journal of Social Issues*, 53(4), pp. 667–81.
Neal-Smith, S. and Cockburn, T., 2009. Cultural sexism in the UK airline industry. *Gender in Management*, 24(1), pp. 32–45.
Pateman, Y.C., 1997. *Women Who Dared: American Female Test Pilots, Flight-Test Engineers, and Astronauts, 1912–1996.* Laguna Woods, CA: Norstahr.
Powell, A., Bagilhole, B.M. and Dainty, A., 2006. The problem of women's assimilation into UK engineering cultures: Can critical mass work? *Equal Opportunities International*, 25(8), pp. 688–99.
PPRuNe Forums (Professional Pilots Rumour Network), 2010. Female pilots ... what do you think? Available at: http://webcache.googleusercontent.com/search?q=cache:http://static.pprune.org/archive/index.php/t-431481.html.
——. 2012. Female pilots should not be allowed in the cockpit. Available at: http://www.pprune.org/pacific-general-aviation-questions/479163-female-pilots-should-not-allowed-cockpit-2.html.
Rabe-Hemp, C., 2008. Survival in an 'all boys club': Policewomen and their fight for acceptance. *Policing: An International Journal of Police Strategies & Management*, 31(2), pp. 251–70.
Reimer, J.W., 1979. *Hard Hats: The Work World of Construction Workers.* London: Sage.
Reinharz, S., 1992. *Feminist Methods in Social Research.* New York: Oxford University Press.
Robinson, J.G. and Mcllwee, J.S., 1991. Men, women and the culture of engineering. *Sociological Quarterly*, 32, pp. 403–21.

Sitler, R.L., 2004. Gender differences in learning to fly. In: M.A. Turney (ed.), *Tapping Diverse Talent in Aviation*, 4th edn. Aldershot: Ashgate. pp. 78–88.

Smart, T.L., 1998. Fast women: Or why women who fly high performance aircraft are fast but not loose. *Australian Military Medicine*, 7(1), pp. 1–10.

Spears, S., 1998. *Call Sign Revlon: The Life and Death of Navy Fighter Pilot Kara Hultgreen.* Annapolis, MD: Naval Institute Press.

Sprague, J., 2005. *Feminist Methodologies for Critical Researchers: Bridging Differences.* Walnut Creek, CA: Rowman & Littlefield.

Strauss, A.L. and Corbin, J., 1997. *Grounded Theory in Practice,* London: Sage.

Turney, M.A. and Bishop, J.C., 2004. Women's learning and leadership styles: Implications for air crews. In: M.A. Turney (ed.), *Tapping Diverse Talent in Aviation: Culture, Gender and Diversity*. Aldershot: Ashgate, pp. 61–75.

Turney, M.A., Bishop., J.C., Karp, M.R., Niemczyk, M.S., Sitler, R.L. and Green, M.F., 2002. National survey results: Retention of women in collegiate aviation. *Journal of Air Transportation*, 7(1), pp. 69–92.

Turney, M.A., Karp, M.R., Bishop, J.C., Niemczyk, M., Sitler, R.L. and Green, M.F., 2002. An applied training model for retention of women in aviation, In: M.A. Turney, M.R. Karp, J.C. Bishop, M. Niemczyk, R.L. Sitler and M.F. Green (eds), *The Interservice/Industry Training, Simulation & Education Conference (I/ITSEC)*.

Whittock, M., 2000. *Feminising the Masculine?: Women in Non-traditional Employment.* Aldershot: Ashgate.

——. 2002. Women's experiences of non-traditional employment: Is gender equality in this area a possibility? *Construction Management and Economics*, 20(5), pp. 449–56.

Williams, C.L., 1989. *Gender Differences at Work: Women and Men in Non-traditional occupations.* Berkeley, CA: University of California Press.

Williams, R., 2003. Women aviators finally fill cockpits of military aircraft. Available at: http://www.defense.gov/News/NewsArticle.aspx?ID=29276.

Yount, K.R., 1991. Ladies, flirts and tomboys: Strategies for managing sexual harassment in an underground coal mine. *Journal of Contemporary Ethnography*, 19(4), pp. 396–422.

Zimmer, L., 1988. Tokenism and women in the workplace: The limits of gender-neutral theory. *Social Problems*, 35(1), pp. 64–77.

Chapter 6
Grounded? Female Pilots, Gender Identity and Integration into the Australian Defence Force

Donna Bridges

Introduction

Gender relations within the Australian Defence Force (ADF) have, in recent years, been under the microscope for two reasons. The first is due to the decision of the Australian government, with full support of the Chiefs of Staffs, to provide women with full employment opportunities in the ADF. Prior to this decision, 93 per cent of jobs were open to women in the ADF, the remaining seven per cent representing roles in the combat arms. Both the announcement and the lead-up to the decision have created debate both within and outside of the defence force. Opponents to the move have expressed fears that women's lack of capacity (physical and psychological) for combat roles will reduce the effectiveness of military operations, will distract men, will incite public outrage and disrupt male bonding. Those who support the lifting of all restrictions on women's service base their arguments on lessons learnt, contending that women's integration in the ADF which has steadily been occurring since the Second World War has not resulted in reduced military effectiveness and they remind dissenters of the necessity for both men and women to pass standards prior to entering the combat arms.

The second reason is media scrutiny into sexual assault and harassment incidents in the ADF. One very high-profile incident occurred amongst Air Force cadets at the Australian Defence Force Academy (ADFA) in March 2011. A male Air Force cadet broadcast live a sexual encounter that he was having with an 18-year-old female member of the ADFA. The Australian Defence Minister announced that the incident would be the subject of an inquiry. In a radio interview, the Minister spoke of the need to instigate 'far-reaching cultural change' in the ADF. Of concern to the Minister was the accountability of individuals in sexual misconduct incidences as well as institutional responsibility (cited in Barclay, 2011). Discipline problems within Defence concerning assault and harassment of female members are in breach of policy and yet are in some ways condoned by the masculine culture and 'boys' club' values of military environments. Ben Wadham (cited in Barclay, 2011) says that incidents such as this are 'consistent and enduring' and are surrounded by a culture that denies them, shrouding them in and secrecy, and ultimately preventing them from being stamped out altogether. The incident sparked the Australian Human Rights Commission's Review into the Treatment of Women in the Australian Defence Force, which was tabled in the House of Representatives in August 2012 (Australian Human Rights Commission, 2012). When the subsequent report was released by Sex Discrimination Commissioner Elizabeth Broderick, it revealed that as many as one in four women in the ADF had suffered some kind of sexual abuse or harassment in the past five years and that 'the covert filming of servicewomen having sex was much more widespread within the military than previously admitted, despite assurances that the 2011 Skype sex scandal was an "isolated" event' (Owens, 2013).

Opening roles to women that have been traditionally associated with male gender identity creates debate amongst critics as to whether women *should* be assigned these roles and also whether they *can* adequately perform them. However, what is of more concern is the welfare of women who enter the hyper-masculine environments of military roles that are associated with masculine gender identity. The roles that the last seven per cent of ADF employments represent will be difficult for women to infiltrate even if they do pass the standards for them. The most significant problems women are likely to encounter will be the masculine culture of the ADF and the compounded issue of workplace cultures within occupations that are associated with masculine gender identity. The tacit acceptance that ADF roles that are traditional masculine strongholds are 'naturally' unsuitable for women will pose extreme difficulties for women as they attempt to integrate into these domains. The paucity of women in roles associated with masculine gender identity in the ADF, such as that of pilot, attest to this.

A history of gender integration in the ADF shows that the lifting of exclusions on women's service does not ensure that women will compete for roles previously unavailable to them or that they will be retained within them (Burton, 1996). Occupations associated with male gender identity have entrenched traditions of intentionally excluding women and simply adding women to these environments does not in itself detract from the belief systems, attitudes and behaviours that are designed to exclude or are the consequences of systemic exclusion. Currently women in the ADF do not serve in notable numbers, and in roles traditionally understood to be masculine domains, the percentage of women is very low (see Department of Defence, 2013). There is also poor representation of women in Defence senior management – for example, all of the six officers at three-star rank are men and of the 39 two-star officers, only one is a women. Of the 139 officers at one-star rank, only 10 are women (Defence Annual Report, 2012–13). As at 30 June 2013, women comprised 14.4 per cent of the Permanent Australian Defence: 18.5 per cent in the Navy, 10.1 per cent in the Army and 17 per cent in the Air Force (Department of Defence, 2013). Presently 93 per cent of all employment categories in the ADF are open to women and the remaining seven per cent are being opened over a five-year period. Women's employment in the ADF is reflective of wider workforce trends, with the majority of women serving in the healthcare field, in administration, supply and personnel.

Whilst there are policy makers and men in positions of power in the ADF who are committed to gender integration, the culture of the ADF is inherently masculine and this means that it favours and rewards masculine values, attitudes and behaviours. It also translates into a culture of resisting the feminine and of constructing feminine values, attitudes and behaviours as inferior to the masculine. The under-representation of women in aviation roles is a double-barrelled problem within the military because both sectors are associated with masculine cultures, male gender identity and sex role stereotypes. Both have traditions that exclude women and resist gender integration.

This chapter addresses the progress of women's integration into roles that have traditionally been associated with masculine gender identity specifically within the ADF and within aviation. I explore and discuss the reasons why, even without restrictions on women's service, roles that are defined as masculine do not attract or retain women in anything other than tokenistic numbers. The masculinised cultures of the military and the aviation industry are considered in terms of how they resist women's participation and how they maintain their gendered identity in the face of increasing pressure to integrate women in greater numbers. This chapter seeks to elucidate the barriers and challenges that female pilots face in the ADF. The most complex of these barriers is the masculine culture of the ADF, which constructs military roles as gendered. The chapter places the role of female personnel in the ADF in societal and political contexts, examining how the military constructs the feminine along lines that are discriminatory and illogical, and how the broader belief systems about gender in the ADF thwart progress toward full gender integration.

The Aviation Industry and Female Pilots in the ADF

All areas of aviation in all three branches of the ADF have been open to women since the 1990s. However, there remain no female fast jet pilots in the ADF and, overall, women comprise few of the overall numbers of service personnel in the role of pilot.

Women are under-represented as pilots within the aviation industry globally (Kristovics et al., 2006). An historically masculine industry, aviation has been found to foster traditionally masculine beliefs, values and attitudes. Miller and Budd found that the role of pilot was one of four occupations believed to be the most strongly sex-stereotyped roles (cited in Miller and Hayward, 2006). Vermeulen and Mitchell (2007) argue that the profession of pilot exists within the patriarchal system where gender is constructed in ways that are contradictory and ambivalent. In aviation, sex role stereotypes are prominent and result in perceptions of gender that 'underpin the professional culture' (Vermeulen and Mitchell, 2007, p. 198).

The aviation industry in Australia is currently unable to meet the growing demand for more pilots (Kristovics et al., 2006). In the ADF the situation is even more dire: 'The retention of experienced pilots has been a perennial problem for all three Services' (Sharp, 2003, p. 187). This issue is caused by several factors: recruitment shortfalls in all three branches, limitations in training capacities for pilots and training failures. There is also the issue of fierce competition from the private sector. Commercial aviation's shortfalls in the pilot profession translates into the sector offering ADF pilots financial incentives to meet recruiting demands (Sharp, 2003).

A shortage of pilots in both sectors would point to there being occupational opportunities for women. However, within the ADF, the masculine culture can be implicated in the under-representation of female pilots in all three branches of the ADF. Restrictions on women's service are not the cause of low numbers of pilots in the ADF. The early 2000s saw approximately 88 per cent of jobs within Defence open to women and it is important to highlight that neither the Air Force, the Navy nor the Army have had restrictions on women serving as pilots in any ADF aircraft since the mid-1990s. In 2000 the first two Royal Australian Air Force (RAAF) F-111 navigators qualified and the Air Force promoted the first female officer to reach one-star rank, Air Commodore Julie Hammer (Hammer reached two-star rank before her retirement). 'By this time the RAAF had seventeen female pilots and navigators, the Army had seven female helicopter pilots, and the RAN four female flight crew, including one helicopter pilot' (Horner, 2001, p. 326). A decade later in June 2011, there were 15 female pilots in the RAAF, the figures showing a deficit in growth in women's employment in the role of pilot (Defence spokesperson, personal communication, 2 July 2012).

Women's Service in the ADF: An Historical Opposition

Graeme Cheeseman, in his submission to the Inquiry into sexual harassment at the ADFA in 1998, said that military culture and its hostility towards women 'are not just the machinations of a few malevolent or chauvinistic servicemen. [But is reflective of] broader political and cultural processes and understandings which stem from Australia's historical circumstances and continue to be reinforced by its military and popular cultures' (Cheeseman, 1998, p. 1). Indeed, Australian culture is built upon images of men in the bush or the outback, and on men together in the trenches (Tacey, 1995; White, 1981). However, folklore has built these images, which are not reality – most Australians live in cities near the sea and only a small number have ever seen active military service. Nevertheless, mythology surrounding the Australian 'digger' and the birth of the Australian nation in Gallipoli provide a foundation for national identity and importantly for Australian military culture (Cheeseman, 1998). David Tacey argues that Australian masculinity 'desires to prove … that it is indeed male … in rituals of combat and battle and overseas in exotic theatres of war' (Tacey, 1995, p. 51). The experience of the digger does not need to pertain to the individual Australian male because it applies to Australian masculinity as a group. Women's experience of war is insignificant because the myth of the digger is about the making of men through battle (Cheeseman, 1998). If it is in theatres of war and in the military that Australian men 'prove' their manhood, then how can women participate? To do so would be to risk the perception of national identity and masculinity itself. Richard White views the digger myth as an Australian 'obsession with masculinity' (White, 1981, p. 136) and, to be sure, Australia has few images of women that represent what it means to be Australian. There are also very few images of Australian women at war.

Despite the omission of women from the national identity and from the collective memory of war, women have served in the military in Australia since the pre-federation era, when they served as nurses in the South African Boer War (1898–1902). Replacing men as medics raised issues for the nurses, who faced considerable resistance from within the Army and from the civilian population. The Army Department contended that soldiers 'preferred to be nursed by male orderlies … [that] women would interfere with the wounded soldiers' freedom and that flirtations would occur' (Adam-Smith, 1996, p. 9). Irrespective of this opposition, the trend to send military nurses to war, accompanying Australian soldiers, was born during the Boer War. Resistance to women serving in the military *in any role* in Australia was also born at this time.

During the Second World War, Australian women trained and served in the roles of nurses, signallers, radio operators, observers, drivers and mechanics. They worked on and operated tractors and other large engines, and were also instrumental in building trucks, tanks and planes. They staffed factories in significantly large numbers, producing uniforms for the troops, weapons and ammunition. In Australia the need for women in war industries was originally less than in countries with greater and more direct participation, so it wasn't until three years into the war that women's services were reluctantly accepted as necessary to the war effort. In 1941 several women's forces were established: the Royal Australian Air Force Nursing Service (RAAFNS), the Women's Royal Australian Nursing Service (WRANS), the Australian Women's Army Service (AWAS) and the Royal Australian Naval Nursing Service (RANNS). The Women's Australian Auxiliary Air Force (WAAAF) attracted the highest number of women, with over 26,000 serving (Adam-Smith, 1996; Bomford, 2001).

Women in Australia worked in unprecedented numbers during the Second World War. They were seen as a reserve force of labour to be used in the exceptional scenario of a national emergency (Smith and McAllister, 1991) and were not taken seriously in their newly acquired roles (Scutt, 1992). Women's work was considered to be less valuable and this bias dictated pay rates, which were set at 50 per cent of the male rate (Scutt, 1992). Women's ability to work without supervision was questioned, as was their physical strength. Women were viewed as being better at tedious, unskilled and routine tasks. The efficiency and productivity of women was considered to be lower than that of men and absenteeism to be higher, though both of these considerations were based in bias against women as a gender and not on fact (Scutt, 1992).

Australian women faced significant opposition when contributing to the actual war effort; the armed forces in Australia were quite resistant to the need for mobilising women. Prominent woman such as Violet McKenzie trained and organised women for the war effort despite opposition and the role being unrecognised and unpaid. A qualified engineer, 'Mrs Mac', founded the Women's Emergency Signalling Corps as well as overseeing training in communications of as many as 12,000 servicemen, while over 1,000 women were to join the women's services as trained wireless telegraphists and signallers. The initial intake was designed to meet a deficiency in the number of male wireless telegraphists; however, women proved themselves proficient in an array of positions that served the war effort (Adam-Smith, 1996).

Many women in the the Second World War Allied forces served in aviation roles. In Britain female pilots worked in the civilian Air Transport Auxiliary, where their roles were to ferrying and transport personnel and resources. In the US the Women's Airforce Service Pilots (WASPs) consisted of 2,000 women who operated over 70 types of aircraft. The Soviet Union is infamous for conscripting female pilots into combat roles. Women formed the all-female fighter regiments, but not without significant opposition. The 588th Night Bomber Regiment, for example, had their first assignment delayed due to the air base commander refusing to let them leave on a mission, stating that their presence was a distraction to men, their discipline poor and their training was inadequate. Opposition towards the 588th Night Bombers was only overcome after they proved themselves in successful battles of the air. In 1943 their success resulted in the distinction of becoming a Guards Unit, the highest honour awarded a regiment (Saywell, 1985, pp. 144–5).

Wartime roles were liberating for women; however, women's military involvement had created hostility about women taking the jobs of men as well as creating workplace and industry issues about equal pay. Consequently, at the war's end, those in power re-established pre-war gender roles and the disbandment of the women's services was one of the first post-war initiatives taken. The attitude that women were not required in the masculine preserve of the military was very soon to be replaced by the reality of personnel shortages in the ADF and in the 1950s all of the women's services were re-established before being integrated in the mainstream ADF during the 1970s and 1980s. In 1977 the RAAF was the first of the three forces to integrate women into the mainstream services and in this same year granted female officers in the RAAF equal pay. Equal pay was granted to all women in the ADF in 1979. The Army integrated women's services into the mainstream ADF in 1984, while the Navy did not do so until 1985. The 1970s and 1980s were periods of significant reform in the ADF in relation to gender integration. In 1975, the year that women in the ADF were granted 12 weeks paid maternity leave, the Chiefs of Staff Committee set up a Working Party to examine and report upon the role of women in the ADF. The ensuing report recommended that women be permitted to serve on active service, but not in a combat role.

Employment categories once closed to women were opened, including engineering and technician roles (Bomford, 2001; Horner, 2001).

In 1984 the Sex Discrimination Act was passed, allowing the ADF exemptions from employing women in combat-related and combat roles, and although women's integration continued to expand with initiatives such as the 1985 decision to permit women officers and sailors in the Navy to serve in seagoing billets, and graduation of the first two women from No. 144 Pilots' Course in Pearce, Western Australia, in 1987 there were also backward steps (Horner, 2001). Ironically, when the Sex Discrimination Act was passed, the ADF became more discriminatory in its employment of women in some areas. Women who had once been employed in combat-related duties – such as transport in the Royal Australian Corps of Transport and the Royal Australian Engineers in the Army – were required to leave these positions (Bomford, 2001).

In 1990 the Chiefs of Staff Committee reviewed the employment of women in the ADF and expanded the number of combat-related positions available to women. This opened positions in the combat aircrew in the Air Force as well as in the Navy and the Army. Fast jets were made available to women in 1995. Prior to this, women were excluded from any duties that would require them to 'work in support of, and in close proximity to, a person performing combat duties' (Department of Defence, 1986).

Women, Work and Masculine Workplace Cultures

The lifting of restrictions on women's service in the ADF reflects broader societal, political and workplace trends. Increases in women's participation in the work sphere has been one of the most significant social changes during the last 50 years and has radically altered the world of work and the structure of society (Summers, 2003). Nonetheless, the sexual division of labour remains difficult to eradicate and women continue to dominate occupations that are low status and low paid (Miller and Hayward, 2006). Resistance to women at work through harassment, discrimination and gender bias are all too often implicated in reasons why women generally do not progress to higher-status and higher-paid positions.

Resistance to women's participation in the work sphere is an historical problem. Women's entry into the university system was resisted successfully until 1882, when they were granted access to Sydney University and slightly later when they were finally allowed into Melbourne University. Early education debates focused on the body as a site of resistance, with opponents to change asserting that a woman's body was not equipped to deal with the exertions of the mind. In some debates it was said that a woman's uterus would shrink or that her reproductive systems be damaged if she were to pursue higher learning (Herbert, 1998, pp. 1–2). Similar arguments are espoused by some military commentators in contemporary debates. Female reproductive organs and the issue of menstruation still receive an unreasonable amount of attention; van Creveld, for example, contends that women's bodies will certainly be damaged if they engage in military operations, saying that women's 'large, pendulous breasts that impede movement and require special attention' (van Creveld, 2000, p. 832) and in the field, he warns, the lack of 'creature comforts' for women invites 'disease of the urinary tract' and sterility (van Creveld, 2000, p. 836).

There are clear links between the slow progression of women in professions that are considered masculine domains and gender bias (Smith and McAllister, 1991). Resistance in occupations such as law and medicine and late access into engineering, the church and the military manifest themselves as 'conscious and unconscious strategies to discourage female participation' (Smith and McAllister, 1991, p. 370). Women in the engineering profession in Australia, the UK and the US continue to work in low-status positions and are typically paid less than men. Equal pay in the civilian sector of engineering is an issue, with women earning up to 40 per cent less than men (Roberts and Ayre, 2002).

Miller and Hayward's research (2006) found that most occupations are associated with sex-role stereotypes. Societal expectations regarding gender and job suitability create the idea of 'men's work' and 'women's work', which perpetuates sex-role stereotypes, and women and men tend to choose roles most appropriate to the sex-role stereotype (Miller and Hayward, 2006). Segregation of the sexes into occupations and gender roles is therefore viewed as the norm and gender identity becomes associated with occupational roles. Within masculine cultures, the values, attitudes and behaviours of men provide the cultural codes for how the workplace functions. In the military, most roles, excluding those in healthcare and low-status administration, are associated with masculinity. Therefore, military attributes such as mate-ship, courage, loyalty and skill become stereotyped masculine qualities, especial to men. The inherent assumption is that women cannot embody these qualities. Women serving in roles that are traditionally associated with masculinity disrupt gendered stereotypes and the established values and practices associated with masculinity.

Male resistance to women integrating into occupations considered masculine occurs for several reasons. One of these is a fear that the occupation will be 'feminised' (Burton, 1991). Certainly, fears that some professions will be accorded less status, value and less financial reward are not unfounded as occupations that are heavily feminised are not afforded the same value as male domains (Burton, 1991). There is the added issue that men who perform the role will be perceived as doing women's work and this can result in men losing job satisfaction because 'part of the satisfaction in some jobs derives from the belief that it is masculine work' (Burton, 1991, p. 6). Van Creveld asserts that when women enter male preserves, prestige and income collapse, making it hard for men to 'mark off any field as their own in order to assert their masculinity' (van Creveld, 2000, p. 831). The need for men to mark off occupational territory to assert their masculinity seems a questionable motive for attitudes and behaviours that resist women's integration, yet the hostility to women entering occupations associated with male gender identity would indicate that the need exists.

Masculine workplace cultures are infused with gender ideologies that are based in stereotypes, ideas, beliefs and assumptions about how men and women should behave rather than the lived reality of how individuals do behave. These notions about gender roles are based in biology, are dichotomous and are assumed to be based in the natural order. But as Cooke says, gender is 'far from being natural, [it] is a cultural code that describes, prescribes, and thus shapes social expectation for sexed bodies' (Cooke, 1996, p. 236). In a social constructivist view, gender is what we do and not what we are – it is not a pre-determined and fixed state of being (Connell, 1987).

How gender is enacted in masculine cultures is complex; it is both overtly and tacitly enforced, and women who enter these areas are required to conform either to feminine stereotypes or to become 'one of the boys'. Within these environments, women themselves report that they feel the need to adjust to stereotypes of gender and to manage their sexuality (Agostino, 1998). The added strain of managing gender – beyond the performance of one's work role – places unnecessary and additional stress on women and leaves them in a position where they feel acutely aware of being different from their male colleagues (Davey and Davidson, 2000). To successfully manage masculine cultures, women negotiate strategies to fit in. Some 'de-emphasise' their female characteristics in physical, sexual and emotional ways (Burton, 1996, p. 97), some women adopt masculine values and behaviours, while others withdraw or become aloof when in the workplace (a strategy that can lead to low-status positions within the profession). The double bind for women's integration is that conforming to feminine stereotypes can perpetuate assumptions and prejudice about women in the workplace and can strengthen hegemonic structures, doing little to change the discriminatory practices within the culture. Conforming to masculine stereotypes and becoming 'one of the boys' can result in women identifying with men and not with other women, which may result in further isolation. Men within masculinised cultures may view a female colleague as an 'honorary man' or as a 'flawed woman' – either way, this perception of women is a barrier to women's success (Powell et al., 2006). The need to conform to masculine values and standards of behaviour has been found to be a contributing factor in women's attrition from aviation (Davey and Davidson, 2000) and from other sectors strongly associated with masculine gender identity such as engineering (Roberts and Ayre, 2002). In engineering, where the workplace culture is described by women in the profession as 'hostile', 'unfriendly' and grounded in the 'priorities, values and life choices' (Roberts and Ayre, 2002, p. 2) of men, the attrition rate of women is astoundingly high. In the research *Women in the Professions: The State of Play Survey Report* (2010) conducted by the Association of Professional Engineers, Scientists and Managers Australia (APESMA), nearly half said that their career was detrimentally affected by the culture of their workplace. In an example of how masculine cultures can impact negatively on women's careers, a staggering 71.6 per cent of engineers felt that their careers would be detrimentally affected if they were to take maternity leave (including unpaid leave) (APESMA, 2010, p. 3).

Although many occupations in the military are open to women's service and have been for some time, those where masculine gender identity is particularly strong remain dominated by men and under-represented by women, and women's participation in these roles is questioned and undermined. For example, the capability of women to fly in combat missions is consistently questioned. In the survey undertaken by Matthews et al. (2009), both male and female college students in the US, West Point cadets and Reserve Officer Training Corps (ROTC) cadets were questioned in relation to their beliefs regarding the suitability of roles for women in the military. The roles included jet fighter pilot and jet transport pilot. The research found that male West Point cadets, a traditionally masculine area of the military, were more resistant to women jet fighter pilots (48.6 per cent) than were male ROTC cadets (45.3 per cent). Male civilian college students were significantly less opposed to women serving in the role (31.6 per cent) and the women from all groups reported an overwhelmingly positive result towards women serving as jet fighter pilots, scoring highest for West Point cadets (94.1 per cent), ROTC cadets (91.2 per cent) and civilians (91.1 per cent) (Matthews et al., 2009, p. 247). The overall score for women serving as a jet transport pilot was favourable in all regards, with approval ratings as follows; male West Point cadets (89.7 per cent), male ROTC cadets (89.6 per cent), male civilian college students (86.2 per cent). Women surveyed were again more positive than men, differing only slightly on their view of the suitability of jet fighter pilots (Matthews et al., 2009, p. 248). The young men in the survey above have no grounds, other than gender bias, to report their view that women are unsuitable to fly as jet fighter pilots or that women are more suitable to fly transport jets. There exists no evidence that women are less capable as pilots than men other than gender bias.

Constructing Gender Difference in the Military: The Body, Morality and 'Esprit de Corps'

In the military the three most powerful arguments against women serving in occupations linked to masculine gender identity are related to physical strength, the morality of women serving in war roles and the issue of male bonding or 'esprit de corps'.

The Body

The size and strength difference between men and women, in terms of averages, is reasonably controversy-free; however, the argument that women's physical differences render them unfit for military roles in not. Military debates about the aptitude of women to achieve in military roles focus on the binary view that sees the male body as strong and useful in war, and the female body as weak and ineffective in war. There is a tendency within the military to revere the physical characteristic of strength that is traditionally associated with the male gender, regardless of whether that strength is required in specific employments. Modern warfare has been changed by technological advances and tasks that once took two or more men to accomplish are now able to be achieved at the push of a button. Modern equipment has also de-gendered war. Military planes, once designed for the larger male body, are now 'designed to accommodate a greater percentage of the female population' (Smart, 1998, p. 11). Where strength is required, such as in the manoeuvring of high-performance aircraft at high speed, it is recommended that 'fitness be judged on a case by case basis, with the acceptance that not all people are capable of flying all types of aircraft and all types of missions' (Smart, 1998, p. 10).

It is reasonable to suggest that physical size and strength are not the most desirable attributes for military personnel to embody; in many situations, intelligence and technical skills are more advantageous and large physical size and enhanced strength are not always required. Furthermore, not all differences in women's constitutions should be constructed as deficiencies. Some of the differences between the sexes put women in a superior position. For example, women are more resilient to fatigue and famine, they have greater levels of endurance and stamina, and are also more resistant to disease and illness (Goldstein, 2001). Where size and strength are required, studies show that training the appropriate women may result in the desired outcomes; a 'study completed in December 1995 by the British Ministry of Defence decided that "by using methods of physical training, women can be built up to the same levels of physical fitness as men of the same size and build". The question is not, then, changing the nature of women, but changing the nature of the military culture in which they attempt to excel' (Brower, 1996, pp. 6–7).

The issue of women's reproductive organs, especially the menstruating body, is consistently raised as an issue when considering whether women can be effective in military employments. These arguments are both alarmist and illogical; for example, Simons (2000) cites a retired general who expressed fears for Navy SEALS training in shark-infested waters when a female colleague is menstruating. Opponents often assert that women need to be more careful than men in relation to personal hygiene. Menstruation, the issue of hygiene and the 'special' attention women must give to it seems a smokescreen that obscures the real issue of gender bias. The real issues are not with the female body, but with the 'construction' of the female body as inferior to the male body. The rehashing of evidence that proves what women can do, and have done in the past, does not go any way to disprove illogical and prejudicial arguments. The answer lies within the culture of Defence and with leadership. As Tracy Smart (1998, p. 14) asserts in relation to female pilots in the ADF: 'The problems relating to physical differences between the sexes can be solved by re-engineering aircraft and safety equipment to accommodate a greater percentage of the population. Most of the specific women's health issues really should be considered on a case by case basis and treated like any other fitness to fly issue'.

Morality

Moral arguments are perhaps the most insidious because they are emotional and based on ideas about what is 'natural' and 'right' in terms of what roles each gender should perform. The protectionism argument, for example, contends that men are 'naturally' protective of women. The issues here are twofold; first, it is believed that the motivation for men to fight wars is to protect women (mothers, wives, sisters, daughters and sweethearts). Therefore, women must remain in need of protection to give men a reason to fight (Cooke, 1996; Peach, 1996). If women fight alongside men in war, then their motivation to fight is diluted. Second, it is argued that women are not naturally suited to the hazards of war and must be protected both from being killed (or taken prisoner) and the act of killing itself. Men, it is proposed, will take inappropriate measures to protect female colleagues and put missions at risk to do so (Hancock, 2000). The idea that men have a monopoly on the protective instinct and that it is focused primarily on women is highly gendered and tells the story of protective instincts only partially. In reality men are also protective towards one another and are rewarded when they 'go to great lengths to rescue, and protect their mates. The idea of men only having a protective instinct towards women is not matched with people's lived realities' (Agostino, 1998, p. 62). Military ethos is clear that it is unacceptable to allow one's male colleagues be killed or taken prisoner and the requirement to protect one another goes beyond gender. Another factor is that the emotion that drives a soldier to protect colleagues is also experienced by women.

Esprit de Corps

An argument raised frequently in military debates about women serving in areas that have been male-only strongholds relates to 'esprit de corps', the male bonding necessary to create and enhance unit cohesion (Goldstein, 2001; Kier, 1999). It is argued that women are incapable of bonding as men do and that they disrupt male cohesion to the detriment of military operations.

Cohesion is social and psychological bonding; it is a connection that individuals within a group feel towards one another and it provides a unified connection to a goal (Goldstein, 2001). The male bonding thought necessary for unit cohesion is 'characterized as camaraderie and team spirit' (Peach, 1996, p. 166). Both of these attributes are important in the military, where war is unpredictable and predictable responses are required from groups and individuals at all times (Kier, 1999, p. 26).

There are two types of cohesion: social cohesion and task cohesion. The goal of social cohesion is closeness, homogeneity and the sense of being one entity. In task cohesion a shared commitment to achieving a task is the goal. It can be argued that social cohesion is an inappropriate goal for military units and that it is not as effective as task cohesion (Kier, 1999). Social cohesion excludes those considered different, hence the proposed idea that men cannot bond with women (Agostino, 1998). It can also have undesirable consequences because of the potential of small cohesive groups to separate from the larger organisation and can become a 'two-edged sword' if connection to the unit results in goals and values that are incongruent with the goals and values of the larger group (Goldstein, 2001). This is evident when soldiers commit, encourage or turn a blind eye to unacceptable behaviour.

Evidence is available that shows that a focus on task cohesion can facilitate gender integration (Kier, 1999). In Britain during the Second World War, mixed-gender AA batteries demonstrated that 'morale, bonding and unit cohesiveness were, if anything, was better than in segregated units' (Nemitschenko, 2001, p. 39). And other studies have shown that mixed units do not exhibit lower levels of task cohesion than single-sex units (see Goldstein, 2001; Kier, 1999). Smart (1998, p. 13) reports on research carried out by the US Air Force (USAF), prior to 1997, amongst pilots that revealed that '97 per cent of males and 98 per cent of females felt comfortable flying in combat with both genders' after having had the experience of doing so.

The focus on social cohesion as necessary for successful military operations misses the opportunity to create cohesion in mixed groups through task cohesion. The argument that men in certain military roles, particularly those in the combat arms, must bond in homogeneous groups perpetuates gender bias. An emphasis on male bonding also alludes to beliefs that women do not bond in cohesive groups or with one another. There is a feeling among military women and women in male-dominated occupations that men are suspicious of women's connections. Hancock asserts that the military may 'need to recognise that bonding between women, as well as between men, is important' (Hancock, 2000, p. 168). Whilst women are deemed inferior for not being able to bond with men, they are actively discouraged from forming bonds with one another. Davey and Davidson (2000) found that women within commercial aviation environments were afraid of being labelled a feminist by male pilots, most of whom vehemently expressed anti-feminist views, because of the hostility and sexist attitudes they would have to confront as a result of being seen as a feminist. Young women in the research conducted by Powell et al. (2006) found that younger women were discouraged from participating in activities with other women due to fears that men would become suspicious of them.

Concluding Thoughts: Changing Institutional Cultures

A review of the literature suggests that in order for women to take their place in combat roles, there need to be changes to the institutional cultures of the military. This suggests that progress may depend on new forms of cultural training, the existence of a critical mass of female pilots, and a concerted and consistent challenge to the deep-rooted belief systems about the inferiority of women in relation to combat and the image of combat as the ultimate masculine protection of women.

Training

Changing institutional cultures is not easy, but this may be the only way forward for sectors that need to facilitate gender integration and increase the number of women within occupations traditionally associated with male gender identity. In the military, one way to smooth the progress of change and to mitigate masculine cultures is to alter the basic training environment. Eliminating sexism and sexist language from training is one way forward for creating cultural change. Warriors are not, after all, born, they are made. Strategies in military training where denigrating the feminine as a way of toughening-up young men are widely used, but are not essential for successful training. In fact, as Wadham (in Barclay, 2011) argues, it may be detrimental to the culture of the organisation. Teaching young men to link aggression with women is not conducive to workplace harmony or equality and in extreme cases may lead them to perpetrate violence against their females colleagues and against civilian women (Snyder, 2003).

Critical Mass

Workplace cultures that are dominated by one group and contain a small minority of another group can tokenise the minority whilst simultaneously 'exaggerating their [own] commonality and the minorities' differences' (Powell et al., 2006, p. 690). Such strategies in masculine cultures make women stand out as being different, construct them as sexual beings rather than as colleagues and can make them the brunt of jokes. In this way the male-dominant culture is 'reproduced and reinforced' (Powell et al., 2006, p. 691). Davison (2007) suggests that a critical mass of women within military roles traditionally staffed by men can address the issue of tokenism and can contribute to the majority accepting the minority (see also Gutek, 1985; Kanter, 1977a).

The theory of achieving a critical mass of women is that it would have the effect of introducing feminine values which would then impact upon the workplace culture. Women's current minority status in the aviation sector and in the military makes them overly visible to their male colleagues and to outsiders. Overt allies are hard to find in this environment. The problem with tokenism is that the dominant culture can worsen as threatened individuals work to secure existing cultural norms. Tokenism doesn't pave the way for other women to enter a 'broken in' environment; rather, the culture becomes self-perpetuating and reinforces low numbers (Kanter, 1977b). Kristovics et al. (2006) found that when men have regular experience flying with female pilots, it instigated positive perceptions of their suitability and ability to perform the role. Achieving critical mass means that all pilots will have the experience of flying with both genders.

A complicating factor for women in the military serving in roles traditionally staffed by men is that there is a lack of informal structures where women can learn from each other, female role models are few and women in positions to mentor other women are scarce. In other male-dominated sectors, women cite the lack of role models and lack of women in senior roles as affecting their career advancement (APESMA, 2010, p. 6).

Combat Restrictions: The Last Stand?

Combat restrictions, regardless of the roles they apply to, have reinforced the belief that women cannot be warriors and are marginal to military operations. Furthermore, the belief system in the military that men are superior and women are inferior has been perpetuated by combat exclusions, reinforcing the masculine culture that resists and excludes women. The ADF is in the process of removing all restrictions on women's service; however, the removal of the restrictions will not in itself change the institutional culture of the ADF. Agostino rightly asserts that full military service will not bring about 'women's emancipation and equality' (Agostino, 2000, p. 75). The acquisition of the entitlement to full military service, free of restrictions and exclusions, will not overcome the masculine culture of the ADF. This has been demonstrated by the continuing representation of women in lower-status positions in Defence and the low numbers of women in aviation and engineering. It is also demonstrated by the persistent complaints of gender bias, discrimination and harassment by military women.

The new legislation that will, over the next five years, liberate Australian military women from restrictions on service does, however, send a powerful message to women and men, both inside and outside of the military. It states clearly that women have earned the right to be considered equal in a military context. This kind of message will have some impact on the culture of the ADF and, combined with initiatives in the basic training environment and focusing on areas such as task cohesion and critical mass, there can be some cautious expectation that institutional change can occur in the ADF.

References

Adam-Smith, P., 1996. *Australian Women at War.* Victoria: Penguin.

Agostino, K., 1998. The making of warriors: Men, identity and military culture. *Jigs*, 3(2), pp. 58–75.

——. 2000. Women in uniform: Challenging feminisms. In: K. Spurling and E. Greenhalgh (eds), *Women in Uniform: Perceptions and Pathway.* Canberra: Australian Defence Force Academy, pp. 64–82.

APESMA. 2010. *Women in the Professions: The State of Play Survey Report.* Melbourne: Association of Professional Engineers, Scientists and Managers.

Australian Human Rights Commission, 2012. *Review into the Treatment of Women in the Australian Defence Force, Phase 2 Report.* Sydney: Australian Human Rights Commission.

Barclay, P., 2011. Military culture. *Australia Talks, Australia Broadcasting Association*. Available at: http://www.abc.net.au/rn/australiatalks/stories/2011/3186072.htm.

Bomford, J., 2001. *Soldiers of the Queen: Women in the Australian Army.* Melbourne: Oxford University Press.

Brower, M.J., 1996. The mother of all future debates: Women in combat. *Minerva: Quarterly Report on Women and the Military*, XIV(3–4), pp. 1–10.

Burton, C. 1991. *The Promise and the Price: The Struggle for Equal opportunity in Women's Employment*. Sydney: Allen & Unwin.

——. 1996. *Women in the Australian Defence Force. Two Studies: The Cultural, Social and Institutional Barriers Impeding the Merit-Based Progression of Women and the Reasons Why More Women are Not Making the Australian Defence Force a Long-Term Career*. Canberra: Defence Centre.

Cheeseman, G., 1998. *Submission to an Inquiry into Sexual Harassment at the Australian Defence Force Academy.* Canberra: Australian Defence Force Studies Centre.

Connell, R.W., 1987. *Gender and Power: Society, the Person and Sexual Politics.* Cambridge: Polity Press.

Cooke, M., 1996. Subverting the gender and military paradigms. In: J. Hicks Stiehm (ed.), *It's Our Military Too! Women and the U.S. Military.* Philadelphia: Temple University Press, pp. 235–69.

Davey, C.L. and Davidson, M.J., 2000. The right of passage? The experiences of female pilots in commercial aviation. *Feminism & Psychology*, 10(2), pp. 195–225.

Davison, S., 2007. Future concepts and force development: The combat exclusion of women in the military, paternalistic protection or military need? *Australian Army Journal*, 4(3), pp. 59–79.

Department of Defence, 1986. *Application of the Sex Discrimination Act to the Australian Defence Force, PERS B/8/86*. Canberra: Australian Department of Defence.

——. 2007. *The Defence Workplace Equity and Diversity Plan 2007–09*. Available at: http://www.defence.gov.au/fr/Reports/Combined_WEDP_20070707.pdf.

——. 2013. *Annual Report 2012–13*. Available at: http://www.defence.gov.au/AnnualReports/12-13.

Goldstein, J., 2001. *War and Gender: How Gender Shapes the War System and Vice Versa.* Cambridge: Cambridge University Press.

Gutek, B.A., 1985. *Sex and the Workplace.* San Francisco: Jossey-Bass.

Hancock, E., 2000. Women as killers and killing women: The implications of 'gender-neutral' Armed Forces. In: M. Evans and A. Ryan (eds), *The Human Face of Warfare: Killing, Fear & Chaos in Battle*. Sydney: Allen & Unwin. pp. 159–76.

Herbert, M.S., 1998. *Camouflage isn't Pnly for Combat: Gender, Sexuality, and Women in the Military.* New York: New York University Press.

Horner, D., 2001. *Making the Australian Defence Force: The Australian Centenary History of Defence*. Melbourne: Oxford University Press.
Kanter, R.M., 1977a. *Men and Women of the Corporation*. New York: Basic Books.
——. 1977b. Some effects of proportions on group life. *American Journal of Sociology*, 82(5), pp. 965–90.
Kier, E., 1999. Discrimination and military cohesion: An organizational perspective. In: M. Fainsod Katzenstein and J. Reppy (eds), *Beyond Zero Tolerance: Discrimination in Military Culture.* Oxford: Rowman & Littlefield. pp. 25–52.
Kristovics, A., Mitchel, J., Vermeulen, L., Wilson, J. and Martinussen, M., 2006. Gender issues on the flight-deck: An exploratory analysis. *International Journal of Applied Aviation Studies*, 6(1), pp. 99–119.
Matthews, M.D., Ender, M.G., Laurence, J.H. and Rohall, D.E., 2009. Role of group affiliation and gender on attitudes toward women in the military. *Military Psychology*, 21(2), pp. 241–51.
Miller, L. and Hayward, R., 2006. New jobs, old occupational stereotypes: Gender and jobs in the new economy. *Journal of Education and Work*, 19(1), pp. 67–93.
Nemitschenko, L., 2001. Is increasing gender equity in the ADF improving operational capability? *Australian Defence Force Journal*, 149, pp. 35–43.
Owens, J., 2013. Independent unit to help with Defence force sex abuse claims. *The Australian*, 27 July. Available at: http://www.theaustralian.com.au/national-affairs/defence/independent-unit-to-help-with-defence-force-sex-abuse-claims/story-e6frg8yo-1226683721362.
Peach, L.J., 1996. Gender ideology in the ethics of women in combat. In: J. Hicks Stiehm (ed.), *It's Our Military Too! Women and the U.S. Military.* Philadelphia: Temple University Press, pp. 156–94.
Pearce, A., Flavell, K. and Dao-Cheng, N., 2010. Scoping our future: Addressing Australia's engineering skills shortage. *Australian National Engineering Taskforce*. Available at: http://www.anet.org.au/?page.
Powell, A., Bagilhole. B.M. and Dainty, A., 2006. The problem of women's assimilation into UK engineering cultures: Can critical mass work? *Equal Opportunities International*, 25(8), pp. 688–99.
Roberts, P. and Ayre, M., 2002. *Counting the Losses. The Careers Review of Engineering Women: An Investigation of Women's Retention in the Australian Engineering Workforce*. Canberra: National Women in Engineering Committee, Engineers Australia.
Saywell, S., 1985. *Women in War.* Toronto: Penguin.
Scutt, J.A., 1992. Inequality before the law: Gender, arbitration and wages. In: K. Saunders and R. Evans (eds), *Gender Relations in Australia: Domination and Negotiation*. Sydney: Harcourt Brace Jovanovich, pp. 266–80.
Sharp, P., 2003. *Report of the Strategic Workforce Planning Review*. Canberra ACT: Commonwealth of Australia.

Simons, A., 2000. Women can never 'belong' in combat. *Orbis*, 44(3), pp. 451–61.

Smart, T.L., 1998. Fast women: Or why women who fly high-performance aircraft are fast but not loose. *Australian Military Medicine*, 7(1), pp. 8–16.

Smith, H. and McAllister, I., 1991. The changing military profession: Integrating women in the Australian Defence Force. *Australian and New Zealand Journal of Sociology*, 27(3), pp. 369–91.

Snyder, C.R., 2003. The citizen-soldier tradition and gender integration of the U.S. military. *Armed Forces & Society*, 29(2), pp. 185–204.

Summers, A., 2003. *The End of Equality: Work, Babies and Women's Choices in 21st Century Australia*. Sydney: Random House.

Tacey, D.J., 1995. *Edge of the Sacred: Transformation in Australia*. Australia: HarperCollins.

Van Creveld, M., 2000. A woman's place: A reflection on the origins of violence. *Social Research*, 67(3), pp. 825–47.

Vermeulen, L.P. and Mitchell, J.I., 2007. Development and validation of a measure to assess perceptions regarding gender-related pilot behaviour. *International Journal of Aviation Psychology*, 17(2), pp. 197–218.

White, R., 1981. *Inventing Australia: Images and Identity: 1688–1980*. Sydney: Allen & Unwin.

Chapter 7
Another Empty Kitchen: Gender Issues on the Flight Deck[1]

Jim Mitchell, Alexandra Kristovics and Leopold P. Vermeulen

Introduction

The occupation of aviation pilot has been, historically, and still is both male-dominated and a gendered (masculine) occupation. Not only is the occupation male-dominated, its 'tools of trade', that is, aircraft, are designed, built and maintained primarily by men for men. In aviation, masculine beliefs, values and perceptions (having the 'right stuff') appear to continue to dominate the industry and the pilot profession. Originating in the US military, the 'right stuff' is characterised by aviators and astronauts who were courageous, single-minded and driven to successfully achieve personal and organisational goals. This perception and behaviour was popularised in movies such as *The Right Stuff* and *Top Gun*, and Wolfe's (1980) book *The Right Stuff*. These, and other stories of heroic exploits such as the aerial combat heroes of the First and Second World Wars, the 'barnstormers' of the 1920s and 1930s and the emergence of the airline sector of the aviation industry, have contributed to a masculine occupational culture that transcends both organisational and national boundaries. For example, airlines were not adverse to utilise the profile of the pilot to promote the organisation and exclude women not only from piloting positions, but also from 75 per cent of all airline positions (Mills, 1998). Mills also indicates that the early corporate image (masculine) adopted by British Airways 'was that of the experienced, heroic and supremely confident pilot' (1998, p. 174). Despite the dominant male culture, female pilots, always in the minority, have also played an often significant part in aviation.

Notwithstanding aviation's history of legendary women aviators, the airline sector has been slow in recruiting, training and advancing female pilots. This has been regardless of the anti-discrimination, equal employment opportunity and affirmative action legislation enacted in many countries. The business

---

1 This chapter is a modified version of a paper that was originally published as: Mitchell, J., Kristovics, A., Vermeulen, L., Wilson, J. and Martinussen, M. 2005. How pink is the sky? A cross-national study of the gendered occupation of pilot. *Employment Relations Record*, 5(2), pp. 43–60. Reprinted and modified here with permission thanks to the Employment Relations Record.

community has instituted many affirmative action programmes and has adopted human resource policies and procedures that meet these legislative requirements. The masculine culture of the industry has led to female pilots experiencing sexism, discrimination, prejudice, hostility and inappropriate discourse (Davey and Davidson, 2000, pp. 198–9). The concept and use of a seemingly harmless protective epithet 'the right stuff' 'becomes, under close scrutiny, the very core of inequality and discrimination based on gender' (Bateman, 1987). Generally, there has been a paucity of articles about the issues faced by female pilots in the industry, although Davey and Davidson's (2000) article provides a well-researched paper on the experiences of female pilots. Turney's (1995, 2000, 2004) research contributes to the discussion.

Female pilots inhabit a profession steeped in patriarchal systems of dominance involving organisational power and labour processes. It is in this domain that there is a prevailing construction of gender involving discourses with various 'forms, structures, variation, contradictions, inconsistencies and ambivalences' (Hearn, 1993, p. 150). Underlying this discourse is perceptions of the airline managers and the pilots. In an organisational or professional setting gender-related perceptions held by people are significant, based on the assumption that these perceptions are influential in determining behaviour (Rollinson, Broadfield and Edwards, 1998, p. 123). Perceptions influence and underpin the professional culture of the pilots and the aviation industry. As masculinity is the dominant perception within the industry, female pilots are faced with a confronting attitude that is often unarticulated but acted out though associated behaviours. In particular, 'sex-role stereotyping is pervasive' (Nicholson, 1996, p. 13) and often women are first identified by sex and, then, by their professional role (Sitler, Turney and Wulle, 1996, p. 333).

Female Pilots in Aviation

An important feature of all societies is for occupations to be segregated by gender and the level of segregation differs between countries. Countries with low Gross Domestic Product tend to have a low level of segregation, while wealthy industrialised countries have at least moderately high levels of segregation (Blackburn et al., 2002, p. 513). This reflected the social structure of societies in which occupations are often prescribed along gender lines. Charles and Grusky (2004, pp. 15–23) identified both horizontal and vertical segregation. Horizontal segregation was based, maintained and reproduced on stereotypes about natural male and female characteristics by which occupations can be regarded as either prototypically male or women. In practice, segregation was influenced by a variety of mechanisms including employer and institutionalised discrimination, the socialisation of sex-typed expectations and preferences, expected levels of sanctions and physicality. Vertical inequalities were based on the cultural belief and ideological form of male primacy in which men were allocated higher status and were 'better suited for positions of authority and domination' (Charles and Grusky, 2004, p. 21).

Flight-crew roles are mainly perceived as a male occupation, while cabin crew is seen as a female domain. The metaphorical glass door to women's entry into professional positions and the glass ceiling that has limited the promotion of women are slowly being eroded. While underlying masculine perceptions are being challenged and as more women achieve access and demonstrate that their gender is not a limiting factor, it would be expected that there would be a concurrent development of equity, although this is not a forgone conclusion. A brief history of female pilots in the US, Australia and South Africa is presented.

The US

The importance of female pilots should not be underestimated. From about 1910 onwards, women in the US overcame a variety of prejudices in order to take to the air. Although it is widely known that Blanche Stuart Scott was the first woman to solo in a heavier-than-air machine, the official credit for becoming the first woman pilot in the US went to Bessica Raiche, who went solo on 16 September 1910 (Cadogan, 1992, p. 39). By the 1930s, women were setting an abundance of aviation-related records. Amongst them was Anne Morrow Lindbergh, who came to share her husband Charles Lindbergh's glory when she helped him map air routes over the Arctic and the Atlantic (Yount, 1995, p. 10).

During the Second World War, American women were recruited to ferry fighter and bomber aircraft from the factories to the airfields and between airfields. Post-war developments included numerous long-distance record flights by women. In the 1950s, Jacqueline Cochran, the first woman to break the sound barrier, competed regularly with Jacqueline Auriol for world speed records (Cadogan, 1992, p. 4). During the 1960s, Geraldine Mock and Joan Merriam Smith competed to be the first female aviator to fly around the world.

Later, during the 1970s and 1980s, Judith Chisholm and Jeana Yeager established further notable long-distance endurance records. Corporate campaigns advocating women for equal rights and equal responsibilities were eventually established and this in turn culminated in the employment of women in civil airliners and military jets. By 1973, the first group of women aviators were accepted into the US Navy. In 1995, the world saw the first female pilot, Eileen Collins, of a space shuttle.

Australia

In Australia, access to airline positions had been denied to female pilots. This was challenged in the courts in a case that lasted three-and-a-half years to 1979. The Wardley/Ansett case legitimised equal employment opportunity legislation and was of historical importance that highlighted the underlying support for such social justice (Dahn, 1997). This opened the glass door of professional opportunity for women to apply for positions as airline pilots and be judged on the requirements for pilots rather than their gender. To date, however, there is a paucity of female pilots in the airline sector. A total of 812 (73.2 per cent) Australian survey respondents indicated that their main area of operation was regular passenger transport (RPT), that is, regional, national and international airlines. Of these, only 53 (6.5 per cent) were female pilots, highlighting that piloting in the airline sector of the industry is still a predominantly male-oriented occupation. Although there are no public domain statistics on the number of female pilots, Helmreich and Merritt (1998, p. 42) indicate that in 1996 only three per cent of airline pilots in the US were women. In Australia today, anecdotal evidence suggests that between three per cent and four per cent of airline pilots are women.

Despite a long history of female pilots in Australia, starting with Florence Taylor in 1909 (see Table 7.1), by 1930 there were only 19 pilot licences issues to women. By the beginning of the Second World War, a total of 162 women had pilot licences (Arnold, 2010). Arnold highlights 100 years of Australian female pilot firsts. Table 7.1 outlines some of those firsts.

Table 7.1 Timeline of Australian female pilot firsts

1909	Florence Taylor: first Australian woman in flight in a glider. Narrabeen sandhills near Sydney, 5 December 1909 (National Pioneer's Women Hall of Fame, 2001).
1927	Millicent Bryant: first Australian woman to obtain a pilot's licence (National Pioneer's Women Hall of Fame, 2001).
1929	Bobby Terry: first Australian woman to own her own aircraft (National Pioneer's Women Hall of Fame, 2001).
1930s	Lores Benney: first Australian woman to fly around Australia, to fly solo from Australia to England, and to fly solo from Australia to South Africa. Irene Dean-Williams:fFirst Australian woman to gain a commercial pilot's licence and also the first woman to fly a solo return trip from Perth to Sydney (National Pioneer's Women Hall of Fame, 2001).
1935	Nancy Bird: organises the first Ladies' Flying Tour in Australia (National Pioneer's Women Hall of Fame, 2001).
1938	Formation of the Women's Flying Club (National Pioneer's Women Hall of Fame, 2001).
1941	Second World War: The Women's Air Training Corps is created and develops into the Women's Auxiliary Australian Air Force. Established 5 March 1941 (National Pioneer's Women Hall of Fame, 2001).
1949	Margaret Clarke: first Australian woman crop-duster and aerial spraying pilot, though she was paid as an unskilled worker as no wage was set for women at that time (National Pioneer's Women Hall of Fame, 2001).
1950	Australia Women Pilot's Association (AWPA), incorporating the Women's Flying Club, is formed (National Pioneer's Women Hall of Fame, 2001).
1960	Olga Tarling: appointed as Australia's first woman air traffic controller at Brisbane Airport (National Pioneer's Women Hall of Fame, 2001).

Table 7.1 Continued

1967	Rosemary Arnold-Harris: Australia's first women commercial rotorcraft pilot (National Pioneer's Women Hall of Fame, 2001).
1974	Christine Davy: first Australian woman passenger pilot (National Pioneer's Women Hall of Fame, 2001).
1980	Deborah Wardley: first Australian woman to fly for a major commercial airline (National Pioneer's Women Hall of Fame, 2001).
1982	Kath Meyering: first Australian woman to fly an ultralight (National Pioneer's Women Hall of Fame, 2001).
1987	Mary O'Brien: appointed as Examiner of Airmen – the highest aviation appointment given to a woman (National Pioneer's Women Hall of Fame, 2001).
1988	Female Pilot Graduations in the Royal Australian Air Force (RAAF) crew (Smart, 1998).
1995	Adelaide hosted the first international conference for women in aviation in Australia (National Pioneer's Women Hall Of Fame, 2001) and first women to be permitted to fly jet fighter aircraft in the RAAF (Smart, 1998).
1999	First Australian women military aerobatic pilot. Graduation of the first women F-111 navigators (Smart, 1998).

South Africa

In South Africa, the story of female pilots is similar, that is, there are very few RPT female pilots. The history of female pilots shows similar anti-female pilot sentiments. After the First World War, many women successfully flew the Europe to Cape Town air route. Their daring and sense of adventure inspired many South African women to join local flying clubs. However, the local student pilot scheme was reserved exclusively for men. Despite the restrictions, women were able to gain licences.

By the late 1930s, Marjorie Egerton-Bird, herself an accomplished 'A' pilot licence holder, made a study of the British state-subsidised Civil Air Guard, with the intention of establishing a similar organisation for women in South Africa (Jameson and Ashburner, 1948, p. 1). Doreen Hooper, an instructor at Grand Central Airport, was approached to head this proposed organisation for female pilots. At a public meeting held in Johannesburg on 6 December 1938, the Women's Aviation Association (WAA) was launched.

The aim of the WAA was to train women to assist in the ground handling of aircraft so as to provide assistance to the Air Force in times of need. The organisation succeeded in its aim by awarding bursaries and attracting subsidies from private organisations (Jameson and Ashburner, 1948, p. 1). By 1939, 300 women had joined the association. Of these, 32 members took turns at ground duties such as cleaning engine parts (this task was thought up by men who felt that the women would not enjoy the dirty work and would thus be discouraged from getting involved in the technical aspects of aviation), swinging propellers and pushing aircraft.

The WAA immediately offered its services to the South African government when war broke out on 3 September 1939. Plans were put forward to train 1,000 women for the South African Air Force and for the creation of a Women's Auxiliary Air Force (WAAF). The formation of the South African Women's Auxiliary Air Force (SAWAAF) was gazetted on 10 May 1940. Upon the completion of their training, WAAF members were transferred to various Air Depots and Air Stations throughout South Africa. By June 1942, there were 34 WAAF camps in South Africa. The WAAFs did valuable work in 75 different career fields, 35 of which were technical. They served as typists, parachute packers, welders, aircraft technicians and fitters, drivers and a host of other trades. They were best liked for their domestic skills in the catering mustering. Pilots of the WAAF flew communication and ferry flights and served as duty pilots and second pilots on the SAAF Shuttle Service. The other fields in which women took to the air were as meteorological assistants on the early morning flights and as photographers on survey flights. By special legislation, WAAF women were allowed to be employed on combatant duties. They served on ack-ack sites on instruments to direct the guns and as searchlight operators (Jameson and Ashburner, 1948, pp. 48–53; Nöthling, 1995).

Although women served in the SAWAAF during the period from 1939 to 1947 and as volunteers in the Women's Defence Corps (WDC) in 1948, it was only on 2 October 1972 that the Minister of Defence granted permission for the appointment of women in the permanent force (Nöthling, 1995). The initial three women to join the South African Air Force in 1974 as permanent force members had all been trained at the Civil Defence College in George. They were all Candidate Officers. On 19 January 1974, 33 women began their Basic Training at the Air Defence School at Waterkloof, Pretoria.

In order to adhere to the equal opportunities policy of the South African government, the SAAF has embarked on a programme to train female aircrew members over a period of time. In 1996 the SAAF recruited the first five women for pilot training and since that time, 15 women have received their wings. Currently 13 still function as pilots in the South African Air Force, with one an instructor pilot. Ten female candidate pilots are currently being trained, though none of the female pilots, both qualified and in training, has been assigned to aviation combat roles (Wilson, 2004, p. 61).

In January 2000 South African Airways (SAA), the country's biggest airline, appointed a team of pilots to spearhead and promote its Pilot Employment Equity Recruitment (PEER) programme. The team was tasked to stimulate an interest in flying among qualifying designated groups as required by the Employment Equity Act. As at October 2004, the airline had 970 pilots in its employ, of which 66 are non-white and only 37 are women. Thus, women constitute a mere 3.8 per cent of the commercial pilots in SAA (Wilson, 2004, p. 61).

The history of female pilots in these three countries highlights both the contributions they made and the struggles they faced in achieving their objectives. Some individuals achieved international recognition, but many simply went about gaining their wings and piloting aircraft. Their history also highlights that female pilots were called upon in times of war to replace men, but were then relegated to 'women's roles' after the conflicts. Their experiences are reflective of the cultural obstacles placed in the way of women to circumvent their becoming successful participants in a masculine occupation.

A Gendered Occupation

Piloting in the airline industry is a 'closed shop'. The recruitment of pilots into airlines requires that all applicants meet certain standards of experience and certification. The low numbers of women who undertake the time-consuming and expensive initial training to become a pilot are reflected in the overall dominance of males in the 'top end' of a piloting career. It would appear that only women with the focus and drive, similar to what is socially accepted and expected in men, but not necessarily women, are able to achieve their career goals. Table 7.2 sets out the minimum cost of licences across the three countries in 2012.

Table 7.2 Minimum licence costs (Australian dollars)

Licence/country	Private Pilot Licence (PPL)	Commercial Pilot Licence and endorsements (CPL)
Australia	$16,000	$25,000
South Africa	$6,600	$43,500
US	$9,700	$50,000

Although the cost of learn to fly is the same for for men and women, in terms of acquiring a Private Pilot Licence (PPL) through to a Commercial Pilot Licence (CPL) with endorsements such as multi-engine and instrument ratings and pilot in command hours, women appear to be at a disadvantage. The actual initial cost to PPL level may be more for female pilots as research has found that women are slower to gain confidence in an plane, require more hours before initial solo flights, but handle aircraft controls more smoothly and have fewer accidents than men (Sitler, 1998, pp. 45–6). Further, completing an additional Airline Transport Pilot Licence (ATPL) can add many thousands of dollars to the cost. For example, in Australia the extra cost for the ATPL is at least $20,000. Individuals and families may desist from investing this amount on young women's careers in what is still seen as a male domain imbued with masculine perceptions.

While equal opportunities and anti-discrimination legislation and corporate policies designed to meet these legislative imperatives have helped to open up occupations they still remain segregated along both horizontal and vertical dimensions. The vertical dimension is a measure of the components of inequality, while the horizontal dimension is a measure of the extent of segregation across occupations (Blackburn et al., 2002, p. 514; Charles and Grusky, 2004). The increasing role of women in previously male-dominated occupations has and continues to question and oppose dominant male perceptions with the processes of recruitment, training and development and career opportunities being challenged.

The Research Profile

The ongoing research underpinning this chapter is based on a survey of aviation pilots in South Africa (644: men 604 (93.8 per cent), women 40 (6.2 per cent)), the US (352: men 206 (58.4 per cent), women 146 (41.6 per cent)) and Australia (1,114: men 972 (87.3 per cent), women 142 (12.7 per cent)), a total of 2,111 usable responses. Because there was no specific conceptual theoretical framework or model with regard to gender-related pilot behaviour, the results of the scientific studies on gender issues in aviation mentioned above were used as points of departure for developing the Aviation Gender Attitude Questionnaire (AGAQ). The original questionnaire consisted of 72 statements (items). These statements refer to behavioural domains of learning ability and learning speed, piloting skills, leadership and decision making, and general prejudices and stereotypes. All the statements (except the demographic variables) were rated on a five-point Likert-type scale to measure the perceptions of participants at an approximate interval level (Vermeulen, Wilson and Mitchell, 2004; Wilson, 2004, p. 184). The aviation industry can be separated into general, commercial and airline sectors, and this chapter addresses these areas. Another major sector is associated with surveillance and protection, and incorporates the armed services and police aviation. Access to this sector was very limited and therefore was not included in the research.

In addition to the statistical analyses in the Statistical Package for the Social Sciences (SPSS) that revealed a two-factor solution of 'flying proficiency' and 'safety orientation', comments were recorded and subjected to qualitative analysis utilising the NVivo software program. Coding of the comments was based on a grounded theory approach. Grounded theory is the approach being taken to draw out the categories inherent in the written comments (Goulding, 2002; Miles and Huberman, 1994; Strauss and Corbin, 1998). According to Haig (n.d.): 'a good grounded theory is one that is: (1) inductively derived from the data, (2) subjected to theoretical elaboration, and (3) judged adequate to its domain with respect to a number of evaluative criteria'. While utilising the quantitative analysis to profile perceptions towards gender, qualitative analysis profiled perceptions expressed in the comments. The quantitative and qualitative analyses will be linked to provide a detailed account of the perceptions and how they impact on the management of flight-deck behaviour towards gender issues. A further aim is to evaluate, both quantitatively and qualitatively, national and cross-national perceptions towards gender in the aviation environment.

As a starting point in identifying categories (nodes) most likely to occur in the data, the two factors identified in the quantitative analysis, that is, Flying Proficiency and Safety Orientation, were adopted. In addition, issues such as Sexism, Femininity, Masculinity, Discrimination, Equality and Teamwork were expected to be addressed and were, although Teamwork attracted few references. Several readings of the comments also identified a number of other themes and were coded accordingly. These categories were Respect, Industry, Profession, Competence, Physical and Mental Strength, Work Orientation, Career Opportunities, Training and Survey. Within several of these categories, subcategories of positive and negative statements, together with strong and weak and low, average and high were identified and coded accordingly, as were general comments about a particular issue. Overall, comments were received, recorded and analysed from Australia (men 326/972 (33.5 per cent), women 84/142 (59.2 per cent): 410/1,114 (36.8 per cent)), South Africa (men 181/604 (30 per cent), women 20/40 (50 per cent): 201/644, 31.2 per cent)) and the US (men 88/206 (42.7 per cent), women 66/146 (45.2 per cent): 154/352 (43.8 per cent)). These nodes have been further grouped into broader themes and these are presented in Table 7.3.

Table 7.3 Themes and nodes

Theme	Node
Flying Proficiency	• Flying Proficiency • Competence • Teamwork
Safety Orientation	• Standards • Performance
Industry	• Industry • Professionalisation • Training • Career • Work Orientation
Gender Issues	• Femininity • Masculinity • Strength (Anthropometrics) • Sexism
Equity	• Equality • Discrimination • Respect
Survey	• Survey

Results

The results presented in this chapter do not attempt to cover all of the findings of the research, but primarily address the qualitative component. The total number of comments for each theme is highlighted in Table 7.4.

Some comments covered several nodes and therefore attracted multiple coding. In total, there were 823 (66 per cent) coded comments from male and 424 (34 per

Table 7.4 **Comments per theme**

	Australia			South Africa			United States			
Theme	**Men**	**Women**	**Total**	**Men**	**Women**	**Total**	**Men**	**Women**	**Total**	**Overall Total**
Flying Proficiency	72 15.5%	22 14.8%	**94** **15.3%** *7.5%*	36 15.3%	5 18.6%	**41** **15.6%** *3.3%*	25 20.2%	22 8.9%	**47** **12.6%** *3.7%*	**182** ***14.6%***
Safety Orientation	20 4.3%	5 3.4%	**25** **4.1%** *2.0%*	27 11.5%	3 11.1%	**30** **11.5%** *2.4%*	12 9.7%	29 11.7%	**41** **11.0%** *3.3%*	**96** *7.7%*
Industry	121 26.1%	33 22.1%	**154** **25.1%** *12.3%*	51 21.7%	4 14.8%	**55** **21.0%** *4.4%*	36 29.0%	61 24.6%	**97** **26.1%** *7.8%*	**306** ***24.5%***
Gender Issues	105 22.6%	37 24.8%	**142** **23.2%** *11.4%*	46 19.6%	4 14.8%	**50** **19.1%** *4.0%*	14 11.3%	40 16.1%	**54** **14.5%** *4.3%*	**246** ***19.8%***
Equity	82 17.7%	27 18.1%	**109** **17.8%** *8.7%*	46 19.6%	8 29.6%	**54** **20.6%** *4.3%*	19 15.3%	73 29.4%	**92** **24.7%** *7.4%*	**255** ***20.4%***
Survey	64 13.8%	25 16.8%	**89** **14.5%** *7.1%*	29 12.3%	3 11.1%	**32** **12.2%** *2.7%*	18 14.5%	23 9.3%	**41** **11.0%** *3.3%*	**162** ***13.0%***
Total	464 100%	149 100%	**613** ***49.2%***	235 100%	27 100%	**262** ***21.0%***	124 100%	248 100%	**372** ***29.8%***	**1247** ***100.0%***

cent) from female pilots. The percentages shown in the men and women columns are the number of comments per theme for that country. The percentages (in bold) shown in the Total columns are the proportion of the total for each country. The percentages (in bold italics) are the proportion of the overall total. Differences in percentages are due to rounding. Each of these themes will now be addressed.

Flying Proficiency

Flying Proficiency refers to how proficient either gender is perceived to be at the task of piloting. The principal elements of this theme relate to learning ability, the speed at which concepts related to flying are understood, decision making in flying, general piloting skills, and the perceived comfort level with regard to stick and rudder controls. These were identified in the nodes of Proficiency, Competence and Teamwork. Competence is reflected in the real attributes of knowledge and/or manual dexterity. While the evaluation of the level of skill is often subjective, a pilot's observations of another's skill depend on his or her training, practice and experience. The comments made throughout are subjective and based not only on experience and observation, but are also modified through the person's perceptions.

The comments from respondents in Australia (15.3 per cent), South Africa (15.6 per cent) and the US (12.6 per cent) in respect of flying proficiency displayed a high level of commonality. Both men and women indicated that gender is not necessarily a factor in determining the flying proficiency of pilots; rather, it is the ability of the individual and their personality that is the determining factor of their proficiency. Examples of poor piloting skills were identified by both men and women, and indications were given that, in some instances, some individuals should have not been allowed to fly. Overall, the majority of comments about the competence of female pilots were positive across all age groups, experience levels and industry sectors. Comments indicated that female pilots were 'good', 'competent', 'outstanding', 'professional' and 'better than the men'. However, female respondents tended to be more positive about their own and other female pilots' ability compared to the responses given by male respondents. Negative comments, all male (Australia 3; US, 4), indicated that female pilots crack under pressure more than male pilots, lack situational awareness and navigational skills and that they make enormous mistakes. One 51-year-old airline pilot said that he had not flown with a good female pilot in 35 years of flying. These negative comments were far outweighed by more positive expressions of female flying proficiency.

Comments concerning competence often indicated different approaches to skill and therefore the control of the aircraft. Male pilots indicated that they believed female pilots lacked an innate sense of the mechanics and dynamics of flight, and this impacted on their assessment of the female pilots' perceived skills. Female pilots, on the other hand, emphasised competence in areas such as leadership and communication skills. They also expressed the view that when flying with different men for the first time, the male pilots appeared apprehensive and seemed to doubt or question the female pilots' ability until the latter demonstrated their competence. Male pilots tended to assume and to take other male pilots' competence and skills as a given or at face value, but female pilots clearly had to demonstrate their skills before acceptance nearly every time they flew in a new cross-gender crew situation. Comments from both male and female pilots indicated that female pilots were different and brought a skill set that was more feminine than masculine into aviation.

Teamwork within aviation is vital to the management of flight of the aircraft. Teamwork exists, whether on a multi-crew flight-deck or between a single pilot and the air traffic controller (ATC). It is important in controlling and utilising flight resources and considerable training in crew resource management (CRM) occurs in the airline sectors. While anticipating many comments relating to teamwork between genders in flying, these failed to materialise. Only three comments from South Africa and eight from the US were identified, of which one and two respectively were from women. Many respondents saw that a positive perception was important in establishing teamwork and that women tended to be more effective in building those relationships. Problems of isolation arose for a female pilot when she was the only women within the group.

Overall, within the theme of flying proficiency, the comments from female pilots reflected a more positive perception towards the capabilities of female pilots than that espoused by male pilots. While some male pilots highly praised the competencies of female pilots, male pilots generally were not as positive in relation to the flying proficiency of female pilots. Unless the male pilots had positive exposure to the capabilities of female pilots, they tended to not regard female pilots as being as proficient as male pilots. This is consistent with the findings obtained from the statistical analyses of the AGAQ (Mitchell, Kristovics and Vermeulen, 2004; Wilson, 2004).

Safety Orientation

Safety Orientation related to perceptions about the level of risk-taking amongst pilots of a particular gender. This included safety consciousness, attention to detail, situational awareness and prudence. The comments were identified as falling into two subcategories of Safety Standards and Safety Performance. Given the high profile of safety within the aviation industry, the number of comments identified as safety related were very low. Overall, safety related comments were very low (Australia 2 per cent, South Africa 2.7 per cent and the US 3.3 per cent, overall 7.7 per cent). This may indicate that, although not 'taken for granted', safety concerns and practices were an expected norm. Comments from Australia (25, 4.1 per cent of the Australian comments) were considerably lower that those from South Africa (30, 11.5 per cent) and the US (41, 11 per cent). This may reflect the fact that in Australia, comparatively, gender does not play a significant part in a pilot's safety orientation.

Respondents, who did comment, however, raised several issues in relation to standards and performance. A consistent concern across the three countries was that of the maintenance of standards. The main thrust of these comments was the belief of systematic double standards. Male pilots expressed the idea that safety standards were being eroded by allowing female pilots latitude in: (a) achieving their licences; and (b) gaining access to flying positions over more qualified male pilots. Item (b) will be considered in more depth in the 'Industry' section below.

The majority of comments on the issue of safety standards came from predominantly male airline pilots across the three countries. Concern was expressed that as long as female pilots were evaluated by and achieved the same standards, everything would be fine. Many indicated that they had seen or believed that female pilots had been treated more favourably in respect of meeting standards by the provision of extra training or allowances made for errors not afforded to male pilots. Safety performance comments mainly came from female pilots across a broader range that included private, instructor, commercial and airline industry sectors. The views expressed indicated that men and women approach safety from differing perspectives. Mn tended to 'take more risks', are 'less attentive' and provided an 'ostentatious display', allowing their ego to override safety. Women tended to 'plan more', are less likely to have 'misplaced confidence' and 'know and fly by the book'.

Although all pilots have a concern for safety, male pilots tended to judge female pilots to be less safe. On the other hand, female pilots had a greater belief in their safety orientation. Again, the comments are consistent with the statistical analysis where women had a more positive perception of their safety. This highlights the different perceptions of risk and approaches taken by men and women to safe practices that are reflected in the different types of accidents experienced by male and female pilots. A study of general aviation crashes in the US has indicated that while there are common causes, there were differences in the types of accident experienced by either gender. Common causes among accidents involving male pilots were inattention and flawed decision making, while for female pilots, mishandling of aircraft kinetics was the most common event. The more serious accidents involving fatalities and serious injuries (19 per cent plus an additional 12 per cent respectively) were with male pilots, while crashes for female pilots were 15 per cent and 7 per cent respectively (Baker et al., 2001, pp. 447–52).

Industry

Included in the overall industry group are the nodes of Industry, Professionalisation, Training, Work Orientation and Career Opportunities. Comments about the industry varied between each country – Australia (25.1 per cent), South Africa (21 per cent) and the US (26.1 per cent) – but overall there were common concerns that aviation remained male-dominated. There were also expressions across all countries that the industry welcomed female pilots, but indicated that it remained a tough industry for them: 'Unfortunately for women, the aviation industry contains plenty of Neanderthal males at all levels'. Australian male pilots tended to be more strident in their opposition to female pilots, considering them to be 'more trouble than they are worth'. Comments from women from Australia and the US indicate that it is hard for female pilots in terms of the prejudices and opposition, particularly from older male pilots. Many female pilots indicated that they continually have to 'prove' themselves to be accepted within the industry. The male-gendered aviation industry in general, and the older contingent of male pilots in particular, tended to regard female pilots with suspicion and occasional hostility. These limitations created by social stereotypes and negative perceptions tended to be overcome by female pilots adopting a professional approach to their work. Being professional and being seen to be professional, according to a cross-section of comments, often negated the stereotypes associated with female pilots.

Comments about the differences between training male and female pilots appeared to be consistent across the three countries. The main distinction was that female trainees tended to rely on the 'book' for understanding of the theoretical aspects of flying, while male trainees tended to be more interested in the practical aspect of flying. A general consensus was that women took longer to achieve the same level of skill as male trainees. At the airline level, some male pilots commented that female pilots were given extra training and allowances made for errors not afforded to male pilots. In Australia and the US, concern was expressed that female airline pilots were being 'pushed through' to meet diversity requirements. In South Africa there was a concern about racial rather than gender differences. Overall, there was a general recognition that men and women learn and process information differently, but that the end result was the same. Female trainees were also regarded as being safer than the 'more macho' approach of male trainees with something to prove.

The general consensus across the three countries was that female pilots work harder than their male counterparts. Statements indicated this was because of perceived difficulties for female pilots or because they had something to prove. The propensity to work harder may reflect an attempt to compensate for the often underlying pervasive masculine and negative view that women should not become pilots. Therefore, women, in order to achieve their goals, did put in considerable extra effort just to be regarded as being equal to male pilots.

Equal employment opportunity (EEO) and affirmative action (AA) legislation has expanded the career opportunities for female pilots across the three countries. However, the impact of this social legislation was highlighted fairly equally by both positive and negative comments. Australian (12.3 per cent +ve, 11.0 per cent -ve), South African (12.7 per cent +ve, 5.5 per cent -ve) and American (13.4 per cent +ve, 11.3 per cent -ve) comments indicated that careers for female pilots had been boosted and that this was good. Not only were there more opportunities within the industry, but promotion opportunities for female pilots had also increased. The negative side revealed that there was resentment that female pilots with fewer hours were given preference over male pilots. Not only were female pilots with less experience given preference, there was also a belief that standards had been compromised. Some indicated that female pilot careers were interrupted by having children and represented a significant cost to the airlines. There were also comments that flying schools and airlines in particular were playing 'political correctness' to avoid any suspicion of 'sexual discrimination' in employment practices. An Australian airline pilot expressed the view that EEO and AA were 'used by the militant feminist lobby unfairly against men and impact unfairly against men in the employment field'. Both positive and negative comments represented a cross-section of perceptions within the aviation domain.

The analyses and discussions thus far have indicated similar perspectives on flying proficiency, safety orientation and industry from both female and male pilots across the three countries. The perceptions, both positive and negative, have not highlighted any gender or country as being distinct or different. Perceptions appear to be more attuned to individual rather than national differences. An explanation appears to be that pilots have a worldwide industry and occupational ethos based on similar training, standards and professional culture. A major influence in this respect is the requirements for international aviation standards and operations generated by the International Civil Aviation Organization (ICAO), of which the three countries are members. Further, the Federal Aviation Administration (FAA) of the US has contributed significantly to the development of operational, training and safety standards. The following two sections differentiate perceptions between Australian, South African and American pilots.

Gender Issues

Nodes covered in gender issues include femininity, masculinity, sexism and strength. Comments on gender issues accounted for 23.2 per cent, 19.1 per cent and 14.5 per cent of Australian, South African and American comments respectively. This represents a clearer indication of different perspectives between the pilots and their country of origin.

Femininity was considered as socially ascribed characteristics, such as caring, warmth and sexually attractive as well as passive, weak and dependent. While the comments were often positive towards female pilots, regular reference was made to the impact, real or imagined, of women's biological functions of menstruation and childbearing on their performance. Australian respondents (14.7 per cent) tended to comment less about these issues than the South Africans (18.0 per cent) and Americans (18.9 per cent). Generally, comments on femininity did equate women's hormonal changes with mood swings, resulting in potential safety problems and poor crew resource management. Female pilots tended to say that emotions were treated as a weakness and their emotions were seen as not being consistent with the 'right stuff'. Some female pilots were seen as having a testosterone-driven ego, but were prepared to use feminine charms where necessary. American comments included the concern that some female pilots used the feminist card to get their way, while some South Africans indicated that female pilots lose their femininity.

Being considered to be 'one of the boys' was not uncommon among female pilots across the three nations. It does appear that female pilots do take on, either consciously or unconsciously, some of the masculine beliefs and behaviours of the occupation. However, very little consideration was given to an individual's variation to the universalised masculine and feminine stereotypes to ascertain whether they did fit the appropriate stereotype (Bird, 2003, p. 580). Research by the US military indicated that while female and male air force pilots are statistically different, the female pilots are more similar to the male pilots than to women in general (King, McGlohn and Retzlaff, 1997, p. 697). This may also be the case where some minority groups, such as female pilots, will attempt to assimilate into the dominant culture in an attempt to lessen or negate the impact of stereotyping and marginalisation. Overall, comments on the strengths and weaknesses of femininity appeared inconsistent with the masculine ethos of the occupation.

Australian comments (3.6 per cent of total) were more concerned with masculinity issues than their South African (1.9 per cent) and American (1.1 per cent) counterparts. Older male airline pilots tended to emphasise male qualities in pilots as being the ideal. Others commented that men had bigger egos and were more likely to take risks or behave aggressively. Although the male pilots gave recognition to the capabilities of female pilots, the men tended to prefer to fly with other male pilots and regularly belittled the different skill sets of female pilots.

Sexist comments, both positive and negative, contributed significantly to the gender issues theme. These comments revolved around sex-role stereotypes in which beliefs about the appropriate roles for males and women were expressed (Kreitner and Kinicki, 1998, p. 164). The positive comments tended to highlight the inappropriateness of stereotypical views of female pilots. Overall, indications were that female pilots were as competent, if not better than their male counterparts, given that there were good and bad pilots of both genders. Australians (3.6 per cent) had more positive comments than the South Africans (2.3 per cent) and Americans (0.8 per cent). Similarly, the negative comments from each of the countries moved in the same direction. These were Australian (9.8 per cent), South African (8.0 per cent) and American (6.7 per cent). Comments such as 'a female pilot = another empty kitchen' and 'if girls were meant to fly the sky would be pink' reflect many of the negative comments across the three countries. Other comments were directed at the attractiveness or otherwise of female pilots, their morals and that the 'facts' confirm that women should not fly. While there is a strong anti-female pilot bias within the occupation, surprisingly, several female pilots reported that they had not experienced or were unaware of any prejudice directed towards them in their flying career. This may well be that these female pilots have embraced the masculinity of the occupation through self-socialisation and that they are a product of the company they keep (Jacklin, 1989).

Given that there are physiological differences between men and women. Physical strength, regarded as a masculine attribute and a feminine limitation, was considered important in piloting by three per cent of respondents. Comments about the physical attributes necessary to fly an aircraft further reflect the stereotyping of women as not meeting these requirements. Safety considerations were a concern that female pilots did not have the strength to manipulate the controls in emergencies and that, generally, women were too short to reach and operate the pedals effectively. Some female pilots admitted that they had some height and strength limitations, but now, with improved computerised servo-mechanical devices, the requirement for physical strength was not an issue. These comments were distributed evenly across the three cultures.

Overall, gender was much more of an issue for Australian pilots than for South African and American pilots. While there were many positive comments about female pilots, there remained a high level of sex-role stereotyping. In piloting, stereotypical masculine attributes were considered to be more important than feminine attributes. Not that these male attributes were highlighted; rather, it was the feminine attributes that were discussed and expressed as limitations. The Australian data indicates a stronger orientation towards masculinity in that country compared to that of South Africa. It appears that in the US, gender, given that the majority of American comments were from female pilots, was not so much of an issue. However, in issues of equity, comments from the American and Australian respondents were reversed, with South African respondents remaining between the two.

Equity

The equity theme consists of equality, discrimination and respect. Across the three nations, it was the South Africans (11.5 per cent), followed by the Americans (10.8 per cent) and the Australians (8.0 per cent), who commented the most on the equality of female pilots. Despite the often limited exposure to flying with female pilots, the vast majority of male pilots indicated that female pilots were just as capable and were often superior in some aspects of flying. American comments on equality, mainly from women respondents, felt that they had been treated equitably in learning to fly and in their operational environment. On the other hand, American female pilots (8.9 per cent) were more prepared to highlight their experiences of discrimination that was based on their gender. These included examples of bullying, both sexual and gender harassment, and outright hostility.

Positive and negative comments were also made about employment quotas from American and South African pilots. The recruitment of female pilots under AA programmes has been seen as an effort to fill quotas. This has led to expressions of resentment and an unfounded belief that female pilots who were hired were incompetent (Vermeulen, Vermeulen and Le Kay, 2004). Issues of both racial and gender quotas were raised in some South African comments. Australian comments were more concerned about the impact of affirmative action and equal employment opportunities. (There are no quotas mandated in Australian anti-discrimination legislation). Claims were made that women now had a distinct advantage in terms of employment and promotional opportunities. For example, women with fewer hours were given preference over men in both employment and promotion; airlines were afraid of accusations of discrimination and thus acted in a politically correct manner. Across the three countries, there were examples of both positive and negative discrimination. Senior (2003) reported that many women experience gender-related obstacles which cause disadvantages, difficulty and distress in career advancement: 'They encounter strong prejudices and preconceptions concerning their abilities and suitability for particular careers. If they are forceful, they violate prescriptions of feminine "niceness". They must choose to be respected but not liked, or liked but not respected' (2003, p. 18). While expressing examples of respect, both given and earned, the comments generally indicated that the female pilots had to be equal to or better than what was expected from male pilots. The female pilots had to be continually judged favourably against the masculine image of a pilot in order to gain respect. There were also indications that female pilots gained respect for their ability to succeed in the traditionally male area of piloting.

Issues of equity, expressed through the comments about equality, discrimination and respect, indicate that the presence of women within the occupation of pilot challenged the masculine beliefs and norms of the domain. Successful female pilots earned a grudging respect provided they met the masculine defined criteria of skill and competence. While their advancement was somewhat welcomed, it drew out negative comments that highlighted the underlying antipathy towards women encroaching into a perceived male preserve.

Survey

Interestingly, the survey itself attracted 13.0 per cent of the total comments. These ranged from 'good survey' to 'waste of time' and 'you can't be serious'. It seems that this survey touched on what was seen as a sensitive issue to a lot of respondents. In both Gender Issues and Equity, proportionally (with the exception of South African women's comments on Gender Issues), comments from women were more numerous than those from men. The survey gave women a voice and they took the opportunity to express their concerns and views about the importance of Gender Issues and Equity in aviation to them.

Most comments on the survey came from Australia (14.5 per cent), with negative comments accounting for 8.0 per cent of these. South Africa (12.2 per cent, 4.5 per cent -ve) and the US (11.0 per cent, 3 per cent -ve) followed, with the balance between the percentage figure being general comments. The general tone of the negative comments was that this subject should be left alone as it was a topic that was best left unexamined. By taking it off the agenda, the issues raised brings to the fore the gendered profile of the occupation. This raises questions that would be, from a masculine perspective, difficult to provide justification for the continuing bias on an individual and organisational level against female pilots. At a deeper level, it challenged male occupational privileges, queried the concept of 'the right stuff' and emphasised the rights and abilities rather than the stereotype of female pilots. To 'give it a rest', as one respondent suggested, is to deny the opportunity to research, raise awareness and challenge the perceptions and stereotypes surrounding the occupation of pilots.

Summary

The occupation of aviation pilot, at first glance, appears to be a bastion of masculinity in which very few women can enter. Those who do choose piloting as a career do so in the face of considerable opposition and hostility from the occupational culture of male pilots. However, the occupation is not exclusively masculine in its orientation. The distribution of positive and negative comments reflects the normality of the distribution of the quantitative results from the survey. There are those who express highly positive comments about female pilots and there are those at the other extreme who are equally negative in their comments, the bulk of perceptions occurring around the mean. The occupation is an arena of contested terrain in which the abilities and, indeed, rights of female pilots are being subjected to considerable debate.

The utilisation of both qualitative and quantitative analyses has enhanced the analyses of the database of the perceptions of pilots. The questionnaire gave respondents the opportunity to express their ideas as well as providing a profile of their gender-related perceptions. While concentrating on the qualitative component in this chapter, the quantitative analysis provided considerable support to the analysis. Overall, there was a tendency for the older male pilots to be anti-women in their opinions, but this was counterbalanced by the perceptions of the younger brigade. The older male pilots often had little or no experience of flying with female pilots and retained a stereotypical belief of the role of women. Importantly, as both men and women have the opportunity to fly together, they become more familiar with the other's capabilities. This leads to a positive change and a breakdown of stereotypical perceptions towards the opposite gender. For male pilots, this means that they are evaluating female pilots more often on their professional competence rather than their sex. It reduces the need for the occupation to be seen as masculine, thus opening the glass door of opportunity to more women wishing to pursue a career in flying. This is also being enhanced by the emergence of female pilots in the military who can become engaged in combat missions. This remains an area of much controversy and debate; however, many countries now allow women access to all roles in aviation, including combat roles.

The cross-national analysis revealed more similarities than differences between the three countries. This appeared to be the result of similar training, types of aircraft flown, industry standards and structure and the internationalisation of the profession of pilot. This finding is consistent with a cross-national study of decision making among pilots from the US, Australia and Norway. The 'activities, roles and expectations of pilots are, to a large extent, the same regardless of where they exercise their skills' (Hunter, Martinussen and Wiggins, 2003, p. 86). On a broader scale, Jones and Smith (2001) found that there is a high level of commonality in the way people from a wide range of countries think about their national identity. Therefore, it would seem that pilots from different countries think about their occupation and gender in similar ways. The role of gender still plays an important part in the perceptions of many pilots. Female pilots, being in the minority, still face many obstacles in achieving their goals. The masculine ethos of the occupation appears to be changing, albeit slowly. This is being enhanced by legislation and organisational practices that outlaw discrimination and at the same time provide career opportunities for women. This, in itself, will not change perceptions. It would seem that when the size of the female cohort in flying reaches some 'critical mass', there will be more acceptance of women as professional pilots rather than the existing view on the stereotypical roles of women.

References

Arnold, R., 2010. *First Females Above Australia.* Balgowlah: Arnold.

Baker, S.P., Lamb, M.W., Grabowski, J.G., Rebok, G. and Li, G., 2001. Characteristics of general aviation crashes involving mature male and female pilots. *Aviation, Space, and Environmental Medicine*, 72(5), pp. 447–52.

Bateman. S., 1987. 'The right stuff' has no gender. *Aerospace Power Journal.* Available at: http://www.airpower.maxwell.af.mil/airchronicles/apj/apj87/win87/bateman.html.

Bird, S., 2003. Sex composition, masculine stereotype dissimilarity and the quality of men's workplace social relations. *Gender, Work and Organization*, 10(5), pp. 579–604.

Blackburn, R.M., Browne, J., Brooks, B. and Jarman, J., 2002. Explaining gender segregation. *British Journal of Sociology*, 53(4), pp. 513–36.

Cadogan, M., 1992. *Women with Wings.* Chicago, IL: Academy Chicago Publishers.

Charles, M. and Grusky, D., 2004. *Occupational Ghettos: The Worldwide Segregation of Momen and Men.* Stanford, CA: Stanford University Press.

Dahn, S., 1997. *Wardley v. Ansett*: An examination and analysis of a leading and influential opportunity case. MBA, University of Melbourne.

Davey, C.L. and Davidson, M.J., 2000. The right of passage? The experiences of female pilots in commercial aviation. *Feminism & Psychology*, 10(2), pp. 195–225.

Goulding, C., 2002. *Grounded Theory.* London: Sage.

Haig, B.D., n.d. *Grounded Theory as Scientific Method.* Available at: http://www.ed.uiuc.edu/EPS/PES-Yearbook/95_docs/haig.html.

Hearn, J., 1993. Emotive subjects: Organizational men, organizational masculinities and the (de)construction of 'emotions'. In: S. Fineman (ed.), *Emotion in Organizations*. London: Sage, pp. 142–66.

Helmreich, R.L and Merritt, A.C., 1998. *Culture at Work in Aviation and Medicine.* Aldershot: Ashgate.

Hunter, D., Martinussen, M. and Wiggins, M., 2003. Understanding how pilots make weather-related decisions. *International Journal of Aviation Psychology*, 13(1), pp. 73–87.

Jacklin, C., 1989. Women and male: Issues of gender. *American Psychologist*, 44(2), pp. 127–33.

Jameson, K. and Ashburner, D., 1948. *South African W.A.A.F.* Pietermaritzburg: Shuter & Shooter.

Jones, F. and Smith, P., 2001. Diversity and commonality in national identities: An exploratory analysis of cross-national patterns. *Journal of Sociology*, 37(1), pp. 45–63.

King, R., McGlohn, S. and Retzlaff, P., 1997. Women United States air force pilot personality: The new right stuff. *Military Medicine*, 162, pp. 695–7.

Kreitner. R. and Kinicki, A., 1998. *Organizational Behavior*, 4th edn. Boston: Irwin/McGraw Hill.

Miles, M. and Huberman, A., 1994. *Qualitative Data Analysis.* Thousand Oaks, CA: Sage.

Mills, A., 1998. Cockpits, hangars, boys and galleys: Corporate masculinities and the development of British Airways. *Gender, Work and Organization*, 5(3), pp. 172–88.

Mitchell, J., Kristovics, A. and Vermeulen, L., 2004. Pilot perceptions across cultures: The Australian perspective on gender perceptions. *26th Conference of the European Association of Aviation Psychologists*, 3–7 October, Lisbon.

Moolman, V., 1981. *Women Aloft.* Alexandria: Time-Life.

National Pioneer's Women Hall of Fame, 2001. High flyers: Australia's women pioneers of aviation. Available at: http://www.pioneerwomen.com.au.

Nicholson, P., 1996. *Gender, Power and Organisation.* London: Routledge.

Nothling C.J., 1995. *Geskiedenis van die Suid-Afrikaanse Weermag. Deel 2: 19-15-1 991.* Pretoria: SAMHIK.

Rollinson, D., Broadfield, D. and Edwards, A., 1998. *Organisational Behaviour and Analysis.* Singapore: Addison-Wesley.

Senior, L., 2003. Challenges facing women at work. *People Dynamics*, 21(9), p. 18.

Sitler, R., 1998. The cockpit classroom: Women's perceptions of learning to fly and implications for flight curriculum and instruction. PhD, Kent State University.

Sitler, R., Turney, M.A. and Wulle, B., 1996. Perceptions reflective of gender-based issues in the aviation and transportation workplace. In: B.J. Hayward and A.R. Lowe (eds), *Applied Aviation Psychology: Proceedings of the Third Australian Aviation Psychology Symposium*. Aldershot: Avebury, pp. 332–42.

Smart, T.L., 1998. Fast women: Or why women who fly high performance aircraft are fast but not loose. *Australian Military Medicine*, 7(1), pp. 8–16.

Strauss, A. and Corbin, J., 1998. *Basics of Qualitative Research.* Thousand Oaks, CA: Sage.

Turney, M.A., 1995. Women's learning and leadership styles: Impact on CRM. In: N. McDonald, N. Johnston and R. Fuller (eds), *Applications of Psychology to the Aviation System. Proceedings of the 21st Conference of the European Association for Aviation Psychology (EAAP).* Aldershot: Ashgate, pp. 262–8.

Turney, M.A., 2000. Attracting women to aviation careers: What recent studies reveal. *Collegiate Aviation Review* (Fall).

——. 2004. *Tapping Diverse Talent in Aviation.* Aldershot: Ashgate.

Vermeulen, L., Vermeulen, P. and Le Kay, U., 2004. The perception of flight instructors with regard to gender-related pilot behaviour. *52nd International Congress on Aviation and Space Medicine*, September, Sun City, South Africa.

Vermeulen, L., Wilson, J. and Mitchell, J., 2004. The measurement of perceptions regarding gender-related pilot behaviour: An exploratory study. *26th Conference of the European Association of Aviation Psychologists*, Lisbon, 3–7 October.

Wilson, J., 2004. Gender-based issues in aviation, perceptions towards women pilots: A cross-cultural analysis. PhD thesis, University of Pretoria.

Wolfe, T., 1980. *The Right Stuff.* New York: Bantam Books.

Yount, L., 1995. *Women Aviators.* New York: Facts on File.

Chapter 8
Flying through Barriers: Identifying Issues for Female Airline Pilots

Jane Neal-Smith

Introduction

Civil Aviation Authority (CAA) statistics state that there were 5,319 men and two women employed as professional airline pilots within the UK commercial industry in 1974 (see www.caa.co.uk/airlinestatistics). The latest statistics indicate that out of 17,056 commercial pilots, 740 are women, numbering just over four per cent (CAA, 2008).[1] These numbers are comparable with other countries; evidence suggests that in Australia, Norway and South Africa, female pilots make up between three and four per cent (Mitchell et al., 2005). The low numbers of female airline pilots has meant that aviation organisational culture has been slow to change. Some airlines have introduced recruitment drives aimed at women by deliberately advertising in women's magazines such as *Cosmopolitan*. However, contemporary images on the World Wide Web still use men to advertise the role of airline pilots.[2] Furthermore, despite adopting positive policies and procedures to address these low numbers, the industry remains dominated by 'masculine beliefs, values and perceptions' (Mitchell, Kristovics and Vermeulen, 2006, p. 36). Moreover, one of the factors which women complain about is the lack of real role models (Walker, 2003), but with low numbers of female pilots, it is hard to find real role models and without role models, it is harder to encourage young women into commercial flying as a career.

Literature on Women's Working Lives

Despite legislation which was brought in during the 1970s (Oakley, 1981), many work spaces still remain segregated, with men concentrated into different and

1 This figure includes the Airline Transport Pilot Licence (ATPL) and the Commercial Pilot Licence (CPL). Figures for the ATPL only indicate that there are 451 female holders out of a total of 12,408.

2 See http://www.acareerchange.co.uk/changing-career-becoming-pilot.html; http://science.howstuffworks.com/transport/flight/modern/pilot.htm; http://www.pilottrainingcollege.com/OurCourses/SchoolLeaverorGraduate.aspx; http://www.ukjobsguide.co.uk/Career-Guide/Airline-Pilot.html; http://www.airleague.co.uk; http://www.gapan.org.

usually more prestigious areas than women (Acker, 1990; Smith, Caputi and Crittenden, 2012). Gendered segregation does not create occupational kudos and economic advantages for women because the more prestigious and better paid jobs are reserved for men (Jarman et al., 1999). Much of the feminist analysis of the position of women in society seeks to understand why women are relegated to certain occupational spaces and why these spaces are devalued through being labelled as women's work. It seems that there is a double bind for women in the labour market: they are located in occupations which demand so-called feminine characteristics, which make them women's work, and then they are seen as less prestigious and well paid than traditional male occupations.

Gender stereotyping is not uncommon and can be found in occupations that are predominantly dominated by one gender (CIPD, 2005; Miller et al., 2004; O'Donnell, 2008; Powell et al., 2004; UK Resource Centre for Women in SET, 2007; Whittock, 2000). Williams (1989) explores the experiences of women employed in the Marines and male nurses, examples of two occupations which have traditionally defined characteristics deemed suitable for each role.

The type of occupations seen as women's work are usually based around caring skills, for example, nursing, or skills based on sexuality, such as cabin crew and waitressing (Game and Pringle, 1983; Hall, 1993; Tyler and Taylor, 1998). In the UK, women's traditional occupations are classified as the '5Cs' (catering, cleaning, caring, clerical and cashiering) and women are encouraged to enter them (CIPD, 2005). Moreover, three-quarters of working women are employed in these five occupational groups (O'Donnell, 2008).

Furthermore, men who work in female jobs are seen as losing status (Game and Pringle, 1983; Williams, 1989). Once an occupation becomes associated with one gender or another, the gender difference eventually becomes seen as a necessary element for employment (Bagilhole, 2002). It also serves to prevent women working in male jobs and vice versa. In the case of engineering, Powell, Bagilhole and Dainty (2008) argue that the image of engineering as a masculine occupation has perpetuated the idea that it is an unsuitable job for a woman. Moreover, these traditional stereotypes serve to reward male jobs because masculine qualities are highly regarded in society (Williams, 1989).

When women move across into what are termed traditional male occupations, they face challenges and also pose them; their presence becomes a threat (Williams, 1989). However, as Bagilhole argues, women are not solely a threat by their presence; it is their 'claims to equality' that their male colleagues find threatening (2002, p. 6). As Chambers (in Davey and Davidson, 2000, p. 197) states, one chief pilot described female pilots as average to above average and thought that if a woman had overcome the barriers to employment, then she must be a good pilot. Moreover, as Mitchell et al. (2005) found in their research into gender issues in Australia, Norway, South Africa and the US, female pilots were required to demonstrate their skills nearly every time they flew with a new male pilot. This did not apply to male pilots.

The UK Aviation Industry: Training and Entry Criteria for Commercial Pilots

In the contemporary aviation industry, there are three main methods of achieving a commercial licence: joining the armed services as a trainee pilot, self-funding towards a commercial licence (CPL or ATPL) or gaining an airline sponsorship. A commercial licence can be gained by completing an approved course of either integrated training or modular flying training and a theoretical knowledge training course. Some airlines offer either part or full sponsorship, but this tends to be very competitive (see www.balpa.org.uk).

After gaining a commercial licence, jobs for first officers (co-pilots) require both a commercial pilot's licence and an instrument rating (IR). Employment depends on supply and demand, and the industry has undergone sporadic periods of unemployment and recruitment (Bruford, 1998; www.prospects.ac.uk). A newly qualified pilot with approximately 200 hours could expect to secure employment with a number of airlines; however, progression to larger, heavier aircraft which operate to faraway destinations usually requires extensive experience. Pilot experience is categorised in terms of numbers of hours flown and as pilots are limited to 900 hours in a rolling year, progressing to long-haul aircraft can take up to five to 10 years (CAP 371, 2004).

Promotion within the airlines is based on seniority and perceived ability within that airline, so female pilots have an equal chance of becoming captains when they attain the right level of seniority; indeed, three women interviewed for this study were training captains. However, because promotion is also based on suitability, places available and seniority, fewer women are likely to be captains because of the relatively short time they have been employed in the industry. Within a large airline, promotion to captain can take up to 10 years. Moreover, larger airlines generally tend to operate larger aircraft, which require more experience. This double bind of the length of time it takes to achieve the hours to fly larger, heavier aircraft plus the time in the airline to gain the seniority means that pilots could expect to be flying for 10–15 years before they can acquire enough experience and seniority to gain a command. Being a captain of a long-haul aircraft 'is considered by many to be the ultimate in career achievement' (Mitchell et al., 2006, p. 37). This means that fewer female pilots are likely to be captains because they have been employed within commercial aviation for a shorter period of time than male pilots and in much lower numbers.

Female pilots were employed before the Equal Opportunities Act 1970 and the Sex Discrimination Act 1975, but their recruitment was due to low numbers of male pilots, which meant that the recruitment pool had to be expanded to cope with the demand. However, the numbers of female pilots has still remained much lower than those of male pilots. In the period from the 1930s to the 1960s, despite women having commercial licences and flying throughout the Second World War, only a handful of female pilots, including Winnie Drinkwater, Grace Brown and

Monique Agazarian, were employed for smaller commercial airlines (Lomax, 1986; Mills, 2006; Redmond, 1997; Simpson, 1996).

This is partly explained because a traditional entry point to the commercial airlines is from military service and the Royal Air Force (RAF) refused to consider women as pilots, hence limiting their access. As a British Women Pilots' Association (BWPA) spokesperson points out, many women were prevented from learning to fly through the RAF or their flying scholarships, which train 500 pilots a year (Thynne, 1987). Whilst traditional explanations for women's work patterns can identify areas of discrimination and highlight prejudices about women that can influence employers, female pilots who have succeeded in gaining their commercial licences have tended to move outside of these and seek employment on the same terms as male pilots. Whilst some women may have suffered discrimination or prejudice during their training or employment, female pilots tend to be more focused on their careers and less focused on their gender. As Davey and Davidson ask:

> We need to consider why the female pilots presented such a positive image of the job and their male colleagues, and downplayed the significance of problems associated with being a woman. Throughout their university education, initial training and employment, female pilots were usually in male-dominated environments. As a result, many women came to identify with their male colleagues, rather than with other women, and to prefer the company of men. (2000, p. 215)

However, whilst feminist analyses of the labour market cannot explain how female pilots came to be employed, they can explain how women may not be able to gain access to a piloting career. The financial costs of flight-crew training, approximately £50,000 to complete an *ab initio* course, present a preliminary barrier (Bruford, 1998). These costs exist for both men and women, but some prejudices may be found in the minds of those in positions to sanction this type of expense, for example, fathers, husbands and partners (Mitchell et al., 2005).

In exploring the backgrounds of female pilots, it is possible to identify areas of their lives which have assisted in their training and subsequent employment in the commercial arena. Parental attitudes, school experiences, personal interests and abilities all impact on career choices (Cubillo and Brown, 2003). Therefore, women may be discouraged from considering flying as a career at a young age. Furthermore, as Bruford (1998) states, the airlines' experience showed that students who had come from an arts background found ground-school training harder than science-orientated candidates; thus, they were more likely to state that potential applicants for sponsorship should have scientific qualifications. Early-life decisions concerning fields of study can result in women opting for subjects less relevant to the labour market (Anker, 2001). Subject choices restrict employer demand and particularly affect their entry into male-dominated fields (Melkas and Anker, 2001). Bagilhole points out that girls are more likely to choose arts-

or humanities-based subjects, so 'they are not prepared for employment in the generally more lucrative scientific, engineering and technical jobs' (2002, p. 30).

Barriers for Female Airline Pilots

Vermeulen and Mitchell point out that 'female pilots have to function in a profession steeped in patriarchal systems of dominance in terms of organizational power and the existing labor processes' (2007, p. 198). Therefore, it is possible that many women interested in private flying or training towards a commercial licence find that there are barriers, both visible and invisible, that exist and that can be discouraging. These barriers generally do not as a rule affect male trainee pilots. Existing studies on gender issues in employment focus on external factors, which may be clustered into attitudinal and structural barriers (Laufer, 2000; Powell, 2000). Attitudinal barriers consist of negative attitudes and stereotypes of women as leaders (Bass, Tomkiewicz and Vaicys, 2001; Ching-Yim and Harris Bond, 2002; Cooper Jackson, 1999; Mostafa, 2003). Structural barriers include inflexible working arrangements and mobility requirements (Davidson and Cooper, 1992). However, discriminatory personnel practices have also been found to persist within recruitment, promotion and appraisal systems and training opportunities, especially for women in non-traditional female jobs (Alimo-Metcalfe, 1995).

For women moving into male-dominated industries, there are certain issues which are invisible within the masculine discourse but which increase pressure on women. These include joining in with the existing (sexist and racist) humour (Davey and Davidson, 2000), performing to and achieving a high standard (Evetts, 1998), adopting conservative dress (Maddock, 1999), dealing with sexualised or masculine language (Rutherford, 2001) and negotiating long work hours (Holley and Simpson, 2001).

The experiences that women have if they learn to fly towards a private licence rather than training with a school from scratch can affect their decision to continue either flying privately or towards a commercial licence. The attitude of flying instructors towards women learning to fly can affect whether a woman feels confident to continue flying. Kohn-Stuart (2000) found that in her sample of New Zealand female pilots, male instructors expected female pilots to have less technical knowledge, their attitudes were more destructive and they tended to provide negative criticism. Furthermore, Walker (2003) notes how in one interview conducted by American private pilot licence (PPL) holder Dr Nancy Fessenden, a female pilot was scared intentionally by the male chief flying instructor.

Research also indicates that female students tend to learn differently from male students. One New Zealand flying instructor found that women tend to be less confident, whereas men tend to be overconfident about their actual ability (Kohn-Stuart, 2000). Helmreich and Merritt (1998) note that this overconfidence is not uncommon amongst (male) commercial pilots, who assume that their ability is unaffected by emergency situations. Research carried out on the characteristics of general aviation crashes shows that male private pilots are more likely to crash because of inattention or flawed decision making, whereas women are more likely to crash due to mishandling the aircraft (Baker et al., 2001 cited in Vermeulen and Mitchell, 2007).

The confidence displayed by many male students combined with extra care taken by female students can reaffirm traditional assumptions and stereotypes about female pilots in the minds of their flying instructors, who treat them accordingly. One of the recommendations made by Kohn-Stuart (2000) was that flying instructors need to be more aware of the possible differences between male and female students. This is supported by Sitler (2004), who found a number of differences between men and women in learning to fly over a 30-year period as a flying instructor in the US.[3] Karp (2004) advocates that in order to meet projected long-term shortages in the commercial pilot population, training centres should be re-evaluating their teaching methods in order to meet students' specific learning needs.

Moreover, if women do ignore negative attitudes towards them flying and continue training, other issues that exist can still act as barriers. Research into the design and layout of aircraft cockpits has shown that they are built around specifications based on male anthropometry, which tend to cause problems for female pilots (Mitchell et al., 2005; Weber, 1997). This is demonstrated by an airline that previously specified a height requirement in its sponsorship scheme for applicants taller than 5 feet 4 inches, which excluded approximately one-quarter of the female population. But the airline stated that this was a requirement because their pilots needed to be able to 'reach the controls of a Jumbo' (Dixon, 1992). One major airline has now reduced the height restriction to 5 feet 2 inches (see www.britishairwaysjobs.com). Kohn-Stuart (2000) notes that in her research female private flyers had to use a cushion in order to reach the rudder controls and brakes on Cessna C152 and C172 aircraft.

The Study: Aims and Methodology

This chapter uses data taken from a much larger study focusing upon women's experiences within the male-dominated industry. As women had been employed within aviation but in a domestic and subordinated position as cabin crew, it is important to examine how aviation employment historically became a site for

3 The differences include: women are slower in gaining confidence; women are more apprehensive and therefore they may be slower to solo; women are quicker to grasp instrument flight; women pilots have fewer fatal accidents; when women learn a procedure, they are more consistent and rarely deviate from procedures; women may be more fearful of stalls, spins and unusual altitudes; women tend to be smoother on the controls; women may have less technical backgrounds; women rarely fly into bad weather; women rarely show off; women rarely fly when intoxicated; and women's flying accidents are more likely to involve landing or taxiing (Sitler, 2004, pp. 82–5).

gendered labour. Interviews were carried out with 17 women who were currently airline pilots or were previously airline pilots and resigned, and three women who were flying instructors, making 20 women in total. There were nine different airlines for which the female airline pilots worked. Some of the women interviewed had worked in different positions within the industry, with three working as cabin crew. When female pilots joined airlines, they were entering into a gendered labour market with a specific gendered organisational culture.

Stroh (2000) states that researchers should try to make interviews with participants into conversations and the majority of the interviews were based on this informal manner. The interviews were semi-structured, with a basic framework of questions. Semi-structured interviewing 'offers researchers access to people's ideas, thoughts, and memories in their own words rather than in the words of the researcher' (Reinharz, 1992, p. 19).

The interview data was 'reviewed' (DeVault, 1996) with the interviewees. Whilst the interviews were written in a semi-structured format concentrating on life history, a grounded approach was used to identify research themes in the interview extracts (Glaser and Strauss, 1967; Lingard, Albert and Levinson, 2008; Stroh, 2000; Tan, 2010). Once the interviews were transcribed and received back from the interviewees, the text was 'coded' into different sections addressing themes.

Analysis and Discussion

Through an analysis of how female pilots gained access to aviation, this section looks to identify the barriers which women face in different areas of the industry and at different stages of their training. By identifying areas in which women can be discouraged from choosing flying as a career, policies can be put in place that can counteract visible and invisible barriers. This section will begin by examining the influences and difficulties women faced on their journey to becoming commercial airline pilots. This is followed by an exploration of barriers, both visible and invisible, that female pilots face at work and an analysis of coping strategies employed to counteract gender issues in the workplace. Finally, this chapter argues that it is the determination and dedication of the women in this study that facilitated their successful careers in the airline industry.

Becoming an Airline Pilot: Influences and Difficulties

Even at an early age, children stereotype work as appropriate for their sex (Miller et al., 2004). However, as Davey and Davidson (2000) note, most female pilots were encouraged by a family member and in nearly all the interviews, female pilots had a family member who was a pilot or who encouraged their interest. Fathers or uncles supported many of the female pilots and this seems to be an important factor towards their decision to train for a professional licence. This male support acts as an 'invitation' into a traditionally male field and sanctions their decision to enter an occupation where the main requirement was to be male. In some cases women were encouraged to obtain their PPL:

> My dad flew privately … So I was brought up hanging around airfields and it was sort of expected that I would get my pilot's licence.[4]

It seems that if young women received encouragement and support about flying, they were able to consider it as a career choice. As this woman explains, she wanted to fly, but did not realise that women could be airline pilots. Once this option was opened up to her by her father, piloting then became a legitimate career choice:

> Um, then I was chatting to my dad about careers and, and when I was a little girl, I will remember this forever, when I said I want to be a stewardess (he worked at the airport you see, he worked in the stores, on the ramp, he did all sorts of things, and my uncle worked there), he looked at me and said: 'Why don't you want to be a pilot?'

Choosing flying as a career was intensified if there is further inspiration, usually from a female pilot in the industry:

> Yeah, so that's where my interest came from, Dad really. I was actually away on a trip with him about eight years ago and there was a female co-pilot on the other crew and it was just talking to her in the bar and I just thought this is a really good job, what an amazing way to make a living, so it was her that inspired me really. I just saw what she was doing and thought that's what I want to do, you know, I'd been interested in aviation because of Dad.

The female pilots interviewed showed that with positive encouragement and in some cases reinforcement by a female role model, flying became a career choice and their career choices were not subject to gender barriers. Other female pilots recalled advice by careers teachers, who had remarked that girls could not fly, but the stewardess route was open to girls:

> I remember when I was at school … which as I say was a very small school and at one of the career things, I must have been about 14 or 15 I suppose, one of the career ladies, I told her I wanted to be a pilot and it was a bit of 'Oh well, I don't think you can, how about being a stewardess?'

For the women who were encouraged to fly at a young age, there may be many more who did not have a role model or family support. It further appears that the

4 All quotes from participants are from interviews with the author conducted in the summer of 2002.

industry at this time was not actively encouraging young women into the industry other than in cabin-crew positions. And, as indicated, many young women received inaccurate careers advice which may have affected their future plans.

After this initial barrier, women considering piloting as a career choice found that others existed further along. Most female pilots had heard of discrimination, usually disguised in recruitment procedures, of airlines that would not employ women, though they were reluctant to recognise it as such, and some experienced issues with male colleagues. One woman applied for sponsorship and found that the airline did not sponsor women:

> There was no space on the form to put you were a girl, you see, so I put the form in and they got as far as taking up the references with my school but then they realised I was at an all-girls' grammar school. I got the letter from them … [it said that the airline] 'sponsor people through … and they do not choose to sponsor females …'. It probably sounds very strange to young girls nowadays but at the time you thought OK that avenue's closed. You couldn't beat a big corporation … If they said they didn't train girls, they didn't train girls.

There were still some men who thought that women were not suitable for the job, despite previous records and achievements (Mitchell et al., 2005). One woman describes how she was told that she would never be able to command an aircraft because in this instructor's opinion, 'it just wasn't physically possible':

> There was one particular instructor … who used to walk over and walk down with me to the flight lounge which is where we did our flight training and he used to say he really admired what I was trying to do and he had nothing against women in flying, but in his opinion I would never be able to command an aircraft because it just wasn't physically possible. He really was not being nasty but [was] only telling me that for my own good. He was the most vocal one who didn't want women in flying … There were two or three known to be – this guy was the ringleader of them – sort of say you won't handle this and won't handle that and it won't be your fault.

Other women experienced discrimination when they tried to apply to airlines for jobs:

> One company I remember, I phoned them up saying I didn't know who to send my CV to, so I phoned up the secretary and got through to someone and said, 'Where shall I send my CV to?' and they just said, 'Oh don't bother' … I remember a … company too. A friend of mine used to fly for them and I remember him saying they would never employ another female pilot because they had had one who had made a complaint against the company about the way she was treated … And they didn't want any special treatment although unofficially they're not employing any more females.

As Vermeulen and Mitchell note, 'arising from (the aviation) discourse are gender-related perceptions that influence airline managers' and pilots' behavior, and that underpin the professional culture of pilots and the aviation industry' (2007, pp. 198–9).

These exist in other forms of 'urban legends' or aviation gossip sometimes termed 'galley FM', which informally operate on a social level within the industry and serve to hinder the employment of female pilots, because most women see applying to an airline known not to recruit women as a waste of time. Thus, with no applications, the 'legend' becomes a form of self-fulfilling prophecy. The airlines then justify this as 'no women apply', so they are unable to recruit them. This then acts as a circle which continues to alienate women. Furthermore, these types of 'legends' also support traditional opinions about female pilots and those airlines which are assumed not to employ them, albeit unofficially, are seen to sanction this type of discrimination.

One female pilot in this research was asked her height before she was invited for an interview:

> And I got a phone call, it was one Sunday evening and a guy saying 'Hallo, I'm the chief pilot of … Airways, how tall are you?'
>
> What?
>
> Exactly, rather surprised it being a late Sunday … Not knowing if this was a joke or not, but it turned out that [the airline] had had a shorter girl who failed a flight test because she couldn't reach all the controls.

These factors can remain in the minds of employers as stereotypes about female pilots and thus hinder their employment in a commercial capacity (Vermeulen and Mitchell, 2007). Even if women overcome these factors and gain a commercial licence, there is no guarantee that further employment barriers will not appear.

Barriers at Work

Employees who believed that women were unable to do the job because the organisational management had pushed this line of labour stratification then had to co-exist with women colleagues when they were recruited as airline pilots. Employees and management who had supported this gender segregation had to cope with a change within their organisational culture when women started to enter the workplace (Ledwith and Colgan, 1996). These 'ways of coping' with women who became airline pilots took two forms: the first was where male colleagues were against the recruitment of women as pilots, but when they had to work with a woman constructed her as being 'alright', even though they disagreed with female pilots in general:

> The guys that I hadn't worked with before, the other captains, some of them were a bit, you know, 'it's a woman, oh dear' ... Before I became a pilot, a lot of people were saying I don't really believe in female engineers or female pilots but you're alright.

The alternative way of coping with a woman in a male-dominated occupation was to ignore gender and focus upon the identity of the job role. To concentrate upon the masculine image bypassed any focus upon femininity and allowed colleagues to ignore the gender of the individual.

Banter and jokes at work are common occurrences used to relieve stress and pressure. However, as Brown (2000) argues, in a male-dominated culture, women are often the subject matter and are excluded from the support and comradeship that humour creates. Collinson (1988) suggests that there can be pressure to conform through tolerating certain types of humour. Furthermore, Davey and Davidson highlight how female pilots were 'forced to laugh' because jokes and pranks were common amongst flight crew, but women who were offended or objected to racist and sexist jokes felt obliged to laugh 'for fear of being labelled feminist, difficult and so on' (2000, p. 211).

Research on workplace humour found that companies can set 'boundaries' defining acceptable humour (Plester, 2009). However, in the following, the female pilot was not offended as she knew the joke was 'meant in jest':

> We're coming off the runway at somewhere or another and I said, 'Shall I clean up', meaning flaps up, you know, and all the bits cos you know, and he started laughing and said: 'Oh you know your place, I should have brought some ironing as well'.

In constructing the joke as not being serious, this female pilot bonded with the male captain and did not make an issue out of the sexist nature of the joke. However, his reaction indicates that he was aware of both her gender and the implications it had on working in a gendered environment. Furthermore, his comment that 'she knows her place' indicated his appreciation of the gender imbalance both within the industry and society and might have possibly been his way of reasserting authority – both professionally and socially.

In some cases the management were aware of gender and potential differences that the recruitment of female pilots could have. However, instead of asking women what existing or potential problems concerned them, they tended to make assumptions based on their existing experiences with women, though not necessarily female pilots. The following comments identify rather more serious aspects of managerial assumptions about women:

> [1] Also they asked: 'When's a girl like you getting married and having kids then?' and I sat there and thought, 'Is this legal? ... No'. I said, 'Well I'm already shacked up with someone for years who supports my career' and that shut them up.

> [2] But I'll tell you something that was asked at the interview, which really pissed me off, um, one of the interviewers said, 'Are you going to have children?' And I said, 'No'.

Even if these issues are not openly spoken of, the hidden assumptions that underpin some interview questions create problems for female pilots. The supposition that young women will want a family is not unusual and in most industries that employ large numbers of young women, a situation can arise where women become either 'women' or 'mothers' (Colgan and Tomlinson, 1996). Research indicates that many women who have children 'choose' either to leave the workplace, work fewer hours or take a less demanding job (Brown, 2010; Lyonette and Crompton, 2008). In contrast, airlines are willing to employ young male pilots who are likely to leave for a better job and this is seen as acceptable, as this female pilot explains:

> And I thought, you are more likely to lose one of your boys at 24 to [a charter airline] than you are to lose me to a child and even if a woman does want to have a baby, she'll come back in a year and you'll have that loyalty because she will want a stable job so it's actually arse about face. I don't understand what their mentality is, yeah you know, we'll hold it against women but we'll employ all these young lads who are young, free and single, who we're going to lose.

Research on gender assumptions in America, South Africa, Australia and Norway found that 'regular reference was made to the impact, real or imagined, of women's biological functions of menstruation and childbearing on their performance' (Mitchell et al., 2005, p. 7). Where a pilot leaving an airline through resignation is perceived by management as a legitimate reason, the potential of leaving for family reasons is not. Furthermore, it is assumed that childbirth will result in significant costs to the airline (Mitchell et al., 2005).

This point is highlighted by a case involving a female pilot suing an airline for disallowing her request for part-time hours in order to care for her daughter (Marston, 2005). The request for part-time hours was initially turned down because her number of flying hours fell below the airline's minimum 2,000 hours needed for 50 per cent contracts. She claimed that the airline's rules breached discrimination legislation because more requests for part-time hours are likely to come from female pilots with children. The airline subsequently lost the case despite arguing that it was about safety and not gender (Womack, 2005). The union's response was to emphasise the changing nature of the pilot workforce and how this creates a need for a change in employment practices for more pilots, not solely for working mothers. However, the 2,000-hour rule was introduced after the request for a 50 per cent contract and the airline argued that it did not exist because there had been no requests to work part time from pilots with low numbers of hours. The airline also 'acknowledged that it had said it would be too expensive to have part-time pilots covering [the female pilot's] duties' (Womack, 2005, p. 6).

Gender Issues: Strategies for Coping in the Workplace

Women who are employed within so-called masculine professions, such as engineering, are often seen as unusual (Evetts, 1998; Powell, Bagilhole and Dainty, 2006; Shortland, 2011). This is because jobs which are seen as 'tough, heavy, dirty and to do with machinery' are loaded with cultural expectations and these do not include women performing the tasks associated with engineering (Evetts, 1998, p. 283). Whilst piloting has seen a move away from actual strength and an involvement in 'dirty' work in recent years (Neal-Smith, 2003, 2004), some jobs, especially in freight transport, did need pilots to become involved outside of their normal requirements, as some of the women's testimonies explain. However, despite becoming more technologically advanced in terms of systems and power-assisted controls, piloting like engineering has retained its masculine discourse and cultural associations, which do not include women.

In examining the strategies used by women in male-dominated industries, Evetts, in her study of women engineers, suggests examining ways in which women 'were active in managing, rather than merely passively adapting to' the existing culture (1998, p. 284). As Maddock points out, whilst women hide their gender in a variety of ways, they also manage their gender: 'being a woman in a male-dominated environment demands handling one's gender in particular ways, with reference to one's interpretation of the prevailing power structure in the organization' (1999, p. 103).

One of the major problems for male pilots was that they were unused to dealing with a woman in their working environment who was not lower in rank and status than they were. Older male pilots 'often had little or no experience with flying with female pilots and retained a stereotypical belief in the role of women' (Mitchell et al., 2005, p. 15). This female pilot notes that:

> One of the things I think is a lot of men, when I first got into flying, their only experience of dealing with women was as a cabin crew member who they'd be perfectly polite to serving them, or their wife, or their daughter. They were not used to dealing with a female in the working environment as an equal colleague. Most of them coped with it very well by pretending you're not female. Once you bring up the big fact of being female, you put them off kilter, particularly the older ones. You put them off balance. I choose not to do that because it makes my working environment easier. Some of the younger ones I've found are quite aggressive.

Most female pilots found that they dealt with the issues of their gender by not playing on it. Whilst female pilots allowed men to be men, they were conscious of not being 'a girl'. In other words, women actively fitted into their environment by altering their behaviour and attitudes, but they also did not 'make a big deal about being a girl'. By managing their gender, female pilots have integrated into a masculine environment. In trying not to change the existing culture, i.e. allowing men to behave as they have always done, women have become accepted or at least female pilots have been treated as pilots rather than as women. Once gender became an issue, existing stereotypes of women and 'male ways of thinking' regarding female pilots surfaced.

This was noticeable on training courses and the women were conscious of not becoming offended by their male colleagues. This does mean that they had to 'fit in' to a certain extent and to accept the culture that was produced by a predominantly male group:

> Practically every course I've been on, 99 per cent of every course I've been on, I've been the only female. I think generally I've tried to fit in with the chaps if I've been on a course, especially if it's been a residential course and they all go down to the bar on an evening and drink beer … I don't sort of sit around telling rude jokes but on the other hand I don't stay in my room and get offended or anything … I do appreciate that some of the chaps try to tame their language when they're around me but I just try to laugh a lot and join in really and on several occasions they've just said I'm an honouree chap; yes, I think you've just got to try and fit in and not get offended.

Whilst the women try to fit in by joining in activities, being professional and laughing at jokes, they construct themselves as being less 'girly' by doing these things. However, as the following extract that describes activities on a trip away from base explains, often the activities tend to be centred on what would be termed as traditional (heterosexual) male interests. The following describes a female pilot who noticed the difference between her choices and those of her male colleagues:

> I would have perhaps gone sightseeing or gone and got a massage or gone shopping and they always seemed to want to head for the nearest bar or lap dancing club or something, but then again if I say, 'Right, I'm not coming, I'm going shopping', they all say, 'Oh, I'll come shopping, I'll come shopping', so maybe they just lack imagination or maybe they thought they have to be this macho man; in fact, secretly they want to do other things as well.

Moreover, whilst the onus of fitting into a male culture was placed upon the women, it is clear that their path was not made easier by airline management. As one female pilot pointed out, the management did not have any idea how to deal with women. In her experience of a training school, she describes what the atmosphere and culture was like:

> No, I don't think they'd any idea. They didn't know what to do. It was a completely strange phenomenon. It was how I imagined the RAF must have been after the Second World War. It was a male club atmosphere. A bit like a boys' school as well. I found it quite juvenile. They used to store up bread rolls to make them hard so they could have good bread roll fights.

How Do Women Overcome Barriers?

The literature explaining women's work patterns and labour market choices does not adequately explain women's move into commercial aviation as airline pilots. The research can explain why women are discriminated against at earlier stages of pilot sponsorship and why women end up in the position of cabin crew. Now, however, legislation has opened up professional piloting positions and women are being recruited, albeit in low numbers, despite discrimination, perceptions and the industry's organisational culture. Thus, how do women move into traditionally masculine occupations despite initial barriers? Cockburn asks in her study of women working in the civil service: 'How is it then, given the disapproval of many men, that women have been admitted in such numbers to the fraternal hierarchy of the Service?' (1991, p. 61).

Cockburn answers herself by placing the emphasis on the women themselves and their drive and determination that have pushed them through the initial barriers. This is also the case for women working in other male-dominated spheres (Shortland, 2011). Mitchell et al. state that 'it would appear that only women with the focus and drive, similar to what is socially acceptable and expected in males but not necessarily females, are able to achieve their career goals' (2005, p. 2). As indicated throughout this chapter, female pilots are dedicated and focused towards achieving their professional licences. Furthermore, as Hakim explains in her category of 'work-centred' women, those who fall into this category tend to invest in 'educational qualifications or other equivalent training for their chosen main activity' (2000, p. 165). As Davey and Davidson (2000) observe, many articles about female pilots state how they tend to be committed to their career, which is highlighted by the amount of time and money spent on training towards their professional licences.

Female pilots who had children balanced childcare with studying for their exams:

> And then studied for all the commercials, did them at home myself, so I worked quite hard for it really, but it was strange really. I used to sit with children on the table with a video while I studied but I really wanted to do it.

Their strength of mind and willpower is evident within these interview extracts and none of the female pilots ever thought that they did anything remarkable in juggling their lives and responsibilities. However, one woman did note that she thought it took a 'boring personality' in order to fly commercially:

> Because I spent four years of my life doing it, you can't do with no money and no time … All the time and I guess when you're 21 to 25, you've got better things to do, going to nightclubs and things like that, which I never did, but, um, that's what it takes, a certain boring personality.

Whether the lack of a social life or material possessions matter more to women is debatable; however, press interviews with female pilots highlight how female pilots were prepared to sacrifice their home to finance their flying (Crosbie, 2001; Dixon, 1992). Furthermore, what was evident in the women interviewed here is that the majority were single when they were studying for their commercial licence. Many women mentioned a significant split with a partner or husband coinciding with their increased interest in flying. In discussing the recruitment of the first female pilots for British Airways, Donne (1987) expressly mentioned their unmarried status and Moore and Barrowclough (1988) in a similar article highlight the difficulties for female pilots of maintaining a relationship because of the 'jealously and bitterness' from male partners who are also pilots. However, this is not unusual for women committed to their career. As Bagilhole (2002, p. 88) notes in her study of female construction workers, women tend to 'adopt career focused lifestyles' because juggling a family or relationship with the commitments attached to their career was simply too difficult.

Summary

This chapter has explored how 20 female pilots achieved their commercial licence, despite barriers that exist and affect aspiring women more than men. In examining existing barriers at different points – for example, the lack of role models, the financial aspects, the specified academic qualifications, attitudes of flying instructors, the cockpit design and existing attitudes of employers – it is possible to identify points where potential female pilots may be discouraged from continuing flying as a career. Furthermore, even if women do train for their commercial licence and achieve employment with a commercial airline, their experiences indicate that gender assumptions about women still exist within the UK commercial industry. These include having to manage their colleagues who may resent their employment, the lack of consideration from the management concerning gender differences, jokes, banter and assumptions made about women in general. This also extends to managing their appearance and personal lives.

The women in this research who successfully became commercial pilots showed high levels of commitment, studying for long periods of time and balancing childcare and exams. However, whilst acknowledging the agency of the women interviewed for the study, this research also identifies barriers which can alienate women either from choosing flying as a possible career choice and/or continuing training for a professional licence. This means that the male-dominated organisational culture within the airlines will remain static, with few women entering the profession to instigate change and that the number of role models for young women will remain low. Airlines need to change not only their recruitment policies and target more women, and this includes a focus on gender and diversity within flying training establishments to prevent women from becoming disillusioned with flying as a professional career, but also the gendered character of their organisations (see Chapter 1 of this book; Mills, 1995).

Acknowledgements

A special thanks to Dr Tom Cockburn for his comments on an earlier draft of this chapter.

References

Acker, J., 1990. Hierarchies, jobs, bodies: A theory of gendered organizations. *Gender and Society*, 4(2), pp. 139–58.
Alimo-Metcalfe, B., 1995. An investigation of female and male constructs of leadership and empowerment. *Women in Management Review*, 10(2), pp. 3–8.
Anker, R., 2001. Theories of occupational segregation by sex: An overview. In: M. Fetherolf Loufti (ed.), *Women, Gender and Work: What is Equality and How Do We Get There?* Geneva: International Labour Office, pp. 129–56.
Bagilhole, B.M., 2002. *Women in Non-traditional Occupations: Challenging Men.* New York: Palgrave Macmillan.
Bass, K., Tomkiewicz, J. and Vaicys, C., 2001. Attitudes toward women and managerial ability of African Americans. *Women in Management Review*, 18(3), pp. 155–8.
Brown, J., 2000. Occupational culture as a factor in the stress experiences of police officers. In: F. Leishman, B. Loveday and S. Savage (eds), *Core Issues in Policing*, 2nd edn. Harlow: Pearson Educational, pp. 249–63.
Brown, L., 2010. The relationship between motherhood and professional advancement: Perceptions versus eeality. *Employee Relations*, 32(5), pp. 470–94.
Bruford, D., 1998. *To Be a Pilot*. Shrewsbury: Airlife.
Ching-Yim, P. and Harris Bond, M., 2002. Gender stereotyping of managers and the self-concept of business students across their undergraduate education. *Women in Management Review*, 17(8), pp. 364–72.
CIPD, 2005. Women & work commission: A fair deal for women in the workplace – an interim statement. In: *Tackling the Pay Gap – Looking Below the Surface*, seminar B6, Conference handbook, Chartered Institute of Personnel and Development Annual Conference, Harrogate, October. London: Chartered Institute of Personnel and Development.
Civil Aviation Authority, 2008. *Pilot Licence Holders by Age and Sex, 2008.* Available at: www.caa.co.uk.
Civil Aviation Authority, n.d. Statistics Personnel Costs (UK and Overseas) 1974–2003. Available at: www.caa.co.uk/airlinestatistics.
Cockburn, C., 1991. *In the Way of Women*. London: Macmillan.

Colgan, F. and Tomlinson, F., 1996. Women in book publishing: A 'feminised' sector? In: S. Ledwith. and F. Colgan (eds), *Women in Organizations: Challenging Gender Politics*. London: Macmillan, pp. 44–77.

Collinson, D., 1988. 'Engineering humour': Koking and conflict in shop-floor relations. *Organization Studies*, 9, pp. 181–99.

Cooper Jackson, J., 2001. Women middle managers' perception of the glass ceiling. *Women in Management Review*, 16(1), pp. 30–41.

Crosbie, P., 2001. I went from check-in girl to jet pilot and now I'm on cloud nine. *The Sun*, 2 January.

Cubillo, L. and Brown, M., 2003. Women into educational leadership and management: international differences? *Journal of Educational Administration*, 41(3), pp. 278–91.

Davey, C.L. and Davidson, M.J., 2000. The right of passage? The experiences of female pilots in commercial aviation. *Feminism & Psychology*, 10(2), pp. 195–225.

Davidson, M.J. and Cooper, C.L., 1992. *Shattering the Glass Ceiling: The Woman Manager*. London: Paul Chapman.

DeVault, M.L., 1996. Talking back to sociology: Distinctive contributions of feminist methodology. *Annual Review of Sociology*, 22, pp. 29–50.

Dixon, B., 1992. Sky is no limit as women take wing. *The Times*, 4 February.

Donne, M., 1987. No title. *Financial Times*, 15 April, p. 8.

Evetts, J., 1998. Managing the technology but not the organization: Women and career in engineering. *Women in Management Review*, 13(8), pp. 283–90.

Game, A. and Pringle, R., 1983. *Gender at Work*. London: George Allen & Unwin.

Glaser, B.G. and Strauss, A.L., 1967. *The Discovery of Grounded Theory: Strategies for Qualitative Research.* New York: Sociology Press.

Hakim, C., 2000. *Work-Lifestyle Choices in the 21st Century*. Oxford: Oxford University Press.

Hall, E.J., 1993. Waitering and waitressing: Engendering the work of table servers. *Gender and Society*, 7(3), pp. 329–46.

Helmreich, R. and Merritt, A., 1998. *Culture at Work in Aviation and Medicine: National, Organizational and Professional Influences*. Aldershot: Ashgate.

Holley, D. and Simpson, R., 2001. One year on: The effects of restructuring on women transport and logistics managers, centre for equality research in business. Research Paper No. 8, November.

Jarman, J., Blackburn, R., Brooks, B. and Dermott, E., 1999. Gender differences at work: International variations in occupational segregation. *Social Research Online*, 4(1), pp. U129–U156.

Karp, M., 2004. Learning style preferences affect training outcomes. In M.A. Turney (ed.), *Culture, Gender and Diversity*. Aldershot: Ashgate, pp. 45–60.

Kohn-Stuart, R., 2000. Gender differences in the cockpit. In: *2000 Asia-Pacific Women in Aviation Conference*, Canberra, Australia.

Laufer, J., 2000. French women managers: A search for equality but enduring differences. In M. Davidson and R. Burke (eds), *Women in Management: Current Research Issues*, vol. II. London: Paul Chapman, pp. 26–40.

Ledwith, S. and Colgan, F (eds). 1996. *Women in Organizations: Challenging Gender Politics*. London: Macmillan.

Lingard, L., Mills, A. and Levinson, W., 2008. Grounded theory, mixed methods, and action research, *British Medical Journal*, 337(7667), pp. 459–61.

Lomax, J., 1986. *Women of the Air*. London: John Murray.

Lyonette, C. and Crompton, R., 2008. The only way is up? An examination of women's 'under-achievement' in the accountancy profession in the UK. *Gender in Management: An International Journal*, 23(7), pp. 506–21.

Maddock, S., 1999. *Challenging Women: Gender, Culture and Organization*. London: Sage.

Marston, P., 2005. Woman pilot sues BA for not letting her reduce hours. *Daily Telegraph*, 10 January, p. 7.

Melkas, H. and Anker, R., 2001. Occupational segregation by sex in Nordic countries: An empirical investigation. In M.F. Loutfi (ed.), *Women, Gender and Work: What is Equality and How Do We Get There?* Geneva: International Labour Organization. pp. 189–213.

Miller, L., Neathey, F., Pollard, E. and Hill, D., 2004. *Occupational Segregation, Gender Gaps and Skill Gaps, Occupational Segregation: Working Paper Series No. 15*. Manchester: Equal Opportunities Commission.

Mills, A.J., 1995. Man/aging subjectivity, silencing diversity: Organizational imagery in the airline industry – The Case of British Airways. *Organization*, 2(2), pp. 243–69.

——. 2006. *Sex, Strategy and the Stratosphere: Airlines and the Gendering of Organizational Culture*. London: Palgrave Macmillan.

Mitchell, J., Kristovics, A. and Vermeulen, L., 2006. Gender issues in aviation: Pilot perceptions and employment relations. *International Journal of Employment Studies*, 14(1), pp. 35–59.

Mitchell, J., Kristovics, A., Vermeulen, L., Wilson, J. and Martinussen, M., 2005. How pink is the sky? A cross-national study of the gendered occupation of pilot. *Employment Relations Record*, 5(2), pp. 43–7.

Moore, M. and Barrowclough, A., 1988. No title. *Mercury* (Hobart), 1 February.

Mostafa, M., 2003. Attitudes towards women who work in Egypt. *Women in Management Review*, 18(5), pp. 252–66.

Neal-Smith, S.J., 2003. The changing image of the airline pilot: Why women pilots no longer have to be 'one of the boys'. Women's History Network University of Aberdeen.

——. 2004. Masculinity and physical labour: The relationship between the changing image of the airline pilot, the employment of female pilots and aircraft technology. *Women and Work Conference*, London, July, Institute for Historical Research.

Oakley, A., 1981. *Subject Women*. London: Fontana Press.

O'Donnell, A., 2008. Gendered choices: Young women's perspectives on non-traditional training and careers in Northumberland. *Education and Training*, 50(6), pp. 474–88.

Plester, B., 2009. Crossing the line: Boundaries of workplace humour and fun. *Employee Relations*, 31(6), pp. 584–99.

Powell, A., Bagilhole, B.M. and Dainty, A., 2006. The problem of women's assimilation into UK engineering cultures: Can critical mass work? *Equal Opportunities International*, 25(8), pp. 688–99.

——. 2008. How women engineers do and undo gender: Consequences for gender equality. *Gender, Work and Organization*, 16(4), pp. 411–28.

Powell, A., Bagilhole, B., Dainty, A. and Neale, R., 2004. Does the engineering culture in UK higher education advance women's careers? *Equal Opportunities International*, 23(7/8), pp. 21–38.

Powell, G., 2000. The glass ceiling: Explaining the good and bad news. In: M. Davidson and R. Burke (eds), *Women in Management: Current Research Issues, Volume 2*. London: Sage. pp. 236–49.

Redmond, A., 1997. Winnie Drinkwater – pioneer pilot. *BWPA Gazette*, Weybridge: British Women Pilots' Association.

Reinharz, S., 1992. *Feminist Methods in Social Research.* New York: Oxford University Press.

Rutherford, S., 2001. Organizational culture, women managers and exclusion. *Women in Management Review*, 16(8), pp. 371–82.

Shortland, S., 2011. Drilling through gender stereotypes: Improving prospects for female expatriation in oil and gas exploration and production? *COERC Seminar*. London Metropolitan Business School, 16 February.

Simpson, A. 1996. Winnie Drinkwater. *The Herald*, 19 October, p. 24.

Sitler, R.L., 2004. Gender differences in learning to fly. In: M.A. Turney (ed.), *Tapping Diverse Talent in Aviation*, 4th edn. Aldershot: Ashgate, pp. 78–88.

Smith, P., Caputi, P. and Crittenden, N., 2012. A maze of metaphors around glass ceilings. *Gender in Management: An International Journal*, 27(7), pp. 436–48.

Stroh, M., 2000. Qualitative interviewing. In: D. Burton (ed.), *Research Training for Social Scientists*. London: Sage, pp. 196–217.

Tan, J., 2010. Grounded theory in practice: Issues and discussion for new qualitative researchers. *Journal of Documentation*, 66(1), pp. 93–112.

Thynne, J., 1987. BA to give women their wings. *Sunday Times* (London), 12 April.

Tyler, M. and Taylor, S., 1998. The exchange of aesthetics. *Gender, Work and Organization*, 5(3), pp. 165–71.

UK Resource Centre for Women in SET. 2007. *The Gender Equality Duty in SET ... and How to Implement It: Good Practice Guide*. Bradford: Resource Centre for Women in SET.

Vermeulen, L.P. and Mitchell, J.I., 2007. Development and validation of a measure to assess perceptions regarding gender-related pilot behaviour. *International Journal of Aviation Psychology*, 17(2), pp. 197–218.

Walker, C., 2003. Why do so few women fly? *General Aviation*, December.

Weber, R.N., 1997. Manufacturing gender in commercial and military cockpit design, *Science, Technology and Human Values*, 22(2), pp. 235–53.

Whittock, M., 2000. *Feminising the Masculine? Women in Non-traditional Employment.* Aldershot: Ashgate.

Williams, C.L., 1989. *Gender Differences at Work: Women and Men in Non-traditional Occupations.* Berkeley, CA: University of California Press.

Womack, S., 2005. BA woman pilot wins right to cut hours by half to care for baby. *Daily Telegraph*, 23 April, p. 6.

PART III
Technical Issues

Chapter 9
Automation in Light Aircraft: A Cross-national Analysis

Alexandra Kristovics, Jim Mitchell, Ronald W. Bishop, Preven Naidoo and Leopold P. Vermeulen

Introduction

The rapid advancements in computer systems and technology in general have had a profound effect on aviation. Voller and Agel-Porte (2002) briefly describe Moore's law, which predicts that the capabilities of digital electronic devices will double every 18 months. The pace of the introduction of advanced aviation technology has been gaining momentum since the late 1990s to early 2000s. Technology that was developed in the military and incorporated in large commercial jets advanced to the point of significant cost reduction to allow the various technologies to be incorporated into light aircraft. As with many industries, new technology has impacted on the attitudes, skills and proficiencies of pilots in the aviation industry. However, advanced technology such as the glass cockpit has been embraced by some pilots more than others.

The reactions to glass cockpits from over 500 commercial pilots surveyed by Hughes (1989) over two decades ago still seem to be valid today. Hughes' findings revealed that although most had positive attitudes towards glass cockpits, pilots also had reservations about losing their piloting skills because of automation. Some were also concerned about automation increasing their workload rather than reducing it, more specifically the time it took to re-programme the computer when encountering situations that called for a change in assigned routes and/or situations. The introduction of the new technology into light aircraft in general aviation has resulted in new and very different human factor issues. This concern has been met with a number of research projects attempting to explore the variables associated with the impact of technology on aviation and pilots in particular.

The aforementioned concerns seem to be echoed in later studies. In evaluating three more recent studies of pilot perceptions of glass cockpits, Mitchell, Vermeulen and Naidoo (2009) found that although most pilots had positive perceptions of glass cockpits, there were a number of concerns that were common among pilots from the UK, South Africa and the US. These were issues related to workload, skills and design. Further qualitative analysis from the South African sample revealed the nature of these issues. While it was acknowledged by the pilots that automation generally reduced levels of workload, negative comments related to

'High workload and stressful situations allow possible error factors to creep in' and 'Biggest negative: the more sophisticated the system, the more stressful it is when it fails!' (2009, p. 22). *Skills* were related to the perceived loss of manual flying ability due to increased reliance on automation and *design* was related to the manufacturer's philosophical approach to aircraft design.

Issues relating to safety and training in glass cockpits have also been highlighted by the Australian Transport Safety Bureau (1991) and, more recently, by the National Transportation Safety Board (NTSB) (2010) in the US. However, the focus of their research was quite different. The former focused on possible limitations on pilot's visual span, both within and outside the cockpit. The glass cockpit windscreen configurations and other physical blockages limit the pilot's view externally. However, Knight (2007) discusses new design approaches that facilitate pilot vision through the introduction of new technology such as synthetic vision and enhanced vision. The safety bodies also acknowledged psychological characteristics, such as the effects of increased workload and the consequences of situations where pilots had been alerted to (or not alerted to) changing circumstances, such as traffic. However, Mosier et al. proposed that a phenomenon termed 'automation bias' may lead to more errors as a result of pilots using 'automated cues as a heuristic replacement for vigilant information seeking and processing' (1998, p. 48). Although Mosier et al. (1998) used a very small sample of commercial pilots (n=25), they found that both experienced and less experienced pilots were adversely affected by automation bias. The study also found that these pilots relied heavily on aircraft automation, leading to automation complacency. Combined with automation bias, automation complacency can lead to poor decision making and reduced situational awareness (Parasuraman and Manzey, 2010). This finding is intuitively contradictory, as the original intention of manufacturers who designed these systems was to improve situational awareness (for instance, by incorporating moving map displays, etc.) and to ease pilot decision making. In addition, Parasuraman and Riley (1997) also argue convincingly that automation has changed the way in which pilots interact with the different aircraft systems, stating that instances of misuse and disuse are common.

The NTSB (2010) undertook a study which assessed pilots transitioning from conventional analogue cockpits to the modern glass cockpits in light aircraft. The project analysed the accident rates of over 8,000 piston-powered aircraft manufactured between 2002 and 2006. It found that although light aircraft using glass cockpits resulted in fewer accidents, the accidents that did occur resulted in more fatalities. Although there have been a few critics of the methodology (e.g., Ison and Decker, 2010), there tends to be general agreement about the need for improved training. This recommendation was also advocated by the Aircraft Owners and Pilots Association (AOPA) Air Safety Foundation (2007). Pilot training, however, becomes more complicated because it not only consists of the transition from analogue to glass cockpits, but pilots may also need to be proficient in systems being developed by competing manufacturers. For example, when Aviation Safety (2009) asked 300 pilots what kind of systems they used, the majority had used Garmin G1000, but others had used Avidyne Entegras, Aspen Evolution, Garmin G600 and Chelton Flight Logic. However, some respondents stated that they had chosen the system, while others indicated that they had no option because the aircraft was bought with the avionics suite pre-fitted. As declared by the NTSB:

> In the past, displays, avionics, and navigation equipment all looked and functioned in a similar manner regardless of the manufacturer. This is not the case with today's advanced avionics systems and displays. Training in the operation of one manufacturer's GPS receiver may not give the pilot sufficient knowledge to safely operate another manufacturer's receiver. This is even more evident with full glass cockpits. Not only does the functionality of PFDs and MFDs vary between manufacturers, but also due to aircraft systems differences, the same avionics equipment in a different type aircraft may function differently. (2010, p. 54)

The transition to glass cockpits, however, involves more than becoming accustomed to new equipment and how to use it. Also involved is a paradigm shift as described by the AOPA Air Safety Foundation:

> The larger definition includes a new mindset for pilots, encompassing a revised view of what constitutes GA flying, with airline-style procedures, regular use of autopilot, and greater dependence on avionics for multiple tasks beyond pure navigation. (2007, p. 3)

This mental shift may not just relate to dependency, but also to a new way of thinking, as suggested by Mosier and her colleagues (Mosier, 2001; Mosier et al., 2007). Mosier suggests that 'the nature of the pilot's cognitive task in the automated cockpit has been altered from a largely intuitive, correspondence-based task to a primarily analytical, coherence-based task' (Mosier, 2001, p. 68). Further, the analytical task becomes somewhat more difficult in glass cockpits, where Mosier (2001) suggests that the apparent simplicity of the surface features hides different pieces of information that may be needed for analytical evaluation of discrepancies or whether it can be found at all, owing to the different and changing formats. Thus, instead of only relying on intuition (or expertise behaviours), glass cockpits require more of an analytical cognitive activity.

The year 2004 saw a rapid rise in the adoption of glass cockpits in general aviation. This trend paralleled the advances in innovative computer technology. For example, in the US, the number of registrations for new conventional and automated aircraft was similar. However, by 2006, the number of automated aircraft had more than doubled, while the number of conventional aircrafts had fallen dramatically (NTSB, 2010). The large increase in the usage of automated aircraft has prompted a different approach to research as well as a number of studies that have focused on pilot perceptions and attitudes towards this new technology.

Some of these have been mentioned above. This chapter seeks to address some of these issues on a cross-national basis.

The Present Study

This study has been undertaken by the University of Western Sydney and Central Queensland University in Australia, together with the University of Pretoria in South Africa. In South Africa, the survey was also endorsed by the South African Civil Aviation Authority (see http://www.caa.co.za) as it aligned very well with the recent inception of its project, General Aviation Safety Initiative (GASI). This project was initiated after the sudden spike in serious accidents and incidents involving general aviation in 2008. The issues that emerged from GASI were categorised as 'flight training', 'aircraft' and 'human factors'. One of the findings found that poor pilot decision making, risk management, poor judgment chains, lack of appropriate threat and error management, and non-existent single-pilot crew resource management skills played significant causal roles in general aviation accident statistics. These human factor variables are also found to emerge when examining the human–machine interface of advanced flight deck systems (see http://www.flightdeckautomation.com).

The focus of the present study explores a relatively new measure of general aviation pilots' perceptions of glass cockpits. This was assessed using the Advanced Cockpit Aircraft Survey (ACAS) developed by Casner (2008). However, Casner did not undertake a factor analysis on his scale and his findings were specific to individual items only. Nevertheless, Casner did suggest that the items belonged to specific dimensions. Table 9.1 shows the items and dimensions.

To date, there has only been one other study that implemented a Casner's measure to differentiate attitudes between male and female pilots (Mitchell, Kristovics and Bishop, 2010). Unfortunately, there were too few participants

Table 9.1 The original ACAS items

General attitudes	6 items
Workload	6 items
Awareness	8 items
Learning	11 items
Retention	4 items
Error	5 items
Safety	7 items
Preference for in flight use	6 items

Note: Item details can be found in Appendix 9.1.

to confirm the factor structure of the scale. The present study therefore aims to examine the factor structure of Casner's measure. The research also seeks to identify similarities and differences in pilots' perceptions cross-nationally. Note that the survey was modified in Australia and South Africa to take account of the different regulatory bodies. For instance, in Australia, the reference to the Federal Aviation Administration (FAA) was replaced by the Civil Aviation Safety Authority (CASA) and in South Africa by the Civil Aviation Authority (CAA).

Method

Participants

In Australia, there were 223 responses. These were from 186 male pilots, 34 female pilots and three who did not indicate their gender. Not all respondents completed their survey forms. Incomplete surveys were removed from the database and the final cohort consisted of 100 male and 22 female pilots. In South Africa, a total of 330 participants answered all or part of the survey. Similarly, incomplete surveys were removed from the database, leaving a cohort of 243 pilots. This consisted of 236 male and seven female respondents.

Table 9.2 on the next page compares South African and Australian male (M) and female (W) pilots' biographical details.

The large standard deviation in the hours flown indicates that the spread of the distribution is substantial, which means that respondents were very diverse in their level of experience. The data for certificates and ratings indicates that many pilots have multiple licences and ratings, and is therefore reflective of their range of flying activities.

Materials

The present study used a measure which was constructed from the 52-item ACAS instrument on general aviation pilots' attitudes towards glass cockpits. Participants were asked to respond to each statement using a five-point Likert scale, where 1 = strongly agree, 2 = agree, 3 = neutral, 4 = disagree and 5 = strongly disagree. However, as most standard measures consist of the item scale being ordered the other way around, the scores were recoded where 1 = strongly disagree to 5 = strongly agree so as to enable the reader to identify that the higher the score, the more likely the respondent would agree with the items. An examination of the ACAS original measure revealed that some of the items needed to be reverse-scored so that all items from the same dimension were allowed to have uniformity in the direction of the responses. For example, item 17 from Casner's measure from the General Attitude dimension was the only one item that denoted a positive evaluation. Therefore, the rest of the items were reverse-scored to be in line with the positive attitude of item 17.

Table 9.2 Participant details

	South Africa (N=243, M=236, W=7)		Australia (N=122, M=100, W=22)	
Average age	M=43 (SD=13.8) W=47 (SD= 8.3)		M=52 (SD=11.8) W=45 (SD= 17.2)	
Average flight hours	M=3,458 (SD=4,947.2) W=4128 (SD=4,079.0)		M=2,679 (SD=3,854.0) W=1,289 (SD= 2,742.0)	
Average hours in 'glass cockpit'	M= 819 (SD=1,826.8) W=289 (SD= 275.6)		M=403 (SD=1,568.5) W=72 (SD=217.5)	
Average hours with at least a panel-mounted GPS	M=1,671 (SD=2,346.0) W=1,371 (SD=3,418.2)		M=740 (SD=1,652.7) W=286 (SD=516.3)	
Certificates and ratings	M	W	M	W
1. Private	86	2	51	12
2. Instrument	16	-	16	-
3. Commercial	43	2	23	5
4. Airline Transport Pilot	56	-	9	2
5. Chief Flying Instructor	11	-	-	2
6. Chief Flying Instrument-Instructor	24	3	1	1
Primary flying activity				
1. Non-scheduled charter	73	4	11	6
2. Scheduled charter operations	7	-	-	-
3. Airline	19	-	3	1
4. Private leisure/sport	109	2	84	14
5. Other	28	1	2	1
Education				
1. High School Certificate	102	3	30	4
2. Diploma	51	1	23	5
3. Bachelor's degree	32	-	24	6
4. Postgraduate degree	51	3	23	7
Computer literacy				
1. Poor	4	-	-	-
2. Average	77	1	18	5
3. Above average	96	6	39	5
4. Excellent	59	-	48	12

Procedure

Casner's reconstructed measure was used to elicit the experiences and perceptions of general aviation pilots with regard to the glass cockpit and to examine cross-national comparisons. The Australian data was collected online via links placed on the websites of the AOPA, the Australian Women Pilots' Association (AWPA), the Sport Aircraft Association of Australia (SAAA) and Recreation Aviation-Australia (RAA). Each of these associations advised members of the research and requested that they complete the survey. Responses were submitted online and collated on Excel spreadsheets.

Similarly, South African data was collected by placing the survey online and inviting pilots to participate. The ACAS was hosted on a web-based system which was accessed by potential respondents via a link found in an accompanying invitation letter. The invitation letter was sent to all South African registered general aviation pilots by the South African Civil Aviation Authority by means of a CAA Aeronautical Information Notice.

The actual response rate for Australia and South Africa is unknown due to the survey being linked to a web-based host. One of the greatest disadvantages of using a web-based survey method is that the researchers have no control over who answers the questionnaire. Nevertheless, the questions were developed in such a way that a closer examination can assist in eliminating participants who did not meet the requirements of the survey. The criteria for inclusion were that each participating pilot had at least a private pilots' licence with an aircraft category and class rating. Student pilots were excluded from the sample.

Results

SPSS 17 was used for the exploratory factor analyses, scale reliabilities, the Welch test and Mann-Whitney U tests. Lisrel 8.5 was used to perform structural equation modelling on the revised scale.

In examining best practices for factor analysis, Costello and Osborne (2005) recommended the use of Maximum Likelihood or Principal Axis Factoring with oblique rotation as the most optimal method of analysis, arguing that most factors from measures used in social sciences would be correlated. Optimal method related to results that tend to be better reproducible for the rest of the population. Costello and Osborne also acknowledge that larger sample sizes are less likely to produce incorrect solutions.

The initial extraction using Principal Axis Factoring (PAF) with Oblimin rotation on the reconstructed Casner 52-item measure failed, owing to more than 25 iterations needed to perform this analysis. The results using PAF and Varimax rotation revealed a 13-factor solution with a number of poor item loadings and many cross-loadings. The results also differed widely from the item pool of Casner's dimensions. Further, initial analyses indicated that there were four communalities that were .25 or below, indicating that these four items contributed very little variance to the structure.

In an attempt to identify items that may not be indicative of the dimension, a series of reliability tests were performed on each dimension of the 52-item data. Some dimensions had good reliabilities, for example, General Attitude had a reliability of .76 and both Awareness and Error had reliabilities of .70. Clark and Watson (1995) recommend a cut-off value of between .70 and .80 to deduce good reliability in a perception measurement scale. In addition, reliabilities of over .90 tend to indicate that items are redundant. However, Workload, Learning, Retention, Safety and Preference for In Flight Use had unsatisfactory reliabilities of .58, .61, .66, .69 and .52 respectively. There were two dimensions, Safety and Preference for In Flight Use, where removal of items would have increased the value of Chronbach's coeffiecient alpha. The low reliabilities, as well as the lack of a stable factor structure for the 52-item scale, led to a decision to revise the scale in an attempt to find a better fit of the items to the dimensions.

Although the lack of a stable factor structure for the 52-item scale may be as a result of low participant rates per item (in this case, seven respondents for one item), the likelihood of getting larger samples from this specialised group may be difficult. Thus, the attempt to produce a shorter measure is warranted.

Revised Scale

Using information from the initial analysis to remove items that did not have strong loadings on any of the factors or that had cross-loadings with other factors, as well as identifying items that, at face value, had similar meanings, the final measure resulted in a 23-item, 6-factor structure (see Table 9.3). Both Maximum Likelihood and Principal Axis Factoring produced identical results, where there were no cross-loadings of above .3. Further, a confirmatory factor analysis using structural equation modelling revealed that the 6-factor structure had adequate goodness of fit indices, that is, c^2 = 575.92, df=215, RMSEA = .067, NFI=.91, NNFI=.93, CFI=.94 (see Sun, 2005 and Schreiber et al., 2006 for discussion on reporting and cut-off scores for goodness of fit indices).

Table 9.3 Revised scale

General Attitude	4 items
Knowledge	4 items
Preferences	4 items
Accident Reduction	4 items
Skill Depletion	4 items
Misuse	3 items

Note: Item details can be found in Appendix 9.2.

Table 9.4 displays the correlations of the latent factors from the confirmatory factor analysis. As one might expect, there was a positive correlation between General Attitude, Skill Depletion and Misuse, suggesting that the more a participant thought that the new technology had become too complex, the more likely they perceived that they may lose their piloting skills, as well as feeling that the new technology could be misused. The negative correlation between General Attitude with Preferences and Accident Reduction suggests that the more the participants thought that the new technology added complexity, the less likely they preferred to fly in a glass cockpit and the less likely they were to believe that the new technology would result in fewer accidents. There was also a positive correlation between Preferences and Accident Reduction, suggesting that those participants who preferred to fly in a glass cockpit were also more likely to believe that the new technology would result in fewer accidents. The participants who were less likely to think that glass cockpits would reduce accidents were also more likely to think that the new technology would be misused, as indicated by the negative correlation between Accident Reduction and Misuse. Further, the positive correlation between Skill Reduction and Misuse suggests that the more likely the participants thought that their skills would be depleted using the glass cockpit, the more they thought that the new technology could be misused.

Table 9.4 Correlations between the latent factors from revised measure

Variables	1	2	3	4	5	6
General Attitudes	1.00					
Knowledge	-.11	1.00				
Preferences	-.48	.29	1.00			
Accident Reduction	-.48	.31	.52	1.00		
Skill Depletion	.56	.13	-.16	-.36	1.00	
Misuse	.45	.11	-.09	-.57	.66	1.00

Table 9.5 shows the coefficients for the standardised factor structure of the revised scale. Although the revised measure showed adequate goodness of fit indices, there were two items that were problematic. Items 8 and 17 of the revised scale had very high measures of uniqueness (.75 and .70 respectively), indicating that they contributed little variance to the measure. Item 8, 'The CASA has provided pilots, students, flight instructors, and examiners with sufficient guidance about flying advanced cockpit aircraft', tends to be the only item that mentions other roles, e.g., instructors and examiners, rather than pilots only. The participants may not have had the knowledge to answer this question appropriately. Item 17, 'I am concerned that flying advanced cockpit aircraft will cause my basic flying skills to deteriorate', was also the only item that related to perceptions of the self rather than other pilots. However, when these items were removed from analysis, the change in χ^2 was not significant and the model tended to be less stable, as indicated by the modification indices from the confirmatory factor analysis results.

The alpha reliabilities for the dimensions of the revised scale dimensions are presented below. As recommended by Clark and Watson (1995) and Schmitt (1996), information on the inter-item correlations and corrected intercorrelations, are also included. For the General Attitude dimension, the alpha reliability was

.76, with intercorrelations between .31 and .55 (mean = .45), and corrected intercorrelations between .47 and .64 (mean = .50). For the Knowledge dimension, the alpha reliability was .68, with intercorrelations between .26 and .43 (mean = .35), and corrected intercorrelations between .40 and .51 (mean = .47). For the Preferences dimension, the alpha reliability was .75, with intercorrelations between .31 and .57 (mean = .44), and corrected intercorrelations between .48 and .69 (mean = .56). For the Accident Reduction dimension, the alpha reliability was .71, with intercorrelations between .30 and .48 (mean = .38), and corrected intercorrelations between .46 and .54 (mean = .50). For the Skill Depletion dimension, the alpha reliability was .75, with intercorrelations between .36 and .53 (mean = .43), and corrected intercorrelations between .48 and .59 (mean = .54). For the Misuse dimension, the alpha reliability was .68, with intercorrelations between .38 and .46 (mean = .42), and corrected intercorrelations between .47 and .53 (mean = .50).

Table 9.5 Coefficients for the standardised factor structure of the revised scale

Item/ Uniqueness	General Attitude	Knowledge	Preferences	Accident Reduction	Skill Depletion	Misuse
1 .32	.83					
2 .42	.76					
3 .51	.70					
4 .65	.59					
5 .54		.68				
6 .43		.76				
7 .56		.66				
8 .75		.50				
9 .15			.92			
10 .51			.70			
11 .43			.75			
12 .63			.61			
13 .53				.69		
14 .63				.61		
15 .63				.61		
16 .43				.76		
17 .39					.78	
18 .61					.63	
19 .31					.83	

Table 9.5 Continued

Item/ Uniqueness	General Attitude	Knowledge	Preferences	Accident Reduction	Skill Depletion	Misuse
20 .70					.54	
21 .44						.75
22 .49						.71
23 .58						.65

Note: Item details can be found in Appendix 9.2.

Differences between Australian and South African Pilots

A series of analyses on the six dimensions of the revised scale was undertaken to explore the differences between Australian (n=122) and South African pilots (n= 243). There has, however, been some debate on the use of applying student's t-test to Likert-based scale designs, with some scholars (e.g., Jamieson, 2004; Seaman and Allen, 2007) arguing that non-parametric tests such as the Mann-Whitney U test should be used for the analysis. Other researchers, however, argue that Welch's t-test can often outperform such tests as the Mann-Whitney U test (e.g., Ruxton, 2006; Kikvidze and Moya-Laraño, 2008; De Winter and Dodou, 2010). Therefore, the analyses to explore the differences between the groups in the present study utilised both Welch's t-test and the Mann-Whitney U test to examine the agreement of findings.

Table 9.6 describes the results from the t-tests which revealed that there was a significant difference between the pilots on five dimensions. South African pilots scored higher than Australian pilots on four of these dimensions, that is, Knowledge, Preferences, Accident Reduction and Skill Depletion. Australian pilots scored significantly higher than South African pilots on General Attitude. For the General Attitude dimension, the results were found using Welch's t-test; t (215.36) = 2.14, p<.05: Mann-Whitney U test: z = 2.23, p = .05. These results indicate that Australian pilots thought that the new technology had become more complex to a greater degree than South African pilots. For the Knowledge dimension, the results were found using Welch's t-test; t (244.90) = -5.03, p<.001: Mann-Whitney U test: z = 4.89, p < .001. These results indicate that South African pilots, more than Australian pilots, felt that there needed to be a focus on providing and evaluating pilot knowledge of glass cockpits. For the Preferences dimension, the results were found using Welch's t-test; t (226.39) = -5.12, p<.001: Mann-Whitney U test: z = 5.09, p < .000. These results indicate that South African pilots, more than Australian pilots, preferred to use the new technology. For the Accident Reduction dimension, the results were Welch's t-test; t (226.69) = -3.66, p<.001: Mann-Whitney U test: z = 3.74, p < .000. These results indicate that South African pilots, more than Australian pilots, felt as if the new technology would result in fewer accidents. For the Skill Depletion dimension, the results were Welch's t-test; t (231.81) = -3.66, p<.05: Mann-Whitney U test: $z = 1.97$, $p < .05$. These results indicate that South African pilots, more than Australian pilots, felt that the new technology would result in a deterioration of manual flying skills. There were no significant differences between the Australian and South African pilots for the Misuse dimension, as indicated by the results from both Welch's t-tests and Mann-Whitney U tests.

Table 9.6 Differences between Australian and South African pilots

Variables	Australia		South Africa		t-value	df	Sign
	No=122 Mean	SD	No=24 Mean	SD			
General Attitude	2.50	.76	2.32	.66	2.14	215.36	.033
Knowledge	3.52	.64	3.88	.65	-5.03	244.90	.000
Preferences	3.79	.67	4.16	.62	-5.12	226.39	.000
Accident Reduction	3.57	.73	3.86	.68	-3.66	226.69	.000
Skill Depletion	3.16	.84	3.35	.80	-1.99	231.81	.048
Misuse	3.76	.76	3.65	.71	1.35	227.24	.177

Differences between Pilots Who are More and Less Experienced in Glass Cockpits

One of the questions asked related to the time participants had spent in a glass cockpit, such as a Garmin G1000. Based on their responses, pilots were divided into four groups. Group 1 consisted of no time in a glass cockpit, Group 2 consisted of 200 hours or less, Group 3 consisted 202–999 hours and Group 4 consisted of over 1,000 hours in a glass cockpit.

In relation to the statistics that were used, there has been some discussion on the robustness of ANOVA versus non-parametric tests, such as Mann-Whitney U Tests and Kruskal-Wallis tests (e.g., Lix, Keselman and Keselman, 1996; Ruxton and Beauchamp, 2008). Lix, Keselman and Keselman suggest that within educational and psychological research, violations are often of sufficient magnitude 'to invalidate the use of the ANOVA F test' (1996, p. 580). They further add that 'violations of the variance homogeneity assumption can have serious consequences for control of the Type I error rate regardless of whether group sizes are equal or unequal, but particularly in the latter case. The effects of non-normality on Type I error performance do not appear to be as severe as those of variance heterogeneity' (1996, p. 612).

Preliminary One-Way ANOVA analyses between Preferences and Accident Reduction revealed that Levene's test of homogeneity was just outside significance, that is, .056 and .053 respectively. Therefore, as suggested by Lix, Keselman and Keselman (1996), the following analyses were undertaken using the Kruskal-Wallis test with alpha set at .05. However, one-way ANOVA analyses with significance levels set at .01 and, using Games-Howell post-hoc analyses, revealed identical results in relation to significant differences between groups. Therefore, Table 9.7 shows the differences between the means from the one-way analyses. The results below relate to the non-parametric tests performed on the variables.

Results revealed that Kruskal-Wallis chi-square approximation, corrected for ties, was significant for General Attitude, χ^2 (3) = 13.34, p = .004; Knowledge, χ^2 (3) = 17.17, p = .001; Preferences, χ^2 (3) = 65.90, p = .000; Accident Reduction, χ^2 (3) = 10.45, p = .015; and Skill Depletion, χ^2 (3) = 10.37, p = .016, but was not significant for Misuse. Six post-hoc comparisons for each dimension were conducted using Mann-Whiney U tests, using an adjusted alpha of .008 (.05/6).

The results revealed a significant difference among groups in a number of different dimensions. Most notable was the Preferences dimension, which suggests that those who had more experience (Groups 3 and 4) in glass cockpits preferred them more than those who had no or relatively low experience with glass cockpits (Groups 1 and 2). In relation to Knowledge, those pilots who were moderately experienced (Group 3) were more concerned about the need for training and increased knowledge of automated cockpits than all the other groups. Pilots with most experience (Group 4) also tended to agree more than other groups that automated cockpits could reduce accidents. Skill depletion also showed that pilots who had the most experience in a glass cockpit (Group 4) were more concerned about losing their piloting skills than those who had moderate experience (Group 3). The effect size between results of Groups 3 and 4 was .26, that is, on the lower

Table 9.7 Difference between means of less and more experienced glass cockpit pilots

Dimension	Group 1 N = 108		Group 2 N = 138		Group 3 N = 61		Group 4 N = 58	
	Mean	SD	Mean	SD	Mean	SD	Mean	SD
General Attitude	2.53^{a}	.66	2.38^{ab}	.67	2.27^{ab}	.73	2.21^{b}	.78
Knowledge	3.60^{a}	.60	3.74^{ab}	.69	4.00^{b}	.62	3.85^{ab}	.68
Preferences	3.85^{a}	.68	3.86^{a}	.61	4.31^{b}	.55	4.52^{b}	.52
Accident Reduction	3.72^{ab}	.64	3.6^{5}a	.78	3.88^{ab}	.66	3.99^{b}	.65
Skill Depletion	3.38^{ab}	.74	3.26^{ab}	.81	3.00^{a}	.92	3.48^{b}	.80
Misuse	3.66^{a}	.73	3.73^{a}	.73	3.73^{a}	.68	3.57^{a}	.77

Note: Group 1 = never used a glass cockpit; Group 2 = up to 200 hours flying in a glass cockpit; Group 3 = between 201 to 999 hours flying in a glass cockpit; Group 4 = 1,000 hours and over flying in a glass cockpit. Different superscripts represent significant differences between the groups. Results are based on differences between the groups set at .01.

side of medium. However, the results also indicated that Group 4 scores were not significantly different from those of Groups 1 and 2. The effect size between results of Groups 3 and 4 was .26, that is, on the lower side of medium.

Differences between Male and Female Pilots

Table 9.8 displays the means and standard deviations among male and female pilots. As can be seen, there were significant differences between men and women on three dimensions, that is, General Attitude, Preferences and Misuse.

In relation to General Attitude, women scored significantly higher than male pilots: Welch's t-test; t (33.52) = 2.21, p<.05: Mann-Whitney U test: z = 2.30, p <.05, suggesting that women tended to agree more than men that advanced cockpit systems had become more complex. Male pilots scored higher than female pilots on Preferences, thus tending to agree more than female pilots for a preference to use automated systems: Welch's t-test; t (363) = -3.36, p<.001: Mann-Whitney U test: z = 3.57, p <.001. Female pilots also scored significantly higher than male pilots on Misuse, suggesting that female pilots tended to agree more than male pilots that advanced cockpit systems could be misused or create more errors: Welch's t-test; t (363) = 1.99, p<.05: Mann-Whitney U test: z = 2.03, p <.05.

Table 9.8 Differences between male and female pilots

Variables	Men		Women		t-value	df	Sign
	No=336 Mean	SD	No=29 Mean	SD			
General Attitude	2.36	.70	2.65	.67	2.20	363	.05
Knowledge	3.76	.68	3.78	.57	.19	363	ns
Preferences	4.07	.65	3.65	.64	-3.36	363	.001
Accident Reduction	3.77	.71	3.65	.70	-.92	363	ns
Skill Depletion	3.27	.82	3.41	.84	.87	363	ns
Misuse	3.66	.73	3.94	.63	1.99	363	.05

Differences between Australian and South African Male and Female Pilots

To examine the differences between the four groups, that is, South African female pilots (Group 1), Australian female pilots (Group 2), South African male pilots (Group 3) and Australian male pilots (Group 4), a series of analyses was undertaken. A one-way ANOVA was undertaken as well as a Kruskal-Wallis test with alpha set at .05. The results from the Games-Howell post-hoc analysis with alpha set at .05 from the one-way ANOVA revealed identical results to the post-hoc Mann-Whitney U tests with alpha set at .008 taken after examining the results from the Kruskal-Wallis analysis. Therefore, Table 9.9 displays the means and standard deviations of the four groups.

The Levene's test of homogeneity revealed that there no significant results for any of the dimensions. Results from the one-way analysis also revealed that there were significant differences between the groups on four dimensions only, that is, Preferences, Knowledge, Accident Reduction and Skill Depletion. However, the analyses from the Games-Howell post-hoc analysis with the more stringent alpha set at .01 revealed no significant differences between the groups on Accident Reduction and Skill Depletion.

For Knowledge, the results revealed that Kruskal-Wallis chi-square approximation, corrected for ties, was significant, χ^2 (3) = 26.12, p<.001. For Preferences, the results revealed that Kruskal-Wallis chi-square approximation, corrected for ties, was significant, χ^2 (3) = 33.85, p<.001. For Accident Reduction, the results revealed that Kruskal-Wallis chi-square approximation, corrected for ties, was significant, χ^2 (3) = 15.34, p<.01. For Skill Depletion, the results revealed that Kruskal-Wallis chi-square approximation, corrected for ties, was significant, χ^2 (3) = 9.99, p<.05. Further analyses were undertaken to examine differences between the groups using Mann-Whitney U tests with alpha set at .008. As stated above, post-hoc Games-Howell analysis with alpha set at .05 revealed identical significant differences between the means of the groups. However, the results below explain those taken from the Mann-Whitney U tests only.

The results for Knowledge using the Mann-Whitney U test: (z = 4.97, p <.001) suggest that South African male pilots agreed more than Australian male pilots that there needed to be more stringent practical tests and learning for advanced cockpit systems. For the Preferences dimension, results revealed that Australian female pilots' scores were significantly different from both South African male pilots (Mann-Whitney U test: z = 4.85, p<.001) and Australian male pilots (Mann-Whitney U test: z = 3.17, p=.002). These results indicate that Australian female pilots tended to disagree more than both South African men and Australian male pilots for a preference to use automated systems. Further, Australian male pilots also scored lower than South African male pilots (Mann-Whitney U test: z = 3.78, p <.001), suggesting that Australian male pilots tended to disagree more than South African pilots in preferring to use automated systems. The results for the other two dimensions of Accident Reduction and Skill Depletion showed significant differences between South African male pilots and Australian male pilots only. For Accident Reduction, the Mann-Whitney U test results (z = 3.21, p <.001) indicated that South African male pilots agreed more than Australian male pilots that advanced cockpit systems are likely to reduce accidents. For Skill Depletion, South African male pilots scored significantly higher than Australian pilots (z = 2.65, p =.008), suggesting that South African male pilots tended to agree more than Australian male pilots that advanced cockpit systems would reduce their flying skills.

Table 9.9 Differences between Australian and South African male and female pilots

Dimension	South African Women N = 7		Australia Women N = 22		South African Men N = 236		Australia Men N = 100	
	Mean	SD	Mean	SD	Mean	SD	Mean	SD
General Attitude	2,61[a]	.69	2.67[a]	.68	2.31[a]	.66	2.46[a]	.78
Knowledge	4.00[a]	.66	3.72[a]	.54	3.88[ab]	.65	3.48[ac]	.66
Preferences	4.18[a]	.76	3.48[ab]	.50	4.16[ac]	.62	3.86[ad]	.69
Accident Reduction	4.11[a]	.35	3.50[a]	.73	3.85[ab]	.68	3.58[ac]	.74
Skill Depletion	3.07[a]	.75	3.52[a]	.85	3.36[ab]	.80	3.08[ac]	.83
Misuse	3.71[a]	.68	4.01[a]	.61	3.64[a]	.71	3.70[a]	.74

Discussion

The main purpose of the present study was to examine the factor structure of a reconstructed ACAS 52-item scale and to make a comparison between pilots in Australia and South Africa, as well as to examine the differences between male and female pilots. However, the analysis did not yield a factor solution indicative of the nine dimensions originally proposed by Casner (2008) and a number of dimensions had very poor reliabilities. The revised 23-item scale with six dimensions produced a stable factor structure using exploratory factor analysis, as well as producing adequate goodness of fit indices using confirmatory factor analysis. Although two of the dimensions (that is, Knowledge and Misuse) from the revised scale had reliabilities less than the acceptable .70 (both at .69), the sub-scale may still be considered useful because of its relatively desirable mean inter-item correlation. Clark and Watson (1995) recommend a mean inter-item correlation of between .15-.20 for scales that measure broad constructs and between .40-.50 for more narrow constructs. The mean inter-item correlations for Knowledge and Misuse were .35 and .43 respectively. 'There is no sacred level of acceptable or unacceptable level of alpha. In some cases, measures with (by conventional standards) low levels of alpha may still be quite useful' (Schmitt, 1996, p. 353). The revised scale also appeared to cover most of the nine dimensions advocated by Casner (2008) and may be a suitable and briefer scale to utilise in future studies.

However, the revised scale did not include any of the items that made up Casner's Awareness dimension. This dimension seems to be warranted in exploring pilot attitudes towards using new technologies. At face value, the heterogeneity of the Awareness dimension of Casner's 52-item scale can be seen by the items. There were items that related to behaviour of the self and items that related to behaviour of others (pilots in general). The items for this dimension also related to depending on the technology (for example, looking outside the window less often [heads-down time] or the possibility of getting lost without the use of the technology), possible dysfunction of the equipment, as well as an evaluation of the equipment being an aid for improved situational awareness.

The revised scale also enabled differentiation between different groups. There were some significant differences between South African and Australian pilots, as well as those who were more and less experienced using glass cockpits. Results from the present study indicated that South African pilots scored significantly higher than Australian pilots in Knowledge, Preferences, Accident Reduction and Skill Depletion as well as significantly lower in General Attitude, that is, automated cockpits becoming more complex. Therefore, South African pilots were more accepting of this technology than Australian pilots, preferring to use more advanced cockpits, as well as feeling that these would reduce accidents. However, South African pilots were more concerned than Australian pilots about losing their basic flying skills.

Among the few researchers that have compared pilots from different countries on their perceptions of advanced technology in aviation were Sherman, Helmreich and Merritt (1997), who found that individualistic and low power distance societies tend to engage more readily with new technology. South Africa is higher in power distance and lower in individualism than Australia, as indicated by Hofstede's website (see http://www.geert-hofstede.com/hofstede_dimensions.php) and should therefore be lower in the Preference dimension than Australian pilots. However, this was not the case and one may need to explore elsewhere for those differences. Even among societies similar in Hofstede's values show a difference. For example, Singh, Deaton and Parasuraman found that 'British pilots prefer to fly advanced automated aircraft on which they rely too much, whereas Americans don't like automated aircraft and they least rely on them' (2001, p. 210). Care should be taken when using Hofstede's cultural model to gain a deeper understanding of behavioural phenomena. Although his findings may be useful for guiding comparisons in this research, critics posit that the model has some crucial flaws based on assumptions and context (McSweeney, 2002). Helmreich and his colleagues point out that one should also explore the impact of other factors such as organisational and professional culture, as well as national culture when assessing pilots' attitudes towards automation and training (Sherman, Helmreich and Merritt, 1997; Helmreich, Merritt and Wilhelm, 1999). However, the majority of the participants from both countries in the present sample consisted of pilots whose main flying activity was in leisure and sport. Therefore, it becomes difficult to try and establish the influence of organisational culture. Perhaps future studies may be able to explore the interaction between national and organisational culture in relation to attitudes towards the use of new technology.

The results from the present study suggest that the more experienced pilots (over 1,000 hours) had a more positive attitude towards glass cockpits, preferred to use the new technology and felt that the new technology reduced accidents, more so than those who had no, a little (less than 200 hours) or some experience as pilots

(201–999 hours). However, it was those who were moderately experienced who tended to be more concerned about the Knowledge dimension. Some researchers have revealed that there might be a cause for concern in these results. For example, Sherman, Helmreich and Merritt found in their study that 'a preference for automation was accompanied by greater confidence (overconfidence/complacency?) in one's automation skills and a heavier reliance on automation' (1997, p. 324, information in brackets was included). Similarly, when Mosier et al. discuss automation bias, they state that: 'In fact, experience and expertise, which might be predicted to make pilots more vigilant and less susceptible to automation bias, were related to a greater tendency to use only automated cues' (1998, p. 59). Thus, if higher scores in the Accident Reduction dimension can be seen as an indicator of complacency, then those more experienced in glass cockpits might be seen as suffering from more automation bias as well as complacency than those with less experience, which Parasuraman and Manzey (2010) found can lead to poor decision making and lack of situation awareness.

The results also suggested that those with most experience in a glass cockpit seemed more concerned with losing their piloting skills than those with moderate experience. Research by the Australian Bureau of Air Safety Investigation (1998) and Mitchell, Vermeulen and Naidoo (2009) over 10 years later indicated that loss of piloting skills was a concern expressed by a number of pilots: 'The opportunities for pilots to maintain their manual flying skills have decreased significantly since the introduction of advanced technology aircraft; for example, improvements in autopilot and auto land systems, airline policies, and long-haul operations have reduced the opportunities for hand-flying' (Australian Bureau of Air Safety Investigation, 1998, p. 29). It may be that those more experienced with glass cockpits have fewer opportunities for hand-flying. From their study and anecdotal evidence, the Australian Bureau of Air Safety Investigation concluded that concerns over the loss may be related to the pilot's natural satisfaction in hand-flying and the need to have these skills should the automated systems fail to function.

In relation to gender, men generally preferred to use more automated systems than women: however, women tended to be more concerned than men with both the complexity of automated systems (General Attitude) as well as the possibility of misusing them (Misuse). When the four groups were differentiated, the finding that Australian female pilots preferred automated systems less than male pilots from both South Africa and Australia (but similar to South African female pilots) may be suggestive of three influences. The first is that, in general, both male and female Australian pilots preferred automated systems less than South African pilots, with Australian female pilots tending to prefer them less than Australian male pilots, so culture plays a role. The second reason why Australian female pilots but not South African female pilots differed from male pilots was because South African female pilots were more likely to be instructors on glass-type cockpit aircraft, that is, 43 per cent of South African female pilots compared to 13.6 per cent of Australian female pilots. In addition, South African female pilots tended to have spent more hours in automated aircraft (Mean=289, SD=275.6) compared to Australian female pilots (Mean=72, SD=217.5). As stated in Mitchell, Kristovics and Mitchell (2010, p. 26):

> Although gender may have an impact on the possible adoption of new technology and, therefore, short-term use, Venkatesh et al. ... indicate that both biological and psychological gender did not have an effect on long-term use. However, short-term use was the only factor that influenced long-term use of new technology.

The issue of gender also becomes increasingly complex. For example, female pilots tend to have to prove themselves as capable, despite their proficiency. As stated by Mitchell, Kristovics and Vermeulen (2006, p. 48), their results indicated that 'many aviation industry pilots had negative perceptions towards female pilots *including* some female pilots themselves'. Therefore, there are differences between male and female pilots regarding perceptions. Future studies may well include female pilots' perceptions of male pilots, a study that has not yet been initiated, suggesting the possibility that researchers may inadvertently reinforce masculine dominance within the aviation area.

Casner (2008) was aware of the items reflecting the pilot's evaluation of their own awareness and that of other pilots. When examining the responses to the two items 'If you turn off my GPS and moving map during a flight, I might be lost' and 'For some pilots, turn off their GPS and moving map during a flight, and they might be lost', he found a significant difference between the responses indicating that pilots perceived themselves more positively than other pilots. Casner attributed this difference to 'unique invulnerability', that is, a 'biased perception is reflected in the common saying, "It won't happen to me", a statement that generally implies that it will happen to others instead' (Perloff and Fetzer, 1986, p. 502). Stewart (2006) reviewed a number of studies which indicated that unique invulnerability was related to risk-taking behaviour in pilots. Therefore, there is merit in the Awareness dimension being included in a pilot's attitude towards glass cockpits, and has empirical support in relation to its utility for measurement. For example, empirical support for awareness and its possible relationship to accidents has been measured as a tendency to look out of the window less often (as indicated by the Australian Transport Safety Bureau [1991] as a potential for accidents) or a dependence on automation (and related 'automation bias' and complacency, as indicated by Mosier et al. [1998] and Parasuraman and Manzey [2010]) and/or comparison of self and other (as per 'unique invulnerability' and its associated risk-taking behaviour, as indicated by Casner [2008] and Stewart, [2006]). Perhaps all three dimensions could be included for future scale development, including the perceived difficulty in changing from a passive system monitor to an active participant in the event of automation failure (Endsley and Kiris, 1995).

The glass cockpit has only impacted pilots in general aviation within recent times and there has been growing research attempting to understand pilot attitudes towards this new and changing technology in aviation. Results from the present study indicated that the need for pilots to have more knowledge and training and subsequent testing was considered more important for those who spent more time in a glass cockpit. However, scores on attitudes towards training and testing from those who had spent the most time in a glass cockpit (Group 4) did not show a significant difference from those who had experienced no or little time in a glass cockpit. These results suggest that those who had most experience may have become a bit more blasé than those who had spent a moderate time using new technology in estimating the need for more thorough training and testing of pilots in the use of glass cockpits than those who had spent a moderate time doing so.

However, in the case of general aviation indicative of most of the participants in the present study, there might be a need to have more comprehensive training on equipment-specific equipment, as noted by the National Transportation Safety Board, which also suggested that training needs should be assessed by aviation bodies and academia that 'would teach pilots "higher-order thinking skills"' (2010, p. i). Unfortunately, the speed of the adoption of the new technology has made assessment of the type of training needs more difficult. As stated above, Mosier and her colleagues (Mosier, 2001; Mosier et al., 2007) suggest that cognitively there has been a change from a largely intuitive, correspondence-based task to a primarily analytical, coherence-based task. However, in reviewing different studies on a lack of awareness in automated systems, Kramer and Weber (2000) point to the difficulty in changing from a passive participant to an active participant when the need arises. Pilots in general aviation should thus be made aware of principles involved in the appropriate use of automation levels. In addition, Kramer and Weber state that 'the human operators are both slower and more error-prone in carrying out these duties than if they had been active participants in the operation of the system rather than a passive system monitor' (2000, p. 795). Therefore, the 'type' of training needed should incorporate cognitive skills, not just the knowledge and ability to use the newer automated systems. The future challenge is to develop a measure that more fully explores the training needs perceptions of pilots with differing experiences of flying automated systems.

Although the results in the present study did reveal a more stable factor structure and acceptable goodness of fit indices for the briefer measure, there were some limitations. Apart from the revised scale not having items that related to Casner's Awareness dimension, all of the items from the revised scale's Preferences dimension related to autopilot and where many pilots may already be very accustomed to this type of technology. The National Transportation Safety Board states that: 'Autopilots and global positioning systems (GPS) in particular have become standard components in the avionics systems of light aircraft' (2010, p. 18). Further, the full glass cockpit continues to grow in light aircraft (National Transportation Safety Board, 2010) and the technology in light aircraft is quickly emulating those found in larger aircraft (Aviation Safety, 2009). Unfortunately, five of the six items from the Preferences dimension from the 52-item scale included autopilot only as the technology being utilised. Therefore, there was little choice in including different systems or different levels of automation for the Preferences attitude. The growth of different systems by different manufacturers may further complicate the selection of items for this dimension. As stated above, the National Transportation Safety Board point out that 'the same avionics equipment in a different type aircraft may function differently' (2010, p. 54), which may confound results in what pilots prefer.

Another limitation to the present study was the assortment of participants in relation to flying hours in general and flying hours in a glass cockpit. The transition to more automation in aircraft means that some pilots may have had extensive flying experience with limited experience in the glass cockpit (or different levels of automation), as well as pilots who may have limited flying experience, but where much of that experience has been in aircraft with more advanced technology. This was the case in the present sample, where a number of participants who had over 1,000 hours of flying experience had very little experience in a 'glass cockpit', such as a Garmin G1000. Similarly, there were participants who had less than 200 total flying hours where much of that time was spent in a glass-type cockpit. Although there was a high correlation between general flying time and time in a glass cockpit ($r=.72$), the heterogeneity of the sample is a cause for concern and prohibits general conclusions about findings, a problem that may be caused by the continued transition to the more automated flight decks. Future studies need to tease out some of those complications regarding levels of experience in automated systems as well as hours spent in them.

In conclusion, the present study was able to present a briefer measure of general aviation pilots' attitudes towards glass cockpits than the one proposed by Casner (2008). Further, the brief measure showed factorial stability as well as adequate goodness of fit indices. The present study was also able to reveal differences between international groups, such as pilots from South Africa and Australia, as well as differences between groups with different levels of glass cockpit experience and gender. The findings with regard to different levels of experience in glass cockpits also showed the advantage of dividing pilots into more groups and may be suggestive of the possible dynamic nature of attitude changes related to experience, a situation that needs to be more fully explored through longitudinal research.

References

AOPA Air Safety Foundation, 2007. Technologically advanced aircraft: Safety and training. Available at: http://www.dviaviation.com/files/45180843.pdf.

Aviation Safety, 2009. EFIS evaluated: Glass cockpits are standard these days, but what do pilots like and dislike about them? And are they safer? We asked pilots to rate the systems. *Aviation Safety*, 29(10), pp. 16–21.

Australian Bureau of Air Safety Investigation, 1998. Advanced technology aircraft safety survey report. Available at: http://www.atsb.gov.au/media/704656/advanced_technology_aircraft_safety_survey_report.pdf.

Australian Transport Safety Bureau, 1991. Limitations of the see-and-avoid principle. Available at: http://www.auf.asn.au/safety/limit_see_avoid.pdf.

Casner, S., 2008. General aviation pilots' attitudes toward advanced cockpit systems. *International Journal of Applied Aviation Studies*, 8(1), pp. 88–113.

Clark, L.A. and Watson, D., 1995. Constructing validity: Basic issues in objective scale development. *Psychological Assessment*, 7(3), pp. 309–19.

Costello, A.B. and Osborne, J.W., 2005. Best practices in exploratory factor analysis: Four recommendations for getting the most from your analysis. *Practical Assessment, Research & Evaluation*, 10(7), pp. 1–9.

De Winter, J.C.F. and Dodou, D., 2010. Five-item Likert items: t-test versus Mann-Whitney-Wilcoxon. *Practical Assessment Research & Evaluation*, 15(11), pp. 1–12.

Endsley, M.R. and Kiris, E.O., 1995. The out-of-the-loop performance problem and level of control in automation. *Human Factors*, 37(2), pp. 381–94.

Helmreich, R.L., Merritt, A.C. and Wilhelm, J.A., 1999. The evolution of crew resource management training in commercial aviation. *International Journal of Aviation Psychology*, 9(1), pp. 19–32.

Hughes, D., 1989. Pilot react to the automated cockpit glass cockpit study reveals human factors problems. *Aviation Week & Space Technology*, 131(6), pp. 32–6.

Ison, D. and Decker, T., 2010. Is glass safer? *Plane and Pilot*, 46(7), pp. 56–9.

Jamieson, S., 2004. Likert scales: How to (ab)use them. *Medical Education*, 38(12), pp. 1217–18.

Kikvidze, Z. and Moya-Laraño, J., 2008. Unexpected failures of recommended tests in basic statistical analyses of ecological data. *Web Ecology*, 8, pp. 67–73.

Knight, J. 2007. The glass cockpit. *Computer*, 40(10), pp. 92–5.

Kramer, A.F. and Weber, T., 2000. Applications of psychophysiology to human factors. In: J.T. Cacioppo., L.G. Tassinary. and G.G. Berntson (eds), *Handbook of Psychophysiology*, 2nd edn. Cambridge: Cambridge University Press, pp. 784–814.

Lix, L.M., Keselman, J.C. and Keselman, H.J., 1996. Consequences of assumption violations revisited: A quantitative review of alternatives to the One-Way Analysis of Variance 'F' test. *Review of Educational Research*, 66(4), pp. 579–619.

McSweeney, B., 2002. Hofstede's model of national cultural differences and their consequences: A triumph of faith-a failure of analysis. *Human Relations*, 55(1), pp. 89–118.

Mitchell, J., Kristovics, A. and Bishop R., 2010. Glass cockpits in general aviation: A comparison of men and women pilots' perceptions. *International Journal of Applied Aviation Studies*, 10(2), pp. 11–29.

Mitchell, J., Kristovics, A. and Vermeulen, L., 2006. Gender issues in aviation: Pilot perceptions and employment relations. *Journal of Employment Studies*, 14(1), pp. 35–59.

Mitchell, J., Vermeulen, L. and Naidoo, P., 2009. Flying glass: A qualitative analysis of pilot perceptions of automated flight-decks after 20 years. *International Journal of Applied Aviation Studies*, 9(1), pp. 13–28.

Mosier, K.L. 2001. Cognition in the automated cockpit: a coherence perspective. *Human Factors and Ergonomics Society Annual Meeting Proceedings*, 45(2), pp. 68–72.

Mosier, K.L., Skitka, L.J., Heers, S. and Burdick, M., 1998. Automation bias: Decision making and performance in high-tech cockpits. *International Journal of Aviation Psychology*, 8(1), pp. 47–63.

Mosier, K., Sethi, N., McCauley, S., Khoo, L. and Orasanu, J., 2007. What you don't know can hurt you: Factors impacting diagnosis in the automated cockpit. *Human Factor: The Journal of the Human Factors and Ergonomics Society*, 49(2), pp. 300–10.

National Transportation Safety Board, 2010. Introduction of glass cockpit avionics into light aircraft. Available at: http://www.ntsb.gov/publictn/2010/SS1001.pdf.

Parasuraman, R. and Manzey, D.H., 2010. Complacency and bias in human use of automation: An attentional integration. *Human Factors: The Journal of the Human Factors and Ergonomics Society*, 52(3), pp. 381–410.

Parasuraman, R. and Riley, V., 1997. Humans and automation: Use, misuse, disuse, abuse. *Human Factors*, 39(2), pp. 230–53.

Perloff, L.S. and Fetzer, B.K., 1986. Self-other judgments and perceived invulnerability to victimization. *Journal of Personality and Social Psychology*, 50(3), pp. 502–10.

Ruxton, G.D., 2006. The unequal variance *t*-test is an underused alternative to Student's *t*-test and the Mann-Whitney U test. *Behavioral Ecology*, 17(4), pp. 688–90.

Ruxton, G.D. and Beauchamp, G., 2008. Some suggestions about appropriate use of the Kruskal-Wallis test. *Animal Behaviour*, 76(3), pp. 1083–97.

Seaman, C.A. and Allen, E., 2007. Likert scales and data analyses. *Quality Progress*, 40(7), pp. 64–5.

Schmitt, N., 1996. Uses and abuses of the coefficient alpha. *Psychological Assessment*, 8(4), pp. 350–3.

Schreiber, J.B., Amaury, N., Stage, F.K., Barlow, E.A. and King, J., 2006. Reporting structural equation modelling and confirmatory factor analysis results: A review. *Journal of Educational Research*, 99(6), pp. 323–37.

Singh, I., Deaton, J. and Parasuraman, R., 2001. Development of a scale to assess pilot attitudes towards cockpit automation. *Journal of the Indian Academy of Applied Psychology*, 27(1–2), pp. 205–11.

Sherman, P.J., Helmreich, R.L. and Merritt, A.C., 1997. National culture and flight deck automation: Results of a multination survey. *International Journal of Aviation Psychology*, 74(4), pp. 311–29.

Stewart, J.E., 2006. Locus of control, attribution theory, and the 'five deadly sins' of aviation. *Technical Report 1182, United States Army Research Institute for the Behavioural and Social Sciences*. Available at: http://www.hqda.army.mil/ari/pdf/TR1182.pdf.

Sun, J., 2005. Assessing goodness of fit in confirmatory factor analysis. *Measurement and Evaluation in Counseling and Development*, 37(4), pp. 240–56.

Voller, V.R. and Agel-Porte, F., 2002. Moore's law and numerical modelling. *Journal of Computational Physics*, 179, pp. 698–703.

Appendix 9.1
The Original ACAS Items

General Attitude	
9	Advanced cockpit systems are becoming too complicated
14	They've gone too far with advanced cockpit systems
17	I look forward to new kinds of advanced cockpit systems
22	The advanced cockpit does not make good use of my basic piloting skills
30	In an advanced cockpit, sometimes I feel more like a 'button pusher' than a pilot
48	Advanced cockpit systems can get you into trouble just as easily as they can get you out of trouble
Workload	
1	Using the autopilot lowers my workload
7	There are too many alerts and warning noises in the advanced cockpit systems
28	I can better control my workload in an advanced cockpit
37	I sometimes spend more time setting up and monitoring the autopilot than I would just hand-flying the aircraft
42	Navigating using GPS lowers my workload
Awareness	
4	My situational awareness is better in an advanced cockpit
15	I always know what mode the GPS and autopilot are in
23	The pilot that uses pilotage (a sectional chart) is going to have better navigational awareness than one who uses a GPS and moving map display
24	It worries me that the GPS, autopilot or other systems may be doing something that I don't know about
25	When I have a traffic alerting system on board, I look out the window less often
29	If you turn off my GPS and moving map during a flight, I may be lost
33	Pilots who use traffic alerting systems have a tendency to look out the window less often
43	For some pilots, turn off their GPS and moving map during a flight, and they might be lost
Learning	
2	New pilots that learn to fly only in advanced cockpit aircraft are going to be lacking some important piloting skills
8	CASA should publish a new pilot handbook to cover advanced cockpit systems
16	There are many things about advanced cockpit systems that can only be learned through experience flying the aircraft

19	The practical test standards need to be expanded to include skills specific to advanced cockpit aircraft
20	There is more for me to learn and remember in an advanced cockpit aircraft
38	There are still features of the advanced cockpit that I don't understand
39	I found everything that I needed to know about advanced cockpit systems in the manufacturer's technical manuals
41	Students learn to fly GPS approaches more quickly than they learn to fly VOR, VOR/DME and localizer approaches
44	The CASA pilot knowledge test (aka 'written exams') should include questions about advanced cockpit systems
47	The CASA has provided pilots, students, flight instructors and examiners with sufficient guidance about flying advanced cockpit aircraft
51	Pilots should not be allowed to act as PIC in advanced cockpit aircraft unless they get an endorsement similar to the one required for high-performance and complex airplanes
Retention	
3	I am concerned that I might become too dependent on GPS, autopilots and other advanced cockpit systems
26	I need to fly more often to maintain proficiency in an advanced cockpit than I do in a conventional aircraft
32	I am concerned that flying advanced cockpit aircraft will cause my basic flying skills to deteriorate
36	I am concerned that today's pilots may become too dependent on GPS, autopilots and other advanced systems
Error	
5	Advanced cockpit systems are going to reduce the number of errors pilots make
6	Using GPS is going to result in fewer accidents
10	Incorrect data entered by mistake is easy to detect in the advanced cockpit
11	I am less likely to make a navigational error or bust an altitude in advanced cockpit
31	Advanced cockpit systems create opportunities to make new kinds of errors
Safety	
13	I feel safer in any aircraft that has a parachute (ballistic recovery system) for the airframe
34	I feel safer in an advanced cockpit aircraft than I do in a conventional aircraft
45	Terrain displays in the cockpit are going to reduce the number of controlled flight into terrain (CFIT) accidents
46	Some pilots will misuse advanced cockpit systems to stretch the boundaries of safety
49	Traffic alerting systems are going to reduce the number of mid-air collisions
50	Cockpit weather systems are going to reduce the number of weather-related accidents
52	GPS is going to reduce the number of accidents

Preference for In-flight Use	
12	I prefer to use the autopilot during a missed approach procedure
18	I prefer to use the autopilot during periods of high workload
21	I prefer to use the autopilot when flying en route
27	I would rather use GPS than VORs to navigate
35	I prefer to use the autopilot when flying an instrument approach
40	I prefer to hand-fly the aircraft (autopilot off) during periods of low workload

Appendix 9.2
Revised Scale

General Attitude	
1.	They've gone too far with advanced cockpit systems (General Attitude)
2.	Advanced cockpit systems are becoming too complicated (General Attitude)
3.	I look forward to new kinds of advanced cockpit systems (General Attitude) – **Reverse score**
4.	There are too many alerts and warning noises in the advanced cockpit systems (Workload)
Knowledge	
5.	CASA should publish a new pilot handbook to cover advanced cockpit systems (Learning)
6.	The CASA pilot knowledge test (aka 'written exams') should include questions about advanced cockpit systems (Learning)
7.	The practical test standards need to be expanded to include skills specific to advanced cockpit aircraft (Learning)
8.	The CASA has provided pilots, students, flight instructors and examiners with sufficient guidance about flying advanced cockpit aircraft (Learning) – **Reverse score**
Preferences	
9.	I prefer to use the autopilot during periods of high workload (Preference for in-flight use)
10.	I prefer to use the autopilot when flying en route (Preference for in-flight use)
11.	Using the autopilot lowers my workload (Workload)
12.	I prefer to use the autopilot when flying an instrument approach (Preference for in-flight use)

Accident Reduction
13. Terrain displays in the cockpit are going to reduce the number of controlled flight into terrain (CFIT) accidents (Safety)
14. Using GPS is going to result in fewer accidents (Error)
15. Cockpit weather systems are going to reduce the number of weather-related accidents (Safety)
16. Advanced cockpit systems are going to reduce the number of errors pilots make (Error)
Skill Depletion
17. I am concerned that flying advanced cockpit aircraft will cause my basic flying skills to deteriorate (Retention)
18. New pilots that learn to fly only in advanced cockpit aircraft are going to be lacking some important piloting skills (Learning)
19. I am concerned that today's pilots may become too dependent on GPS, autopilots and other advanced systems (Retention)
20. I am concerned that I might become too dependent on GPS, autopilots and other advanced cockpit systems (Retention)
Misuse
21. Advanced cockpit systems create opportunities to make new kinds of errors (Error)
22. Advanced cockpit systems can get you into trouble just as easily as they can get you out of trouble (General Attitude)
23. Some pilots will misuse advanced cockpit systems to stretch the boundaries of safety (Safety)

Note: The information in brackets relates to the items that came from the dimensions of Casner's 52-item scale dimensions.

Chapter 10
Gender Issues in Usability of Glass Cockpit for General Aviation Aircraft

Ioana Koglbauer, Reinhard Braunstingl, Klaus Fruehwirth, Eric Grubmueller and Siegfried Loesch

Introduction

According to international studies (Mitchell et al., 2005), female pilots represent less than five per cent of the pilot population worldwide. Female pilots are also underrepresented or lacking in the samples of pilots who participate in the evaluation of aviation equipment or flight training programmes. Thus, human–machine interfaces of aircraft or aircraft cockpits, which essentially influence pilot performance (Trollip and Jensen, 1991), were designed and tested merely with male pilots. Previous research has documented gender differences in using aircraft (Baker et al., 2001) and computers (Beckwith et al., 2005; Grigoreanu et al., 2008, 2009), showing that each gender has its own benefits and limitations in terms of using new technologies.

In a long-term study over 30 years, Sitler (2004) found gender-specific strengths and weaknesses in learning to fly. Female flight students were found to be slower in gaining confidence and had less technical background and experience with technology. However, female flight students enjoyed the use of procedures more, operated the controls more smoothly and took fewer risks than male flight students.

Gender diversity in pilot crew behaviour, leadership, judgment and management of flight situations has been revealed in several studies (Turney et al., 2002; Turney and Bishop, 2004). According to Turney and Bishop (2004), for male pilots, it was more important to make important contributions and seek challenges, whereas for female pilots, the reduction of risks was more important. Female pilots considered that they had to work harder than male pilots at learning technical information and they were continuously under stress to earn the respect of their men crew-mates.

Apparently, gender differences are fading out in more specialised fields such as combat aviation, where female and male pilots have passed several selection phases and have more homogenous training. The findings of Caldwell and LeDuc (1988) confirm this view, showing that there were no significant gender differences in performance and errors of fatigued female and male combat pilots during simulated flight, in conditions of 40 hours' sleep deprivation. However, female pilots reported less tension and anxiety and more vigour than male pilots, results that were considered to be biased by women's tendency to suppress any 'complaining' that might question their capability to perform the job.

An evaluation of gender differences in pilot errors which contributed to general aviation aircraft accidents was performed by Baker et al. (2001) with data from 144 female and 287 male pilots collected in the period between 1983 and 1997. Results showed that landings with gear up, erroneous Instrument Flight Rules (IFR) approaches, collisions, flawed decisions and inattention were more frequent in crashes involving male pilots, whereas loss of control on landing and take-off were more frequent in crashes involving female pilots. Wrong handling of aircraft kinetics was the most frequent kind of error in crashes involving both genders. However, in crashes involving female pilots, there were significantly more errors in handling aircraft kinetics than in crashes involving male pilots.

The design of new cockpit systems and automation needs to take these human performance limitations into consideration, including the above-mentioned gender differences, in order to provide pilots with the optimal resources for information processing and action. Regardless, further research is necessary for designing cockpit systems and automation which enables optimal usability for both female and male pilots. Nevertheless, an essential source of information is also provided by aviation studies that do not have a gender dimension yet. For example, actual benefits and limitations of cockpit automation were summarised by Fennell and Pruchnicki (2009) on behalf of the International Airline Pilots Association. The role of automation, in the view of airline pilots', should be to complement the strength of humans and to protect against their limitations, to improve utilisation and control of aircraft, and to solve problems. Automated systems must allow pilots to control them at any level and therefore they should provide the pilot with appropriate feedback, clear indications of present and expected future status, meaningful alerts and warnings. There were requirements to industry to perform usability evaluations with pilots in all stages of systems development and in conditions of both normal and emergency operations. Furthermore, the airline pilots warned against using overtraining as a substitute for poor human factors design.

As a recent National Transportation Safety Board (NTSB) report (2010) shows, the introduction of glass cockpit in light aircraft has not brought with it the expected safety improvement. Besides improved training programmes for pilots in using glass cockpit devices, another area of optimisation would be that of the human–machine interface. Usability of similar glass cockpit systems can be different and can lead to different results in commercial and general aviation. Airline pilots generally receive more flight training and perform more hands-on training for managing abnormal procedures in flight simulators than general aviation pilots. Commercial aircraft are always flown by crews and are more complex than general aviation aircraft, which are merely flown by one pilot. Therefore, the needs of general aviation pilots in terms of cockpit resources can be totally different from those of airline pilots. Thus, the design of glass cockpit systems and the transfer of systems from commercial to general aviation aircraft need to take organisational and individual aspects as well as technical differences into consideration.

Evidence for pilots' concerns about the complexity and new learning challenges posed by advanced cockpits in general aviation and the danger of becoming 'out-of-the-loop' and too reliant on the systems was presented by Casner (2008). Attitudes towards advanced glass cockpit systems were evaluated with 134 general aviation pilots who had different levels of experience with glass cockpits (from 0 to 4,200 hours) and GPS (from 0 to 5,000 hours). Results also showed that the pilots would prefer to fly most of the time an aircraft equipped with advanced glass cockpit systems, especially with GPS and autopilot. Pilots considered that autopilot and GPS would reduce workload and errors, and would improve situational awareness and safety.

Mitchell, Kristovics and Bishop (2010) evaluated gender differences in attitudes towards advanced glass cockpit systems such as GPS, moving map, traffic alerting systems and hazardous air display systems with 100 male and 22 female general aviation pilots. Generally, they have found positive attitudes towards glass cockpit, but pilots expressed some concerns about its efficacy and utilisation. There were differences: male pilots agreed significantly more than female pilots that their situational awareness and safety were better when using a glass cockpit as compared to a conventional one, but expressed some concerns about too much reliance on the glass cockpit. Female pilots expressed significantly stronger concerns than male pilots about using the glass cockpit, which would require more training to maintain proficiency and would lead to trouble, loss of flight skills and could make one too dependent on it.

Human factors and especially gender diversity in using aircraft cockpits are research fields that need more exploration in order to inform the design of future glass cockpit systems. This research is part of a joint academic and industrial project to investigate and implement gender diversity issues in designing a Flight Guarding System (FGS) for glass cockpits. The principal aim is to increase usability and acceptance of female and male pilots for new glass cockpit systems. The long-term aim is to make flight and general aviation aircraft which are used for *ab initio* flight training more attractive to both women and men, and to enlarge the market for aircraft products and services.

FGS is a new glass cockpit system providing electronic warnings and cautions, recommendations and electronic aids for configuring the aircraft for specific flight phases (i.e. take-off, climb, cruise, approach, landing and so on). Furthermore, FGS provides precise and structured information for managing the electrical system in normal and emergency operation. FGS can be operated in automatic and manual modes. In this study we investigate if there are passive barriers (Kilbourne and Weeks, 1997) for female and male pilots in using the FGS prototype in manual and automatic mode during normal and abnormal operation. The results will be used to optimise the design of functions and indications of the system in order to allow an optimal use of cockpit resources for pilots of both genders.

Method

Participants

Pilots were recruited from flight clubs and pilot associations from Austria, Germany and Switzerland. Ten female pilots aged between 21 and 62 (M = 41.90, SD = 14.54) and 10 male pilots aged between 18 and 54 (M= 37.20, SD = 12.50), all licensed and active pilots, volunteered for the experiment. Age differences between women and men did not reach statistical significance [F(1,18) = .60, p = .44]. The groups of women and men were matched according to qualification, total flight, glass cockpit and simulator time. As the medians show, more than half of the pilots had little or no experience with glass cockpit or certified flight simulators. All participants were in possession of a current private pilot licence, four pilots had an IFR rating (two women and two men) and two pilots had an airline pilot licence (one woman and one man). As Table 10.1 shows, female pilots had in mean 407 total flight hours (SD = 564.62), whereas male pilots had in mean 469 total flight hours (SD = 853). The female pilot group had in mean 37.20 hours (SD = 110) and the male pilot group had in mean 29.30 hours' (SD = 62.29) experience with glass cockpit. All pilots owned a computer and used it weekly for private purposes or at work. Female pilots used a computer in mean 24.72 hours weekly (SD = 6.61) and male pilots' average weekly use of a computer was 30.60 hours (SD = 6.84). Differences between the groups in respect of total flight, glass cockpit, certified simulator and computer usage time calculated using the Wilcoxon test did not reach statistical significance.

Procedure

In the beginning all pilots were asked to read and sign an informed consent form that described the experiment as a cockpit evaluation and optimisation study. Considering individual differences in learning style, we provided each pilot with written instructions for using the device and for the task, followed by a briefing and a hands-on session. In the hands-on session, all pilots performed every configuration of the aircraft (before start, after start, engine run-up, taxi, line-up, climb, cruise, approach, final, after landing and parking) using the FGS. For familiarisation with the electrical page of the Primary Flight Display (PFD), pilots were requested to switch devices on and off, and to take notes of the electrical consumption of devices and the status of energy supply units on a protocol. Differences between the manual and automatic mode and the procedure to control automation were explained and probed by each pilot using the FGS. This procedure was found by all pilots to be sufficient to learn the functioning of the system and to proceed to evaluation.

Table 10.1 Descriptive variables of the pilot groups

Variable	Gender	Mean	SD	Median	Minimum	Maximum
Total flight time (hours)	Women	424.44	198.67	250.00	100.00	2,000.00
	Men	469.00	269.86	125.00	80.00	2,850.00
Total glass cockpit time (hours)	Women	41.33	38.64	.00	.00	350.00
	Men	29.30	19.69	1.50	.00	200.00
Total moving map time (hours)	Women	18.89	16.53	.00	.00	150.00
	Men	35.00	19.56	5.00	.00	200.00
Total GPS time (hours)	Women	117.78	35.93	100.00	.00	350.00
	Men	333.50	274.31	50.00	20.00	2,800.00
Total simulator time (hours)	Women	10.56	6.26	.00	.00	50.00
	Men	24.50	16.80	.50	.00	170.00
Average weekly computer hours	Women	24.72	6.61	20.00	1.00	60.00
	Men	30.60	6.84	30.00	3.00	84.00

The test procedure consisted of configuring a virtual single engine light aircraft for all phases of flight, including a missed approach and a go-around. Therefore, the test sequence had a fixed order of configurations: before start, after start, engine run-up, taxi, line-up, climb, cruise, approach, cruise, approach, final, go-around, climb, cruise, approach, final, after landing and parking.

The procedure for abnormal operation included an alternator failure which was induced by the experimenter at the time when pilots completed the first cruise configuration. It was not possible for pilots to bring the alternator to function again, and therefore they had to switch off devices in order to save energy for completing the test sequence until parking.

Configuring the aircraft during normal operation, as well as configuring the aircraft and management of the electrical system during alternator failure, was performed in both manual and automatic mode, resulting in the following blocks: manual-normal, manual-failure, automatic-normal and automatic-failure. The presentation orders were randomised across participants, but were yoked across genders.

Equipment

The device was implemented in the research simulator of the Institute of Mechanics at Graz University of Technology. The system interface included a Primary Flight Display and manual switches of devices (lights, flaps, trims, transponder, radio and so on). An instructor station was connected to the simulator, allowing the experimenter to induce alternator failures.

Dependent Measures

Performance

Performance was evaluated using self-ratings of the pilots as part of NASA-TLX (Hart and Staveland, 1988). In addition, the duration to complete the task was used as an objective measure of performance. Task duration was the time between the beginning and the end of each block, triggered manually by the experimenter and recorded concomitantly with ECG data of pilots using the Polar RX800C heart monitor.

Workload

Six dimensions of workload (mental demand, physical demand, temporal demand, performance, effort and frustration) were rated post-trial by the pilots using the NASA-Task Load Index (Hart and Staveland, 1988). Pilots rated each dimension using a Likert scale from -5 (very low) to +5 (very high).

Psychophysiological Activation

Pilots cardiac activity was recorded using a thorax belt with incorporated electrodes and a sender which sent data to the Polar RX800C heart monitor. Heart rate data of the pilots was recorded for each block and the triggers were set manually by the experimenter at the beginning and end of each block. Mean heart period or inter-beat-interval (IBI) in milliseconds and the heart rate variability (HRV) as the root mean square of successive differences (RMSSD) were calculated for each block using the Polar software. In addition, for each pilot we performed five rest measurements of two minutes, which were recorded between blocks in a standard order. The first rest measurement was used only for familiarisation of the pilots with this type of recording. IBI and HRV data of 40 second-intervals in the middle of each rest measurement were used for standardising physiological data. This data standardisation method (Koglbauer et al., 2010) was necessary for gathering group differences despite highly divergent individual differences. Each individual value was standardised using the formula $z_j(\text{IBI}) = (\text{IBI}_j - M_j) / SD_j$, where $z_j(\text{IBI})$ was the standardised value for subject J, IBI_j was the raw value of subject J, M_j was the mean rest value and finally SD_j was the standard deviation of the individual rest values. This formula was also applied to HRV data.

Situation Awareness

Situation awareness was evaluated using a modified version of SASHA_Q (Jeannott, Kelly and Thompson, 2003), which included items related to the use of a device or of automation. Pilots rated post-trial each item on a Likert scale from -5 (low) to +5 (high). The items include self-ratings of situation awareness, pilots' ability to anticipate the evolution of the situation, planning and organising ahead, the occurrence of unexpected events, too much focusing on an isolated aspect, forgetting, difficulties in finding information or elements, paying too much attention to the device and the influence of the device to improve understanding of the situation.

Emotion

Emotions were evaluated after each block by the pilots using the positive and negative affect scales (PANAS; Watson and Clark, 1988) with 10 items each. The positive affect scale (PA) included feelings of being active, alert, attentive, determined, enthusiastic, excited, inspired, interested, proud and strong. The negative affect scale (NA) included feelings of being irritable, distressed, upset, guilty, scared, hostile, nervous, jittery, afraid and ashamed. Pilots rated the intensity of their actual emotional state for each item using a five-point scale from 1 (very slightly or not at all) to 5 (extremely). For each scale was calculated an average (e.g., positive and negative) positive emotion and negative emotion score.

Usability

A modified version of the usability evaluation form of Chin, Diehl and Norman (1988) was applied at the end of the experiment. Usability dimensions evaluated were the understanding of functions, general impression, display indications, terminology and information, system capability and learning. Each question had a rating scale differentiating between two adjectives (e.g., difficulty -5 on the left and easy +5 on the right).

Acceptance

Acceptance of the device was assessed by means of an evaluation form that was adopted with some modifications from Jensen, Guilkey and Hunter (1988). The form contained multiple-choice items for evaluating to what degree the device was helpful to pilots, their willingness to use the device in the future or recommend the device to other pilots and, finally, their expectation about other pilots' reactions to the device. Free-response questions were used to solicit pilot input regarding what they liked best and least about the device, as well as desirable functions/indications, which the device does not provide yet. Pilots were also questioned about the contribution of the device in terms of increasing or jeopardising flight safety.

Statistical Analysis

Gender differences in performance, psychophysiological activation, workload and situation awareness were analysed in a design with repeated measures having mode (manual versus automatic) and type of operation (normal versus abnormal) as within-subjects factors, and gender as a between-subjects factor. Gender differences were analysed using the main factor gender and Greenhouse-Geisser tests for the interactions between mode and gender, operation and gender, and mode, operation and gender. In addition, overall analyses of main effects of mode and operation and of the interaction term mode and operation are presented. Gender differences in usability ratings were analysed by means of multivariate and univariate tests. A descriptive data analysis was selected (Abt, 1987) adopting an α-level of .05 and presenting results with statistical probabilities up to p = .10. Qualitative data obtained for various aspects of acceptance are presented descriptively.

Results

Analyses of the Main Operation Effects and Interactions between Gender and Type of Operation

A significant main effect of operation on self-ratings of performance [F(1,18) = 5.04, p = .037] was found, performance being worse during abnormal (M = 1.32, SD = .48) than during normal operation (M = 2.37, SD = .42). As expected, pilots needed less time to complete the task during normal (M = 383.21, SD = 17.67) than during abnormal operation (M = 445.85, SD = 26), differences resulting in a significant main effect of operation [F(1,18) = 12.14, p = .003].

Mean and standard deviations for different measures of performance, workload, emotion and psychophysiological activation (IBI and HRV) of each gender group are presented in Table 10.2. The results show that differences between female and male pilots in self-ratings of performance and in the duration to complete the task in normal and abnormal operation did not reach statistical significance.

There was a significant main effect of operation on mental workload [F(1,18) = 4.60, p = .046], as pilots reported higher mental workload during abnormal (M = .80, SD = .56) than during normal operation (M = -.30, SD = .58). Pilots rated their effort higher during abnormal (M = -.52, SD = .56) than during normal operation (M = -1.80, SD = .53), revealing a significant main effect of operation on effort [F(1,18) = 6.66, p = .020].

Further analyses show a significant main effect of operation on pilots' ratings of time pressure [F(1,18) = 4.56, p = .047], which were significantly higher during abnormal (M = -1.42, SD = .56) than during normal operation (M = -2.22, SD = .48). No main operation effects on physical workload were revealed. There were no significant gender differences in terms of mental and physical workload or in time pressure and effort during normal and abnormal aircraft operations.

A significant main effect of operation on frustration was revealed [F(1,18) = 6.30, p = .022]. Pilots' frustration was significantly higher during abnormal (M = -1.85, SD = .51) than during normal operation (M = -2.95, SD = .50). There were

Table 10.2 Subjective ratings of performance, workload and emotion and objective measures of task duration, standardised psychophysiological activation of female and male pilots in different modes and types of operation

Mode		Manual mode				Automatic mode			
Operation		Normal operation		Abnormal operation		Normal operation		Abnormal operation	
Measure	Gender	M	SD	M	SD	M	SD	M	SD
Performance	Women	2.60	1.43	0.90	2.38	1.50	3.24	1.50	1.96
	Men	3.10	2.08	0.90	3.18	2.30	2.63	2.00	3.06
Duration (sec)	Women	374.89	57.11	457.11	113.43	336.89	59.39	411.89	116.30
	Men	448.00	120.55	485.50	141.52	373.10	83.54	428.90	132.91
Mental demand	Women	-0.80	2.94	1.40	2.37	0.80	3.33	0.60	3.10
	Men	-1.00	2.79	1.10	3.03	-0.20	2.74	0.10	2.92
Physical demand	Women	-2.00	2.54	-1.50	2.84	-2.40	3.06	-1.90	2.85
	Men	-2.70	2.11	-2.00	2.58	-2.20	2.57	-2.30	2.31
Temporal demand	Women	-1.50	2.17	-1.20	2.70	-1.70	2.54	-0.90	3.28
	Men	-2.30	2.50	-1.60	2.50	-3.40	2.01	-2.00	2.54
Effort	Women	-2.00	2.71	-0.90	2.88	-2.70	2.71	-0.80	2.44
	Men	-0.70	2.95	0.20	2.97	-1.80	2.25	-0.60	2.59
Frustration	Women	-3.10	2.42	-1.80	2.62	-2.70	2.87	-1.30	2.50
	Men	-3.20	1.99	-1.30	3.33	-2.80	2.53	-3.00	2.67
Negative emotion	Women	1.12	0.13	1.13	0.16	1.17	0.30	1.17	0.21
	Men	1.15	0.15	1.25	0.42	1.09	0.10	1.14	0.23
Positive emotion	Women	3.46	0.75	3.50	0.77	3.64	0.61	3.53	0.76
	Men	3.89	0.63	3.65	0.62	3.83	0.45	3.91	0.64
Δ IBI (msec)	Women	-4.23	1.65	-2.82	1.11	-3.93	1.50	-2.72	1.21
	Men	-5.95	1.57	-3.81	1.05	-5.75	1.43	-4.15	1.14
Δ HRV (msec)	Women	.44	.92	.59	1.12	.28	1.01	.31	.87
	Men	-1.49	.87	-1.41	1.06	-1.72	.95	-1.85	.83

Note: Performance, mental, physical and temporal demand, effort and frustration were rated on a scale from -5 (very low) to +5 (very high). Positive and negative emotions were rated on a scale from 1 (very slightly or not at all) to 5 (extremely).

no main effects of operation on pilots' positive emotion. Effects of the interaction between gender and operation on measures of positive and negative emotion did not reach significance.

Apparently there was a significant effect of operation on standardised IBI (milliseconds) [$F(1,17) = 16.63$, $p = .001$]. The heart period of the pilots was lower during normal (M = -4.96, SD = 1.07) than during abnormal operation (M = -3.37, SD = .77). There was no main effect of operation on HRV (MSSD). Furthermore, no significant effects were revealed from analyses of the interactions between gender and operation on the measures of IBI (ms) and HRV (MSSD).

Generally, there were significant main effects of operation on different aspects of situation awareness related to the use of the device. Mean scores and standard deviations of different aspects of situation awareness in female and male pilots are presented in Table 10.3. Pilots rated their situation awareness lower during abnormal (M = 2.06, SD = .48) than during normal operation (M = 2.80, SD = .35), the effect being marginally significant [F(1,18) = 3.05, p = .099]. The effect of the interaction term between gender and operation did not reach significance for situation awareness.

Table 10.3 Ratings of situation awareness of female and male pilots when using the device in different modes and types of operation

Mode		**Manual mode**				**Automatic mode**			
Operation		**Normal operation**		**Abnormal operation**		**Normal operation**		**Abnormal operation**	
Measure	**Gender**	**M**	**SD**	**M**	**SD**	**M**	**SD**	**M**	**SD**
Prediction	Women	1.89	3.02	-0.56	2.51	2.67	2.06	-0.56	2.74
	Men	1.90	2.64	0.00	3.02	2.00	2.40	1.50	2.92
Planning ahead	Women	1.78	2.95	0.22	1.99	2.67	1.50	-0.44	2.88
	Men	3.30	1.06	1.60	2.50	2.70	1.25	1.30	2.36
Unexpected events	Women	-3.00	2.50	1.00	2.45	-2.78	1.86	0.67	2.12
	Men	-2.20	2.57	0.20	3.16	-1.10	2.81	0.20	3.19
Focus on details	Women	-3.56	1.59	-1.00	2.24	-3.67	1.94	0.33	1.73
	Men	-1.70	2.00	-0.90	2.77	-3.00	1.63	-1.30	3.43
Forgetting	Women	-2.56	3.00	0.44	2.24	-2.89	2.42	0.11	2.26
	Men	-2.20	3.49	-1.50	3.57	-0.30	2.95	-2.10	3.25
Difficulties in finding	Women	-2.67	2.24	-2.67	1.87	-4.00	1.22	-1.11	2.42
	Men	-2.10	3.45	-2.30	2.91	-1.70	2.26	-2.80	2.86
Focus on device	Women	-1.33	3.04	-1.33	3.00	-2.44	2.60	-0.67	2.35
	Men	-2.40	2.88	-3.10	1.91	-2.40	2.80	-2.30	3.13
Device improved SA	Women	1.56	1.88	0.44	3.05	1.56	2.92	0.89	2.85
	Men	2.30	2.91	2.40	2.72	2.50	2.55	1.60	3.03
Situational awareness	Women	2.89	1.76	1.67	1.87	2.22	1.64	1.78	1.64
	Men	3.30	1.57	2.00	2.91	2.80	2.10	2.80	2.30

Note: Items were rated on a scale from -5 (low) to +5 (high).

There was a significant main effect of operation on pilots' ratings of anticipation [F(1,18) = 17.44, p = 001]. Analyses show that during abnormal operation, pilots could predict less (M = .09, SD = .46) than during normal operation (M = 2.11, SD = .45) the evolution of the situation. As Table 10.3 shows, female pilots rated their capability to predict the evolution of the situation higher than male pilots during normal operation in automatic mode, but during abnormal operation they evaluated their capability to predict the evolution of the situation lower than their male counterparts [F(1,17) = 2.86, p = .10]. Further analyses showed significant main operation effects on pilots' capacity to organise and plan ahead and in being surprised by events [F(1,18) = 21.22, p = .00001 and F(1,18) = 25.49, p = .00001, respectively]. Lower ratings for planning ahead were observed during abnormal (M = .66, SD = .40) than during normal operation (M = 2.61, SD = .32). There was no significant interaction term between gender and operation for planning ahead.

Pilots reported being more surprised by events during abnormal (M = .51, SD = .46) than during normal operation (M = -2.26, SD = .42).

As illustrated in Figure 10.1, female pilots reported fewer unexpected events during normal operation than male pilots, but during abnormal operation they were surprised by more unexpected events than male pilots [F(1,17) = 2.87, p = .10].

There were significant main effects of operation on focusing on isolated elements of the situation and on forgetting [F(1,18) = 21.81, p = .00001 and F(1,18) = 4.26, p = .054, respectively]. Pilots were more focused on isolated elements of the situation (M = -.71, SD = .54) and reported having forgotten more (M = -.76, SD = .56) during abnormal than during normal operation (M = -2.98, SD = .34, and M = -1.98, SD = .51, respectively).

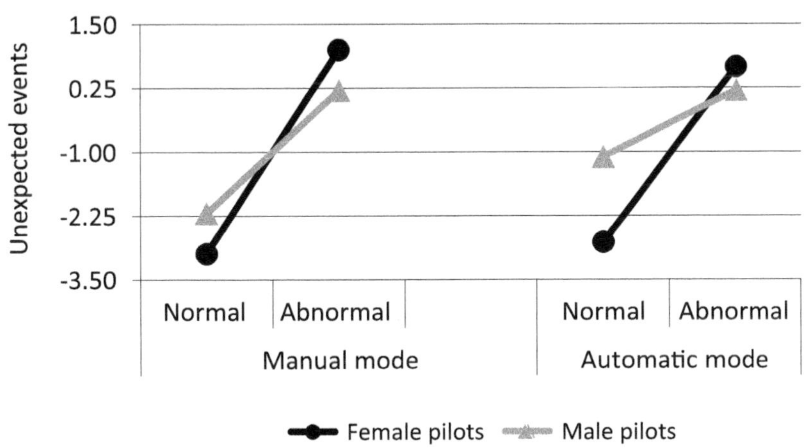

Figure 10.1 Mean self-ratings for the occurrence of unexpected events of female and male pilots in different modes and types of operation (ratings from -5 low to +5 high)

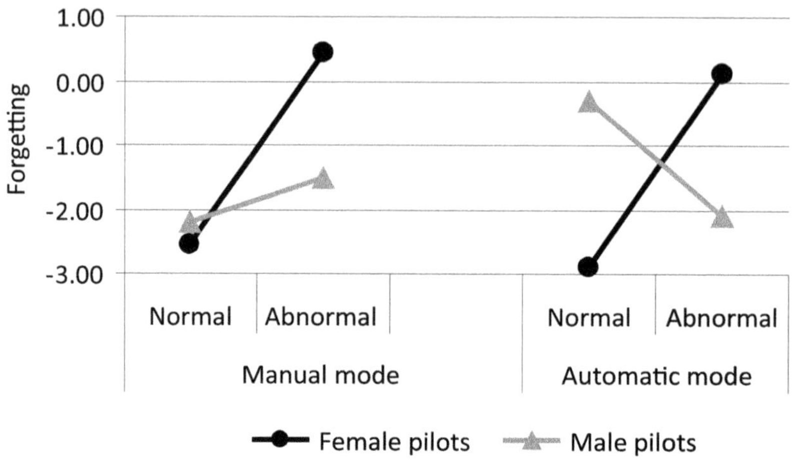

Figure 10.2 Mean self-ratings of forgetting of female and male pilots in different modes and types of operation (ratings from -5 low to +5 high)

During normal operation, female pilots were less focused on a singular aspect of the situation, but during abnormal operation, they were more focused on one aspect than male pilots [$F(1,17) = 4.37$, $p = .052$]. As shown in Figure 10.2, male pilots forgot more than female pilots during normal operation, especially in automatic mode, and forgot less than female pilots during abnormal operation in both modes [$F(1,17) = 8.96$, $p = .008$].

There were no significant main operation effects on pilots' reported difficulty in finding display elements, on pilots' excessive focus on the device and on the reported contribution of the device to improve pilots' situation awareness. Nevertheless, female pilots reported higher concentration on the device than male pilots during both normal and abnormal operation [$F(1,17) = 5.17$, $p = .036$]. During normal operation, female pilots had fewer difficulties in finding display elements, but during abnormal operation they had more difficulties in finding display elements than male pilots [$F(1,17) = 15.87$, $p = .001$].

Analyses of Main Mode Effects and Interactions between Gender and Mode

There was no significant main effect of the mode of control on pilots' performance self-ratings. However, analyses show that pilots needed significantly more time [$F(1,18) = 10.88$, $p = .004$] to accomplish the task in manual ($M = 441.37$ sec, $SD = 22.58$) than in automatic mode ($M = 387.69$ sec, $SD = 21.38$). The interaction term between gender and mode for the performance self-ratings and for the duration to complete the task did not reveal significant results.

The main effect of control mode on effort reached marginal significance [$F(1,18) = 3.71$, $p = .07$], showing pilots' tendency to expend more effort in manual ($M = -.85$, $SD = .53$) than in automatic mode ($M = -1.47$, $SD = .50$). Further comparisons for mental, physical and temporal demand did not reach statistical significance. There were no significant interaction effects between gender and mode on effort, or on mental and physical workload and time pressure.

Pilots positive emotions were stronger when using the device in automatic ($M = 3.72$, $SD = .13$) than in manual mode ($M = 3.62$, $SD = .15$), resulting in a significant main effect of the control mode on pilots' ratings of positive emotion [$F(1,18) = 5.79$, $p = .027$]. Results for negative emotion ratings did not reach statistical significance. Further analyses of the interaction term between gender and mode revealed no significant differences in self-ratings of positive and negative emotion of female and male pilots for different operation modes.

Analyses of main mode effects and those of interaction terms between gender and mode for the IBI (ms) and HRV (MSSD) did not reveal significant effects.

In general, main effects of control mode on different aspects of situation awareness did not reach statistical significance. Male pilots reported the tendency to focus more on an isolated aspect of the situation than female pilots when using the manual mode, whereas in the automatic mode, female pilots felt more distracted by particular elements than male pilots [$F(1,17) = 3.87$, $p = .066$]. The ANOVA revealed no other significant differences of situation awareness in female and male pilots in different modes (automatic vs. manual). Generally, the effects of interaction terms between gender and mode on pilots' anticipation, planning and organising ahead, on forgetting, on difficulties to find information or elements, on paying too much attention to the device, as well as on the estimated device contribution to gain a better understanding of the situation did not reach statistical significance. Reported occurrences of unexpected events did not differ significantly in various modes and types of operation.

Analyses of Interactions between Mode, Type of Operations and Gender

There were significant interaction terms between mode and of operation on pilots' performance [$F(1,18) = 5.37$, $p = .032$]. Pilots' self-ratings of performance during normal operation were higher in manual ($M = 2.85$, $SD = .39$) than in automatic mode ($M = 1.90$, $SD = .66$). However, during abnormal operation, pilots rated their performance higher in automatic ($M = 1.75$, $SD = .57$) than in manual mode ($M = .90$, $SD = .62$). No significant interaction term between system mode (manual vs. automatic) and operation (normal vs. abnormal) was found on the duration to complete the task. Further analyses revealed that gender differences in performance and in duration to complete the task in different operations and modes did not reach statistical significance.

Significant interaction between modes and types of operation were found on pilots' mental workload [$F(1,18) = 4.39$, $p = .039$]. Mental workload of the pilots during normal operation was higher in automatic ($M = .30$, $SD = .68$) than in

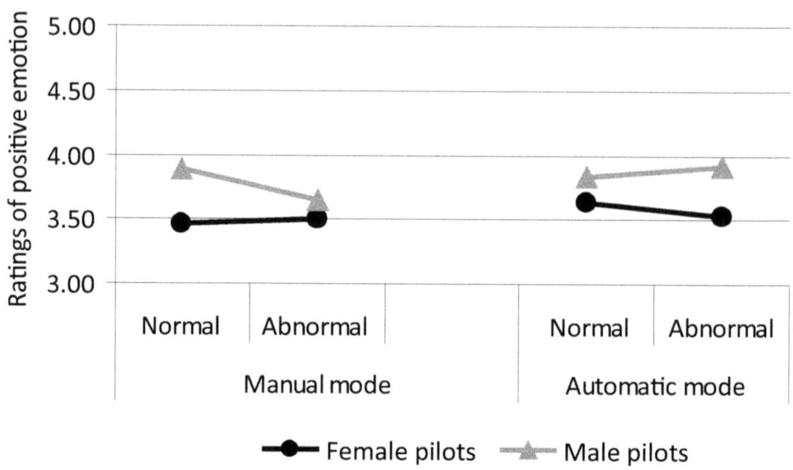

Figure 10.3 Mean self-ratings of positive emotion of female and male pilots in different modes and types of operation (ratings from 1 very slightly or not at all to 5 extremely)

manual mode (M = -.90, SD = .64). Nevertheless, during abnormal operation, mental workload was lower in automatic (M = .30, SD = .68) than in manual mode (M = 1.25, SD = .60). There were no significant interactions between operation and mode for physical and temporal demand, or for effort. Further analyses showed that triple interaction terms between gender, operation and mode for the measures of mental and physical workload, time pressure, effort and negative emotion did not reach statistical significance.

No significant interaction terms between mode and operation were found for measures of positive and negative emotion. Nevertheless, the analysis revealed a significant triple interaction term among gender, system mode and type of operation [F(1,18) = 5.71, p = .028] on pilots' ratings of positive emotion. During normal operation, female pilots showed stronger positive emotion when using the device in automatic than in manual mode, whereas male pilots showed stronger positive emotion when using the device in manual than in automatic mode (Figure 10.3). During abnormal operation, female pilots showed similar levels of positive emotion when using the device in manual and in automatic mode, whereas male pilots showed stronger positive emotion when using the device in automatic than in manual mode.

Effects of interaction terms between mode and operation and gender, mode and operation on pilots' heart period and HRV did not reveal significant effects.

Furthermore, there were no significant interaction terms between system mode and type of operation on different aspects of situation awareness. As Figure 10.4 illustrates, female pilots reported fewer difficulties to find display elements during

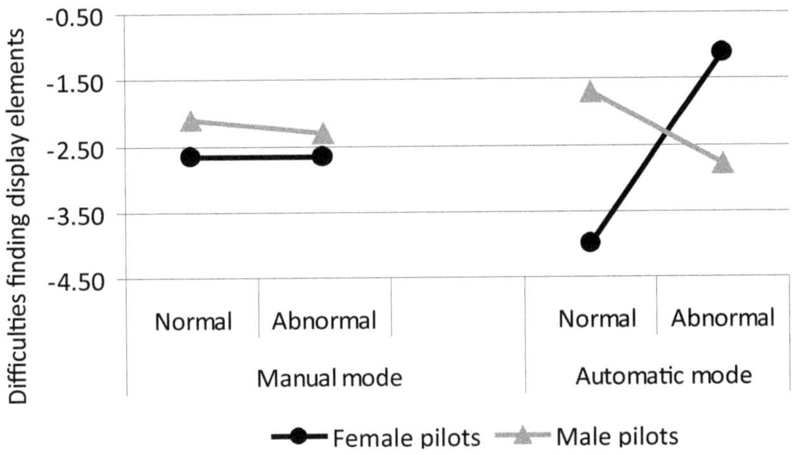

Figure 10.4 Mean ratings of difficulties in finding display elements of female and male pilots in different modes and types of operation (ratings from -5 low to +5 high)

normal operation in both modes and during abnormal operation in manual mode [F(1,18) = 4.78, p = .043].

However, during abnormal operation in automatic mode, female pilots had more difficulties than male pilots in finding display elements. Effects of the interaction terrm among gender, system mode and type of operation on other dimensions of situation awareness did not reach statistical significance.

Analyses of Overall Gender Differences

There was no significant main gender effect on pilots' performance ratings or on duration to complete the task. Analyses for the measures of effort, time pressure, mental and physical workload revealed no significant overall gender effect. Similarly, no main gender effect was found for the measures of positive and negative emotion, or for the measures of psychophysiological activation (IBI and HRV).

Nevertheless, a tendency was found in male pilots to plan and organise ahead more than female pilots during abnormal operation in both manual and automatic modes, and during normal operation in manual mode [F(1,18) = 3.82, p = .067]. However, during normal operation in automatic mode, male and female pilots reported similar capacity to plan and organise ahead. Generally, no main gender effects were revealed on other aspects of situation awareness related to the use of the device.

Multivariate analysis of gender differences in usability revealed a significant main gender effect [F(6,3) = 3.01, p = .045]. As Table 10.4 shows, female pilots rated in general the usability of the FGS higher than male pilots. However, univariate analyses confirmed gender differences only for the information and terminology used [$F(1,18) = 4.01$, $p = .060$]. Univariate analyses of gender effects on ratings of general impression, display indications, understanding of functions, system capability and learning did not reach significance.

Table 10.4 Mean and standard deviations of usability scores in female and male pilots

Gender group	Female pilots		Male pilots	
Measure	**M**	**SD**	**M**	**SD**
General impression (-5, awful, +5 wonderful)	2.87	1.85	2.16	1.99
Display indications (-5, difficult, +5 easy)	3.85	0.96	3.53	1.04
Terminology and information (-5, confusing, +5 clear)	4.34	0.45	3.39	1.43
Learning to use the device (-5, difficult, +5 easy)	2.98	1.96	3.14	1.53
System capability (-5, not useful, +5 very useful)	3.90	1.20	3.14	1.74
Understanding of functions (-5, difficult, +5 easy)	4.73	0.29	4.63	0.61

Qualitative Analyses of Pilots' Acceptance of the FGS

With respect to the degree of usefulness of the FGS, five female pilots reported that the device had been extremely useful, two reported that it had been helpful, two reported that it had been neutral and one reported that it had not been useful. On the other hand, two male pilots reported that the FGS had been extremely useful, seven reported that it had been helpful and one male pilot reported that it had been neutral.

In considering the use of the FGS in the future, if they would have the possibility, seven female pilots answered that they would definitely use the device, two answered maybe and one answered no. Six male pilots confirmed that they would use the device in the future, three answered maybe and one was not sure if he would use it.

Most of the female pilots (9) and all male pilots (10) reported that they would positively recommend the device to other pilots and one female pilot reported that she would not recommend it.

When asked how they think the device would be received by other pilots, two female and two male pilots answered very positive, seven female pilots and eight male pilots answered positive, and one female pilot answered neutral.

Female pilots specified 30 and male pilots specified 28 best functions and indications of the device. On the top list were the configuration checklists (mentioned by nine female and six male pilots), the monitoring and warning function (mentioned by nine female and six male pilots) and the operating concept (mentioned by seven female and eight male pilots). The architecture of the electrical system of the aircraft was put on the top list by four male and four female pilots. Furthermore, the recommendation function was put on the top list by four female and three male pilots. Automation was put on the top list by one female and one male pilot. Furthermore, the control of automation was considered by one female pilot as being one of the best functions.

Least useful or disturbing functions and indications of the device were also identified. Female pilots reported nine disturbing indications related mostly to colours and font size used, and to automation. Male pilots reported eight disturbing indications related to automation and terminology.

When asked to specify four functions or indications which they would like to have in the future, 25 answers were provided (12 from female pilots and 13 from male pilots). Support of the device in managing abnormal procedures was demanded by five female and nine male pilots. Five minor display changes were demanded by female pilots and three were demanded by male pilots. Support in communication with air traffic control and support in navigation were requested by two female pilots and one male pilot.

Finally, pilots were asked to evaluate and bring forward arguments for the contribution of the FGS to assuring and/or jeopardising their own personal safety. Nine out of 10 female pilots reported that the device was beneficial to safety because it prevented the forgetting of actions, it provided monitoring and warning, and it gave recommendations to manage different situations. However, one female pilot considered that the device did not contribute to safety due to automation, which might induce complacency in pilots. All male pilots reported that FGS contributed to safety because it prevented forgetting, simplified cockpit procedures, reduced workload, and improved monitoring of aircraft and detection of failures. However, safety concerns were also expressed by male pilots with respect to possible excessive focus on device and on automation.

Discussion

The primary goal of this research was to identify overall effects of automation and type of operation and gender differences in the usability of a new glass cockpit system and to implement gender diversity issues, complementary to other human factors issues for further optimisation of the system. Thus, we performed a scenario-based evaluation in a flight simulator including normal and abnormal procedures and two different modes of control, automatic and manual.

For normal operation of the electrical system, the FGS provided a menu with electronic checklists, contextualised recommendations and status indications. For abnormal operation, a new cockpit interface was designed to provide pilots with a greater amount of information in a more precise and contextualised manner. The results of the evaluation showed that the electronic checklists, the warning system and the architecture of the electrical system were considered most helpful by both female and male pilots. However, some deficits of the system were found with respect to automation. Pilots were concerned about excessive attentional demands posed by automation and about the risk of overreliance on automation. Despite several studies that revealed a general pilot concern about becoming too reliant on glass cockpit systems (Casner, 2008; Mitchell et al., 2010), we see that there is still space for improving such a system.

Abnormal operation that involved the management of a simulated alternator failure concomitant to configuring the aircraft was associated with an overall decrease of performance and an increase of effort, mental workload, time pressure, task duration and frustration in all pilots. Contrary to our expectations, the subjective increase of workload was not associated with diminished heart period and HRV of the pilots. During abnormal operation, pilots reported lower situation awareness, less anticipation and less planning ahead than in normal operation. They encountered more unexpected events, were more distracted by isolated aspects and forgot more than during normal operation.

No significant gender differences in performance, workload, emotion and psychophysiological activation could be found between normal and abnormal operation. However, the situational awareness related to the use of the FGS of female pilots was better in normal operation and worse in abnormal operation as compared to the situational awareness of male pilots.

In case of alternator failure, female pilots reported stronger shortcomings as they gained less information and could predict less than male pilots when using the new system. Generally, male pilots could benefit more from the information provided by FGS during abnormal operation than female pilots. However, male pilots as well as female pilots expressed the wish to receive more support from the FGS in managing abnormal procedures.

During normal operation, female pilots could benefit more of the FGS as they felt more capable to anticipate, encountered less unexpected events and forgot less than male pilots. Female pilots were also less focused on isolated aspects and reported fewer difficulties in finding display elements than male pilots during normal operation. However, a possible limitation might be the fact that female pilots reported more concentration on the device and less planning ahead than their male counterparts during both normal and abnormal operation.

In respect of the mode of control, our findings revealed the overall main benefits of cockpit automation being to reduce duration and effort associated with the task and to raise stronger positive emotion in pilots, as compared to the manual mode of control. However, a tendency in male pilots to benefit more from cockpit automation was found, as their reports of being distracted by isolated elements were lower than those of female pilots when using this mode. Female pilots had the advantage of being less distracted by isolated elements when using the manual mode. No significant main effects of the mode of control were found on performance self-ratings, mental, physical and temporal workload, psychophysiological activation and negative emotion. Furthermore, gender differences in performance, mental, physical and temporal workload, psychophysiological activation and negative emotion did not reach statistical significance.

The use of automation led to different effects on pilots' performance and workload in different types of operation. During normal operation, pilots' performance was better and mental workload was lower in manual than in automatic mode. During abnormal operation, the use of automation had a positive effect on pilots' performance and on decreasing their mental workload. Although the use of automation poses new demands on pilots who have to control automation in addition to their normal flight tasks, during abnormal operation, automation has the benefit of reducing higher workload imposed by concurrent tasks of flying and carrying out abnormal procedures.

Further analyses showed interesting interaction effects between operation, gender and mode. Female pilots reported stronger positive emotion when using automation during normal operation, whereas male pilots experienced greater positive emotion when using automation during the abnormal operation. Generally, male pilots reported greater positive emotion than female pilots when using the new device.

Overall ratings of usability of the FGS were higher in female pilots than in male pilots, especially for terminology and information of the interface. The results of qualitative analyses clearly indicate a positive contribution of the FGS to improve pilots' safety. Pilots reported that the new device prevented them from forgetting actions, provided useful recommendations to manage different situations and assisted them in monitoring the aircraft. Pilots also reported additional benefits of the device in simplifying cockpit procedures, decreasing workload and facilitating the recognition of warnings and cautions. However, the evaluation also revealed limitations of the FGS and areas of improvement.

Application

The principal application of this formative evaluation study was to inform the design process in respect of safety-relevant and gender diversity issues that require further optimisation of the FGS. Our final aim was to design a FGS that meets operational requirements and preferences of both female and male pilots, and to overcome passive barriers in using new glass cockpit technologies.

Our findings show that all general aviation pilots could use more cockpit resources to improve their performance and reduce workload when managing abnormal procedures. Facilitation of better situation awareness when using the system for managing technical failures is required, especially for female pilots. As female and male pilots explicitly demanded, the new system will include structured checklists for the management of abnormal procedures. Thus, pilots will not rely entirely on remembering knowledge-based procedures or reading aircraft handbooks in emergency situations, but will be provided by the FGS with contextualised 'to do' lists. This measure is not meant to eliminate pilots' before-flight preparation and knowledge of the handbook of their aircraft; rather, it should be seen as an additional safety measure, as a back-up system.

Furthermore, the shortcomings in situation awareness observed in male pilots during normal operation and the feeling of female pilots of being excessively concentrated on the device indicate the necessity to improve the interface in some points. One possible solution might be to provide pilots with aural and visual signals instead of visual information only. As analyses of qualitative data show, male pilots also suggested particular changes in terminology used and in display indications. The results also show that additional changes are necessary to improve the utilisation of automation during normal and abnormal procedures.

The main benefit of this study resulted from the evaluation of basic structures and functions of the FGS in different modes of control and types of operation. On the other hand, the limitations of this research were the evaluation of the system on-ground only and the specification in the experimental procedure of the control mode to be used in each block.

The findings of this study will be used to optimise the new glass cockpit system which will be re-evaluated with pilots, women and men. Future evaluations will include in-flight tests and a session in which pilots are free to choose if and when they use automation.

Acknowledgements

We gratefully acknowledge the Austrian Federal Ministry for Transport, Innovation and Technology and the FEMtech Programme for supporting this research (Project No. 561022). The authors would also like to thank the unnamed pilots for their participation in the experiment and their invaluable inputs and suggestions.

References

Abt, K., 1987. Descriptive data analysis: A concept between confirmatory and exploratory data analysis. *Methods of Information in Medicine*, 26(2), pp. 77–88.

Baker, S.P., Lamb, M.W., Grabowski, J.G., Rebok, G. and Li, G., 2001. Characteristics of general aviation crashes involving mature male and female pilots. *Aviation, Space and Environmental Medicine*, 72, pp. 447–52.

Beckwith, L., Sorte, S., Burnett, M., Wiedenbeck, S., Chintakovid, T. and Cook, C., 2005. Designing features from both genders in end-user programming environments. *Proceeding of the IEEE Symposium on Visual Languages and Human-Centric Computing*, Dallas, TX, 24–26 September.

Caldwell, J.A., Jr. and LeDuc, P.A., 1988. Gender influences on performance, mood and recovery sleep in fatigued aviators. *Ergonomics*, 41(12), pp. 1757–70.

Casner, S., 2008. General aviation pilots attitudes toward advanced cockpit systems. *International Journal of Applied Aviation Studies*, 8(1), pp. 88–112.

Chin, J.P., Diehl, V.A. and Norman, K.L., 1988. Development of an instrument measuring user satisfaction of the human-computer interface. *Proceedings of SIGCHI*, pp. 213–18.

Fennell, K., and Pruchnicki, S., 2009. Aviation automation design and implementation: The need for human factors considerations. *Proceedings of the International Symposium on Aviation Psychology*, Dayton, Ohio, pp. 299–304.

Grigoreanu, V., Brundage, J., Bahna, E., Burnett, M., Eirif, P. and Snover, J., 2009. Males and females script debugging strategies. In: *Lecture Notes. Computer Science, End-User Development*. Heidelberg: Springer Berlin, pp. 205–24.

Grigoreanu, V., Kulesza, T., Bogart, C., Rector, K., Burnett, M. and Wiedenbeck, S., 2008. Can feature design reduce the gender gap in end-user software development environments? *IEEE Symposium on Visual Languages and Human-Centric Computing*, pp. 149–56.

Hart, S.G. and Staveland, L.E., 1988. Development of NASA-TLX (Task Load Index): Results of empirical and theoretical research. In: P.A. Hancock. and N. Meshkati (eds), *Human Mental Workload.* Amsterdam: North Holland Press, pp. 239–50.

Jeannott, E., Kelly, C. and Thompson, D. 2003. The development of situation awareness measures in ATM systems. *EATMP Report*. Eurocontrol HRS/HSP-005-REP-01.

Jensen, R.S., Guilkey, J.E. and Hunter, D.R., 1988. *An Evaluation of Pilot Acceptance of the Personal Minimums Training Program for Risk Management.* Washington DC: Federal Aviation Administration, DOT/FAA/AM-98-6.

Kilbourne, W. and Weeks, S., 1997. A socio-economic perspective on gender-bias in technology. *Journal of Socio-Economics*, 26(3), pp. 243–60.

Koglbauer, I., Kallus, K.W., Braunstingl, R., Wurmitzer, K. and Boucsein, W., 2010. Evolution of pilots' performance and psychophysiological state in managing unusual attitudes, full stalls and spins during simulator training and real flight tests. *Proceedings of the 29th Conference of the European Association of Aviation Psychology*, Budapest, September, pp. 339–44.

Mitchell, J., Kristovics, A. and Bishop, R., 2010. Glass cockpits in general aviation: A comparison of men and women pilots' perceptions. *Gender Work and Organisation Conference*, Keele University, June, pp. 21–3.

Mitchell, J., Kristovics, A., Vermeulen, L., Wilson, J. and Martinussen, M., 2005. How pink is the sky? A cross-national study of the gendered occupation of pilot. *Employment Relations Record*, 5(2), pp. 43–7.

National Transportation Safety Board, 2010. Introduction of glass cockpit avionics into light aircraft. Available at: http://www.ntsb.gov/publictn/2010/SS1001.pdf.

Sitler, R.L., 2004. Gender differences in learning to fly. In: M.A. Turney (ed.), *Tapping Diverse Talent in Aviation: Culture, Gender and Diversity.* Aldershot: Ashgate, pp. 77–90.

Trollip, S.R. and Jensen, R.S., 1991. *Human Factors for General Aviation.* Englewood Cliffs, NJ: Jeppesen Sanderson Inc.

Turney, M.A. and Bishop, J.C., 2004. Women's learning and leadership styles: Implications for air crews. In: M.A. Turney (ed.), *Tapping Diverse Talent in Aviation: Culture, Gender and Diversity*. Aldershot: Ashgate, pp. 61–75.

Turney, M.A., Bishop, J.C., Karp, M.R., Niemczyk, M.S., Sitler, R.L. and Green, M.F., 2002. National survey results: Retention of women in collegiate aviation. *Journal of Air Transportation*, 7(1), pp. 69–92.

Watson, D. and Clark, L.A., 1988. Development and validation of brief measures of positive and negative affect: The PANAS scales. *Journal of Personality and Social Psychology*, 54(6), pp. 1063–70.

Chapter 11

Glass Cockpits in General Aviation: A Comparison of Male and Female Pilots' Perceptions[1]

Jim Mitchell, Alexandra Kristovics and Ronald W. Bishop

Introduction

Commercial, large jet aviation has been utilising an expanding range of advanced technology such as GPS (Global Positioning System), AP (autopilot), MCDU (multi-purpose control display unit), FMC (flight management computer), EFIS (electronic flight instruments system), PFD (primary flight display) and HUDs (heads-up displays) on flight decks for over 20 years. This technological application has been labelled the 'glass cockpit' and has been the subject of much research over this period (Wiener, 1988; James et al., 1991; Rudisill, 1995; Singh, Deaton and Parasuraman, 2001; Naidoo, 2008; Mitchell, Vermeulen and Naidoo, 2009). Similarly, the paucity of female pilots in large commercial jets has been explored (Kristovics et al., 2006; Mitchell et al., 2005; Vermeulen and Mitchell, 2007). The new technology continues to be developed and applied to the military, commercial and the general aviation field. General aviation includes all aviation operations, but excludes scheduled commercial airlines and military aviation. It includes business flying, agricultural aviation, personal flying for pleasure and sports, bush flying, gliding and flying by flight-training institutions (Kumar, DeRemer and Marshall, 2004). Experimental aircraft and very light jet aircraft are recent additions to general aviation (Cobb, Thomas and Cobb, 2007).

More recently, manufacturers of light aircraft have been introducing versions of this technology, including GPS, AP and the Traffic Alerting System (TAS) into the general aviation (GA) and recreational aviation (RA) sectors. These are referred to as advanced cockpit systems. Advanced cockpit aircraft means any aircraft, old or new, that includes at least a panel-mounted GPS receiver unit and an AP. The new cockpit systems might also include electronic flight instruments, a moving map, traffic alerting system, hazardous weather system, terrain warning system

1 Originally published as Mitchell, J., Kristovics, A. and Bishop, R. 2010. Glass cockpits in general aviation: A comparison of men and womale pilots' perceptions. *International Journal of Applied Aviation Studies*, 10(2), pp. 11–30. Reprinted here with permission thanks to *International Journal of Applied Aviation Studies*.

or a complete glass cockpit. Therefore, general aviation and recreational pilots are being exposed to a new raft of innovations in light aircraft flight deck design. Recent research (Casner, 2005, 2008; Dekker and Nahlinder, 2006) has examined pilots' perceptions of the new technology and some implications for training new pilots. The aims of this research are to develop a greater understanding of the perceptions of pilots, as a community of end users, towards automation on the flight deck of GA and RA aircraft in Australia using this framework. More specifically, the research will address the relationship between female pilots and the new technology, and compare their perceptions with those of male pilots.

Women and 'Those Flying Machines'

Within international, domestic and regional aviation domains, there is a paucity of female pilots. Estimates put the numbers to be less than five per cent of the worldwide total pilot population (Mitchell et al., 2005). In Australia, the current number of licence holders for the piloting of planes, helicopters and balloons is 40,734 men and 2,382 women. Women represent 5.85 per cent of all licence holders (Stewart Cameron, CASA, personal communication 26 February 2010). This is an unfavourable comparison with other non-traditional occupations such as engineering, where, for example in Australia, women comprise 10 per cent of the engineering workforce (Engineers Australia, 2006). The reasons for the low numbers of women entering into the commercial flying field remain unresolved. This is despite more than three decades of affirmative action, equal employment opportunity legislation and organisations providing opportunities for women. In engineering, Faulkner indicated that women and girls are not interested in design roles and 'that the symbolic association of masculinity and technology must be operating strongly' (2006, p. 143). Similarly, Mitchell et al. (2005) found that Australian data indicated a pronounced orientation towards a masculine culture within piloting. This is despite the evidence of legendary women aviators and their contribution to aviation (Moolman, 1981; Cadogan, 1992; Yount, 1995). Thus, piloting remains less attractive to women than other non-traditional occupations including engineering.

The significance of air transportation cannot be overestimated in terms of the economic and social impact to society. From the early days of powered flight women have been involved in its development and acceptance. Female pilots (aviatrixes) help 'fuelled an immense popular passion for flying and captured the imagination and hearts of the masses' (Millward, 1998–9, p. 1). It is from this point that female pilots, having demonstrated that flying was safe, began to be marginalised by the aviation industry. Millward's (1998–9, p. 13) research indicated that female pilots were portrayed either as 'woman in pursuit of diversion' and 'woman in pursuit of fortitude'. Women between the First World War and the Second World War were portrayed as not being serious about the economic rewards of flying, but merely flew for sport and pleasure. As a result, many women's contributions to flying were written out of the history of aviation. As Millward (1998–9, p. 14) pointed out, 'while women can occasionally be incorporated into a masculine discourse, the reverse seldom occurs'. Airspace, at that time, came to be and largely remains under masculine control and the domain of men.

Classifying female pilots as seeking either diversion or fortitude helped reinforce the notion that women were not meant to fly aircraft. They were the recipients of gender bias evaluations based on their excursions into a male-dominated occupation and 'man's work'. These successful female pilots were then subjected to a discourse that favoured male attributes and were therefore criticised for violating gender prescriptive norms (Heilman et al., 2004). For women, stepping outside the bounds of gender-specific stereotypes generates forms of social censure including disapproval, negativity, being cold, poor group members and interpersonally wanting. They can be seen as 'bitter, quarrelsome, selfish, deceitful and devious' as well as counter-communal (Heilman et al., 2004, p. 417). These negative epithets are usually not applied to the successful man operating in a male gender-specific domain. Prototypically, men are applauded for being assertive, competitive, agentic and controlling, while women are stereotyped as pro-social and communal (Lammers, Gordijn and Otten, 2009). This stereotypical bias against successful female pilots led to their contribution to aviation to be downgraded and/or ignored in the development of aviation.

Not only were women 'written out' of aviation history, aircraft cockpit design was engineered with a bias against women's bodies. This bias was confined not only to the military but also to commercial aircraft. Aircraft cockpits were designed and built to conform to male anthropometry (Weber, 1997). As Araújo (2008, p. 483) pointed out: 'the relative subordination of women thus concerns not only the production of technology and science but also its practical utilization'. The design of cockpits has acted as a barrier to the inclusion of female pilots in military and commercial aviation and therefore helped to preserve the cockpit primarily as a male domain. However, in light aircraft, cockpit design had fewer physical limitations for women. Cockpit space, although always confining, is personal space, whether the cockpit seating layout is singular, paired or tandem. Instrumentation, relative to large aircraft, was basic and the required physicality of strength, leg and arm reach required for large aircraft was generally not an issue except for exceptionally short people. But flying has a duality of space. There is the envelopment of the pilot within the aircraft and the expansiveness of seemingly unlimited airspace surrounding the aircraft. The duality and use of this airspace then depends upon how it is being utilised by the pilots. It could be because of the pilot being employed and engaged in commercial activity, the pilot's participation in a sporting event or a pilot's engagement in leisure or personal flying.

Women and Technology

Feminist studies into the relationship between women and technology have spanned several decades. A critical argument in women's relationship with technology is that technology and its development is male-dominated and therefore it enhances men's power. Much of the writing has been based on the premise that 'the cultural association between masculinity and technology in Western society is hard to exaggerate' (Grint and Gill, 1995, p. 3). Articles on the 'social shaping of technology' or 'constructivist' theory of technology emphasise the dominance of masculinity in the development of technology (Wajcman, 2005). Rather than women being the developers of technology, they are mainly consigned to the role of end users, be it in the home or the workplace. Edited books by MacKenzie and Wajcman (1985, 1999), Grint and Gill (1995), Fox, Johnson and Rosser (2006) and Wyer et al. (2009) are some of the many contributions to the understanding of that relationship which embeds technology in a masculine frame.

Feminist writers bring many perspectives to analyses of the interactions between women and technology. Bryson (1999) discussed various approaches and recognised that each approach can be complementary or antagonistic. Similarly, Rosser (2006) recognised that there are many divisions within the feminist approach to understanding the relationship between women and technology. Each perspective brings with it its own 'ways of seeing' and interpreting the impact of technology in such terms as patriarchy, culture, class, power, race, inequality, occupations and structural issues relative to gender. Similarly, other approaches, informed by constructivist thought, include ways of 'doing gender', 'performing gender', 'positioning gender' and 'practicing gender' (Poggio, 2006).

Orlikowski criticised the social constructivist approach, indicating that it does not take into sufficient consideration the role of the end user of technological artefacts, technology-in-practice. She goes on to say:

> in both research and practice we often conflate two aspects of technology: the technology as *artefact* (the bundle of material and symbol properties packaged in some socially recognizable form, e.g., hardware, software, techniques); and the *use* of technology, or what people actually do with the technological artefact in their recurrent, situated practices. (2000, p. 408)

The choice of various technologies and technologies-in-practice involves both choosing the type of technological artefact and identifying how the user will interact with and apply any number of applications. Accordingly, technologies-in-practice are those 'rules and resources' based on the 'skills, knowledge and assumptions' held by the user and developed by their ongoing interaction with the properties and norms or protocols of each artefact (Dery, Hall and Wailes, 2006, p. 232).

On a more psychological level, and one that does not dispute Orlikowski's (2000) argument, are the findings of Venkatesh, Morris and Ackerman (2000) and Venkatesh et al. (2004). They investigated gender differences in individual decision-making processes in technology adoption using the theory of planned behaviour as the basis of their studies. Initially, Venkatesh, Morris and Ackerman (2000) found that women tended to have what they termed a 'balanced' approach to adopting new technology; that is, they were most influenced by subjective norm and perceived behavioural control. In contrast, attitude was the only influencing factor for men. Attitude relates to the perceived ease of use and the usefulness of the technological base being introduced. Subjective norm relates to 'perceived opinions of referent others' (Mathieson, 1991, p. 176). Perceived behavioural control relates to perceived 'perception of the availability of skills, resources and opportunities' (Mathieson, 1991, p. 176). As Venkatesh, Morris and Ackerman (2000) suggested, these findings support the gender schema theory. Their literature review indicated that men were more inclined towards a preoccupation with work, accomplishment of objectives and eminence, and were achievement motivated. Other masculine traits included dominance and assertiveness, being instrumental, task-oriented, more likely to rebel and more likely to emphasise outcomes over process. In contrast, they related to women having characteristics such as expressive behaviour, being more compliant in receiving and acting on orders, relationship oriented, interpersonal goals, increased awareness to social cues and having a greater process orientation.

One of the limitations of the findings above was addressed by a later study by Venkatesh et al. (2004), who not only explored the difference between men and women based on biological sex, but also incorporated a measure of gender identity. They found that masculine individuals showed the same pattern above for men, that is, influenced by attitude only. Feminine individuals were most influenced by subjective norm and perceived behavioural control, where attitude was not significant. However, for androgynous individuals (where participants exhibited both male and female traits), results indicated that attitude, subjective norm and perceived behavioural control were all significant. Their research also showed that a large percentage of women (67 per cent) in their sample could be classified as androgynous. Also, Venkatesh, Morris and Ackerman (2000) found that factors such as income, organisational level, education and computer self-efficacy were all found to be not significant as predictors of intention of use.

Within the context of general aviation and recreational aviation, which may be considered a masculine industry, the implementation of advanced technological developments, represented by a range of artefacts identified above, presents the opportunity to compare what male and female pilots, a community of users, say they do in relation to the new electronic systems being implemented in light aircraft.

The Present Study

The present study builds on recent findings (Casner, 2008) carried out by NASA in the US into GA pilot perceptions of glass cockpits in light aircraft that examined the benefits and limitations of the use of this technology. Casner (2008) identified nine topic areas arising out of the research: (1) general attitudes about advanced cockpit systems; (2) workload; (3) situational awareness; (4) learning; (5) retention; (6) error; (7) safety; (8) preference for in-flight use; and (9) overall preferences. The focus of the present study, however, is to examine these issues in relation to female pilots in comparison to that of men's perspectives and is based on data collected from an Australian sample.

The research used a mixed-method approach. Quantitative data was drawn from the multiple choice questions and the qualitative data drawn from the free comments that participants wrote at the end of the survey. In this approach the quantitative and qualitative methods are used in conjunction with one another. Results from both areas are integrated and are aimed to complement each other (Steckler et al., 1992).

Method

Participants

Overall, there were 223 responses. These were from 186 male pilots, 34 female pilots and three who did not indicate their gender. Not all respondents completed their survey forms. Incomplete surveys were removed from the database and the final cohort consisted of 100 male and 22 female pilots. Table 11.1 highlights their biographical details.

Materials

The present study used the identical 52-item NASA survey on pilot attitudes towards glass cockpits. Participants were asked to respond to each item using a five-point Likert scale, where 1 = strongly agree, 2 = agree, 3 = neutral, 4 = disagree and 5 = strongly disagree. Therefore, the lower the score, the more the pilots agreed with the statement represented by the item. One further item, 'How do you think advanced cockpit systems will affect the number of aircraft accidents?', had a different response set. Participants had to choose from six responses, that is, 'significantly reduce accidents', 'somewhat reduce accidents', 'will not affect accidents', 'somewhat increase accidents', 'significantly increase accidents' and 'unsure'.

In addition, further items gathered data related to primary flying activity (e.g., private/leisure, scheduled charter operations, etc.), age, sex, educational background, certification and total flight time – including time flying with a glass cockpit. Participants were also asked about their preference between the different advanced systems, such as GPS, AP, hazardous weather display, moving map, terrain warning and traffic alerting system. Further, a space for comments was added to allow pilots to express their views on issues that were or may not have

Table 11.1 Participant details

	Women (N=22)	Men (N=100)
Average age	44.8	51.9
Average flight hours	1289	2679
Average hours in 'glass cockpit'	72	403
Average hours with at least a panel-mounted GPS	286	740
Certificates and ratings		
1. Private	12	51
2. Instrument	-	16
3. Commercial	5	23
4. Airline Transport Pilot	2	9
5. Chief Flying Instructor	2	-
6. Chief Flying Instrument-Instructor	1	1
Primary flying activity		
1. Non-scheduled charter	6	11
2. Scheduled charter operations	-	-
3. Airline	1	3
4. Private leisure/sport	14	84
5. Other	1	2
Education		
1. High School Certificate	4	30
2. Diploma	5	23
3. Bachelor's degree	6	24
4. Postgraduate degree	7	23
Computer literacy		
1. Poor	-	-
2. Average	5	18
3. Above average	5	39
4. Excellent	12	43

been addressed in the survey questions. These comments were then utilised as the basis for the qualitative analyses. The NVivo 8® software package was utilised to analyse the qualitative data.

Procedure

The data was collected online via links placed on the websites of the Aircraft Owners and Pilots Association (AOPA), the Australian Women Pilots' Association (AWPA), the Sport Aircraft Association of Australia (SAAA) and Recreation Aviation-Australia (RAA). Each of these associations advised members of the research and requested that they complete the survey. Responses were submitted online and were collated on Excel spreadsheets.

Results

Quantitative

The data from the 52-item questionnaire was analysed using SPSS 17. The original intention of performing a factor analysis on the questionnaire was not possible owing to the small size of the sample. In reviewing the required sample sizes for factor analyses, Mundfrom, Shaw and Ke (2009) stated that the minimum that has been suggested was three per item, which for the 52-item questionnaire would be a minimum of 156 participants. Unfortunately, the present sample of 122 prohibited analysis for the factor structure. Therefore, the following analyses were undertaken on an item-specific basis.

When sample sizes are uneven, as in the case of the present study, where there are 100 men and 22 women, most statisticians recommend the use of non-parametric tests such as Mann-Whitney tests (Kikvidze and Moya-Laraño, 2008). However, when Kikvidze and Moya-Laraño (2008) compared these two procedures with uneven sample sizes and unequal variances, they found that the t-tests produced lower percentage of Type I error rates compared to the Mann-Whitney tests. There was little difference between the two procedures for Type II error rates. Simply, Type I errors refer to seeing a difference between two samples when there is none (false positives) and Type II errors refer to not seeing a real difference between two samples when there really is a difference (Borg and Gall, 1989). Therefore, the following analysis on the items was undertaken using independent t-tests, which, according to Kikvidze and Moya-Laraño (2008), would reduce the incidence of 'false positives'.

In relation to which advanced cockpit system men and women preferred, the majority of both men and women preferred the GPS. For women, 63.6 per cent preferred the GPS, 9.1 per cent selected AP and 9.1 per cent selected the moving map. Men showed a similar pattern, where 54 per cent chose the GPS, 19.0 per cent selected AP and 19.0 per cent selected the moving map. More women preferred (13.6 per cent) the traffic alerting system than men (4 per cent). Hazardous air display systems were preferred by 3 per cent of men and 4.5 per cent of women.

The item of whether advanced cockpits would increase or decrease accidents was scored from 1 = significantly decrease accidents to 5 = significantly increase accidents (no one had chosen 'unsure'). The result from an independent t-test with α set at .05 showed no significant difference between men and women; $t(120) = .21$, $p = .83$. The mean for men was 1.88 ($SD = .33$) and the mean for women was 1.86 ($SD = .35$), indicating that both men and women thought that advanced cockpit system would 'somewhat' to 'significantly' decrease accidents.

Table 11.2 shows the items of the questionnaire and the difference between the means for male and female pilots. As can be seen from the table, 11 of the items showed a significant difference between men and women. All analyses on the items below were undertaken using independent t-tests with α set at .05. Items

Table 11.2 Differences between male and female responses

	Variables	Men (100)		Women (22)		Sign
		Mean	SD	Mean	SD	
General attitudes						
9	Advanced cockpit systems are becoming too complicated	3.18	1.09	3.05	.90	ns
14	They've gone too far with advanced cockpit systems	3.77	.98	3.59	.91	ns
17	I look forward to new kinds of advanced cockpit systems	2.14	.93	2.41	.96	ns
22	The advanced cockpit does not make good use of my basic piloting skills	3.07	1.11	2.77	1.15	ns
30	In an advanced cockpit, sometimes I feel more like a 'button pusher' than a pilot	3.35	1.11	2.91	1.11	ns
48	Advanced cockpit systems can get you into trouble just as easily as they can get you out of trouble	2.46	.98	1.91	.75	$p = .006$
Workload						
1	Using the autopilot lowers my workload	1.62	.69	2.05	.57	$p = .005$
7	There are too many alerts and warning noises in the advanced cockpit systems	3.36	1.00	3.09	.92	ns
28	I can better control my workload in an advanced cockpit	2.43	.91	2.73	.93	ns
37	I sometimes spend more time setting up and monitoring the autopilot than I would just hand-flying the aircraft	3.29	.98	2.82	1.05	ns
42	Navigating using GPS lowers my workload	1.87	.66	2.27	.93	ns

Table 11.2 Continued

	Variables	Men (100)		Women (22)		Sign
		Mean	SD	Mean	SD	
Awareness						
4	My situational awareness is better in an advanced cockpit	2.33	1.21	2.91	1.20	p = .042
15	I always know what mode the GPS and autopilot are in	2.25	.95	2.32	.84	ns
23	The pilot that uses pilotage (a sectional chart) is going to have better navigational awareness than one who uses a GPS and moving map display	3.15	1.18	2.77	.97	ns
24	It worries me that the GPS, autopilot or other systems may be doing something that I don't know about	3.38	1.00	3.00	.93	ns
25	When I have a traffic alerting system on board, I look out the window less often	3.51	.99	3.23	.92	ns
29	If you turn off my GPS and moving map during a flight, I may be lost	3.95	.88	3.77	1.11	ns
33	Pilots who use traffic alerting systems have a tendency to look out the window less often	3.00	.98	2.68	.78	ns
43	For some pilots, turn off their GPS and moving map during a flight, and they might be lost	2.43	1.04	1.91	.61	p = .003
Learning						
2	New pilots that learn to fly only in advanced cockpit aircraft are going to be lacking some important piloting skills	2.51	1.08	1.91	.92	p = .017
8	The CASA should publish a new pilot handbook to cover advanced cockpit systems	2.63	1.14	1.95	.78	p = .002
16	There are many things about advanced cockpit systems that can only be learned through experience flying the aircraft	2.01	.77	2.09	.87	ns
19	The practical test standards need to be expanded to include skills specific to advanced cockpit aircraft	2.26	.92	2.00	.87	ns
20	There is more for me to learn and remember in an advanced cockpit aircraft	2.34	.90	2.00	1.02	ns
38	There are still features of the advanced cockpit that I don't understand	2.53	1.06	2.09	.92	ns

Table 11.2 Continued

	Variables	Men (100)		Women (22)		Sign
		Mean	SD	Mean	SD	
Learning (Cont.)						
39	I found everything that I needed to know about advanced cockpit systems in the manufacturer's technical manuals	3.07	1.08	3.27	.88	ns
41	Students learn to fly GPS approaches more quickly than they learn to fly VOR, VOR/DME and localiser approaches	2.81	.71	2.64	.49	ns
44	The CASA pilot knowledge test (aka 'written exams') should include questions about advanced cockpit systems	2.54	1.00	2.77	1.02	ns
47	The CASA has provided pilots, students, flight instructors and examiners with sufficient guidance about flying advanced cockpit aircraft	3.35	.78	3.59	.67	ns
51	Pilots should not be allowed to act as PIC in advanced cockpit aircraft unless they get an endorsement similar to the one required for high-performance and complex airplanes	2.79	1.16	2.32	1.09	ns
Retention						
3	I am concerned that I might become too dependent on GPS, autopilots and other advanced cockpit systems	3.12	1.05	2.50	1.14	$p = .015$
26	I need to fly more often to maintain proficiency in an advanced cockpit than I do in a conventional aircraft	3.00	1.08	2.32	.84	$p = .006$
32	I am concerned that flying advanced cockpit aircraft will cause my basic flying skills to deteriorate	3.33	1.10	3.00	1.02	ns
36	I am concerned that today's pilots may become too dependent on GPS, autopilots and other advanced systems	2.70	1.07	2.50	1.14	ns
Error						
5	Advanced cockpit systems are going to reduce the number of errors pilots make	2.85	1.09	3.05	1.13	ns
6	Using GPS is going to result in fewer accidents	1.98	.91	2.09	.92	ns

Table 11.2 Continued

	Variables	Men (100)		Women (22)		Sign
		Mean	SD	Mean	SD	
Error (Cont.)						
10	Incorrect data entered by mistake is easy to detect in the advanced cockpit	3.27	.95	3.50	.74	ns
11	I am less likely to make a navigational error or bust an altitude in advanced cockpit	2.44	1.10	2.50	.96	ns
31	Advanced cockpit systems create opportunities to make new kinds of errors	2.22	.94	2.00	.62	ns
Safety						
13	I feel safer in any aircraft that has a parachute (ballistic recovery system) for the airframe	3.08	1.14	3.00	1.23	ns
34	I feel safer in an advanced cockpit aircraft than I do in a conventional aircraft	2.84	.98	3.36	.90	p = .023
45	Terrain displays in the cockpit are going to reduce the number of controlled flight into terrain (CFIT) accidents	2.44	1.05	2.50	.86	ns
46	Some pilots will misuse advanced cockpit systems to stretch the boundaries of safety	2.21	.87	2.05	.84	ns
49	Traffic alerting systems are going to reduce the number of mid-air collisions	2.44	.97	2.32	.72	ns
50	Cockpit weather systems are going to reduce the number of weather-related accidents	2.39	.97	2.36	.85	ns
52	GPS is going to reduce the number of accidents	2.92	.98	3.14	1.04	ns
Preference for in-flight use						
12	I prefer to use the autopilot during a missed approach procedure	3.17	.92	3.59	.73	p = .047
18	I prefer to use the autopilot during periods of high workload	2.00	.94	2.36	.85	ns
21	I prefer to use the autopilot when flying en route	2.09	.93	2.55	1.01	p = .043
27	I would rather use GPS than VORs to navigate	2.05	1.02	2.00	.97	ns
35	I prefer to use the autopilot when flying an instrument approach	2.86	.93	3.14	.71	ns
40	I prefer to hand-fly the aircraft (autopilot off) during periods of low workload	2.68	.99	2.32	.89	ns

1, 8, 43 and 48 were analysed using the t-test for unequal variances because of violation of the assumption of homogeneity.

There were five items in which the men's scores were significantly different to women's scores, indicating that men agreed more with the statement than women on the following items:

Item 1	Using the autopilot lowers my workload, $t(35.77) = -3.019$, $p = .005$.
Item 4	My situational awareness is better in an advanced cockpit, $t(120) = -2.051$, $p = .042$.
Item 12	I prefer to use the autopilot during a missed approach procedure, $t(120) = -2.004$, $p = .047$.
Item 21	I prefer to use the autopilot when flying en route, $t(120) = -2.042$, $p = .043$.
Item 34	I feel safer in an advanced cockpit aircraft than I do in a conventional aircraft, $t(120) = -2.296$, $p = .023$.

Women's scores were significantly different from men's scores on six of the items. Women agreed more with the statement than men on the following items:

Item 2	New pilots that learn to fly only in advanced cockpit aircraft are going to be lacking in some important piloting skills, $t(120) = 2.426$, $p = .017$.
Item 3	I am concerned that I might become too dependent on GPS, autopilots and other advanced cockpit systems, $t(120) = 2.473$, $p = .015$.
Item 8	CASA should publish a new pilot handbook to cover advanced cockpit systems, $t(43.14) = 3.332$, $p = .002$.
Item 26	I need to fly more often to maintain proficiency in an advanced cockpit than I do in a conventional aircraft, $t(120) = 2.774$, $p = .006$.
Item 43	For some pilots, turn off their GPS and moving map during a flight, and they might be lost, $t(51.75) = 3.131$, $p = .003$.
Item 48	Advanced cockpit systems can get you into trouble just as easily as they can get you out of trouble, $t(38.53) = 2.938$, $p = .006$.

Qualitative

Various qualitative analysis procedures and interpretive techniques are available. In order to bring structure and meaning to the large volume of collected data in this study, it was decided to employ computer-aided qualitative data analysis software. This is typically used in projects that have non-numerical, unstructured data, such as data in the form of text, e.g., transcripts from interviews, essays, written comments, graphics and other multimedia formats. NVivo 8® is a software program for qualitative text analysis and is designed to assist researchers organise, manage, code and analyse qualitative and mixed-methods research data. This program can be used to facilitate the uncovering of the multifaceted themes hidden in the data or to allocate the data to pre-determined categories.

Written responses by men (63/185: 34 per cent) and women (13/34: 38.2 per cent) were extracted from the survey. The qualitative analysis was conducted through NVivo 8®. Casner's (2008) categories were entered as tree nodes and the content of the comments allocated to the various nodes. In addition to the tree nodes, 'child nodes' or subcategories were added to the tree nodes of General Perceptions, Retention and Safety. These child nodes were Positive and Negative Perceptions, Reduced Skill Levels and Decreased Safety respectively. These were added to reflect the varying perspectives that were identified within the comments.

Comments made by both male and female pilots tended to be brief, and focused on particular aspects of the technology and its application. This amount of qualitative data has limited the analysis and therefore the results can be considered exploratory rather than definitive.

General Perceptions about Advanced Cockpit Systems

The qualitative analysis revealed a mixture of both positive and negative perceptions of advanced cockpit systems. Both male (21 comments) and female (3 comments) pilots were mainly positive in their perceptions about the cockpit systems. Comments from men included 'Glass Cockpits are awesome', 'the glass cockpit makes me more confident in the systems I am trusting to keep me in the air', 'I believe that Glass cockpits will make better pilots. There is no guessing or any confusion, you can never have enough information' and 'I would prefer a glass cockpit because you get more performance figures that you can manage in-flight'. Female pilots had fewer comments; however, the indication was that 'they can only enhance the flight'. While both groups of pilots were generally positive, some expressed reservations about the new technology. Typically, men said 'I believe they are of benefit, but can cause us to be a bit reliant', 'glass moving map etc is great but I am wary of me and my pilots becoming too reliant on it', while women indicated that 'Glass cockpits are inherently neither good or bad' and that 'if the pilots use them as they should be used'. These comments indicated that perceptions were positive; however, there were some reservations about their efficacy and use.

With fewer comments (8) on the negative side, the focus for men was that 'Glass cockpits are a distraction' and that there were difficulties operating across different brands. For example, 'Glass cockpit ie Garmin 1000 etc is vastly different to Advanced cockpit ie Autopilot, VOR, GPS' and 'glass cockpits could be more intuitive, and standardised across brands' and 'Glass cockpits should resemble analog [sic] cockpits with as little button pushing as possible'. Female pilots (2) commented 'I really don't find digital displays do much for me, the analogue dials give me a really good indication of what's going on … and I don't have to worry much about electrical failure etc', 'each system is very different both in display and controller requirements' and 'Will be just as lethal in the hands of cashed up private pilot who has minimal ability or understanding and big ego'. Among both male and female pilots, there is a cross-section of perceptions about the new technology being installed in general aviation and recreational aircraft. Overall these perceptions are positive, but with some doubts being raised as to their efficacy and to the standardisation of the operation and displays of various brands.

Workload

Pilot workload is an issue across all fields in the aviation domain and the survey sought comments on how advanced cockpit systems may affect workload. Workload in the aviation domain 'refers to the combined mental and perceptual demands imposed by the time critical pressures of the flight environment' (Hitchcock, 1999, p. 313). Only male respondents (6) commented briefly on workload in a positive manner: 'Any device that reduces pilot workload makes for safer flight', 'Anything that has the potential to reduce workload and provide good positive feedback to pilots is worthwhile ... a glass environment reduces workload and makes the task much easier' and a warning – 'the increased sophistication and complexity of cockpit systems for the pilot (who now has to act as computer operator in addition to PIC [Pilot in command])'.

Situational Awareness

Flying an aircraft requires the pilot or pilots to maintain a high level of situational awareness. Situational awareness is 'the perception of the elements in the environment within a volume of time and space, the comprehension of their meaning and the projection of their status in the near future' (Endsley, 1999, p. 258). On the positive side, male pilots (10) gave recognition to the enhancement of situational awareness. Comments included: 'The benefits of improved situational awareness in advanced cockpit aircraft are beyond dispute', 'just upgraded to a full glass panel to improve safety and situational awareness' and 'Very expensive, but it has greatly enhanced situational awareness'. Again, words of caution were evident: 'Glass offers significantly enhanced geographical situational awareness ... but also breeds complacency about looking out the window', 'I don't think glass cockpit technology enhances PIC situational awareness', 'Glass cockpits, apart from readability, if taken too far can focus attention inside the aircraft instead of outside', 'I worry that in busy airspace pilots will tend to use/look/play/admire their electronic systems instead of keeping a good lookout' and 'They should be looking outside, not watching TV'. Similarly, female pilots (2) were reticent about the improvement in situational awareness: 'In saying that, the moving map I'm used to seeing is used purely for situational awareness and never relied upon' and 'I am concerned that there will be too much "heads inside" rather than looking outside'.

Learning

In this survey, learning refers to how advanced cockpit systems might affect the way pilots train and maintain proficiency. This category attracted the most overall comments, with men (20) and women (11) raising issues about training in advanced cockpit systems. Clearly, the emphasis on training indicated that pilots were aware of the need for in-depth training to acquire the appropriate level of knowledge about the various electronic systems. Arising out of this, a major concern from both male and female pilots was the lack of a formalised training programme for advanced cockpit systems together with a subsequent licence endorsement from the Civil Aviation Safety Authority (CASA). One woman commented: 'A glass cockpit needs a rating like IF flying'. Others commented that 'CASA or the respective flying schools utilising Glass cockpit aircraft need to run ground courses and practical courses that let the student know the limitations of their instruments' and 'CASA could develop an online course for providing further instruction'. Comments such as 'CASA, operators and pilots need to work together to ensure pilots are familiar with the operations of each specific system' and 'Suggest it would be difficult for CASA to do much in terms of ground study because each system has its own idiosynchrosies [sic]. The existing requirements for use of GPS/RNAV under Instrument Flight Rules (IFR) are a bit of a joke – if they were serious, they'd require a ground school for each specific type of GPS system' came from male pilots.

Both male and female pilots gave indications that training in conventional cockpits should precede training on advanced systems. Comments from women included: 'In the initial stages of flying I believe traditional methods of navigation etc should always be the foundation of knowledge with more technologically advanced methods maybe being introduced to complement that later down the track', 'I believe new pilots should be trained using old "steam gauges" and only after a period of learning should glass cockpit instruments be introduced' and 'I think that the PPL licence should include training in the use of GPS'. Men commented that 'all pilots need to learn normal analog [sic] cockpits first', 'Ground familiarisation (aka the Garmin simulator) is invaluable', 'I think that it is beneficial for pilots to be trained on basic instrumented aircraft before they fly with moving map displays etc' and 'Learning glass cockpit operations after being trained on the older analogue instruments is part of the on-going learning experience of aviation'.

Retention

Retention is about retaining knowledge and skills related to advanced cockpits. Here again, both men (15) and women (2) pilots had mixed views on the impact of advanced cockpit systems on the retention of knowledge and flying skills. Female pilots said: 'It is the skill level of the operator which determines how effective it is. I love "glass" but am concerned that little use of functions may be easily forgotten and hard to call upon when urgently needed' and 'having all the electronics in the world will not stop a pilot from ignoring the systems "alarms", it may encourage some to become slack with their flying skills'. Male pilots indicated that: 'Like everything else, there will be enormous variation between individual pilot aptitudes in adapting to the capabilities of advanced cockpits', 'I try to maintain basic skills, but when busy sometimes you do just rely on the equipment' and 'any of these type of technology are an aid to the pilot but should not replace proper piloting skills/training or proper airmanship'.

Other male pilots were more direct: 'Yes, we see basic pilot skills getting worse from people who have only learnt in a glass aircraft – particularly nav. Yes, their situational awareness is often better from good use of glass. Until it goes blank', 'Currency is important when using the systems, particularly where IFR flight is concerned. The current trend towards providing low time students with advanced avionics should be considered as it could definately [sic] result in pilots with reduced piloting skills' and 'However i [sic] see limited hour pilots place too much reliance on the automated systems and they do not learn airmanship or handling capabilities in an emergency situation. Map reading skills also disappear rapidly after licence qualification'.

Error

Error refers to how advanced cockpit systems will affect pilot error. This area attracted the least number of comments; only four men wrote comments. Comments included: 'Poor pilot decision making/choices will still be the reason for most accidents … but unfortunately people will find ways to make new errors and dumb choices', 'The problem with planes with glass cockpits is that different brands of glass cockpits can have subtle differences in the way they operate. This can cause confusion when flying different planes' and 'Some pilots, regardless of what is occurring in and out of the cockpit will end up crashing because they fail to manage themselves wisely'.

Safety

Safety is a high priority in aviation. The survey sought to examine pilots' beliefs about how advanced cockpit systems would impact on safety. Thirteen male pilots and no female pilots addressed the issue of safety in their comments. Again, their comments reflected mixed perceptions concerning the safety aspects of the glass cockpit. Positive comments included: 'Technology should help to decrease accidents', 'Technology provided by the advanced cockpit is of great benefit for safe piloting', 'I fly high performance single with GPS moving map advanced autopilot and weather at command instrumnt [sic] and have just upgraed [sic] it top a full glass panel to improve safety' and 'can only see it as good and positive move to safer flying'. Others appeared to be more reticent, saying: 'I believe the systems to be much safer, however i [sic] see limited hour pilots place too much reliance on the automated systems', 'makes for safer flight in IMC but there will always be mavericks and mncho [sic] men doing it the hard way' and 'The attitude and professionalism of the pilot has more to do with safety of flying either system'.

Others saw in the use of advanced cockpits the potential for a decrease in safety: 'Without having duplicated "glass" systems I am not yet convinced that the same level of safety is obtained', 'Most mid air collisions in Australia are at GAAP reporting points and traffic alerts will not reduce them', 'VFR is see and avoid, not to be "told" that there is something there and then avoid it' and glass cockpits have 'the potential for distraction'.

Preference for In-Flight Use

This examined pilots' preferences for when to use advanced cockpit systems during flight. Pilots had little to say in when they actually used the systems. Comments included: 'The auto pilot allows for vertical navigation and go around', 'I recently fitted the Dynon auto pilot which makes cross country so relaxing', 'I have Storm Scope, which is seldom used, but essential when it is' and 'While I have a gps I only use it as a back up, not as my main navigational aid'. These comments came only from the male pilots with no comments from female pilots.

Discussion

The main focus of the present study was to explore the possible differences between men and women based on Casner's (2008) measures of pilot attitudes towards advanced cockpit systems. Although the primary objective was to confirm Casner's proposed factors, the small number of pilot responses prohibited this analysis. Therefore, differences between men and women were undertaken on items rather than Casner's proposed factors.

While elements of the advanced technology are available, ranging from a GPS system to a full glass cockpit, male and female pilots have both similar and differing perceptions of the application of and benefits associated with its use. The use of such technology is predicated upon a level of computer literacy. Both men (82 per cent) and women (77.3 per cent) rated themselves above average or excellent in computer literacy. No one rated themselves as poor. Thus, respondents could be assumed to have a familiarity with and experience in the use of these artefacts.

By adopting Mathieson's (1991) definition of attitude to technology-in-use – that is, the perceived ease of use and its usefulness – men found it more useful in terms of lowering their workload (item 1), increasing their situational awareness (item 4), an aid during missed approach procedure (item 12) and flying en route (item 21). However, these comments relate to usefulness rather than perceived ease of use. In General Perceptions, qualitative analyses of men's comments revealed that although men found these advanced systems more useful, they were also concerned about becoming too reliant on them. Qualitative analysis also revealed that there were difficulties in moving from one brand to another, which may impact on the relative ease of use. This also raises the question whether a larger sample of men would indicate that there were more opportunities in the use and purchase of other systems relative to the smaller sample and possible opportunities for women. Thus, future studies may need to include a different number of trialled systems and whether this may have an influence on perceptions of ease of use.

Quantitative analyses also revealed that women were more concerned than men in relation to losing some important pilot skills, both in general (e.g. items 2, 3 and 43) and in their own flying (item 26). Past studies have indicated that when male pilots judged female pilots' abilities in a positive manner, they were more 'accepted' by male pilots. Davey and Davidson found that: 'By demonstrating a high level of skill, the first female pilots were able to establish reputations for themselves as good pilots' (2000, p. 207). In addition, Moore (1999) found that women in a masculine occupation (police in her study) developed a greater sense of occupational identity when participating in professional courses. Thus, pilots' attitudes towards technology-in-use (Mathieson, 1991) may be more complex than initially proposed, that is, it may well need to consider aspects of perceptions of 'value' within a person's occupational identity, as indicated for female pilots.

In line with the above, female pilots were concerned with both Learning and Retention. Items 2 and 8 in Learning and items 3 and 26 in Retention were statistically different. Women displayed concern for both themselves and other pilots in asserting that there should be more training and possible certification for advanced cockpit systems. The concern for learning was matched by the recognised need for retaining the operational information required to maintain currency on their licence and the use of the artefacts when flying. In terms of technology-in-practice, many female pilots lacked the same level of experience as that of male pilots (see Table 11.1). While generally positive over a range of items, women recognised the need for improved and follow-up training to assist in the retention of skills and knowledge. This view is supported by the National Transportation Safety Board (NTSB) in the US (NTSB, 2010). Familiarity with the artefacts, developed through training and practice, assists in developing confidence in the pilot's ability to recognise and deal with the various situations he or she may face.

Safety within aviation is of primary concern to all sectors of the domain. For item 34, men's score was significantly different from those of women, indicating that they felt safer in an aircraft with advanced cockpit systems. There was a general belief that the introduction of advanced cockpit systems would result in the reduction of mid-air collisions, weather-related accidents and accidents in general. There was also concern that some pilots would stretch the boundaries of safety using the new cockpits. Words of warning were made in respect of too much reliance on the systems and the attitude of pilots. However, the lack of any female responses for error and safety aspects in the qualitative findings can either indicate that men were more concerned about these aspects or that the women had already indicated their attitude about this through other means. For example, women agreed more than men on item 48, 'Advanced cockpit systems can get you into trouble just as easily as they can get you out of trouble'. On face value, this item may reflect a safety or error perception, but this item was part of the General Attitude factor. Thus, the need to confirm the factors proposed by Casner (2008) becomes necessary.

While both men and women felt that advanced cockpit systems would decrease accidents, recent preliminary research by the NTSB has indicated that single-engine light aircraft 'had no better overall safety record than airplanes with conventional instrumentation' (NTSB, 2010). Their study covers the accident rates of over 8,000 light aircraft between 2002 and 2006. In this study it was found that there was a higher fatality rate in aircraft with advanced cockpit systems than that of similar planes with conventional or round dial instruments. The enquiry recommends additional training and endorsement of licences, a position strongly supported by female pilots in the survey. However, the situation may be more of one where pilots become too complacent or prone to risk-taking when using these new devises, an aspect that was suggested by both men and women in the qualitative analysis. This situation was most apparent in the research undertaken by Casner, who stated:

> In a previous study, pilots who used GPS and moving map displays estimated their navigational awareness to be greater than that of pilots who navigated using a sectional chart and pilotage in a conventional cockpit ... Believing their awareness to be superior in the presence of a GPS and moving map, these pilots appeared to assume a less active role in the navigation process. When put to a practical test of navigational awareness, these pilots in fact performed worse than pilots who used pilotage to navigate, and quickly lowered their awareness estimates. Pilots who navigated using a sectional chart and pilotage performed better than they expected, and subsequently raised their estimations of their own awareness ... These results suggest that pilots' beliefs and attitudes about advanced cockpit systems can sometimes be powerful determinants of pilot behavior and performance in the cockpit. (Casner, 2008, pp. 88–9)

Casner further adds that pilots in their research acknowledged some of the pitfalls of the advanced cockpit systems and that an important part of training should be to help pilots to 'more accurately assess their own vulnerabilities' (2008, p. 110).

While these results give an indication of differences in perceptions, there is a limitation in the data due to the small numbers of female pilots who responded, the discrepancy in numbers between men and women in the ratio of 5:1. Given that females represent less than six per cent of the total number of licensed pilots in Australia, research in this domain will continue to have these small numbers. Another limitation seems to be the concept of previous experience of using an advanced cockpit system. One may question what kinds of advanced systems have been used and for how long, as well as experience with different brands. On average, women have less experience in a glass cockpit and flying with at least a panel-mounted GPS (as seen in Table 11.1). Unfortunately, there is little information to indicate whether this is because they are not interested (thus affecting behavioural intention) and prefer to use the conventional cockpit. Other aspects may relate to whether they may or may not have the funds to purchase the equipment or whether they have only used one brand of equipment. Although gender may have an impact on the possible adoption of new technology and therefore short-term use, Venkatesh, Morris and Ackerman (2000) and Venkatesh et al. (2004) indicate that both biological and psychological gender did not have an effect on long-term use. However, short-term use was the only factor that influenced long-term use of new technology.

Conclusion

The present study provided an opportunity to compare the perceptions of male and female pilots in respect of the new technology being incorporated in general aviation aircraft. Generally referred to as advanced cockpit systems or glass cockpits, there is an expanding range of artefacts that are available or that pilots are using in their flights. For male and female pilots, technology-in-practice is routinely enacted in every flight. Pilots may choose, or not choose, to use an artefact, but if they do so, they are deliberately choosing how they will interact with that artefact (Orlikowski, 2000). This is evident in the quantitative and qualitative responses to the survey.

While generally positive in relation to the use of artefacts, both men and women were selective in terms of when and how to use the technology – particularly the AP. Comparison of the qualitative and the quantitative data indicates that both male and female pilots, as a community of users, tend to have a general positive perception of the new advanced cockpit systems.

References

Araújo, E.R., 2008. Technology, gender and time: A contribution to the debate. *Gender, Work and Organization*, 15(5), pp. 477–503.

Borg, W.R. and Gall, M.D., 1989. *Educational Research: An Introduction*, 5th edn. New York: Longman.

Bryson, V., 1999. *Feminist Debates*. Houndmills: Macmillan.

Cadogan, M., 1992. *Women with Wings*. Chicago: Academy Chicago Publishers.

Casner, S., 2005. The effects of GPS and moving map displays on navigational awareness while flying under VFR. *International Journal of Applied Aviation Studies*, (5)1, pp. 153–65.

——. 2008. General aviation pilots' attitudes toward advanced cockpit systems. *International Journal of Applied Aviation Studies*, 8(1), pp. 88–113.

Cobb, R., Thomas, J.L. and Cobb, L.A., 2007. The very light jet arrives: Stakeholders and their perceptions. *Journal of Air Transportation*, 12(1), pp. 87–97.

Dekker, S. and Nahlinder, S., 2006. Introduction of technically advanced aircraft in ab-initio flight training. *International Journal of Applied Aviation Studies*, 6(1), pp. 131–44.

Dery, K., Hall, R. and Wailes, N., 2006. ERPs as 'technologies-in-practice': Social construction, materiality and the role of organisational factors. *New Technology, Work and Employment*, 21(3), pp. 229–41.

Endsley, M., 1999. Situational awareness in aviation systems. In: D. Garland., J. Wise and D. Hopkins (eds), *Handbook of Aviation Human Factors.* Mahwah, NJ: Lawrence Erlbaum. pp. 257–76.

Engineers Australia, 2006. *The Engineering Profession: A Statistical Overview*, 4th edn. Victoria: Engineers Australia.

Faulkner, W., 2006. The power *and* the pleasure. In: M. Wye., M. Barbercheck, D. Giesman, H.O. Ozturk and M. Wayne (eds), *Women, Science and Technology*, 2nd edn. New York: Routledge, Pp. 143–56.

Fox, M.F., Johnson, D.G. and Rosser, S.V. (eds), 2006. *Women, Gender and Technology.* Urbana: University of Illinois Press, pp. 13–46.

Grint, K. and Gill, R., 1995 *The Gender-Technology Relation.* Basingstoke: Burgess Science Press.

Heilman, M.E., Wallen, A.S., Fuchs, D. and Tamkins, M.M., 2004. Penalties for success: Reactions to women who succeed at male gender-typed tasks. *Journal of Applied Psychology*, 89(3), pp. 416–27.

Hitchcock, L., 1999. Pilot performance. In: D. Garland., J. Wise. and D. Hopkins (eds), *Handbook of Aviation Human Factors.* Mahwah, NJ: Lawrence Erlbaum, pp. 311–26.

James, M., McClumpha, A., Green, R., Wilson, P. and Belyavin, A., 1991. *Pilot Attitudes to Flight Deck Automation.* London: Royal Aeronautical Society.

Kikvidze, Z. and Moya-Laraño, J., 2008. Unexpected failures of recommended tests in basic statistical analyses of ecological data. *Web Ecology*, 8, pp. 67–73.

Kristovics, A., Mitchell, J., Vermeulen, L., Wilson, J. and Martinussen, M., 2006. Gender issues on the flight-deck: An exploratory analysis. *International Journal of Applied Aviation Studies*, 6(1), pp. 99–120.

Kumar, B., DeRemer, D. and Marshall, D., 2004. *An Illustrated Dictionary of Aviation.* New York: McGraw-Hill.

Lammers, J., Gordijn, E.H. and Otten, S., 2009. Iron ladies, men of steel: The effects of gender stereotyping on the perception of male and female candidates are moderated by prototypicality. *European Journal of Social Psychology*, 39, pp. 186–95.

MacKenzie, D. and Wajcman, J. (eds), 1985. *The Social Shaping of Technology.* Milton Keynes: Open University Press.

——. (eds), 1999. *The Social Shaping of Technology*, 2nd edn. Buckingham: Oxford University Press.

Mathieson, K., 1991. Predicting user intentions: Comparing the technology acceptance model with the theory of planned behavior. *Information Systems Research*, 2(3), pp. 173–91.

Millward, L., 1998–9. The 'aerial eye': Gender and the colonization of airspace. *Michigan Feminist Studies*, 13. pp. 1–18.

Mitchell, J., Vermeulen, L. and Naidoo, P. 2009. Flying glass: A qualitative analysis of pilot perceptions of automated flight-decks after 20 years. *International Journal of Applied Aviation Studies*, 9(1), pp. 13–28.

Mitchell, J., Kristovics, A., Vermeulen, L., Wilson, J. and Martinussen, M., 2005. How pink is the sky? A cross-national study of the gendered occupation of pilot. *Employment Relations Record*, 5(2), pp. 43–60.

Moolman, V., 1981. *Women Aloft*. Alexandria: Time-Life.

Moore, D., 1999. Gender traits and identities in a 'masculine' organization: The Israeli Police Force. *Journal of Social Psychology*, 139(1), pp. 49–68.

Mundfrom, D.J., Shaw, D.G. and Ke, T.L., 2009. Minimum sample size recommendations for conducting factor analyses. *International Journal of Testing*, 5(2), pp. 159–68.

Naidoo, P., 2008. Airline pilots' perception of advanced flight deck automation. MA thesis, University of Pretoria.

NTSB, 2010. NTSB study shows introduction of 'glass cockpits' in general aviation airplanes has not led to expected safety improvements. Press release, 9 March.

Orlikowski, W., 2000. Using technology and constituting structures: A practice lens for studying technology in organizations. *Organization Science*, 11(4), pp. 404–28.

Poggio, B., 2006. Editorial: Outline of a theory of gender practices. *Gender, Work and Organization*, 13(3), pp. 225–33.

Rosser, S., 2006. Using the lenses of feminist theories to focus on women and technology. In: M.F. Fox., D.G. Johnson. and S.V. Rosser (eds), *Women, Gender and Technology*. Urbana: University of Illinois Press, Pp. 13–46.

Rudisill, M., 1995. Line pilots' attitudes about and experience with flight deck automation: Results of an international survey and proposed guidelines. *Eighth International Symposium on Aviation Psychology*, Columbus, Ohio State University, 24–27 April, pp. 288–93.

Singh, I., Deaton, J. and Parasuraman, R., 2001. Development of a scale to assess pilot attitudes towards cockpit automation. *Journal of the Indian Academy of Applied Psychology*, 27(1–2), pp. 205–11.

Steckler, A., McLeroy, K.R., Goodman, R.M., Bird, S.T. and McCormick, L., 1992. Towards integrating qualitative and quantitative methods: An introduction. *Health Education Quarterly*, 19(1), pp. 1–8.

Venkatesh, V., Morris, M. and Ackerman, P., 2000. A longitudinal field investigation of gender differences in individual technology adoption decision-making processes. *Organizational Behavior and Human Decision Processes*, 83(1), pp. 33–60.

Venkatesh, V., Morris, M., Sykes, T.A. and Ackerman, P., 2004. Individual reactions to new technologies in the workplace: The role of gender as a psychological construct. *Journal of Applied Psychology*, 34(3), pp. 445–67.

Vermeulen, L. and Mitchell, J. 2007. Development and validation of a measure to assess perceptions regarding gender-related pilot behavior. *International Journal of Aviation Psychology*, 17(2). pp. 197–218.

Wajcman, J., 2005. *TechnoFeminism*. Cambridge: Polity.

Weber, R., 1997. Manufacturing gender in commercial and military cockpit design. *Science, Technology and Human Values*, 22(2), pp. 235–53.

Wiener, E.L., 1988. Cockpit automation. In: E.L. Wiener. and D.C. Nagel (eds), *Human Factors in Aviation.* San Diego: Academic Press, pp. 433–61.

Wyer, M., Barbercheck, M., Giesman, D., Ozturk, H.O. and Wayne, M. (eds), 2009. *Women, Science and Technology*, 2nd edn. New York: Routledge.

Yount, L., 1995. *Women Aviators.* New York: Facts on File.

PART IV
Taking Action

Chapter 12

Leaving Gender 'In': The Royal Australian Air Force's Project to Increase the Representation of Female Pilots

Deanne Gibbon

Introduction

On 4 April 2013, the Chief of the Air Force, Air Marshal Geoff Brown, launched a glossy magazine called *Flying Solo: A Handbook for Women Pilots*, which was designed by military female pilots, for female pilots. The Chief's willingness to publish a document that frankly and fearlessly addresses some of the confronting barriers and challenges faced by female pilots in the Australian Defence Force (ADF) prompted me to reflect on just how far the Australian Air Force has come in terms of cultural reform over the past few years. Air Force's willingness to actively address some of the known challenges facing women working in the non-traditional employment role of pilot reflects a significant cultural and ideological shift that, just five years ago, would have been rejected as 'inequitable', 'too radical' and frankly unnecessary.

While this chapter discusses strategies and tactics designed to improve female pilots' experiences in the ADF, these targeted strategies do not negate the necessity for much wider cultural reform. Each programme discussed here fits into the holistic cultural reform programme that Defence is currently progressing, '*Pathway to Change*'. This reform dialogue addresses inclusivity, appropriate workplace behaviours and the leadership interventions required to ensure women and other groups of personnel are accepted as full and equal partners in the Defence workplace. The larger cultural reform initiatives have not been discussed in this chapter but do work alongside the programmes outlined here. If the current reform programmes succeed, perhaps many of the targeted interventions and schemes detailed in this chapter will be rendered unnecessary.

This chapter details the Royal Australian Air Force's practical response to the findings of an Air Force-sponsored doctoral research project addressing women's under-representation in piloting in both civil and military aviation. The detailed results of this project have been discussed in Chapters 2 and 5 of this book. The broader research theorises that organisations must consider and address all aspects of the 'choice versus constraints' challenge when seeking to increase women's participation in non-traditional careers and occupations.

The Air Force has certainly applied that theoretical premise to this project by addressing the full spectrum of recruiting/attraction constraints (choice) and workplace barriers (constraints) currently preventing higher numbers of women from joining the Air Force and remaining in the Air Force for long-term careers. The Air Force's multifaceted response, although still at the early stages, is showing signs of significantly increasing women's representation in Air Force piloting roles over the next five years.

Early indications are extremely positive. When the Air Force started its action plan in 2010/11, women comprised 2.4 per cent of Air Force pilot roles; today this representation is 3 per cent (4 per cent if just counting Officers with less than 10 years' experience).[1] While this change may seem insignificant, there have been no female pilot resignations for 12 months and Air Force pilots are increasingly opting to remain in service after having children, a point where, historically, they have sought resignation (Air Force retention data for pilots, sourced January 2011). This improved retention, coupled with forthcoming recruiting initiatives launching in 2013, looks likely to double women's representation in Air Force flying roles within the next two years. Given women's historically low representation in this field, this will be an impressive achievement.

A Feminist Approach: Leaving Gender 'In'

Many of the initiatives detailed in this chapter have been designed to meet the needs of female workers and reflect an acknowledgement that 'treating everyone the same' (which in the Air Force has meant treating everyone as men) has not proved effective as a means of increasing women's participation in non-traditional employment fields. By leaving gender 'in' and acknowledging the differences that exist between male and female workers, the Air Force has (perhaps inadvertently) moved towards policies and practices that can only be described as 'feminist' in application.

Feminism and Air Force service may seem strange bedfellows, given that military service, worldwide, is renowned as being 'hyper-masculine' (Solaro, 2006) and steeped in 'hegemonic masculinity' (Hinojosa, 2010; Kronsell, 2005; Zeigler and Gunderson, 2005), a gender practice which guarantees the dominant position of men and the subordination of women (Connell, 2005). Whilst this form of acute and pervasive masculinity is prevalent across most areas of the ADF, it has been reported as 'extreme' in both military and civil aviation contexts (Ashcraft, 2005; Barrett, 1996). For this reason, it has been rewarding to see the Air Force so willingly embrace aspects of feminist ideology in the application of this project.

In the past, like many other military organisations, the ADF's approach to integrating women into non-traditional employment roles has entailed 'opening the door' and allowing (sometimes grudgingly) women to enter. As with most

1 Data provided by the Directorate of Workforce Planning, 11 April 2013.

patriarchal organisations, there has been minimal 'recognition that women's work experience may be different to that of men's as a result of power relations that differentiate society at large' (Wilson, 1996, p. 825). The challenges faced by pioneering women entering highly masculinised workplaces have been largely invisible in the ADF. Although the ADF has traditionally applied the principles of 'equality as sameness', in reality, true equality is almost impossible for women who represent a miniscule portion of the workforce (Bagilhole, 2002; Kanter, 1977).

Previous studies have shown that in order to integrate into the masculine Defence context, women have been required to 'act like men and to strive to achieve the same career goals in the same fashion as men without the benefits men take for granted' (Agostino, 2000, p. 78). They have had to manage complex negotiations of femininity (Bridges, 2005; Burton, 1996) without female peers, instructors, role models and mentors to guide their journey into highly masculinised training institutes and workplaces. While many resilient, amazing women have certainly 'survived' and sometimes 'thrived' in Defence working contexts, survival can come at significant personal cost. The women interviewed in this study have spoken extensively of consequences borne from harassment, extreme exclusion, fighting to be accepted and compromising their own values in order to be accepted by the dominant group.

From a structural perspective, in the past, military policies and models for career progression have been built to accommodate the needs and patterns of the majority male worker. There has been minimal flexibility to encompass the differing needs of female workers, especially around periods of maternity and post-maternity employment. It should be noted that these highly inflexible structures have also proven limiting to some men, who, for various reasons (such as illness, injury, caring responsibilities or needing to accommodate their partner's career) may also be unwilling or unable to follow rigidly structured career pathway:

> we're in an environment that is run by men, designed for men and that's just the way it is, you know. (Mindy, student ADF pilot)

This research project determined that women who are unable or unwilling to adapt to the highly masculine context will be discarded during their training, may leave military service at the end of their contractual obligation or may choose to leave the non-traditional employment role (pilot) in favour of a more *welcoming* military context. Historical retention data for female pilots shows that even amongst those who manage to *survive* the initial years as a pilot, very few remain in the Air Force beyond their contractual obligation. Those who do stay often leave at the point of having children.

This project represents a significant point of departure from the traditional military model of just 'opening the door' and allowing women to enter. The Air Force has 'left gender in' throughout this project, from the project's inception to delivery, accepting at all stages that actively addressing women's gender-specific challenges and barriers is absolutely critical to the project's success. This approach supports the widely held feminist contention that 'we must recognise the ideologies of difference which define us as men and women and the inequality this produces' (Wilson, 1996, p. 825).

The initiatives detailed in this chapter have been developed by women, for women, in response to qualitative research for women, at all times keeping women's 'issues, experiences and concerns at the centre' (Hesse-Biber and Yaiser, 2004, p. 3). Gender perspectives were kept at the 'heart of the inquiry', another defining feature of all forms of feminist research (Reinharz, 1992). This research sought to make 'women's invisible experiences visible' (Gray, 2007, p. 225) and, in doing so, has fundamentally changed the Air Force.

There has finally been an acknowledgement within the Air Force that men and women are not 'exactly the same' and expecting women to operate in male paradigms, without support, is actually *unequitable.* To truly diversify our workforce, we must build recruitment, retention and support policies and structures designed to accommodate the needs of *all* workers, not just the dominant male majority.

In the Beginning

The project commenced with the clearly articulated intent to increase women's representation in Air Force piloting roles. This intent was not based on political correctness or social justice agendas, but stemmed from a tangible capability need. Very few people have the physical and psychometric requirements to 'make the grade' as a pilot in the Australian Air Force and of those who do, even fewer are capable of succeeding as a fighter pilot. Australian fighter pilot training is amongst the most arduous in the world, resulting in extremely high-calibre pilots, but a limited pool of fighter pilot graduates. For the past decade, the Air Force has had significant concerns that the number and quality of potential pilot candidates entering recruiting would not meet the growing demand for high-calibre fighter pilots.

With so few pilots being women (as compared to 17 per cent across the wider Air Force), women are considered an as-yet-untapped source of future pilots, especially noting that worldwide, girls are increasingly reaching parity with or are outperforming boys in pilot-necessary subject areas like maths and physics (Ceci and Williams, 2011). Women have also proven themselves to be extremely capable pilots in a range of flying contexts (Gilmartin, 1992; Grant, 2002; Haynsworth and Toomey, 1998; Pateman, 1997). McGlohn et al. contend that in military aviation, while men may have the egocentric 'right stuff', women 'appear to have more of what may be the "good stuff"' (1996, p. 14). Accordingly, only accessing half of Australia's population can be likened to fishing in half of the ocean; there is a whole half an ocean of fish that the Air Force just isn't accessing at the moment. The most capable fighter (pilot) fish may be swimming in the in the other half of the ocean!

There were also ongoing concerns about the retention rates in piloting. Where women had risen to the highest echelons of the Air Force in other occupational groups (including non-traditional fields like engineering), few female pilots had remained in the Air Force for long-term careers. Pilots are also the pool from which most of our senior leaders are drawn; greater leadership diversity will require efforts to attract and retain female pilots. With diversity in leadership and decision making a growing consideration for all organisations, Air Force leaders are conscious that the current leadership team is largely homogenous. Homogeneity has not been an issue in the past, but is increasingly problematic for an organisation seeking to position itself as progressive, inclusive and reflecting the community it exists to defend.

Sponsoring a senior officer, and feminist researcher, with a passion for gender diversity and an interest in women working in non-traditional employment fields to undertake this research was the first step towards generating the action necessary to address this problem. This was also a positive sign that the Air Force was taking the challenge of increasing the numbers of women in piloting quite seriously and was prepared to make a significant investment to achieve their desired outcome.

The Research Journey

After reviewing the literature, I decided that the research should encompass all aviation contexts to enable comparisons between aviation contexts and to ascertain why civil aviation has a higher number of female pilots entering and remaining in piloting careers. Studying the barriers and challenges facing women across different aviation contexts also ensured a point of difference between this study and other studies focusing on female pilots; all previous research into aviation has focused on either military or civil aviation, but never both.

This research to determine and critically discuss ongoing barriers preventing higher numbers of women from entering and remaining in the piloting profession began with two simple goals:

- to contribute to ongoing theoretical debates about gendered occupations/organisations and the barriers faced by women who choose non-traditional careers;
- to provide a research foundation for future strategies that will enable organisations to attract and retain higher numbers of women to non-traditional employment roles.

The first of these aims makes clear the theoretical positioning and academic contribution of the thesis. The second aim encapsulates the intended practical or 'action orientation' that was an important goal from the outset, and the intention to improve women's experiences in Air Force aviation and increase their overall representation was of paramount importance to every stage of the research conceptualisation and development.

In sum, the research followed a qualitative feminist design and methodology, which primarily centred on 75 female pilots' (past, present and future) lived experiences through various stages of flying across different flying contexts. The other empirical component of the study entailed a series of focus groups with women and girls from various contexts, including high schools, the Air Force's one-year GAP year programme and students at the Australian Defence Force Academy (ADFA), to ascertain their views of flying as a possible career choice. Interviews and focus groups were conducted by the primary researcher.

All interviews and focus groups were digitally recorded and subsequently transcribed verbatim. Initial themes and categories for analysis were drawn from both re-listening to the original recordings and coding the transcripts using a modified grounded theory inductive coding approach (Charmaz, 2006; Strauss and Corbin, 1997).

The First Steps Towards Action

Once some of the early data had been transcribed, coded and analysed, an 'interim report' was presented to the then-Director General of Air Force Personnel, Air Commodore John Hewitson. This report was somewhat emotively entitled 'Disturbing Research Findings', because many of the findings were indeed disturbing to me as a woman, mother, researcher and Air Force Officer. It was clear that some of my Air Force colleagues were facing some significant challenges in both learning and working contexts, and I was not prepared to wait until the research's conclusion to act. The findings detailed in this report enabled the Air Force's hierarchy to appreciate some challenging realities of women's integration into ADF piloting roles and created impetus for prompt change.

This research and other influencing factors resulted in the Air Force establishing a new directorate that was dedicated to progressing gender and other diversity initiatives. The Directorate of Workforce Diversity was established as a small but highly motivated team of diversity enthusiasts. Our first major project was to address some of the issues discovered through the previous two years of my doctoral research.

It was at this point that the Air Force made another decision that has proved to be an invaluable 'lesson learnt' for other organisations and occupational groups seeking to generate greater diversity. This decision was to engage, as the project manager, the Air Force's most senior woman pilot (who was still relatively junior, given that woman pilots tend not to remain in the Air Force) and a hugely influential role model. True to the principles of feminist research, I had connected quite deeply with Squadron Leader Samantha Freebairn through our interview and I knew her to be very passionate about resolving some of the gender-based issues that she herself had experienced through her pilot training and early career.

It is difficult to overstate Sam's importance to the project: her piloting networks, her subject-matter expertise, her professional credibility and her sheer dynamism were absolutely essential to the project's success. Non-pilots simply would not have had the buy-in and access afforded to Sam. I also suspected that female pilots would have been very distrustful of any gender-diversity initiatives 'thrust upon them' by a non-pilot outsider, however well-intentioned and well-researched. Sam was able to garner widespread support for the work we were doing and engaged the entire female pilots' network, including Army and Navy pilots, in support of the initiatives we were developing and progressing.

As a result of this engagement and 'consciousness-raising' (Fonow and Cook, 1991, p. 3), initiatives developed throughout the project were well supported by most other female pilots; this was critical to the project's success, especially to the buddy and mentoring schemes that will be further discussed below. Human resource interventions developed and delivered by the personnel most impacted by the interventions are likely to be far more accepted than those developed and 'sold' by 'outsiders'. The Air Force is actively applying this finding to a range of other diversity projects.

The Chief of the Air Force's personal commitment to the initiatives developed over the past few years has also been crucial at every stage of this project. This highlights another key consideration for organisations seeking cultural change; in the face of strong cultural resistance to change, public and irrefutable senior leadership 'buy-in' is of critical importance to success (Trice and Beyer, 1991). This project could not have succeeded without the staunch commitment of the Chief, his senior leadership team and both Directors General of Personnel Air Force (currently Air Commodore Bob Rodgers).

Actions to Increase Women's Representation in Air Force Piloting

Reducing Visibility

> not very many girls in the squad(ron), there was only myself and (another female pilot) there for quite some time, again everyone always knew what you were doing, you know. (Lisa, former AF pilot)

Heightened visibility is a widely renowned issue facing women working in non-traditional employment (Bagilhole, 2002; Kanter, 1977). With few women entering military flying, the women going through course were highly visible. Many interviewees spoke of the negative impact of this visibility, such as being the source of gossip, having all mistakes known about instantly and not being able to 'fly below the radar' in terms of flying performance and social activities.

The research also determined that women on course with numbers of other women, or posted into areas with at least a few other woman pilots, felt less visible and alone. Even if they were still highly visible, interviewees reported that having other women around made an enormous difference to their well-being:

> And, in fact, (another female pilot) was there when I first arrived there. So that was very helpful because she was obviously already in the squadron. And I honestly never had any problems at the squadron … I think, probably the difference when I went through, we'd already had people like (respected female pilot) and all that going through, and she definitely held her own. (Jess, former AF pilot)

While being on course with other women did not always result in close friendships, there is little doubt that higher numbers will reduce the visibility of being a singular woman pilot or one of only two or three pilots. Beyond visibility, there was some anecdotal evidence that additional numbers of women may improve female pilots' success:

> I had a chat to the CFI (Chief Flying Instructor) at 2FTS just before I left … I mean, this is just his word but he said statistically the girls that are on-course on their own seem to fail more than the girls that are on-course with another girl … we lost a girl the course after us, two courses after us they lost another girl and they were both singular girls on-course. (Yasmine, junior AF pilot)

The findings of this research, coupled with recommendations from the Review into the Treatment of Women in the ADF Phase 2 Report (Australian Human Rights Commission, 2012), prompted the Air Force to develop a quite significant human resource intervention targeting employment groups with few, if any women.

The intervention was mandated through a Personnel Branch Directive, which stated that 'where possible, and where there is no disadvantage to individual women', critical mass should be created by posting women to a smaller number of squadrons. The second part of this directive requested that 'where possible, and where there is no disadvantage to individual women', attempts should be made to panel numbers of women onto the same training courses.

The aim of this directive is to try to reduce women's extreme visibility and isolation on course and in posting locations. Its creation was informed by Kanter's well-proven assertion that 'a group member's awareness share, averaged over shares of other individuals of the same social type, declines as the proportion of total membership of the category increases, because each individual becomes less surprising, unique or noteworthy' (1977, p. 971). The directive also sought to provide enhanced opportunities for women to work and study alongside other women who were perhaps experiencing similar challenges pertaining to their gender (a 'safety in numbers' approach).

Whilst well-meaning, this change was not without controversy. A number of men and female pilots argued that 'clustering' women into specific locations would diminish the reputation of the squadron that inherited the women, ultimately making it a less desirable posting for all pilots. These concerns support the research arguing that feminine is considered 'inferior' in military constructs (Boldry, Wood and Kashy, 2001; Karst, 1991) and Reskin's (1988) premise that women's entry into non-traditional workplaces and occupations automatically reduces the prestige of that context.

Some female pilots also felt that 'clustering' women in specified locations would impact their ability to progress to squadrons and associated aircraft platforms, where there were few or no female pilots. Other concerns stemmed from a perception that female pilot trainees would have to 'wait in line' for significant periods of time to commence their training, thus disadvantaging them as compared to their male peers.

While these concerns have validity when the policy changes are viewed in isolation, there was intent by the Air Force to significantly increase the numbers of overall female pilots, which can only occur if more are recruited. With higher numbers of female pilots coming through training and being posted in larger numbers to all squadrons, the fears about disadvantaging individual women and creating 'ghettos of chick pilots' (as one male pilot so succinctly phrased it) will hopefully prove unfounded.

However, in the interim, the words 'where possible and where there is no disadvantage to individual women' were included to ensure that women were not disadvantaged. Personnel in support of this policy change feel that it will make a real difference to women's ability to succeed through flying training and ensure they feel less 'alone' and visible in their subsequent posted locations.

Loneliness, Isolation and a Lack of Peer Support

Ibarra (1993) notes that women's limited access to or exclusion from informal interaction networks in organisations can be problematic to their progress and success. Numerous female pilots interviewed in this study certainly expressed feelings of intense loneliness through various career stages. This loneliness was particularly acute during both phases of their flying training, where they have limited access to friends and family outside the intensive flying training environment:

> Being the only girl on course I felt quite alone, but anyway, getting through pilot's course was, I still don't know how I did it, to this day. It was tough. I just studied my toosh off. I guess maybe because I didn't have that stability, someone else to lean on, like it really affected me. (Bianca, junior AF pilot)

> … have I felt ostracised? Yes I have … To be honest with you I expected it to be the way it was, which is unfortunate but at least you don't go in there going oh I'll get a fair go. (Andrea, ADF student pilot)

Although less isolating than their training experiences, the workplace also proved a very lonely place for many female pilots, even when they had numerous male friends and colleagues who supported them:

> It was very lonely at work. But then I had my friends that I relied on, like the guys there, and I knew people were looking out for me. (Tara, AF pilot)

> We'd go around trips, and all the pilot guys organised they all do something; they don't invite me. (Margie, junior ADF pilot)

The policy changes designed to ensure that women go through their training with other women and are posted to workplaces with other women should help to ease this loneliness, but our team felt that more direct action was required to create networks for women working in flying and other non-traditional occupations across the Air Force. Research into the role of women's networks in masculine organisations supported the importance of affording women opportunities to interact and bond with like-minded women for workplace support, advancement, nurturing relationships and career satisfaction (Hanson, 2000; Metz and Tharenou, 2001).

Additional focus groups with non-pilot Air Force women, coupled with findings from academic literature and organisational 'best practice' case studies, prompted the development of a specialised local networking programme for all Air Force women, called WINGs (an acronym for Women's Integrated Networking Groups). WINGs began in 2011 as a trial programme, but is now run bi-monthly in every Air Force base location around Australia. The groups provide an opportunity to interact with other ADF women (public service, Army and Navy women attend WINGs in some locations), hear from guest speakers, discuss issues of interest or concern, share information and generally create a forum where friendships and mentoring relationships can form.

Noting the needs of female pilots going through flying training, a senior ex-Air Force woman pilot was engaged to run WINGs at the flying school in Tamworth, an activity that has been extraordinarily successful and well-supported by female students at the school. The sessions have covered areas of need, ranging from developing confidence, women's learning styles and strategies for negotiating femininity in male-dominated contexts. On occasion, instructors have been invited to participate in order to learn about some of the additional challenges faced by their women students.

WINGs, like any programme designed to support military women, has not been without its critics. Holding 'women's groups' throws the strongly held military 'equality as sameness' ideology into utter disarray, resulting in feelings of distrust, paranoia and, in some cases, anger from men and women who decry the need for such groups. In male-dominated contexts, men find women's relationships with other women very threatening and respond by preventing women from engaging with all-female groups (Cockburn, 1991; Katzenstein, 1998). In her 1996 study of ADF culture, Burton also noted that 'any formal or informal attempts to provide support or mentors for women is likely to incur male hostility and resentment' (1996, p. 59).

Ironically, while the importance of 'male bonding' is often provided as a valid reason to exclude women from military service, 'male soldiers seem categorically unable to perceive or forgive a similar need in women … they often possess an irrational fear of women's groups, believing that, in their midst, men will be plotted against or perhaps worst of all, be rendered unnecessary' (Barkalow, quoted in Katzenstein, 1998, p. 84).

Male resistance to the new and unusual concept of 'women's bonding' took many forms in the Air Force, such as derogatory remarks in the workplace, referring to meetings as 'secret women's business', 'old chooks club' and 'whinging mother's group'. Others made an effort to express their concerns via emails to our team. Some senior women were the greatest antagonists, fearing that the groups would only serve to further polarise military women and prevent their full integration.

We acknowledged these concerns, but remained committed to the programme; we kept the focus on supporting those Air Force women who valued the rare and precious opportunity to connect with other women in a supportive, safe environment. I have often reflected that prior to undertaking this research, as a successful integrator into military culture (a 'survivor and thriver'), I may have once also disagreed with any notion to create separate activities for women.

That said, women like myself working in highly feminised fields within the military, such as health, education, administration and logistics, are simply not as exposed to the same challenges experienced by our colleagues working in non-traditional areas. As WINGs has grown in size and popularity and once men realised that we weren't actively plotting their demise, the outcry quietened somewhat, although there is still a level of discomfort and distrust across the organisation.

Flying Females Breakfasts

Beyond WINGs, and to motivate and provide support the younger ADFA women who have not yet commenced their flying training, in 2011, the Air Force began running annual 'Flying Females' breakfasts at ADFA. These breakfast afforded younger women an opportunity to informally meet and speak with more senior women from aviation roles (pilots and Air Combat officers), as well as to interact with other ADFA women from different year levels and services.

Again, the feedback from this initiative has been overwhelmingly positive. Through the breakfasts, a number of more senior aircrew women have started actively mentoring the younger women they have connected with, which has again created a sense of solidarity and 'sisterhood' amongst flying women. The 'women's breakfast' concept looks likely to be extended to other women in other non-traditional fields (such as engineering) at ADFA, based on the very positive feedback garnered through the programme.

Australian Women Pilots' Association (AWPA) Membership

The AWPA is a civilian networking organisation for female pilots. In 2010, the Air Force began funding membership of the AWPA for all Air Force female pilots in order to extend pilot networks and create opportunities for Air Force members to be inspired by other woman pilots (and vice versa). The links forged between the AWPA and the Air Force have grown stronger over the past few years, due to this and other activities designed to promote greater interaction between the two organisations, including Air Force-funded scholarships for AWPA members.

Women's Development Forum

To further encourage networking between women across all Air Force workplaces, in 2012, the Air Force held its inaugural 'Women's Development Forum', a two-day conference which was themed 'Surviving and Thriving in Non-Traditional Employment'. The conference was an outstanding success, tackling hard-hitting relevant topics with key speakers and panels comprised of a range of different women sharing their experiences. A highlight of the conference was our guest speaker, Deborah Lawrie (née Wardley), Australia's first commercial airline pilot, who regaled the audience with highly amusing anecdotes about her life and career as a woman pilot. Positioning female pilots at the same table for the conference dinner created further networking opportunities, many of which have been maintained post-conference.

Role Models and Mentors (Air Force Buddy Programme)

For female pilots, who have very limited opportunities to meet more senior female pilots, they treasured any opportunity to fly with or even just talk to another more senior woman. In our interviews, female pilots directly quoted advice they had received from other female pilots during their careers, suggesting the level of value placed on these interactions:

> Briefly once, but (female pilot mentor) she did tell me, she goes you can't sweat the small stuff and everything that gets in your head in the small stuff. If they break your leg, sweat it, now it's getting violent, but she said everything in here is you, so you have to control that … I honestly think … that little bit of advice, don't sweat the small stuff and don't let them get in your head just was probably enough. (Harriet, AF pilot)

Women who had little or no access to piloting role models felt that access to a role model or female flying instructor would have been very beneficial:

> But I know that if there was an (ADF) pilot – someone that had gone through all of that shit, and been able to sit there and listen to us and was willing to do that

> role too … and just be there for the girls whenever they do want to cry. (Cindy, ADF pilot)

This study clearly identified the need for women in non-traditional employment to have access to have tangible role models and mentors, a finding well-supported by past research (Ahuja, 2002; Chesler and Chesler, 2002; Whittock, 2002). To generate further targeted mentoring and role modelling opportunities beyond WINGs, 'Flying Females' breakfasts and the women's forums, in 2012, the Air Force trialled a programme called the WINTER-BP (Women in Non-Traditional Employment Roles – Buddy Programme).

This programme was trialled by Samantha, who personally undertook to mentor two women students undertaking flying training in order to assess the impact of the mentoring relationship on their success and experience in training. Through her network with these two women, Sam found herself actively mentoring a number of women at Tamworth, providing them with advice, a friendly empathetic ear, discussing learner style strategies and, more importantly, bolstering their confidence through critical stages of their training. Post-programme evaluations suggest that the women being mentored actively attribute their success on course to Sam's influence.

Training Female Pilots – A Guide for Instructors

A review of data pertaining to the learning context revealed a range of gender-based challenges beyond cultural and social barriers, including learning style concerns, confidence issues, instructors who were unable to cope with women's tears, inappropriate instructor behaviour and so on:

> And the girls do tend to have, and I know I did, and I know (name removed) did and I know other girls have more confidence problems. If you can teach them in a slightly different way to build up that confidence because a lot of the blokes I think are quite good at deflating the confidence on pilot's course then that would really help. (Margaret, former AF pilot)

> I think it is and interesting enough they don't actually test your learning style … because I don't think they've tailored the training to take into account that females do learn differently to males. (Bianca, junior AF pilot)

In response to this research, a number of female pilots have worked together to create a guide for military flying instructors at all stages that addresses the possible differences between female and male pilot trainees and provides instructors with practical information and helpful tips for instructing their female students. One of the Air Force's most experienced female flying instructors contributed significantly to this guide, contributing her perspective regarding the numerous social and cultural challenges that may be faced by pilots undertaking training.

It is hoped that this guide will enhance instructors' understanding of their female students and enable them to build strategies for bringing out the best in every student. The guide may also be useful to helping male pilots understand that while outcomes and standards can be the same, the route taken to achieve them might be different for female students.

Flying Solo

As noted in the opening paragraphs of this chapter, *Flying Solo*, a handbook for female pilots, was developed on the basis of research findings from this study. The handbook is highly visually appealing, resembling a women's magazine with numerous pictures and stories of inspiring pilots at all career and life stages. The magazine's styling was deliberate, normalising the role of women in flying by placing military pilots in the context of a female-orientated magazine. It tackles the 'hard issues' in a direct way, including strategies for managing some of the complex social situations on the course, dealing with inappropriate behaviour, addressing confidence issues, practical study techniques and a range of helpful, targeted advice from more senior pilots. We hope that male pilots will read *Flying Solo* and develop some sense of the challenges faced by women through their non-traditional careers.

One of the main features of the guide is a list of currently serving and past ADF female pilots and their contact details, if women need an empathetic ear or advice at any stage of their flying careers. *Flying Solo* was 'market tested' on a range of audiences prior to productions, including older teenage girls, future ADF pilots at the ADFA and experienced ADF pilots, to ensure that it was appealing to as wide an audience range as possible. Our team feels very proud of this document, which we hope will challenge some of the less inclusive practices of some aviation workplaces.

Structural Barriers Relevant to Parenting

This research determined that parenting was a substantial barrier to female pilot retention that required urgent and targeted mitigation strategies if women were to pursue long-term careers in the Air Force. Few female pilots remained in the Air Force flying roles after having children, citing the following as the main reasons:

- a lack of access to meaningful part-time work;
- the inability to return to their flying career from where they 'left off' prior to their pregnancy;
- a lack of access to support structures and childcare that could accommodate non-standard 7 am–6 pm workdays; and
- feeling like a burden to their workplaces on confirmation of pregnancy and whilst on maternity leave, due to policies that do not allow them to be replaced or 'back-filled' while pregnant or on maternity leave.

The Air Force required a comprehensive range of strategies to mitigate this long list of issues.

Perception of Burden

Current policies preventing women from being posted or replaced were designed to protect women from being moved out of their position once pregnant, but this means that Commanders are required to carry a vacancy during a pilot's pregnancy and subsequent maternity leave. Other pilots are then required to 'carry the load' of a pilot who is unable to fly. In Defence, women are grounded on confirmation of pregnancy, so this may result in women being unable to fly for one–two years (or longer, depending on the length of maternity leave).

For female pilots who fight, from their first day of training, to be accepted as full and legitimate members of their flying teams, the idea of filling a flying position whilst unable to fly is simply untenable. Women interviewed in this study preferred to leave the Air Force prior to or shortly after having children, rather than become a 'burden', perceived or otherwise, to their workplaces:

> [On considering leaving after having a baby] I think that it's maybe – well, on my part, it's because I don't want to let them down. It's – I'd love to stay (in the ADF) … because I love my job. I love it. (Anne, junior ADF pilot)

This perception of being a 'burden' to the workplace, however inaccurate, needed to be removed. The only way to achieve this was to change the policy to enable squadrons to replace women unable to fly due to pregnancy and maternity leave. In 2012, the Directorate of Personnel issued a directive allowing women in a range of non-traditional occupations (operational occupations with less than 10 per cent women) to remain in their squadron as an 'additional asset' on confirmation of pregnancy, thus enabling their position to be temporarily filled by another member.

This policy means that rather than feeling like a non-flying burden, pregnant pilots can undertake a range of ground-based squadron duties while their flying duties are facilitated by an extra pilot posted into the squadron. We are hopeful this policy change will improve women's willingness to remain in flying squadrons through their period of pregnancy and maternity leave, whilst also providing one option for part-time employment once they return to work.

Career Flexibility: Add-on Return of Service Obligation

The current career progression pathway for pilots offers very little room for any deviation from the model. Career gates must be passed at specific career stages and failure to do so results in the inability for pilots to continue their operation flying career. The model is designed to maximise the Air Force's return on investment for training – pilots need to have sufficient tenure at the end of each training course to ensure the Air Force's financial commitment is justified.

Having a baby at any stage of a pilot's early or middle career stage, before they attain sufficient captaincy hours on their chosen platform, can be disastrous to pilots seeking a long-term flying career. We observed first-hand experience of this while Sam was working on our project. She had fallen pregnant whilst undertaking her captaincy training on the C17 aircraft and been advised that due to her seniority, and without captaincy on her aircraft type, her options to continue flying as an operational pilot were very restricted and it looked as though her C17 career might be over.

This news was obviously disappointing, as Sam had expressed aspirations of progressing into a leadership role on C17s, as the squadron Executive Officer or as a Flight Commander, which required her to have attained captaincy on the C17 at her previous rank. Sam's personal case prompted the development of a further directive stating that women are to be afforded every opportunity (and the training/retraining required) to 'resume their career from when it was stalled due to pregnancy and maternity leave, regardless of rank, experience or time out of their primary employment role'. This policy was, once again, aimed at all occupations with less than 10 per cent women.

Due to this policy change and some further negotiation with Squadron executives, Sam was permitted to return to her C17 flying career and has been allowed to pursue Captaincy, even though her current seniority is higher than would normally be acceptable when undertaking a Captaincy conversion. This sets a precedent likely to also afford men opportunities to maintain their flying careers after career breaks attached to parenting, injury, illness or accompanying their partners on posting overseas. This new flexibility also affords pilots the option to seek a ground-based, non-flying posting during the early years of parenting, to accommodate part-time and flexible work, with a view to returning to operational flying at a later time. These policies mean that female pilots will no longer have to delay motherhood until their early forties to avoid compromising their Air Force flying careers.

Part-Time and Job-Share Models

There are currently very limited options for male or female Air Force aircrew personnel to work part-time, as the current construct is based on a 'days-per-fortnight' model that doesn't fit with most operational flying requirements. The 'roster on-roster off' model instigated by Virgin Australia, which operates on a month-on, month-off basis, is a vastly preferable model, allowing pilots to undertake the full suite of flying within the month in which they are 'operational'. Virgin pilots spoke of implementing a system of alternating months between two flying parents so that one parent was always at home to care for children.

There are factors complicating any changes to part-time arrangement for the Air Force, involving the Defence Act and pay systems that are too complex to detail here. That said, the Air Force, the Army and the Navy are all collectively working towards a range of changes that will accommodate greater flexibility for all Defence members, including:

- different constructs for part-time, including month-on, month-off and job-share options, grounded month on/off (which enables two pilots to alternate flying and grounded months to accommodate carer responsibilities);
- greater access to fly-in, fly-out working models that may enable pilots to base themselves near family for greater support;
- encouraging Commanders to accommodate flexibility by revising their work structures and systems; and
- providing financial support for 24-hour childcare, including live-in help where needed.

Flying through Parenthood

One of the key points arising from mothers across all aviation contexts was the lack of advice and information about pregnancy and maternity leave from other female pilots who had 'been there and done that'. In response, the Air Force has developed a guide called 'Flying through Parenthood', which details practical tips, strategies and advice for aircrew women, their managers and human resource staff, regarding a wide range of factors relevant to female aircrew. This booklet includes practical advice received from numerous sources, including pilot mothers, who were very keen to share their 'lessons learned' with their colleagues.

Attraction and Recruitment

Initiatives designed to retain female workers are largely superfluous if there are few female workers to retain, rendering attraction and recruitment as critical to any successful diversity intervention. The Air Force's actions to attract more women into flying roles was based on a number of key findings from the research, which can be summarised as follows:

- The 12-year contract period for military aviation is a huge disincentive for women.
- The majority of Army pilots interviewed in this study decided to fly only after discovering, almost inadvertently, they had an aptitude through routine testing at Duntroon's Royal Military College.
- Women undertaking third year of the Bachelor of Aviation undergraduate degree course were extremely concerned about sourcing the requisite flying hours required to become competitive for commercial airline employment.
- Women's dreams of flying were inspired by either a tangible event (like visiting the flight deck during a flight) or some form of flying exposure.

It was a practical 'hands-on' experience, often in their teenage years that confirmed their desire to fly.
- Women and girls view flying, and particularly flying in the Air Force, as a highly masculine job that is 'difficult', 'dangerous' and 'not a job for me'.

Air Force Actions to Improve the Recruitment of Women Already Intent on Becoming Pilots

The Changed ROSO Model

Almost every civilian woman pilot interviewed for this study cited the 12–14-year contractual commitment (or Return of Service Obligation (ROSO)) as the main factor preventing them from pursuing a military flying career. Most had initially investigated the ADF option, discovered the lengthy commitment and decided not to take their application any further. The ROSO is currently so lengthy because flying training is expensive, and the Air Force needs assurances regarding its 'return on investment'.

Although 'Generation Y' is renowned for its propensity for high job turnover and disinclination towards long-term employment commitments (McCrindle, 2006), older pilots (40+) interviewed in this study had also rejected the Air Force due to the lengthy contracted commitment. The Air Force has also become aware that the ROSO is serving as a deterrent for many male pilots, perhaps due to their Generation Y tendencies, especially with the fee-help BAv option making flying training more accessible and affordable. Once, military service was the only way for the less affluent to achieve their dream of flying, but this is no longer the case.

Some senior Air Force pilots believe that the current lengthy ROSO is unnecessary as a retention tool, as prior to the 10-year point, very few pilots will achieve the required number of captaincy hours and licences to make them competitive for airline employment, which is where the majority of pilots go after leaving the Air Force. ADF pilots are also extremely well remunerated compared to their peers in general aviation, so leaving the Air Force for poorly paid work whilst gaining the required hours/licences is unlikely to be appealing.

The Air Force has taken action to address the issue of a lengthy ROSO by developing a reconfigured model for applying the ROSO so that it appears far less intimidating to potential recruits. Under this new model, the ROSO will be significantly reduced to less than five years. However, to progress their careers after this point, pilots may be asked to commit to further ROSOs along the way in order to protect Air Force's return on investment.

There is some risk when applying this model; however, as stated previously, the likelihood of pilots resigning from the Air Force before they can be employed in well-paid civilian flying roles seems low. The Air Force considers this risk to be negligible, when compared to the benefits of accessing a much larger pool of potential pilot candidates through the recruiting process, enabling the Air Force to select the 'best and brightest' men and women from a much larger component of the population.

The Graduate Pilot Scheme

The Graduate Pilot Scheme (GPS) was approved by the Chief of Air Force in 2012 and was implemented in 2013. The scheme has been developed in direct response to other research findings from this study, which show that third year Bachelor of Aviation students find it extremely difficult to source quality flying opportunities that will enable them to achieve their ambition of commercial pilot employment.

These are women who are mature, have flying experience, are adept at operating in masculinised aviation contexts, have well-developed networks/ friendships with other female pilots, are confident in their own abilities and have succeeded in degree level studies of aviation theory. They may be ideal Air Force pilot candidates, noting that more mature women with previous aviation or Air Force exposure have proven more successful in ADF flying training than their less experienced female peers.[2]

The GPS entails recruiting women in the latter years of their BAv programme (second and third years) and enabling them to fulfil the practical flying component of their degree through the Air Force. Griffith University in Queensland has confirmed that it will provide the final year's flying accreditation on successful graduation for ADF flight training, which means the students will still attain their BAv degrees from Griffith University (the Air Force is liaising with other universities to extend the GPS more broadly).

The Air Force seeks to recruit 'multiples' of female BAv students and ensure they remain together for their training, thus also ensuring a level of peer support and reduced visibility/pressure whilst undergoing training. The Air Force believes that the scheme will be attractive to BAv students for a number of reasons, but primarily because on successful graduation from 2FTS (the second phase of ADF flight training), The Air Force will pay off their entire student debt, which can be around $120,000 for some students.

The hope is that the reduced ROSO commitment and the ability to gain much-needed early-career flying experience will create interest in this scheme, with the Air Force funding 14 GPS pilots in the 2013/2014 financial year. If only half of these graduate, this would still be a significant increase to the Air Force's female pilot numbers (currently there are only 21 female pilots in the Air Force).

AWPA Scholarships

To increase civilian pilot's awareness of military flying careers and afford the Air Force with opportunities to promote flying careers across AWPA networks, in 2012,

2 The Pilot Technical Data brief was provided by DOPHA in August 2011; the brief utilises data collected from 2,648 ADF pilot applicants from 1996 to 2011.

the Air Force began funding a number of financial scholarships for civilian flying students. The scholarships are awarded annually at the AWPA conference, providing another opportunity to promote military aviation careers to AWPA members.

Air Force Actions to Overcome Negative Perceptions and Create 'I Can Do this' Moments

Overcoming Negative Perceptions and Creating 'I Can Do this' Moments

'Difficult' 'dangerous' and 'not a job for me' are complex perceptions to overcome, as is the stereotype that piloting is a 'male' occupation. The Air Force's traditional response to changing negative perceptions has been through targeted marketing campaigns, but this research suggests that it will take more than marketing to dispel a girl's strong perception about flying.

As noted in Chapter 2 of this book, there are many reasons why young people 'rule out' occupations they deem 'gender inappropriate'. Military flying was perceived as an untenable option for almost all of the women and girls who partook in the high school focus groups, including girls with substantial aviation exposure through aviation high school. This finding was supported by focus group marketing research conducted by Horizon for Defence Force Recruiting in 2012, which lists the perception of being unachievable as a main deterrent for girls looking at Air Force careers. Civil aviation has also been found to suffer from negative perceptions borne from gender perceptions, with Mitchell el al. noting that 'the occupation of pilot seems to be much less attractive in terms of a chosen career for females … the issue of gender perceptions still has importance for the aviation industry today' (2005, p. 44).

Of more concern were the maths/science-inclined women already serving in the Air Force. They had passed through the barrier of entering one large field of non-traditional employment (military service), but most showed no inclination towards flying. Women who had joined the gap year with the intention of becoming pilots had changed their minds, deterred by their exposure to the 'arrogant, dismissive' pilots they had encountered. This research proved that exposure to strong female pilot role models was not enough to change girls' views about flying being 'not a job for me', supporting Byrne's theory that access to role models is inadequate as a means of *attracting women to non-traditional careers* (1993). Focus group research in this study showed that exposure to 'amazing' female pilots made many girls felt that flying was even less tenable: 'she was amazing, but I could never be that amazing'.

Research has shown that changing negative perceptions about non-traditional roles mandates a more practically oriented 'hands-on' targeted approach and a multifaceted strategy aimed at different groups of women and girls (Maher, Corbit and Wofford, 2008; Rosser, 2001). The Air Force has a number of exciting concepts designed to encourage higher numbers of women and girls into flying roles.

The findings about Army pilots substantially influenced the Air Force's planned response to this research, as they proved that 'discovering' an aptitude for flying as an adult could mitigate the 'lifelong' dream motivation noted by most other pilots from all aviation contexts. This finding influenced the development of the Air Force's plan to attract higher numbers of women to flying.

'Jet Camp' and 'Flying Start'

Research into attracting women into other non-traditional fields requires 'hands-on' exposure to create those 'I can do this' moments (Rosser, 2001; Yilmaz, 2010). With this in mind, and targeting high school girls in Years 10–12, the Air Force has developed the concepts of 'Jet Camp' and 'Flying Start' as both a means of creating an interest in Air Force flying careers and creating those 'I can do this' moments so critical to women and girls selecting a non-traditional career.

The camp/experiential concept has proven highly successful when attracting women into other non-traditional fields such as engineering (Gilbride et al., 2007; Outlay, Ambrose and Chenowith, 2012). Gilbride et al.'s research into the success of a summer camp for mathematics/science-inclined girls showed that 60 per cent of attendees chose to pursue engineering careers and cited the camp experience as a key factor in their decision (1999). Doerschuk et al. (2007) noted similar positive experiences with one-week camps designed to attract girls into computer science, and a number of US military pilot biographies cite 'space camp' as a key factor in their decision to fly.

The Jet Camp concept is a one week-school residential programme, alternatively held at RAAF Amberley and RAAF Williamtown, where attendees will be exposed to fast jets. Up to 24 girls aged 15–17 will be selected for the programme on the basis of their maths/science ability, physical prowess and leadership skills. The selection process is aimed towards ensuring only those girls most suitable for Air Force entry will attend the camp, thus minimising the risk of building an unattainable dream for camp attendees. Key components of the camps will be an opportunity for girls to undertake a flight in a military aircraft, as well as an opportunity to pilot a flight simulator, hopefully creating the 'I can do this' moment needed to incite an interest in pursuing an Air Force flying career.

A shorter version of the camp concept is the one-day 'Flying Start' experiential, which is based on the same premise of creating 'I can do this' moments in an Air Force pilot simulator. Post-experience, the intention is to remain engaged with attendees during the remainder of their schooling, to ensure they retain the Air Force as a consideration once they complete Year 12. If they seek to join, the Air Force will attempt to place them on training courses with their Jet Camp/Flying Start peers.

Although these activities may not offer the Air Force immediate returns in terms of pilot recruitment, it is hoped that in the years to come, this concept, which will be delivered to around 48 girls each year, will dramatically increase the numbers of girls interesting in joining the Air Force, either as pilots or perhaps other aviation occupations.

Blanket Aptitude Testing

The number of Air Force women who expressed a reluctance to at least try the pilot aptitude testing due to their perception of difficulty was concerning. How many women currently serving in the ADF might have an excellent aptitude for flying, but have never attempted the tests? Many of the men serving in non-pilot Air Force roles, such as Air Combat Officers (formerly Navigators and Air Defence Officers), Engineers and Air Traffic Controllers initially sought pilot entry, but may have lacked the flying aptitude to progress down this career pathway. This research, coupled with data from Defence Force Recruiting (DFR), determined that few Air Force women actively considered pilot as a viable option when deciding on their Air Force career pathways, whereas the opposite is true for men.[3]

As such, there may be numerous future pilots in our midst, but the Air Force has previously had no means of identifying them. To counter this, from 2014, the Air Force, like the Army, intends to offer an opportunity for all ADFA students who have not previously attempted the tests to undertake initial aptitude testing to ascertain their flying aptitude. In seems likely that of the 60–80 or so girls studying at the ADFA at any one time, a portion of them will have an aptitude for flying, especially maths/science-inclined women enrolled in engineering and other science-orientated degrees.

Targeted Marketing Campaigns (Women in Non-Traditional Employment Roles (WINTER))

For the past 12 months, DFR has been developing a series of marketing campaigns designed to attract women into a range of non-traditional employment roles, including pilot, other aircrew, engineering and technical trades. The tag-lines of these campaigns have been specifically designed to mitigate women's and girls' known perceptions about careers in Air Force non-traditional employment roles.

Conclusion

As organisations struggle to diversify their workforces, not just in terms of gender but also cultural, religious, sexual and all other forms of diversity, the approach used by the Air Force provides an example that may be useful to other organisational and occupational contexts. This model entails thoroughly researching the issue from two distinct perspectives. The first of these is choice – discovering why an occupation does not appeal to the target audience and factors important to the members of the target audience already in that role. The second aspect involved 'constraints' – the barriers and challenges potentially preventing target audience

3 Data provided by Defence Force Recruiting in 2010.

members from remaining in the occupation for long-term careers through different career and life stages.

Once the choice and constraint barriers are known, organisations must then devise holistic strategies and interventions designed to mitigate *both* choice and constraint barriers. Simply attracting higher numbers of a target demographic to a role is not enough if cultural and structural barriers work to impede their integration and progress. Focusing on training and retention, without consideration of other critical factors, is unlikely to result in increases in a target demographic. Success requires all aspects of the puzzle to be addressed.

Finally, this approach requires analysing the points of divergence across different types of workers, their beliefs, needs and challenges, in order to develop tailored workplace solutions designed to meet a range of workers' needs. In this particular feminist case study, the Air Force needed to accept the complexities of 'surviving and thriving' as a woman pilot in the Air Force, and actively develop workplace solutions to meet the needs of these inspiring women through a range of life and work stages. Finally, this research shows the power of gaining senior leadership commitment and stakeholder buy-in when supporting widespread cultural change, as resistance to any form of targeted intervention is likely to be strong.

The Air Force's approach to this one particular case study has had a wider-reaching impact than just the pilot workforce. The theoretical and practical 'lessons learned' through this research journey have been actively applied to other areas of non-traditional employment across the whole of Defence, including the ADF's recent project to remove the remaining gender restrictions from frontline employment roles. This project also kept gender at the heart of the inquiry, and rather than just 'opening the door' and allowing women to enter, as has been traditional practice in the ADF, the project was managed very carefully and gave full consideration to the likely challenges and barriers faced by pioneering women entering these roles for the first time, amongst much resistance from some factions of the organisation.

I believe we are entering a new age for diversity in the ADF, where difference is accepted and welcomed, and the differing needs of workers are actively supported through targeted interventions. In time, perhaps valuing 'sameness' will become secondary to inclusive behaviours that value difference and the benefits that diversity brings to organisations. If there is strength in diversity, these can only be positive changes that will enhance the ADF's capability both now and in the future. It has been my great pleasure to be a part of this journey.

References

Agostino, K., 2000. Women in uniform: Challenging feminisms In: K.L. Spurling and E. Greenhalgh (eds), *Women in Uniform: Perceptions and Pathways*. Canberra: School of History, University College, UNSW, pp. 64–82.

Ahuja, M.K., 2002. Women in the information technology profession: A literature review, synthesis and research agenda. *European Journal of Information Systems*, 11(1), pp. 20–4.

Ashcraft, K.L., 2005. Resistance through consent? Occupational identity, organizational form, and the maintenance of masculinity among commercial airline pilots. *Management Communication Quarterly*, 19(1), pp. 67–90.

Australian Human Rights Commission, 2012. *Review into the Treatment of Women in the Australian Defence Force, Phase 2 Report*. Sydney: Australian Human Rights Commission.

Bagilhole, B.M., 2002. *Women in Non-traditional Occupations Challenging Men.* New York: Palgrave Macmillan.

Barrett, F.J., 1996. The organizational construction of hegemonic masculinity: The case of the US Navy. *Gender Work and Organization*, 3(3), pp. 129–41.

Boldry, J., Wood, W. and Kashy, D.A., 2001. Gender stereotypes and the evaluation of men and women in military training. *Journal of Social Issues*, 57(4), pp. 689–705.

Bridges, D.V., 2005. The gendered battlefield: Women in the Australian Defence Force. PhD thesis, University of Western Sydney.

Burton, C., 1996. *Women in the Australian Defence Force: Two Studies*. Canberra: Director Publishing and Visual Communications, Defence Centre.

Byrne, E.M., 1993. *Women and Science: The Snark Syndrome.* London: Falmer.

Ceci, S.J. and Williams, J.M., 2011. Understanding current causes of women's underrepresentation in science. *Social Sciences – Psychological and Cognitive Sciences*, 108(8), pp. 3157–67.

Charmaz, K., 2006. *Constructing Grounded Theory: A Practical Guide through Qualitative Analysis.* London: Sage.

Chesler, N.C. and Chesler, M.A., 2002. Gender-informed mentoring strategies for women engineering scholars: On establishing a caring community. *Journal of Engineering Education*, 91(1), pp. 49–55.

Cockburn, C., 1991. *In the Way of Women: Men's Resistance to Sex Equality in Organizations.* Basingstoke: Macmillan.

Connell, R.W., 2005. *Masculinities*, 2nd edn. Berkeley, CA: University of California Press.

Doerschuk, P., Jiangjiang, L., Mann, J. 2007. Pilot summer camps in computing for middle school girls: From organization through assessment. Proceedings of the 12th annual SIGCSE conference on Innovation and Technology in Computer Science Education (ITiCSE'07), September 2007, 39(3), Dundee, Scotland, 4–8.

Fonow, M. and Cook, J.A. (eds), 1991. *Beyond Methodology: Feminist Scholarship as Lived Research.* Bloomington: Indiana University Press.

Gilbride, K., Kennedy, D., Waalen, J. and Zywno, M., 2007. A proactive strategy for attracting women into engineering. *Canadian Journal of Counselling and Psychotherapy*, 39(3), pp. 4–8.

Gilmartin, P., 1992. Women's performance in desert storm helps lifts barriers in military civilian market. *Aviation Week & Space Technology*, 136(2), pp. 62–3.
Grant, R., 2002. The quiet pioneers. *Air Force Magazine*, 85(12), pp. 34–8.
Gray, P.S., 2007. *The Research Imagination: An Introduction to Qualitative and Quantitative Methods*. Cambridge: Cambridge University Press.
Hanson, S., 2000. Networking. *Professional Geographer*, 52(4), pp. 751–8.
Haynsworth, L. and Toomey, D., 1998. *Amelia Earhart's Daughters.* New York: Morrow and Company.
Hesse-Biber, S.N. and Yaiser, M.L., 2004. *Feminist Perspectives on Social Research.* New York: Oxford University Press.
Hinojosa, R., 2010. Doing hegemony: Military, men, and constructing a hegemonic masculinity. *Journal of Men's Studies*, 18(2), pp. 179–94.
Ibarra, H., 1993. Personal networks of women and minorities in management: A conceptual framework. *Academy of Management Review*, 18(1), pp. 56–87.
Kanter, R.M., 1977. Some effects of proportions on group life: Skewed sex ratios and responses to token women. *American Journal of Sociology*, 83, pp. 965–90.
Karst, K.L., 1991. The pursuit of manhood and the desegregation of the armed forces. *UCLA Law Review*, 38, pp. 499–581.
Katzenstein, M., 1998. *Faithful and Fearless: Moving Feminist Protest Inside the Church and Military.* Princeton: Princeton University Press.
Kronsell, A., 2005. Gendered practices in institutions of hegemonic masculinity: Reflections from feminist standpoint theory. *International Feminist Journal of Politics*, 7(2), pp. 280–98.
Mahar, J., Corbit, M. and Wofford, J., 2008. Virtual outreach through virtual worlds: A model for attracting and keeping women in computing. *Proceedings of World Conference on E-Learning in Corporate*, ed. Bonk et al, AACE, Chesapeake, VA, p. 1036.
McGlohn, S.E., King, R.E., Retzlaff, P.D., Flynn, C.F. and Butler, J.W., 1996. *Psychological Characteristics of United States Air Force Pilots*. San Antonio, TX: Air Force Materiel Command, Brooks Air Force Base.
McCrindle Research., 2006. *New Generations at Work: Attracting, Recruiting, Retraining and Retaining Generation Y*. Baulkham Hills Australia: McCrindle Research.
Metz, I. and Tharenou, P., 2001. Women's career advancement: The relative contribution of human and social capital. *Group & Organization Management*, 26(3), pp. 312–42.
Mitchell, J., Kristovics, A., Vermeulen, L., Wilson, J. and Martinussen, M., 2005. How pink is the sky? A cross-national study of the gendered occupation of pilot. *Employment Relations Record*, 5(2), pp. 43–7.
Outlay, C., Ambrose, P. and Chenowith, J., 2012. Overcoming gender stereotype entry barriers to computing degree programs: The cybergirlz program experience. *Journal of Computing Sciences in Colleges*, 28(1), pp. 33–8.

Pateman, Y.C., 1997. *Women Who Dared: American Female Test Pilots, Flight-Test Engineers, and Astronauts, 1912–1996.* Laguna Woods, CA: Norstahr.

Reinharz, S., 1992. *Feminist Methods in Social Research.* New York: Oxford University Press.

Reskin, B.F., 1988. Bringing the men back in: sex differentiation and the devaluation of women's work. *Gender & Society*, 2(1), pp. 58–81.

Rosser, S.V., 2001. Women confronting the new technologies. *Women's Studies Quarterly*, 29(3–4), pp. 164–86.

Solaro, E., 2006. *Women in the Line of Fire: What You Should Know About Women in the Military.* Emeryville, CA: Seal Press.

Strauss, A.L. and Corbin, J., 1997. *Grounded Theory in Practice,* London: Sage.

Trice, H.M. and Beyer, J.M., 1991. Cultural leadership in organizations. *Organization Science*, 2(2), pp. 149–69.

Whittock, M., 2000. *Feminising the Masculine? Women in Non-traditional Employment.* Aldershot: Ashgate.

——. 2002. Women's experiences of non-traditional employment: Is gender equality in this area a possibility? *Construction Management and Economics*, 20(5), pp. 449–56.

Wilson, F., 1996. Organizational theory: Blind and deaf to gender? *Organization Studies*, 17(5), pp. 825–42.

Yilmaz, M., 2010. Hands-on summer camp to attract K-12 students to engineering fields. *IEEE Transactions on Education*, 53(1), pp. 144–51.

Zeigler, S.L. and Gunderson, G.G. 2005. *Moving Beyond G.I. Jane: Women And The U.S. Military*. Lanham, MD: University Press of America.

Chapter 13
The Teaching Women to Fly Research Project

Penny Rafferty Hamilton

Introduction

Only around six per cent of American pilots are women (Women in Aviation International, 2010). Why is that number so abysmally low over a 100 years after Harriet Quimby became the first woman in the US to earn a pilot's certificate (Lebow, 2002)?

In 2011, for the first time in American history, women earned more advanced college and Bachelor's degrees than men (Yen, 2011). In 2005, American women accounted for 30 per cent of all lawyers. Their numbers in law school increased from 3.7 per cent in 1963 to more than 47 per cent in the academic year 2006 and 2007. Women in medical school increased from 5.8 per cent in the academic year 1960 and 1961 to almost 49 per cent in 2005 and 2006, and are now 32 per cent of all physicians and surgeons. Female pharmacists increased from 30 per cent in 1985 to 48 per cent in 2005. Yet, women still trail behind men in business, science, engineering and aviation (AFL-CIO, 2008; Cauchon, 2009; Collins, 2009). In 2007, only 4.2 per cent of all aircraft pilots, captains and flight engineers are women (AFL-CIO, 2008).

Even in vocations as sailing, motorcycle riding, and skydiving, participation by women has increased significantly compared to aviation (Motorcycle Industry Council, 2009; Smith, 2009). Because this suggests that women are underserved and, perhaps, little understood by general aviation flight schools, the Teaching Women to Fly Research Project was developed.

Research Project Overview and Methodology

The Teaching Women to Fly Research Project, partially funded through an Alfred L. and Constance C. Wolf Aviation Fund grant, focused on women's motivations, positive and negative flight training experiences, and barriers to general aviation success. The research began in the autumn of 2008.

After a literature review, a short open-ended survey consisting of 15 questions for female general aviation flight students and pilots, and a similar 12-question survey for flight instructors were developed. The questionnaire could be completed via the Internet, written responses and/or personal interview.

Using published email, telephone and US postal addresses, over 300 on-airport flight schools nationwide were contacted asking for participation in the research. Many web-based message boards for various aviation groups were used to announce the study. Over 100 female flight students, geographically distributed throughout the US, who were registered in the Federal Aviation Administration's database, were also contacted by mail asking them to share their views and experiences.

Each participant was pre-qualified by contacting the researcher first by email or telephone before a questionnaire was released to them. During the period from 2008 to 2010, 54 female flight students and women who started flight training but did not certificate, and 157 female pilots, some with advanced ratings in helicopters, soaring, commercial and military aviation, volunteered to complete the questionnaire and/or be interviewed. In addition, 52 female and 33 male flight instructors shared their insights by completing a questionnaire. Over half of the flight instructors participated in personal interviews.

In the fall of 2010, the 296 survey responses were tabulated. Based on frequency of responses, those ideas were condensed down into the 'Top 10 Barriers Which Stop Women from Learning to Fly' and the 'Top 10 Ways to Increase Female Success in General Aviation Flight Training'. Also, 101 ideas were generated on how to increase the number of female pilots.

Major Findings

The Top 10 Barriers which Stop Women from Learning to Fly

1. Lack of money for flight training.
2. Instructor–student communication incompatibility. Men and women communication patterns differ significantly (Gray, 1992).
3. Instructor-Interuptus: instructors leave flight instructing to take airline or charter service jobs, often requiring the flight student to start over with another instructor. This is time-consuming, expensive, and discouraging.
4. Lack of female mentors and support systems to encourage the flight student. Several recent gender studies have documented the importance of mentoring for women to succeed in business and science careers (Brennan, 2009; Donner, 2010; Hutson, 2009).
5. Personal lack of confidence in their ability and a fear of flying, especially stalling the plane too early in the training process. One of the flight instructors participating in the study said:

> In my own experience as a student, and now as a flight instructor, I think many male flight instructors don't understand that the female brain reacts

> to things differently. Women are frequently less confident and much more critical of their own abilities. I almost quit early on because my instructor did not understand that each comment he made upset me and tore down my confidence. Not that the comments were necessarily incorrect, but that the way he said them made it seem like I was more wrong than I actually was. When I instruct, I spend a lot of time building up my female students to recognise what they are doing correctly.

6. Lack of experience with and knowledge of mechanical systems. Another instructor in this study with advanced ratings commented:

> Women have had much less exposure to the functional aspect of the way things work, and tend to tune out when discussion are based on the way an engine or generator works.

7. Lack of map-reading experience and orienteering skill sets. A male flight instructor participant explained:

> Women often come to the airport for flight training already at a disadvantage as compared to men because young men learn a lot about aviation before they learn to fly the real thing. How many women build or fly aircraft models?

8. Flight schools are perceived as indifferent. A woman pilot and skydiver said:

> It is not just the decoration in the flight schools, it is the atmosphere, conversation and social activities. Skydiving is much more social and hangar talk is centred on the experience and the future of skydiving. At many pilot meetings, the older males reflect on war-time flying stories. Because most women have no combat history, they stand silent.

9. Outstanding historic and contemporary female pilots are largely unknown as role models to non-aviator women.
10. Lack of emotional support from family and friends, who perceive flying as too dangerous.

If these barriers erode or destroy the woman's perception of the benefit of or her confidence to achieve the goal of pilot certification, then she either never begins flight training or drops out (Patterson et al., 2008).

Top Ten Ways to Increase Success in General Aviation Flight Training

1. Solve the lack of money problem by creating a low-interest revolving loan programme for flight training, not associated with community colleges and university programmes. Aviation manufacturers and aviation groups need

to realise they have a vested interest in increasing the number of general aviation pilots, especially women. By pooling resources, general aviation manufacturers and aviation organisations can partner to create a fund which can grow overtime, with interest and principal paybacks, creating more funds for future flight students.

2. Expand general aviation training scholarships, grants or low-interest loans. These need to be expanded for women over 50 wanting to start or complete flight programmes. Most of the current programmes target a younger demographic, especially aviation career-oriented younger women.
3. Develop a no-cost, readily available database of female mentors for pilots in training. Promote this mentor network constantly through flight schools and the aviation media. Focus on the success stories, especially using social media networking.
4. Create an online support community for female pilots in training at no cost to them. An older woman in the study shared:

> It would help so much to have a support group or someone to talk to who is as inexperienced as I am … even if I could email someone, I would. Something like an online sport pilot or newbie club.

5. Develop female-friendly flight training with more simulator time and increase women's confidence levels by building on what they already know, instead of going strictly by the Federal Aviation Administration (FAA) curriculum steps. Flight schools, instructors and the FAA need to recognise that women and men have different learning styles and strengths. Instead of the one-size-fits-all flight training syllabus, the sequence of instruction needs to be flexible to acknowledge differences in learning styles. One style is not better than the other, they are just different.
6. Individualise and personalise the flight training process with additional self-study options. To increase map-reading and orienteering skills, offer interesting no-cost ways to learn geography and map reading with online learning such as www.nationalgeographic.com or www.knowledgehouse.info.
7. Increase confidence and competence levels with aviation mechanical systems through low- or no-cost self-study training to close any workshop gap. Some flight students have not had the opportunity to develop mechanical skills. Form study groups or teams for hands-on training.
8. Create a friendly atmosphere with more emphasis on enjoyment of the flying and social experience. It is in the self-interest of flight schools to look at each female student as a potential Amelia Earhart. Walls of the flight training facility should be decorated with photographs of smiling students of both genders and outstanding general aviation pilots and aviation heroes, such as Women Airforce Service Pilots (WASPs).
9. Encourage pilot-in-training and instructor compatibility. Allow the student to feel comfortable with an easy transition or change to a different flight

instructor. Flight schools must understand that graduating more pilots creates a stronger aviation and airport community. Just as college alumni supporters cheer for their alma mater, female pilot graduates can make a huge positive impact on the Fixed Base Operator (FBO) future success. Recently flight schools and instructors have been invited to join the expanding no-cost network called 'Certified Woman Friendly Flight Training Facility' at www.womenofaviationweek.org, which communicates that women are welcome. Founded by Flight Instructor Mireille Goyer, many projects encouraging women to celebrate the aviation spirit worldwide are promoted.

10. Celebrate smaller milestones along the way to pilot certification. Reward the journey and make it fun. Many respondents reported that the aviation community provided the important emotional support often lacking from family and friends.

If only one-third of one per cent of the US population hold private pilot certificates and if only six per cent of those are female pilots, then they are indeed special. The desire to achieve and to be special may be a major benefit, making the time, effort and expense of learning to fly worthwhile for them (Patterson et al., 2008).

101 Ideas to Increase Women's Success in General Aviation

What aviation organisations can do

1. Large aviation associations and aviation manufacturers can create low-interest loan programmes for private pilot training.
2. General aviation interest groups need to encourage either the US Department of Education loan programme administrators or Congress to expand low-interest student loan programmes to include flight training. If flight students are affiliated with a community college or university aviation programme, student loans are available. However, at many on-airport programmes and with private flight instruction, women report difficulties in securing funds for aviation training.
3. More financial aid and scholarships need to be made available for women at Part 61 flight schools as an approved Trade School. Current student loan programmes often require higher interest rate loans for the financing of aviation training.
4. Late in 2010, Congress amended the Post-9/11 Veterans Educational Assistance Improvements Act of 2010 to broaden its provisions, which will now allow veterans to pursue flight training in some circumstances. This is an encouraging step to increase the number of female veterans in aviation (at the time of the initial Teaching Women to Fly Research Project, these educational benefits were not easily available).
5. The Military Spouse Career Advancement Account (MyCAA) grant needs to be reinstated and allow Part 61 Flight Schools to qualify.

6. More Military Base Recreation Departments need to start aero clubs. This will encourage military families/dependants to get involved with aviation and will increase the number of women in aviation.
7. Under 2007 legislation, federal student loan borrowers, who work in public service jobs for at least 10 years, qualify for loan forgiveness. With the expected shortage of airline pilots, legislation to include aviation training loans in student loan forgiveness programmes should be started now.
8. Scholarships for women over 50, who are not affiliated with a University Flight Programme, are very limited. Training grants should be available to encourage this demographic to earn their wings at the local flight school. Many women indicated a strong lifelong desire to become a pilot. Family obligations often required this goal to be put on hold. Now is their time to learn to fly. Many current scholarship programmes target only a younger, career-oriented demographic.
9. Aviation associations or local pilots can form aero clubs to keep down the cost of flying and aircraft ownership. Aero club members could encourage and mentor less experienced pilots, plan social flying events and focus on family activity and friendship building.
10. Expand programmes to have female pilots available to mentor students. One pilot said:

    > my flight training was one of the most wonderful things I have ever done. But I can also tell you that it really did feel like the loneliest thing I have ever done. It would have helped, if I had a community of female pilots close at hand who reached out to me.

11. Local general aviation training programmes, especially sport pilot, should be widely promoted. Aviation insurance companies should reward and encourage two-pilot families with significant insurance premium discounts.
12. Create a toll-free telephone crisis line. Female flight students could call the confidential line to share their experiences.
13. Create a non-profit online group with a good moderator to provide support for female pilots in training.
14. Market/target risk takers, such as women in parachute clubs, motorcycle clubs, martial arts clubs and gun clubs, with invitations to take an introductory flight lesson. One female pilot suggested marketing flight training as an adventure, especially to professional women, who have the means and freedom to develop their passions. Invite these women to local aviation meetings and airport events.
15. Organisations such as Women in Aviation International (www.wai.org), the 99s (www.ninety-nines.org), Whirly Girls (www.whirlygirls.org), Women Soaring (www.womensoaring.org), Women in Corporate Aviation (www.wca-intl.org) and the International Aviation Women's Association (www.iawa.org) should link websites with free listings for women instructors and

female-friendly websites, and should publish local meeting and conference information. These groups can cosponsor events and training.

16. Women in airline careers, such as flight attendants, baggage handlers, customer service gate agents and mechanics, should be invited to aviation meetings and offered introductory flight training.
17. Airlines should offer subsidised flight training education benefits to employees. Aviation-related businesses should consider this employee benefit too.
18. Female pilots and organisations should network with other women's organisations, such as the Red Hat Society. Invite them to hold a luncheon at the airport, especially in a hangar. Have female pilots participate in the meeting. Donate flight instruction or orientation flights as door prizes.
19. Reach out to charitable groups. Stories of female pilots should be placed in these organisations' publications. The local news media should be informed that a female pilot is using general aviation to participate in charity flights. Organisations such as Pilots N Paws and Cloud Nine Rescue Flights need to be promoted in aviation publications so that female pilots can respond. Angel Flight and many other important charitable organisations should partner to introduce female pilots to non-aviator audiences.
20. In marketing aviation services to women, use photographs of smiling female pilots. Both mature and younger women should be featured in flight training materials.
21. Stories of successful female pilots need to be brought to the attention of the local and national media and women's periodicals.
22. Sport pilot training needs to be widely promoted. Sport pilot graduates should speak to non-pilot women's groups to share their experience. Earning a pilot's certificate is achievable for women at any age, especially in the newer sport pilot planes and training programmes.
23. A free online Teaching Women to Fly – Improving Communication continuing education flight instructor training programme needs to be developed and made easily available.
24. To increase women's competence and confidence levels with aviation mechanical systems, low- or no-cost self-study training DVDs should be offered.
25. Groups could be formed around special interests such as grandparents flying to connect to other grandparents and grandchildren to spread the joy of flying. Other affinity groups that have already been formed, such as Ladies Love Taildraggers, need to be promoted and sponsored.
26. Girls need to meet female aviation role models. The power of early childhood exposure to general aviation for girls is very important. Aviation groups, businesses and advertisers should sponsor girls-fly programmes on cable outlets targeted at the teen market. Films as *The Aviators*, *Pearl* and *Breaking Through the Clouds*: *The First Women's National Air Derby* need to be promoted and broadcast (Faber and Mazlish, 2005).

27. In targeting buyers, research indicates that men want to know about the product's speed, size and options. However, women relate to how it will make their lives better or easier (Haberkorn, 2006). Perhaps, this is a clue as to how more women can be attracted to general aviation. Aviation manufacturers, advertisers and flight training schools should focus on its value to improve their quality of life.
28. A listing for female-friendly flight instructors should be made easily available to prospective pilots in training before they begin flight instruction. Because finding a compatible flight training programme or private instructor is critical to the woman's success, the listing needs to be made available at no cost to future students and for flight instructors.

What flight schools and flight instructors can do

29. The flight training industry and the FAA need to recognise the need for flexibility in the instruction syllabus. The flight training sequence of instruction needs to allow for individualisation and personalisation based on the student's learning styles and experiences. One size does not fit all.
30. Create a more female-friendly atmosphere at the flight centre with photos of successful, smiling female pilots getting in planes and at the controls, instead of only the cold, framed art of jets and rockers barreling through the sky with no people in the pictures.
31. Training materials and flight school marketing materials need to show both genders enjoying the experience of flight training. Both genders should be pictured as pilots in training, instructors and in career roles such as air controllers, airport managers and aircraft sales.
32. Instructors should give positive feedback, especially for well-executed procedures. This allows the flight student to build confidence.
33. When speaking about the training experience, use personal pronouns such as 'we' and 'us'. Women tend to focus on building friendships, relationships and emotional connections (Brizendine, 2006; Eliot, 2009).
34. Linguistic research (Eliot, 2009) reveals women tend to use apologetic language as 'I am so sorry, but I don't understand'. They tend to start sentences with questions. Some men misinterpret this pattern of communication, which can lead to instructor–flight student incompatibility.
35. Research indicates women are more sensitive to voice tones, body language and facial expressions. They require good eye contact to feel they are actually being listened to (Gray, 1992). Instructors should be aware of various communication styles.
36. Flight school owners and managers should ask students for feedback on their flight school experiences and instructors. Flight schools need to be more interested in customer service. This follow-up is essential if a female flight student drops out of training (Koonce, 2002).

37. Give flight students a greater sense of control by allowing them to talk to the flight instructors, instead of just being assigned the next instructor in line. Instructor–student compatibility is critical to success.
38. Flight schools should have a very short form which asks students about their preferred learning styles. This will improve communication.
39. In addition to learning styles, a cursory look at the student's tolerance for risk needs to be done. Just as financial organisations perform risk assessment to help individuals plan for investment/retirement, an individual student flight training plan can be mapped out with the pilot-in-training (Tileston, 2005).
40. Educational research indicates that when a manual task is paired with a mental task, learning is strengthened (Churches and Terry, 2007). Incorporating verbal, auditory and kinetic explanations increases information retention.
41. Flight students respond to positive instruction. When explaining what needs to be done, instructors should use positive language and provide visual and written instructions. Research indicates (Brounstein, 2001) that if a negative description is used to describe what should not be done, the image of the negative or incorrect behaviour is planted in the mind. For example, by saying 'don't land short', the image of this negative stays in the mind. A positive image would be to say: 'Roll the plane gently on the centreline.'
42. When a student's instructor leaves flight instructing, give a free or lower-cost orientation with a new instructor so she can determine if they are compatible. In addition to good customer service by the flight school, this provides a sense of control and personalisation for the flight student.
43. Develop a buddy network where a more advanced student or a pilot can mentor a newer student, if only by telephone or email. Friendships are key to enjoying the general aviation experience.
44. Establish monthly or quarterly student and instructor success events where milestones can be celebrated as a group in a less tense environment than the cockpit. Friendships based on a shared interest in aviation can be established. One pilot suggested: 'The flight school might make it easier to communicate with other students who would like to study or socialise together.'
45. Celebrate the journey and small milestones. Just as the whole baseball team runs to home plate to celebrate a home run, the pilot-in-training who completes her solo should have a clapping crowd waiting for her as she deplanes or walks into the flight school. But smaller milestones should be celebrated with fun pins, baseball caps, etc. The flying journey should be a good experience. One pilot reported that she flew from a small, community airport. When she was on her third touch and go during her solo, the tower radioed her. She could hear the applause over her radio. Over 10 years later, she still reflects about how much the personal support and encouragement from the entire aviation team meant to her.
46. Photos of female flight school pilots in training at the controls, pre-flighting the plane, etc. can be posted on the school bulletin board, school website and other electronic communications.

47. Flight schools should develop alumni groups/clubs where networking can be accomplished. Also, future students can be recruited and referred through the alumni.
48. Instructors should not yell. Research on the effect of stress on flight instructor behaviour revealed that instructors in high-stress situations, especially air training, tended to be irritable and more impatient with students (Machado, 2009). Instructors should take a few minutes to talk with the student about her feelings too. A long-time flight instructor advised: 'Acknowledge if you were terse or appeared to be angry, you are sorry. You were just having a difficult day. Be sure she knows it is not her fault'. A female study participant, who holds several soaring world records, shared her first private pilot flight training experience:

> I ended my flight training when the instructor yelled at me 'You don't know how to fly!' I can't imagine how devastating that experience would be if it was my only flight experience.

49. Find out about the student's past experiences to build communication bridges which relate specifically to that experience. If a football analogy is used, women are less likely to understand because they probably lack that experience. However, they have had plenty of other experiences which can be used to transfer to flying skills.
50. Instructors should not show off on the first, second or even third air training lesson. Some women in the Teaching Women to Fly Research Project reported fear as a factor in their flight training. Some women described flight instructors who bank too steeply or perform death stalls as *fright instructors.*
51. Depending upon the student pilot's risk tolerance and experience, flight simulator training should be offered early on in the process. Many women have never used computer applications such as Microsoft Simulator.
52. Determine what the student knows and her general aviation experience before introducing her to air work. One woman in this study was immediately taken for an orientation ride. The instructor yelled at her when she did not follow his direction to follow the VASI in. She had never heard of a VASI before. Beginners need to clearly understand equipment and procedures.
53. Several women indicated that when they started air training and even ground school, they had difficulty with the new jargon. One did not know FBO meant Fixed Base Operator/Operation. Providing a commonly used list of aviation flying abbreviations at the beginning of the training would be helpful. A fun classroom exercise could be to see how many students could identify (or guess) what AOPA, EAA, WAI, FAA, FSDO, ADO and many other commonly used aviation acronyms mean.
54. One pilot stated: 'In ground school I felt like Alice in Wonderland because I did not go to boy school. I never heard of right-y tight-y, left-y loose-y. It was a completely and, I mean completely, new language'. Engines, maps

and compasses all need to be physically present in the classroom to help crystallise the abstract and foreign concepts. Several study participants suggested a lending library of DVDs to reinforce the classroom materials at their own pace.

55. Most of the women who begin flight training are self-starters. If map reading and geography skills need to be strengthened, suggest no-cost online sites listed at www.nationalgeographic.com or the public library. Recommend computer skill games related to increased spatial skill sets.
56. Because air traffic control (ATC)/radio communications can be difficult, a microphone in class can be used to demonstrate quick, short delivery. The Aircraft Owners and Pilots Association (AOPA) Air Safety Institute's Say it Right: Mastering Radio Communication online course is a great place to build skills.
57. Because studies (Brizendine, 2006; Gurian et al., 2001; Moir and Jessel, 1991) indicate that women have often developed less spatial ability, don't ask her to turn north during the flight. Pair the directions with: 'Let's head north or toward that railroad bridge. Can you see that bridge?' Women typically navigate using landmarks that can be seen and heard or smelled. Men are more likely to use absolute direction such as north or south or absolute distances as miles or city blocks (Sax, 2005.)
58. Instructors need to be confident that their student pilot can actually see over the panel. Booster seats and pedal extenders should be made available to flight students through the flight school.
59. Have someone call the student to check how they are. Students need to feel the flight school is personally interested in them and their progress (Desruisseaux, 2011).
60. Gender research studies indicate differences in the way men and women learn (Pease and Pease, 2001; Tannen, 1990; Turney, 2004). Many flight students benefit from visual and tactile reinforcement when learning maths and science and spatial skills. Simulators should have real yokes and panel instruments so that student pilots can really get the feel. Don't just talk about reading the compass – have a compass to demonstrate.
61. Some studies indicate that women tend to be left brain dominant (Brizendine, 2006; Eliot, 2009; Sax, 2005). They tend to have superior verbal, listening and writing skills. To build early confidence, flight instruction exercises should incorporate these areas first.
62. In *Words that Work* (Luntz, 2007), studies reveal that women generally respond better to stories, anecdotes and metaphors, while men are more fact-oriented and statistical. Be upbeat about other successful female aviators.
63. Take a photo of the student pilot smiling at the controls, even if that photo needs to be taken while still on the ground. Give it to her to post everywhere she will see it. As you see yourself, so you will be. If you think you are a pilot, you will succeed. Encourage positive self-talk and focus on what they are doing correctly.

64. If your student population allows, offer study groups for various phases of flight training. Introduce students to each other. They might form their own study group.
65. After the in-flight training lesson, have a private area away from the cockpit and flight line, even if it is just a table in the coffee room, where the lesson can be reviewed. Emphasise positive performance.
66. Use echo communication, where some of the student's words are echoed back in your response. This confirms the listener is really listening to what was just been said. This is a very useful communication technique (Brounstein, 2001).
67. Having a mnemonic to practise and memorise for various phases of flight training is very helpful. It is a mental checklist.
68. Having the instructor tell, show and use the same terms establishes a pattern to model. For example, the instructor could review the steps for take-off on the ground before the engine starts. Using the same words, terms and sequence, the instructor should model a correct take off. Then, when it is the student pilot's turn to take off, evaluate using the same words, terms and sequence. It is easier to model correct behaviour.
69. If the student has a question which is outside of the FAA curriculum sequence, it should be acknowledged with some basic information. This demonstrates that the instructor is actually listening to the student. If the instructor's response is 'we will get to that later', it can be interpreted as dismissive and condescending. Individualise the instruction.
70. Words have impact. Using the term 'pilot-in-training' or even 'student pilot' indicates that success and certification are the planned outcome.
71. Sport pilot needs to be presented as an option, especially if that student might face medical issues. Women over 50 appear to be an overlooked segment, with many having a lifelong dream of becoming a pilot.
72. Flight schools need to know what financing programmes are available. According to several responding to this study, many flight schools expect the student pilot to arrange payment on their own. Flight schools should have an updated list of scholarships, grants and loans available.

Ergonomics can be improved

73. The newer planes have adjustable seats, but the older models still have seats which do not easily accommodate shorter legs and smaller bodies. Flight schools should consider loaning out booster seats and pedal extenders to students.
74. Male instructors need to be made aware that if the female flight student cannot see over the panel, she will have difficulty. Women need to know that seat cushions as Oregon Aero pillows and others can make the cockpit more comfortable. One pilot said she took the seat cushion off the couch in

the FBO's lounge each time she flew. Another pilot reported using boat float cushions, which are not very expensive. Another said in her survey response:

> I think that when more women become pilots, the cockpit environment will accommodate women's physical stature more accurately. Until then, we have to adjust. It helps to know other women pilots, just to be able to express how difficult it is to learn and complete a rating. Most of the male pilots can't relate to the struggle.

75. Plane designers need to incorporate newer technology, such as moveable rudder pedals, especially in rental and training aircraft.
76. Keeping a small step ladder near the flight line makes it easier for women to check fuel levels instead of having to balance on the struts. Another step stool/ladder near the fuel facility would be helpful and add to safety.

Building for the future: What pilots and aviation organisations can do

77. More pilots need to help girl scouts with their aviation badges. Also, more female pilots need to volunteer to speak to classrooms about aviation and careers. More female pilots need to volunteer with the Experimental Aviation Association Young Eagles programme, museum aviation summer camps and aviation exploring.
78. Working with their local schools, local pilot volunteers should provide classroom aviaton educational materials which also teach maths, reading and reasoning skills. Pilots should volunteer to mentor and assist in the classroom with these exercises.
79. Working with local school boards and administrators, aviation magnet schools and aerospace academies can be developed. Models such as Shawnee High School Jefferson County, Kansas, and Ross Shaw Sterling High School in Houston, Texas and others should be cited to school leaders. Georgia adopted a four-year high school aviation curriculum to focus on job skills and career classes.
80. More female pilot role models need to be seen in magazine articles and advertising for products.
81. The stories of the important contributions made by the brave and talented WASPs of the Second World War need to be included in history discussions and classroom education at all grade levels. Many stories are shared on www.wingsacrossamerica.us, which honours and preserves the important contributions of female Air Force service pilots.
82. Research in gender issues indicates that boys and girls typically play with different toys (Eliot, 2009; Orenstein, 2011). Rather than trying to have young girls play with planes if they would rather play with a doll, why not offer them a general aviation pilot doll? Currently only female flight attendant dolls and male airline pilot dolls are available. Several years ago, Barbie Career

doll did offer a female airline pilot doll. Mattel indicates that the doll is out of production and no longer available. A female general aviation pilot doll could have pilot pals, an airplane hangar and even a new plane. Girls Explore has a mission to sell dolls which reach out to a young girl's imagination to inspire her to achieve greatness. Aviation dolls depicting historic pilots as Bessie Coleman and Amelia Earhart are sold by online retailers.

83. Mattel has an annual Career Barbie online voting competition. An organised campaign to have a general aviation Barbie Pilot should be started. If Barbie Dentist, Barbie Computer Engineer, Barbie Animal Trainer and Barbie Gymnast are options for this programme, just the awareness created by a Barbie Pilot could be helpful to young girls considering their future careers.
84. General aviation female pilots need a social media presence. If breast cancer survivors can build a battalion of pink sisters to support them and provide information as they journey to survivorship, social media, such as Facebook and Twitter, can be used as a pilot-in-training reaches her flying milestones. This can be helpful to her and encouraging to others, who might not have considered pursuing aviation. Social media allows for interactive communication.
85. Pilots without partners matching service needs to be developed so that pilot buddies can be connected to promote flying and the social aspects and fun of general aviation. It does not have to be a dating service, just a chance to fly socially. This would bring down the cost of flying with cost sharing and would encourage newer aviators to partner with mentors.
86. Promote information about high-profile women who are pilots. If young women knew that Angelina Jolie and Hilary Swank are private pilots, a lot more excitement from young women about flying might result. Successful role models are very important. Television shows at the Smithsonian Channel's *Women in Science* expand career horizons.
87. More female pilots, aviation organisations and businesses need to support the highly successful Girls with Wings project (www.girlswithwings.com). Encouraging young girls to pursue aviation careers by introducing female aviation professionals early in their decision-making process opens up career options for young women.
88. Because pilots are more likely to respond to local invitations to promote their community airport and aviation, a free online aviation speakers bureau needs to be created for aviators to register as speakers on various topics. This site needs to be available at no charge to civic club programme planners and educators.
89. Pilots of both genders need to personally meet with the local high school counsellors, who are so important in career decisions of students. Aviation training, scholarship and career information needs to be provided to them for their files for student counselling. Photos of both genders need to be featured in this career information.

90. Aviation needs community outreach. Hosting booths at shopping centres, high school and college athletic events are examples. Potential female flight students can often be reached at these locations, especially with security issues making airports less accessible to the general public.
91. Host an aviation art show at a local gallery or public library. An aviation art competition might be included. The theme of famous female aviators would provide an important focus on outstanding pilots. Suggest a great aviation book to the local book club and participate in their discussion. Or volunteer to read an aviation story at the local library children's storytime.
92. Pilots should take every opportunity to promote the value of general aviation. If they have a business or medical office reception area, put out *AOPA Pilot*, *Sport Pilot*, *Flying Adventures* and *Flying* for reading materials. Wear aviation pins and badges in social settings to encourage discussion about aviation. This might get a non-pilot interested in pursuing flying.
93. More women need to volunteer with the Civil Air Patrol (CAP). CAP provides an excellent introduction to the flying experience. Female pilots can be role models for all the cadets. Other CAP volunteers share aviation and leadership experiences (see http://www.gocivilairpatrol.com).
94. Sexual harassment is often experienced by women in a male-dominated industry (Gutek and Morasch, 1982). Several respondents mentioned examples of sexual harassment. Serious thought needs to be given as to how individuals and organisations can address the need for a professional training and working environment that is free from sexual harassment.
95. Studies indicate girls can perform maths problems as well as boys if the problems are on a topic of interest to them (Hutson, 2009; Phillips, 1991; Sax, 2005). For example, ask: 'What is the price of a new sweater if it is on sale at 30 per cent off the original price of $55? But if you use your frequent shopper card, which gives you an additional five per cent reduction off the sales price, and the sales tax is 3.5 per cent, what do you pay?' More girls can solve the problem than boys. How aviation is presented is very important to get the girls interested. Saying Angelina Jolie just bought a new plane, then presenting options of where she can fly to the movie set with the fuel her plane has on board gets a young girl's attention.
96. Pre-paid tuition and flight training funds placed with private flight instruction schools needs to be better protected, especially in a difficult economy. Flying is expensive. When offered the opportunity to pre-purchase instruction and plane rental, safeguards need to be established because many students have been financially ruined when their flight training funds were lost as a result of the school closing unexpectedly.
97. If local media celebrities are pilots, that accomplishment needs to be promoted in their station bios. Aviation organisations need to reach out to them as high-profile role models, especially female pilots.
98. The Teaching Women to Fly Research Project revealed that 43 per cent of female pilots participated in organised sports programmes such as

basketball, volleyball, softball, soccer, track and cycling. Because the 1972 Title IX legislation, sports programmes have offered risk and team sports opportunities and social experience for young women (Ladda, 2012). General aviation marketing and female pilot organisations should target organised high school and collegiate women sports programmes with the general aviation message.

99. Female pilots and aviation training information should be made available to female students in information technology, computer programming, engineering, and construction programmes because they may have stronger spatial skill sets and interest in mechanical and detailed procedures as are found in flight training.
100. Because other women may be reluctant to venture onto the airport alone, pilots need to personally invite them to aviation meetings or events at the airport and should offer to go with them on an orientation flight.
101. Aviation organisations and individual pilots need to donate age-appropriate library materials about successful and famous female pilots, especially Women's Airforce Service Pilots (WASPs) to their school libraries. Back issues of *AOPA Pilot*, *EAA Sport Pilot*, *Flying*, *99 News* and *WAI Aviation for Women* magazines can be donated to the pre-school for the children to cut out the planes and pretend to fly them. Current aviation magazines should be donated to the local community library for the reading rooms. Flight schools should also have a lending library and reading room. One newer female pilot suggested: 'If the weather stops your flight lesson, read flying-related books and magazines to keep up the right mindset'.

Going Forward With Future Studies

The Teaching Women to Fly Research Project findings suggested several studies that other aviation education researchers might consider to build on this original research:

- Do female general aviation students have a higher success rate (solo or earned private certification) if they participate in ground school first before air training?
- Do female general aviation students have a higher ground school success rate if taught in a classroom/seminar setting vs. self-study?
- Do female general aviation students with simulator hours before air training have a higher success rate than those with air training only?
- Do female general aviation students have a higher success rate with male or female instructors?
- Is the success rate higher with either gender of instructor in private instruction vs. flight school setting?

- Do female general aviation students have a higher success rate in college/university programmes vs. FBO/on-airport flight schools? If so, is it because of more easily available financial assistance? Is it that college/university programmes tend to point towards aviation careers? Is it the more social interaction setting of the classroom and campus of college-based programmes?
- The following should be another area of study: even though this and past research has indicated that a male pilot family member or close friend has a very strong positive influence on a woman's decision to pursue flight training and to succeed, is it because there are just more male pilots and a female pilot partner/family member/mentor has just as strong, if not greater influence, on flight training decisions?

  - Is it because a male pilot introduced the woman to flying, perhaps in a gradual process and the comfort level was increased over time (as in the story of the boiled frog!)?
  - Was it that she has access and perhaps less expense to general aviation experience because a plane was more readily available, and rental expense and even instructional time was less costly?
  - Was it that often families owning a plane are in a higher income bracket, so therefore flight instruction/training cost was not as burdensome?
  - Does having a pilot as a relative or friend normalise the desire to pursue certification? Is the family more supportive of the decision to pursue certification/flight training?
  - Would any of the above be the same or even more encouraging to a woman if her family member aviator was a woman?

- What is the difference in the success rate of female flight students, if any, with male vs. female flight instructors?
- What might be the difference, if any, in success rates of female flight students given a male pilot mentor vs. a female pilot mentor?
- What role might participation in organised athletics/sports play in the success rate of female flight students? In a post-Title 9 era, are female athletes more confident and comfortable with risk activities? It is a well-known recruiting fact that Army recruiters for the Armor Branch have display booths at Monster Truck events. Do successful female pilots demonstrate an affinity for certain organised or risk sports?
- Because the general aviation flight training dropout rate appears to be around 70 per cent, do female students have a higher dropout rate than male students?
- This research indicates that women tell their flight instructors that the major reason they pursue flight instruction is personal satisfaction. How can this motivation best be used to recruit and retain women in general aviation?

Because women are excellent pilots and flying is a life-changing experience, they should be encouraged to learn to fly at every opportunity.

References

AFL-CIO Department of Professional Employees (2008). *Professional Women: Vital Statistics Fact sheet.* Washington DC: DPE Research Department.

Brennan, A., 2009. Encouraging pilot hopefuls. *State Aviation Journal*, August/September. Available at: http://www.stateaviationjournal.com.

Brizendine, L., 2006. *The Female Brain.* New York: Morgan Road Books.

Brounstein, M., 2001. *Communicating Effectively for Dummies.* New York: Wiley.

Cauchon, D., 2009. Women gain in historic job shift. *USA Today*, 3 September, p. 1.

Churches, R. and Terry, R., 2007. *NPL for Teachers: How to Be a Highly Effective Teacher*. Bethel, Connecticut: Crown House.

Collins, G., 2009. *When Everything Changed: The Amazing Journey of American Women from 1960 to the Present.* New York: Little Brown and Company.

Desruisseaux, J., 2011. 101: A primer for instructors on customer service. *MENTOR*, February, pp. 10–15.

Donner, R., 2010. The next generation. *Aircraft Maintenance Technology*, April, p. 4.

Eliot, L., 2009. *Pink Brain, Blue Brain: How Small Differences Grow into Troublesome Gaps – And What We Can Do About it.* New York: Houghton Mifflin Harcourt.

Faber, A. and Mazlish, E., 2005. *How to Talk So Teens Will Listen and Listen So Teens Will Talk.* New York: HarperCollins.

Gray, J., 1992. *Men are from Mars, Women are from Venus.* New York: HarperCollins.

Gurian, M. and Henley, P. with Trueman, T., 2001. *Boys and Girls Learn Differently! A Guide for Teachers and Parents.* San Francisco: Jossey-Bass.

Gutek, B.A. and Morasch, B., 1982. Sex-ratios, sex-role spillover, and sexual harassment of women at work. *Journal of Social Issues*, 38(4): pp. 55–74.

Haberkorn, J., 2006. Does it pass the wife check? *Washington Times*, 21 January. Available at: http://www.freerepublic.com/focus/f-chat/1562457/posts.

Hutson, M., 2009. Mathematical model: Teaching girls that brains and beauty are compatible. *Psychology Today*, July–August: pp. 33–4.

Koonce, J.M., 2002. *Human Factors in the Training of Pilots.* Bocan Raton, FL: CRC Press.

Ladda, S., 2012. Examining Title IX at 40: Historical development, legal implications, and governance structures. *President's Council on Fitness, Sports & Nutrition: Research Digest*, 13(2): pp. 10–20.

Lebow, E.F., 2002. *Before Amelia: Women Pilots in the Early Days of Aviation.* Washington DC: Brassey's.

Luntz, F., 2007. *Words that Work.* New York: Hyperion.

Machado, R., 2009. Time builders and ruined dreams. *AOPA Pilot*, October, p. 38.

Moir, A. and Jessel, D., 1991. *Brain Sex: The Real Difference between Men and Women.* New York: Carol Publishing.

Motorcycle Industry Council, 2009. The motorcycle population is growing with more women and younger riders, Available at: http://curvesahead.net.

Orenstein, P., 2011. *Cinderella Ate My Daughter*. New York: HarperCollins.

Patterson, K., Grenny, J., Maxfield, D., McMillan, R. and Switzler, Al., 2008. *Influencer: The Power to Change Anything*. New York: McGraw-Hill.

Pease, A. and Pease, B., 2001. *Why Men Don't listen and Women Can't Read Maps: How We're Different and What to Do About it*. New York: Broadway Books.

Phillips, L., 1991. *The Girls Report: What We Know and Need to Know About Growing up Female*. New York: National Council for Research on Women.

Sax, L., 2005. *Why Gender Matters: What Parents and Teachers Need to Know About the Emerging Science of Sex-Differences*. New York: Random House.

Smith, W.R., 2009. She's at the helm and loving it! *Great Lakes Boating Magazine*, February, pp. 11–13.

Tannen, D., 1990. *You Just Don't Understand: Women and Men in Conversation*. New York: Ballantine Books.

Telfer, R. and Biggs, J., 1988. *The Psychology of Flight Training*. Ames, IA: Iowa State University Press.

Tileston, D.W., 2005. *10 Best Teaching Practices: How Brain Research, Learning Styles, and Standards Define Teaching Competencies*. Thousand Oaks, CA: Corwin Press.

Turney, M.A (ed.), 2004. *Tapping Diverse Talent in Aviation: Culture, Gender, and Diversity*. Burlington, VT: Ashgate.

Women in Aviation International, 2010. Women in aviation: the facts. Available at: http://www.wai.org/resources/facts.cfm.

Yen, H., 2011. Women surpass men in advance degrees. *Seattle Times*, 26 April, p. 18.

Conclusion

> On a coastal sand dune at Kitty Hawk, NC on December 17, 1903 two brothers realized mankind's dream to fly. Not as well known is the part their sister, Katharine, played in their success. (Stimson, 2013)

Katherine Wright is said to have contributed much to the efforts of her two brothers in terms of emotional and intellectual support (Stimson, 2013), adding to their scientific knowledge and even financial needs (Holden and Griffith, 1991). For her contribution to aviation, alongside Wilbur and Orville, Katherine was awarded the French Legion of Honour. When the Wright airplane manufacturing company was formed in 1909, 'Katherine became an officer in the company and served as secretary to the executive committee' (Stimson, 2013). To his credit, Orville often spoke of his sister's role in his success, stating that: 'When the world speaks of the Wrights it must include my sister; she inspired much of our effort' (quoted in Holden and Griffith, 1991, p. 35). Interestingly, 'Katherine was active in the suffrage movement' and was supported by both her father and Orville, who, on at least one occasion, joined her on a demonstration for women's rights on the streets of Dayton, Ohio, where they lived (Stimson, 2013).

In a similar vein, Mabel Hubbard, the wife of Alexander Graham Bell, inspired some of her husband's inventions and helped finance his aviation company (Holden and Griffith, 1991). Yet neither Mabel Hubbard nor Katherine Wright has received much attention in the history of aviation over the ensuing century. Indeed, over much of the second half of the twentieth century through to today, there have been a growing number of books (including this one) devoted to celebrations of female flyers and their 'untold' stories (Cadogan, 1992; Curtis, 1985; Holden and Griffith, 1991; Lauwick, 1960; Render, 1992; Spring, 1994). There have also been a number of articles that have sought to explain the reasons why women have been excluded or marginalised from key areas of aviation (largely piloting and engineering, but also from other aspects of commercial and military aviation) and ignored, neglected and/or marginalised in histories of civil and military aviation (Barry, 2007; Durepos et al., 2008; Helms Mills, 2002; Mills, 2006; Neal-Smith and Cockburn, 2008; O'Brien, 1983).

Throughout the literature on gender and aviation, a number of points have been raised by feminist and other gender equity scholars and practitioners to explain the absence of women in piloting. These include such things as organisational culture, formative contexts and societal values, technical skill and ability, the association of flying with danger and warfare, and associated cultural factors such as symbolism, attitudes and language (or jargon).

In this edited collection we have attempted to bring together a number of these key issues in one book to lay out the overall challenges to those fighting to ensure a gender-equitable industry.

Gender, Social Values and Cultures

Much of the early attempts to develop heavier-than-air flights occurred at the beginning of the twentieth century, when social values across Europe, North America and parts of the then British Empire stressed the value of domesticity and women's place in the home (Weeks, 1990). Nonetheless, a few women – usually from the rich and upper classes – did manage to take part in the fledgling enterprise, including several destined to become well-known (at least at the time) aviatrixes. With the character of the industry at the time, often developed out of small workshops and enterprises, there were no organisational or industry-wide cultures directly associated with aviation (although there were powerful, all-male aviation associations that did play an important gatekeeping role – see Cadogan, 1992). Three things may have served to enhance the future limitation of women's ability to enter the field: 1) the increasing technical nature of airplane development and the limited access of women to those skills (Cadogan, 1992); 2) the association of flying with danger – a large number of aviators lost their lives in early attempts at flight (Ellis, 1980; Foster, 1990); and 3) the onset of the First World War, which increasingly came to associate flying with masculinity and the image of the warrior (Beauman, 1971; Escott, 1989; Mills, 2006). In the UK, the First World War served to crystallise the association of flighting with men and masculinity, and saw the paradox of the establishment of the Women's Royal Air Force in 1918 alongside the further banning of women from combat roles and even being carried as passengers on non-combat flights (Beauman, 1971). At the war's end, the fledgling commercial aviation industry in the UK was founded and staffed by men who oversaw and led the military air forces and/or who were pilots and engineers in those military air forces (Penrose, 1967; Pudney, 1959). Less than a handful of women served in the early post-Second World War commercial ventures and only as secretarial and office help (Mills, 2006). Eventually, in 1924, with the establishment of Imperial Airways (IA), a rule was introduced that restricted piloting and engineering work to those who has served in the military air services, i.e., men (Mills, 2006). The doors were, however, opened to the employment of greater numbers of female office staff (Mills, 2006). However, with its esprit de corps based on military air force camaraderie and numerous wartime symbols (e.g., uniforms, converted bombers and hangers), a particular form of masculinist culture took hold in the airline (Mills, 2006).

Shortly after the establishment of IA and a number of other airlines throughout Europe, international aviation bodies were established, including the International Commission for Air Navigation (ICAN), which, among its early pronouncements, banned women from the flight crew of commercial airlines (see Mills, 2006).

The Culture of Organisation

Issues of social values and organisational culture are raised by several of the chapters in this edited collection. As we saw in Chapter 1, for instance, Weigand et al. focus on the role of organisational cultures in constructing different forms of discrimination (according to gender, race, ethnicity, class and nationality) at different points in time. They argue that discriminatory practices need to be examined in context and over time to track the way they become established, modified and changed. They argue that this knowledge can help us to identify particular strategies for dealing with intersecting aspects of discrimination. In the process they draw attention to the need to examine the complexity of discrimination that, at one point, may see white men favoured over black men and all women, but at the same time may see all men favoured over all women. An example would be the practices of the US Air Force during the Second World War, which saw a separate unit for black flyers alongside a continued ban on women from joining the air force as pilots (Francis, 1993). Thus, discriminatory practices need to be examined from various contexts and outcomes.

Keeping us focused on the centrality of organisational culture, Bridges' (Chapter 6) examination of gender issues in the Australian Defence Force (ADF) reveals various aspects of symbolism that discourage women from joining and hinder those who do join the ADF. She particularly draws our attention to the role of actors within organisational culture in the form of men who draw on cultural archetypes of the military as a masculine pursuit to 'resist' women's efforts to join and integrate in the ADF.

The broad issue of social values also came up, but from a different perspective, in Chapter 2 by Gibbon, who focuses on how young Australian women come to perceive civil and military piloting as difficult and dangerous and (stereotypically) a male profession. Gibbon alerts us to the need for greater socialisation of women and more exposure to related aspects of flying that can engender a much-needed enthusiasm for the profession. To some extent, this echoes the work of Wallace (2009a; 2009b) on women in accounting. Wallace argues that while serious barriers to female partnerships still remain in accounting, we need to understand the choices made by women to not seek promotion in the industry.

Women, Men and Gender Dynamics

While some of the chapters focus on gender and the social construction of masculinity and femininity, other chapters return us to the lived experiences of women in regard to aviation: a timely reminder of the tension between constructivist arguments about the differences between women and women/men and men/men and women, and the need for a women's voice perspective to translate experiences into political action (Calás and Smircich, 1992).

Tracy Smart's examination (Chapters 3a and 3b) of perceived female weaknesses (both physical and mental) is traced in large part to unscientific accounts rooted in cultural values. She argues that, nonetheless, certain physiological differences between men and women need to be kept in mind when discussing improvements in design (i.e., cockpit and flying suits) to accommodate these differences in order to improve women's experiences of flying. Indeed, one of the earliest examples of the influence of social values over scientific knowledge can be traced back to the 1924 ICAN decision to ban women from flying based on the argument (backed at that time by medical science) that women's menstrual cycle made them unfit for flying during certain parts of the month (see Mills, 2006). Nonetheless, long after this particular 'scientific' fact was revealed as false, bans of female pilots persisted long into the post-Second World War era, although some small airlines in the UK and the US did hire female pilots in the 1930s (Cadogan, 1992).

Attitudes are the focus of the chapter by Reynolds et al. (Chapter 4), looking specifically at how male pilots in the US, and in other cross-cultural studies, feel about the idea of female flyers. Reynolds et al., like Smart, argue that male bias towards female flyers should be fully explored through the study of the masculinist culture of aviation ventures.

In Chapter 8 by Jane Neal-Smith, attitudes to aviation are again to the fore, this time remaining us of the need to explore how women feel about the industry. Here the focus is on gaining an understanding of why certain women persevere in spite of the male character of the aviation, indicating that the British female flyers that she interviewed were particularly dedicated and determined to enter aviation and succeed. She also reminds us that while we can learn from the women who enter aviation, attention also needs to be given to factors influencing those women who turn away from aviation due to existing barriers.

Focussing on this latter point, Gibbon (Chapter 5) raises the issue of structural and power barriers to female entry and retention in Australian military and civilian aviation. She gets us to focus our attention on the strategies that (numerically, structurally and culturally) dominant groups often use to retain their dominance. Specifically she focuses our attention on how new and junior career female pilots face cultural and attitudinal forms of pressure that can potentially drive them out of flying. Gibbon also reminds us of the tension between the needs of aviation (as currently structured) for full-time, dedicated career people and the needs of some young women to take 'time off' for childbirth and motherhood. In her focus, Gibbon reminds us of Kanter's (1977) classic work on power and structure and its continued relevance today – 37 years later!

Shades of Kanter (1977) are also found in Mitchell et al. (Chapter 7), where the authors remind us of the long-established argument that organisational change needs to move beyond tokenism to counter stereotypical views in aviation. Mitchell et al. contend that the process of change needs to be accompanied by the recruitment of substantial numbers of women and that even a relatively small number can be seen to have effected change (see also Gutek, 1985). Increasing numbers of female pilots can be seen not only to engender greater resistance from some male pilots (see also Bridges in Chapter 6) but also, paradoxically, serve to weaken stereotyping. Finally, Mitchell et al. return us to the issue of cultural archetypes and remind us that the masculine imagery of aviation has gone through various iterations, including the notion of 'the right stuff', with its complex mix of danger, professionalism, heroism and technical proficiency. To change the industry, such archetypes need to be unravelled and dissociated from masculinity

From Glass Ceiling to Glass Cockpit

The fact that perceptions of women's differences from men have been used to keep them out of aviation does not mean that there are no physiological or experiential differences. As several of our contributors point out, those differences are reasons for ergonomic, attitudinal and/or cultural change, not exclusion.

Three chapters raise the question of differences between male and female pilots in regard to the adoption of new technologies. Here the glass cockpit becomes a kind of metaphor for gender dynamics in aviation: not a metaphor of exclusion – as in the notion of the 'glass ceiling' (Morrison et al., 1987). In fact, the glass cockpit refers to a real material innovation that nonetheless also serves, in the following chapters, as a metaphor for a space for understanding how gender differences can be understood and mediated.

One of the three studies, by Koglbauer et al. (Chapter 10), focuses on apparent gender differences in regard to accidents and the improvement of cockpit design. The authors argue that rather than being ignored, gender differences need to be understood and incorporated into new technologies. A similar argument is made by Kristovics et al. (Chapter 9) and Mitchell et al. (Chapter 11), who focus on the reported differences between male and female pilots, respectively in Australia and South Africa, and in the US. They make two main observations. The first is that in order to simultaneously improve aviation technology and more equitable aviation processes, it is important to understand that there are reported gender experiences and attitudes. The second is to note their finding of cultural differences between the three countries, suggesting that gender differences vary depending on deep-rooted cultural values and experiences.

Looking Forward

This collection was conceived as a way to further jump-start the recruitment and retention of more women in aviation, especially piloting. To that end, we brought together a group of male and female scholars and practitioners from academia and aviation. While the record of aviation is abysmal in regard to the recruitment of women in piloting, the situation is not universally bleak. There have been certain changes over time and some variance between different countries in their approach to female recruitment. That some of the various research findings have and are being applied in aviation is evidenced by our remaining two chapters (Chapters 12 and 13) that report on ongoing projects. In the first of the two, Gibbon's (Chapter 12) evaluation of an Australian Air Force project suggests that one way forward is to consider both choice and constraint factors as part of an overall recruitment strategy. This is very much in line with the overall contributions of this book that look at both of these approaches. In the final chapter (Chapter 13), Hamilton discusses the lessons from a US project that gave weight to women's motivations to fly and the specific barriers to their success. This generated three important lists that reinforce many of the points made throughout this book. The first list is 'The Top 10 Barriers that Stop Women from Learning to Fly' and the second is 'Top Ten Ways to Increase [Women's] Success in General Aviation Flight Training', while the third was a list of '101 Ideas to Increase Women's Success in General Aviation'. Readers will hopefully note the overlap between those lists and much of what has been said throughout the preceding chapters. Our hope is that this edited collection will spur not only critique but more especially much-needed changes within aviation. We would like to think that future books will not need to focus on the absence of female pilots, but rather on studies undertaken within aviation to effect an increasing number of steps towards gender equity.

References

Barry, K.M., 2007. *Femininity in Flight: A History of Flight Attendants*. Durham, NC: Duke University Press.

Beauman, K.B., 1971. *Partners in Blue: The Story of Women's Service with the Royal Air Force*. London: Hutchinson.

Cadogan, M., 1992. *Women with Wings*. London: Macmillan.

Calás, M.B. and Smircich, L., 1992. Using the 'F' word: Feminist theories and the social consequences of organizational research. In: A.J. Mills and P. Tancred (eds), *Gendering Organizational Analysis*. Newbury Park, CA: Sage, pp. 222–34.

Curtis, L., 1985. *The Forgotten Pilots*. London: Eastern Press.

Durepos, G., Helms Mills, J. and Mills, A.J., 2008. Tales in the manufacture of knowledge: Writing accompany history of Pan American World Airways. *Management & Organizational History*, 3(1), pp. 63–80.

Ellis, F.H., 1980. *Canada's flying heritage*. Toronto: University of Toronto Press.

Escott, B.E., 1989. *Women in Air Force Blue*. Northampton: Patrick Stevens.

Foster, J.A., 1990. *The Bush Pilots*. Toronto: McClelland & Stewart.

Francis, C.E., 1993. *The Tuskagee Airmen*. New York: Branden Publishing Co.

Gutek, B.A., 1985. *Sex and the Workplace*. San Francisco: Jossey-Bass.

Helms Mills, J., 2002. Employment practices and the gendering of Air Canada's culture during its Trans Canada Airlines days. *Culture and Organization*, 8(2), pp. 117–28.

Holden, H.M. and Griffith, C.L., 1991. *Ladybirds: The Untold Story of Women Pilots in America*. Mt. Freedom, NJ: Black Hawk Publishing Co.

Kanter, R.M., 1977. *Men and Women of the Corporation*. New York: Basic Books.

Lauwick, H., 1960. *Heroines of the Sky*. London: Frederick Muller.

Mills, A.J., 2006. *Sex, Strategy and the Stratosphere: Airlines and the Gendering of Organizational Culture*. Basingstoke: Palgrave Macmillan.
Morrison, A., White, R. and Van Elsor, E., 1987. *Breaking the Glass Ceiling*. Reading, MA: Addison Wesley.
Neal-Smith, S. and Cockburn, T., 2008. Cultural sexism in the UK airline industry. *Gender in Management: An International Journal*, 24(1), pp. 32–45.
O'Brien, G., 1983. Negotiating order in the workplace: The case of the air hostess. *Journal of Irish Business and Administrative Research*, 5(2), pp. 3–13.
Penrose, H., 1967. *British Aviation: The Pioneer Years*. London: Putnam & Co. Ltd.
Pudney, J., 1959. *The Seven Skies*. London: Putnam.
Render, S., 1992. *No Place for a Lady: The Story of Canadian Women Pilots 1928–1992*. Winnipeg: Portage & Main Press.
Spring, J., 1994. *Daring Lady Flyers: Canadian Women in the Early Years of Aviation.* Lawrencetown Beach, NS: Pottersfield Press.
Stimson, R., 2013. The Wright Brothers plus one: The influence of their sister. Available at: http://wrightstories.com/the-wright-brothers-plus-one-the-influence-of-their-sister.
Wallace, P., 2009a. Career stories of women professional accountants: Examining the personal narratives of career using Simone de Beauvoir's feminist existentialist philosophy as a theoretical framework. *Qualitative Research in Organizations and Management: An International Journal*, 4(1), pp. 62–84.
——. 2009b. Why do women CAs leave public accounting firms before reaching the partnership level? Stories told by women CAs provide different answers to this same old question. *Canadian Journal of Administrative Sciences*, 26(3), pp. 179–96.
Weeks, J., 1990. *Sex, Politics and Society*, 2nd edn. London: Longman.

Index

For Product Safety Concerns and Information please contact our EU representative GPSR@taylorandfrancis.com
Taylor & Francis Verlag GmbH, Kaufingerstraße 24, 80331 München, Germany

www.ingramcontent.com/pod-product-compliance
Ingram Content Group UK Ltd.
Pitfield, Milton Keynes, MK11 3LW, UK
UKHW022007180926
475701UK00003B/244
* 9 7 8 0 3 6 7 6 7 0 1 0 8 *